3000 800024 93873

St. Louis Community College

D0142949

WITHDRAWN FV

 St. Louis Community College

Forest Park
Florissant Valley
Meramec

Instructional Resources
St. Louis, Missouri

Back to Birmingham

BACK TO BIRMINGHAM

Richard Arrington, Jr., and His Times

.

Jimmie Lewis Franklin

The University of Alabama Press

Tuscaloosa & London

Copyright © 1989 by
The University of Alabama Press
Tuscaloosa, Alabama 35487–0380

All rights reserved

Manufactured in the United States of America

Library of Congress Cataloging-in-Publication Data

Franklin, Jimmie Lewis.
  Back to Birmingham.

  Bibliography: p.   Includes index.
  1. Arrington, Richard.   2. Mayors—Alabama—
Birmingham—Biography.   3. Afro–Americans—Alabama—
Birmingham—Politics and government.   4. Birmingham
(Ala.)—Politics and government.   I. Title.
F334.B653A774 1989   976.1′781063′0924 [B]   88-29589
ISBN 0-8173-0435-5

British Library Cataloguing-in-Publication Data available

Designed by Laury A. Egan

To

two sisters, Annie and Fannie, who never lost faith,

and to

Elouise, a niece, who knew the essence of family love

Contents

Illustrations

Preface

During the 1960s, Birmingham became a major battleground in the struggle for human rights in the American South. Undoubtedly, it was one of the most segregated cities in the United States, and its name became virtually synonymous with violence and the callous suppression of black civil rights. The unrelenting fight for racial equality in Alabama brought significant results with the passage of national legislation that directly addressed the issue of injustice in American society. Federal laws gave blacks long-overdue civil rights and the ballot, which further increased their political consciousness and their participation in the democratic process.

In October 1979, the city that had once used dogs and fire hoses to crush protest demonstrations elected a black mayor, Richard Arrington, Jr. A man of quiet demeanor, Arrington was born in the small, rural town of Livingston, less than 150 miles from the office he now occupies in downtown Birmingham. Although he lived through the era of the civil-rights revolution in the South, he played little direct part in it as an activist, but Arrington was destined to bring about historic changes in the city that for years had defied racial harmony. Hardly anyone who knew him intimately expected the shy, scholarly Arrington to pursue politics, especially in Birmingham, Alabama.

This study of Richard Arrington is not conventional political or civil-rights history, but rather the story of a man who has demonstrated incredible faith in his region and in its people. Not surprisingly, there is in this work a subtle yet powerful subtheme that often appears with remarkable clarity, namely, *sense of place*, a quality that enables a person to claim sentimentally a portion of the natural and human environment. Too often writers who have examined black southerners have failed to give adequate emphasis to the attachment of blacks to the land, to place. Because of the presence of southern racism, perhaps, those authors have ignored the incorporation by blacks of many regional values and ways of living that had little to do with racial proscription but made them southerners, the same as their white brethren. The excitement of Arrington, then, is also the excitement of a region, of a people and a city that have undergone radical social and political transformation in the last two decades.

It is hoped that *Back to Birmingham* will appeal to both the general reader and the serious student of American society. The book endeavors to bridge what I consider an essentially artificial gap between so-called popular and scholarly history. It is guided by the assumption that Americans of whatever description can find satisfaction in comprehending social change and that they are buoyed by the individual triumph of those who beat the odds.

I have been the fortunate beneficiary of awards that made possible this study. A Ford Foundation Fellowship sponsored through the National Research Council enabled me to complete a large portion of the research for this biography while I worked on a related project at the University of Alabama during the 1982–83 school year. Dean Russell Hamilton and the University Research Council at Vanderbilt also provided funds that permitted me to complete the final revisions of the book.

It is impossible to thank all the persons who aided me in my research. My greatest indebtedness, of course, is to the subject of this work and his family, who suffered the disruptions that invariably accompany such an enterprise. I am also grateful to the many persons who talked to me (many of them more than once) and who opened for examination their public and sometimes their private lives. Without the cooperation of many individuals at Birmingham City Hall, this study would have met with failure. I must single out Jessie Huff, an aide to Mayor Arrington, who assisted me in acquiring the mayor's public papers and eased my path to other sources. Marvin Y. Whiting, Tom Haslett, and Jane Keeton at the Department of Archives and Manuscripts of the Birmingham Public Library not only rendered invaluable service but took time to explain much about the city's politics and history. Sandra Henderson, formerly of the Birmingham Public Library, also rendered invaluable aid. George and Connie Franklin always graciously made their home and their table available to me, and rarely did I ever discover a reason to refuse their invitation to a good home-cooked meal.

Appreciation must also go to a number of other very special people. My former colleague in the speech communications department at Eastern Illinois University, Tom Worthen, offered helpful advice on technical aspects of the manuscript, and his wife, Brenda, patiently typed many drafts of individual chapters and the final two revisions of the complete work. Wolfgang Schlauch, also at Eastern Illinois, read practically all of the manuscript and, despite our friendship, never abandoned his critical literary standards. Sally Miller and Kiddy Moore of the Vanderbilt history department typed several of the chapters of this book and much of the correspondence connected with the production of the study. Anna Luton, administrative assistant in my department, endured my grumbling about heavy committee assignments and other obligations that were conspiring to defeat the writing of *Back to Birmingham*. Paul Conkin and Dewey Grantham, my colleagues and good friends at Vanderbilt to whom I turned repeatedly for advice, must be elated to see the completion of this book. I also want to thank my editors, Craig Noll and the staff of The University of Alabama Press, whose patient work greatly improved the literary quality of this study, and whose efforts kept me from a number of logical inconsistencies.

As always, my wife, Golda, demonstrated a tolerance that only an author can truly appreciate. She survived revamped monthly budgets to take me "back to Birmingham" for research, and she endured those terrible shifts in moods that only a loved one can comprehend or tolerate. Her patience and understanding of my mission carried me through the darkest nights. I am grateful.

Back to Birmingham

1

Depression and Segregation: Background in Sumter County

.

When Richard Arrington took the oath of office as Birmingham's first black mayor in November 1979, he still carried memories of his family's life in western Alabama. Time had eclipsed much that had taken place in his native county of Sumter, but history had indelibly imprinted many sharp images. Although he had left rural Livingston at an early age, subsequent trips back home helped him to appreciate the challenges the small town had offered his parents as they struggled to survive on the land and as they worked to help create a sense of community in the tiny place with its agrarian values. Through his parents, Arrington came to know the real meaning of "sense of place" and what the love of one's "home place" meant to those who had lived close to the soil.

The years in Sumter immediately prior to the birth of Richard Arrington, Jr., in October 1934, were filled with hardship and suffering. Like other citizens across the country, Alabamians struggled to understand the terrible calamity that came with the disastrous crash of 1929, and they fought to eke out a precarious existence from a rural economy that had stubbornly defied economic diversification. Their anticipation of building a new society that included both a balanced agriculture and industry had gone unrealized, despite admonitions from some southern leaders for more than half a century. Although possessed with great courage, these descendants of Sumter families who had helped clear the for-

3

est and work the soil of the state found it difficult to endure the deep fear and the economic and psychological pain of the depression. In reality there was more to fear than fear itself. There was the matter of survival.

Sumter County had long depended upon agriculture for its livelihood, and it symbolized the dependence upon a one-crop, cotton economy. Some people, however, saw cotton as a burden to the region. The notices of foreclosures in Livingston's *Our Southern Home* told an ugly tale not only of national economic tragedy but of the burdensome weight of cotton upon an entire southern region. Much like their pre–Civil War brethren, some Sumter residents contended that their troubles grew from northern exploitation. A critic wrote in 1944, for example, that, "if some means could be devised to keep . . . the net profits made by northern and eastern corporations in this state," Alabama would soon become "one of the wealthiest states in the nation." The argument sounded a familiar note, but it hardly addressed the central issues that had kept the region economically backward and that had made the South the nation's number-one economic problem, before the depression caused even greater trouble.

Optimism, however, continued to exist among Alabamians, despite difficult economic times. A Livingston resident echoed the spirit of hope that prevailed among many citizens when she wrote, "Here in Alabama we can carry two crops in a year, and sometimes three, and we can work out-of-doors nearly everyday in the twelve months." Self-reliance would lift them from their desperate condition. She challenged her neighbors to greater industry, encouraging them to grow vegetables and fruits. Alabamians could whip the depression if they "quit being down-hearted" and worked fervently to bring the state back to prosperity. The depression, however, had root causes that went deep, and it would take more than optimism and a determined spirit to bring about a new, vibrant economic order.

Blacks in Sumter had been deeply mired in poverty long before the 1929 catastrophe. They had come to the county with white settlers in the early nineteenth century, and they had been part of the institution of chattel slavery in the Old South that created fortunes for a few planters in Alabama's Black Belt. Certainly, the depression struck blacks and whites throughout the South with devastating force, but its impact upon blacks only served to make them more economically subservient. The hope of giving blacks their own land during an earlier period of American history had died on the altar of party politics and the eventual failure of Reconstruction during the 1870s. "Forty acres and a mule" had remained part of the wishful thinking of those blacks, who recognized that no real emancipation could come without a solid economic foundation. Ironically, southern blacks did work and live on the land for many years, but it trapped them in a terrible net of poverty.

By the 1930s, law and custom had clearly fixed the place of black people in Alabama society. Since the 1896 *Plessy* Supreme Court decision, legalized segregation had kept blacks and whites separated in social relations and in public accommodations. Significantly, *Plessy* reinforced long-held racial attitudes about blacks, for it inscribed the notion of inferiority. The decree itself was direct in its pronouncement of a social principle, though it was hardly in line with democratic tenets. Given racial thought in the latter part of the nineteenth century, the Court's stance mirrored the beliefs of most whites in the North and the South and in many other parts of the world.

Law alone, however, has never been the sole guide to behavior in American society. Indeed, custom often proves a more important influence than statutes. Southern lawmakers passed numerous segregation ordinances that forced whites and blacks to "stay in their place," and out of fear of the tragic consequences for disobeying existing custom, most people respected them. Truly, each generation of southerners needed no laws to direct their behavior. Conversation at the dinner table, at picnics and baseball games, and at other activities helped to teach children the mores and folkways that told black and white people of their opportunities and their limitations. Although signs appeared in Livingston and throughout the South with the designation "white" and "colored," in most cases they were unnecessary, except for people generally unfamiliar with the region.

While on rare occasions blacks and whites did meet together at special events, a rigid standard of behavior controlled these contacts. Even in such settings whites did not act in a manner that conveyed to blacks the notion of racial equality. Significantly, most blacks, including community leaders, soft-pedaled the idea of "social equality," although they may have been determined advocates of racial justice and fair play. White southerners viewed social equality as anathema, for it evoked notions of racial intermingling and intermarriage, which to them spelled "mongrelization." The southern way of life, built upon the assumed supremacy of white people, called for racial purity, and that requirement demanded the continued separation of the races. Few white southerners saw any glaring inconsistency between their way of life, democratic principles, and a Judeo-Christian ethic that prided the ideal of brotherhood. With each passing year whites developed more of a sentimental and psychological attachment to the system, and many had a considerable economic stake in its maintenance. Little wonder that some southerners were willing to kill to defend the region's belief and to keep the advantages society gave to them. Blacks, of course, did not passively accept this system, and in many subtle ways a number of them protested the unequal treatment and injustice that existed.

Ernestine Bell and Richard Arrington, Sr., grew up in the old southern system. They felt the restrictions imposed by a segregated society, but racial oppression did not crush their pride and self-esteem. Both their families had lived in rural Sumter County for a period that stretched back to slavery, but they were also the product of many of the agrarian values that molded white Livingstonites. But their striking difference in opinion on racism and Jim Crow radically separated them from those of white Livingston residents. An appreciation for the land, hard work, and a belief in an orthodox Christian faith composed central features of Sumter County life; and both the Bells and Arringtons reflected those qualities readily associated with white southerners.

The Bell household never knew grinding poverty, although existence on a small, family farm often proved difficult. Ernestine's father, Ernest F. Bell, worked thirty or forty acres as a tenant; like most farmers, he grew cotton, but he also reserved some land for garden crops. Contrary to a popular notion about southern farms, cotton did not grow "up to the door of the Bell house." Corn, sweet potatoes, peanuts, and vegetables provided food for the table and for canning. Three Bell children—Ernestine, Eloise, and Clyde—learned about farming by working in the fields; and getting up early in the morning to "beat the sun" became a ritual for young Ernestine as she went to chop cotton in the late spring and early summer. And at harvesttime she worked late into the afternoon to pick the fleecy, white staple so closely identified with the South and the economy of the region.

A close family life of discipline, order, and religious faith characterized the Bell home. The two sisters and their brother enjoyed a happy childhood, but their parents expected strict adherence to Christian principles. Since the Bells were devout Baptists, the children had to participate in church activities, especially Sunday morning services. Although their father had a quiet demeanor, he was a strong authority figure who tolerated "no back talk." The children's mother, Cleopatra Bell, an extroverted woman with a big, infectious smile, was no less concerned about discipline, but she spent most of her time taking care of the family and explaining the "facts of life" to her offspring. With a tenth-grade education she could have qualified to teach in the black schools of the state during that period, but she never applied for a teaching certificate.

Sumter County had limited educational opportunities for black children. Yet, there existed an almost fanatical desire among some black parents for formal education that would improve the lot of their children and black people generally. The Bells, much like their neighbors, had a profound faith in learning, and the family had developed a tradition of education long before Ernestine's birth in October 1914. As a child, the young girl had regularly gone to school with a great aunt who resided in the Bell house and who taught in the black schools of Livingston. Indeed, Ernestine's grandfather, D. S. Jones, had been the first black to graduate from Selma University, later earning distinction as an educator in the Alabama schools.

The background of Richard Arrington, Sr., did not provide a striking contrast to that of Ernestine Bell's. Much like the parents of the woman he would later marry, his family farmed seventy-five acres near York, Alabama, a small town in Sumter County, ten miles from Livingston. A large household of fourteen people taxed the resources and the ingenuity of the Arringtons, but vegetables from the garden and some cows, hogs, and chickens kept the family supplied with food. In his youth, Richard plowed the fields along with his father, Matthew, attended the stock, gathered fuel, and worked as a blacksmith, a job he continued to hold for many years. Although the Arringtons had a high regard for learning, they did not have the educational tradition of the Bells. Richard's formal sixth-grade training, however, belied his native intelligence and a wide range of skills. Despite having only a modest farm income, Matthew and his wife, Barbara, taught the Arrington children the middle-class virtues of industry, self-respect, and pride.

The families of Ernestine Bell and Richard Arrington, Sr., had lived within a few miles of each other in Sumter, but the two did not meet until Richard's brother suggested it in the latter part of 1929. Upon returning from Birmingham, where he had been working, Richard attended a school-closing concert held in a country church outside Livingston. And it was here, with Ernestine's father close by in his Model T, that the two met. Impressed with their first contact, the young man borrowed his father's car and visited Ernestine again on the Sunday following the concert. Since she was still attending boarding school in Livingston, it was possible to see her only on Wednesday nights or Sundays. A courtship of two years gave the young lovers ample time to explore each other's values and to discuss plans for the future; and it also gave Ernestine time to finish her high-school work before embarking upon married life.

Tragedy, however, visited the Bell family and temporarily altered future plans. When he was not busy farming, Ernestine's father cut logs for a living and performed other odd jobs for additional income. In December 1933, while cutting timber, a tree fell on Ernest Bell, killing him instantly. Just five months earlier his wife had succumbed to illness. Ernestine faced not only sorrow but full responsibility for her younger brother and sister and the household. Grief made preparation for marriage more difficult, at a time when more immediate problems stared her in the face. Ultimately Ernestine had to make a decision about her wedding and whether to remain on the land that her family had worked for many years, a farm that had become known as "Bell's Place," although her father had never really owned it.

The love Richard and Ernestine had for each other created its own special joy and they decided to marry. The death of Ernestine's mother and father had been hard to accept, and it was impossible to hold her wedding in the church of her parents' funeral. Therefore, she and Richard joined hands at the Bell place. When the Reverend R. F. Thomas accepted their vows on 19 December 1933 to remain loyal to each other, he sealed a marriage that has continued for over a half century.

Life posed considerable hardships for the Arringtons in those trying years of the Great Depression, but they managed to survive off the land. Following their marriage, they lived on the Bell farm with Ernestine's sister and brother as part of the household. Richard willingly shouldered his new responsibilities, acting as both husband and father. With implements left by Ernestine's father, the family did what it knew best—farm—and with resourcefulness provided food and shelter and a limited amount of comfort for their household.

Living expenses exhausted practically all of the income of the youthful Arringtons. Rental of the land on the Bell place came to fifty dollars a year, not an exorbitant figure at that time for both acreage and the use of a house. Seed, fertilizer, tools, and other necessary items, however, proved very expensive. With cotton selling for forty-five to fifty dollars a bale during the depression, the return from the Arringtons' few acres was indeed small. They did most of their shopping for basic foodstuffs at the country store owned by Tom Mellon, their Livingston landlord. While prices were "kind of high," they were probably no more expensive than at similar stores that dotted the southern landscape. Indeed, the Arringtons believed that Mellon dealt fairly with them in the rent he charged and by permitting them to remain on the Bell farm. Like most cash tenants in the South, the Arringtons fared much better than the large number of sharecroppers who found themselves perpetually in debt to the country store and unable to move because of special state or local laws.

The New Deal farm programs of the 1930s did not significantly affect the Arringtons' lives as farm tenants. However, they responded positively to the admonitition of Franklin Delano Roosevelt and his call for courage in defeating the economic depression. Like other blacks, they had reason to hope that the dawning of a better day would come with the institution of new government policies. The Agricultural Adjustment Act, one of many alphabetic agencies established during the New Deal, aimed to raise prices of reducing agricultural production. The Arringtons indirectly participated in the program, but it netted them little. Unfortunately, the measure hardly achieved its objective, and in time it ran afoul of the United States Supreme Court, which ruled it unconstitutional.

Prior to the passage of the AAA, the family farmed about twenty-seven acres, but the landlord, a participant in the New Deal program, reduced that amount to five acres. And since the Arringtons received only a small price for their cotton, this change drastically reduced their income. However, they were not subjected to the harsh treatment and outright thievery that characterized the relationship between some landowners and tenants. In parts of the South, landlords denied tenants income from the government and callously drove them off the land. Others permitted farm workers to remain but charged them high rents and even higher prices for goods and services provided them. Responsive to southern votes and attitudes, Roosevelt and the New Dealers did not bring maximum pressure upon landowners to obey the law.

The president's New Deal program, with its broad objective of relief, recovery, and reform, affected practically every community in America, even small Livingston. Since government policy curtailed cotton production, Richard Arrington and his family had to turn to the raising of watermelons, sweet potatoes, beans, corn, and other garden crops. Although they lived off the farm, they still needed cash. After establishment of the Works Projects Administration (WPA), Richard joined that agency, repairing rural roads at a pay of three dollars a day. He found the Civilian Conservation Corps much more attractive, but unlike some blacks in Livingston, he never worked in that program. His tenure with WPA, however, was short-lived, lasting only about a month.

The Arringtons' meager income left little money for Ernestine's "shopping sprees." Austere though life was in the 1930s, she did manage to buy "a choice item or two every now and then." Even shopping in small Livingston was a special treat in those days; and to travel to Meridian, Mississippi, a town thirty miles to the west, was a special delight. Ernestine always made the best of it. Over the years she got to know some of the best clothing stores in Meridian, such as the highly fashionable Marks Rothenberg, the preeminent name in clothing stores in the east-central part of the state. Rothenberg catered mostly to professionals, both blacks and whites, but it also attracted Ernestine, who had an eye for "good merchandise." And since she rarely had the opportunity to visit "first-class shops," she went unhurriedly about her business while in the city, although she did not spend hard-earned money recklessly. Pleasure came not only from buying at Rothenburg's but from shopping at the huge department store, which took up a large portion of a block in Meridian's downtown area.

Livingston, of course, did not have businesses that compared favorably with the big stores in much larger Meridian. But it did possess a magnetic attraction for rural Sumter countians who needed a social outlet but could not travel far from home. Restaurants and places of entertainment were rigidly segregated (as in Meridian), and blacks had to seek services in the few places owned by other blacks. In the Livingston of this period most black establishments were found along Day Street, a very special place for blacks who lived within the town as well as for those who visited from the rural areas. Saturday gatherings provided a wholesome social diversion for those who came to "downtown" Livingston. People would arrive early in their horse-drawn wagons and would remain until late afternoon. "Sin always lurked around the corner," as bootleggers industriously and ingeniously peddled their booze in prohibition Alabama. Although the town was supposedly "bone dry," those who wanted their spirits lifted had little trouble purchasing liquor along Day Street or elsewhere in the city. One well-known bootlegger courageously sat along the streets of Livingston and profitably sold his "white lightning" while eating candy from a barrel.

Ample opportunity did exist for enjoyable and wholesome recre-

In 1957, Livingston's Franklin Street had changed very little from the time that the Arrington family had left the city. (Courtesy of John Craiger, Livingston, Alabama)

ation during a visit to town. Farmers gathered to discuss crops, economic hardship, and whether they would stick with "6-8-4" fertilizer or "lay aside" a section of their acreage to regain fertility after years of growing cotton. Recent sermons, revivals, and quartet singing, especially "battles of music," occupied the attention of locals, who felt the need for conversation or outright debate. Women talked of canning, sewing, the rearing of children, and the best way to combat certain illnesses. Marriages, births, and deaths also held the interests of a rural people who lived close to the land and, despite distance, close to each other in a society still unaffected by the depersonalization of urban existence.

Much of social life for the Arringtons and other blacks centered in the church, but other activities provided an occasional outlet. Attending "preaching" on Sundays constituted almost a requirement for all blacks, whether or not they claimed to know the Lord. Sunday worship services provided an important opportunity for local gossip or the chance to continue yesterday's conversation from the town square. It was also a time, especially after the harvest, to wear new outfits and to see new wagons or new pregnancies. Small and restless children found it a happy time to break away from the relative isolation of the farm and to join others of their age in merriment. Adolescents seized the opportunity to cast glances at the opposite sex and, shyly and unpretentiously, to court. Revivals offered a special time for visiting and camaraderie, and often as many came to witness the conversion of lifelong sinners as came to "feel the presence of the Lord." These meetings gave a kind of psychic release from the pressures of a long, hard growing and harvesting season, but they also fostered a sense of community by bringing together people of similar values. The black church, as unorganized as it may have appeared to some, represented a powerful force in the lives of black people. Later it would assume a central place in the reformation of southern society and in the lives of young leaders.

Social life in Livingston often served as a means of fostering cooperation and promoting fundamental values. The winter season in the South, although not bitterly cold, restricted the mobility of southerners and, consequently, social visiting. But "hog-killing time," Ernestine Arrington recalls, offered an opportunity for neighbors to get together to break the dreaded isolation that came with cold weather. "Preparing a hog" required a certain ritual that transcended mere slaughter. On the night prior to the killing, an owner and his family would prepare the knives, pots, and other instruments needed for the event. The head of the household or a son would chop wood to boil the water and to make the lard from the hog's fat. Early the next morning friends from the community would gather in anticipation of the forthcoming killing, but considerable discussion ensued before the hog met its eventual fate. The men often pondered whether to use a gun or an ax on the animal that would later provide delicious meat for the winter. As a matter of established practice, the hog's owner did the slaughter, but the task sometimes fell to a more youthful, or braver, member of the group. Once killed, the hog was hung for cleaning, a process that took plenty of hot boiling water. The fire under these pots also warmed those who gathered to exchange stories or to speculate on local matters.

The women took an active part in the preparation of the meat for storage. They cleaned chitterlings ("chitlins"), and they made the various table-sized cuts for cooking. Oftentimes they would prepare "cracklings" from the pork skin that remained after the fat had been boiled. "Packing," or preserving the meat, and curing it became a virtual art to Ernestine, who found real pleasure in storing pork for later use. The Arringtons enjoyed the sense of community and cooperation that a hog-killing affair strengthened as much as they did the experience of preparing meat for later use.

Children and their "proper Christian upbringing" were important in the rural lives of those who gathered for hog killings and other social activities in southern society. Richard Arrington, Sr., had come from a large family of fourteen children, and he looked forward to rearing his offspring with the values that had molded his life and that of his wife. Understandably, he greeted the news of Ernestine's first pregnancy with "great joy," and he experienced even greater happiness when she eventually gave birth on 19 October 1934 to a healthy, ten-pound boy who was named for his father. Two and a half years later he felt equally proud at the arrival of another son, James. But Richard Arrington, Sr., had little hope for the boys as farmers, for he did not want them to witness the difficult life he had encountered on the land. From the beginning, their mother recalled later, "we wanted to make life better for them than it had been for us." But that dream seemed distant at the time, for, despite Roosevelt's hopes, the American economy still hung precariously in the balance, still tipped as much toward possible economic disaster as it was toward bright hope and prosperity. The year 1934 had not been a very good one for the United States and Sumter County. The birth of Richard Arrington, Jr., however, had brought happiness to his parents, and it had given them greater incentive to carve out a good, secure future.

The difficulties of rural life during the depression were lost upon young Richard Arrington, and he mostly remembers a very happy childhood in Livingston. His rather rustic surroundings, however, made a deep impression on the young boy, who had already begun to develop an appreciation for the things around him. Long after he had left Livingston, he could still recall his rural home, a somewhat typical abode for blacks of that era. His place had windows constructed of lumber that opened and closed "much like doors." Off to the side of the kitchen there stood a smokehouse, to which his mother had easy access. The interior of his dwelling had walls papered with pages from a Sears Roebuck catalog, and the living room had a large fireplace and a big bed in it. At some distance there stood a barn for the cattle and an outhouse, which appeared more remote as night approached. In the yard there sat a large, black washpot that despite its relatively small size, seemed to dominate a nearby area reserved for chopping wood. The boy's father and his friends had dug a well adjacent to the house which provided water until pollution made it unsafe. Little Richard then had to travel a mile to acquire water from a spring, but that task did not frighten him, since the spring was located near the home of a favorite uncle, affectionately referred to as "Flute." The small boy sometimes rode a horse without a saddle, but he occasionally found getting back on the animal impossible without assistance.

After his family had moved from Livingston, Richard periodically returned to the town of his birth, and it was then that his view of the area became sharper. While he was there, he and brother James lived with paternal grandparents. Despite some loneliness at being away from home, both the boys looked forward to these visits "to the country." They appreciated the fun of rising early in the morning to go to the fields or to check on the chickens or cattle. Sometimes they would slip down to the creek and "take a dip" into the forbidden waters. Like most youngsters, the boys roamed the woods and fields, inspecting the flora and fauna with childlike curiosity. The world of nature intrigued them, and their youthful inquisitiveness later grew into a deep, scientific interest that shaped their professional lives. They also liked adventure and daring, and a good ripe watermelon invited the attention of anxious boys, who could not resist plucking and eating the tasty treat.

For a period of nearly ten years after the Arringtons left Sumter, the boys returned to their old home place. Summers in Livingston gave them an opportunity to rejoin young relatives of the same age. But despite the positive features of the delightful visits, there were some shortcomings. Frightened of the dark, Richard would sometimes cry at night as he talked of home; recovery usually followed with daylight. James still remembers the strange and irritating sounds of cricket noises "out in the country," the often-stifling smell of poison on cotton, and the creaking of his grandfather's house as the winds beat against the lumber. In more courageous moments, the boys sometimes played a game of "ghost," assured of the security offered by those who loved them. The experience greatly resembled that of viewers of a horror movie, who watch with alternating pleasure and fear from within the modern cinema.

From the birth of Richard Arrington, Jr., to 1940, the country struggled to overcome the depression; and the New Deal did realize some success. However, the terrible economic experience still lingered, and it faded completely only with America's involvement in World War II. Yet, the depression never stifled the desire of the senior Richard Arrington for a better life, and as the country crept slowly out of the economic doldrums, it seemed possible that existence would improve, even in Livingston. But race and a rural economy would still circumscribe existence in the small town. While his blacksmith's shop and odd jobs offered a chance for additional income, Richard Arrington, Sr., desired more productive employment—good, steady wages, and security for his family. To "pull up stakes," however, required more than economic resources, for a sense of place and sentimental attachment had always been a key consideration in the choice to "stay put" or to "move on" to a new location where others perhaps did not share similar values.

The hope of better opportunities and a more secure economic life steadily pulled at Arrington. Ernestine had also tired of the farm, although she dreaded the thought of leaving behind relatives and friends. New friendships would emerge in time to end any loneliness for those she would leave behind in Sumter. When her husband's brother sent Richard a bus ticket to come to Fairfield, an industrial town adjacent to Birmingham and dominated by the steel industry, the prospect of his getting employment there delighted her. A job there in one of the mills could mean a new life, a steady income, and other advantages rural life did not offer. The Arringtons then, had become upwardly mobile, a part of the continuing story of American life that had long composed a central feature of its history. The senior Arrington, however, did not assign great phil-

16

osophical significance to his decision to move from Livingston. He simply desired a better life.

Moving from Sumter generated much discussion in the Arrington household during the summer of 1940. The youth of the two boys, of course, prevented a profound grasp of the meaning of a move. Preparing to leave was "an exciting time for me," Richard Arrington, Jr., later said, for it provoked a sense of adventure, a feeling that his family was "tackling the unknown." Beyond visits to downtown Livingston, the young boy had never taken any trips. Although only 120 miles separated their small town from the city of Fairfield, the journey seemed much farther to Richard and James. The family's departure in late evening also produced some anxiety, as Richard and James prepared to ride in the back of their Uncle Jonathan's fashionable Model T, which now had a bed mattress on top. Their mother, affectionately called "Peach" by close friends, shared her sons' excitement and some of their anxieties, but she found reassurance in her husband, who understood something about "the ways of the city." Moreover, Uncle Jonathan, who lived in Fairfield, "knew his way around" and could ease the transition into a fast-moving, urban world. A new place and a new life lay ahead.

2

The Quest for Excellence:
From Fairfield to Leadership

.

As his Uncle Jonathan's car sped toward Fairfield, young Richard Arrington may have thought of what he had left behind in Livingston. Gone now were those days when his elders sat on rural porches, read their Bibles, sang hymns, or casually talked with friends about crops, the weather, or local gossip. Gone, too, were his small friends with whom he played children's games on the hot, summer days for which Alabama is famous. Gone, too, were the delightful gatherings at Shiloh Baptist Church, where he craved and received more attention than he perhaps deserved from kindred and friendly neighbors. The embraces of those who knew him best did not easily fade as his uncle's Model T made its way through the countryside, northeast toward Birmingham, "the steel capital" of the South. The security he had felt in Livingston at the sound of his nickname "papa," and that of "Joe," for his brother, James, continued to provide him some comfort, since his family and others persisted in using the terms. An aunt had given Richard his nickname when she observed the little boy's mature behavior as he played the role of father administering punishment to an errant child. Time in its own sure way would partially eclipse thoughts of Livingston, but many memories of the country town would remain.

If young Richard's mind caught fleeting glimpses of the past as he traveled away from Sumter, he had no unusual fear of his new home, Fairfield, a suburb of Birmingham. His new place would bear little similarity to his rural Livingston, which had been the center of his family's life before the move to the city. Years later he recalled that "there was a kind of excitement about this new venture." With an eye for detail that characterized his adult life, he noted that "the thing I remembered most is arriving at our new home at night and going to sit on the steps of our porch; and I could hear something which I later discovered was the Number 7 streetcar." Of course, little Arrington had never seen a streetcar, a city convenience Livingston did not have or need. A kind of mystery, he said, surrounded the whole experience. But reckless adventure had played no role in his parents' decision to move from their Sumter environment. Here now was a new home, a new job for his father at Tennessee Coal, Iron and Railroad Company (TCI), and an inviting new challenge similar to the ones other Americans had faced as they searched out their place on new frontiers of life.

TCI stood at the center of the Fairfield economy, and for thirty-five years it was the source of the Arringtons' livelihood. With the increasing demand of steel, the city grew as migration to the Birmingham area increased. TCI had come to the area in 1886 and had bought out several local companies in the Birmingham district. In 1891, the president of TCI, Nat Baxter, Jr., negotiated an important deal that gave the company additional strength and assured its solvency. When TCI encountered serious economic difficulties, Baxter approached Henry F. DeBardeleben (the powerful steel magnate who had built Bessemer, Alabama, a city adjacent to Fairfield) about a possible deal that would aid both entrepreneurs. Baxter persuaded the usually crafty and perceptive DeBardeleben to accept $8 million worth of TCI securities for $10 million worth of good stock in the DeBardeleben Coal and Iron Company. DeBardeleben did not know that TCI was practically broke! The virtual absorption by DeBardeleben's company enabled TCI to recapitalize at $120 million and gave the company increased power and a "staggering monopoly on the Birmingham district."

TCI, however, could not escape the embrace of a more powerful company, one with a name that became inextricably linked with the Birmingham-Fairfield economy. Convinced that TCI, with a debt in the millions, could not survive the panic of 1907 and that its failure would increase the severity of the crisis, the ultrarich financier J. Pierpont Morgan asked President Theodore Roosevelt to accept a merger of United States Steel and TCI. Contrary to some advice, President Roosevelt, noted as a "trust buster," approved the merger. Although TCI's estimated assets amounted to more than $1 billion dollars, United States Steel purchased the company "for a song," paying a little over $35 million for it. "Why had US Steel purchased TCI," asked the critics of the merger? The company answered that it had made the deal as a "public service" to avoid more severe problems, to prevent a "general industrial smash up." Genuine progressives who had as their aim the regulation of the growth of monopoly remained unconvinced. Even in Alabama mixed opinion prevailed over the long-range effects of the deal. Some believed that the steel industry in the Birmingham area would suffer because of United States Steel's Pittsburgh plants. One local editor however, thought the purchase would "make Birmingham hum as it never hummed before"; another wrote, with sometimes typical southern overstatement, that it would make the district the greatest steel manufacturing center in the universe.

The Birmingham district did become a notable steel center, and the demand for the hard metal to build automobiles, durable products, and rapidly expanding American cities attracted large numbers of workers to the area. Limited housing often posed a problem. The original plan for Fairfield, formerly called Corey, did not provide for low-income housing for TCI employees, a number of whom were immigrants or blacks. During World War II, TCI purchased land to build a "model village—Westfield" to house workers. This community, located roughly a mile from Fairfield, had schools and churches and a recreational area with an abundance of trees, a feature that also characterized Fairfield with its many parks. When Richard Arrington, Sr., made the decision to move to the Birmingham area, he declined the opportunity to live in housing specifically for company employees.

Housing for blacks in Fairfield did not compare favorably with that of whites, but the relative newness of the city's housing stock made it considerably better than that of rural Alabama towns. Fortunately, the senior Arrington was able to find accommodation for

The streetcar tracks on this 1945 tree-lined Fairfield Street resemble the ones young Richard Arrington, Jr., saw when he came to the city. (From the Photographic Collection, Department of Archives and Manuscripts, Birmingham Public Library, Birmingham, Alabama.)

his family in Fairfield on Avenue "H," in a quiet, working-class, residential area. He rented a "double tenant" home from a landlord who lived in an adjacent house. While many of the men who resided in the community worked at TCI, others had employment elsewhere. A few professional blacks, principally teachers and ministers, also had homes scattered throughout the area. Although the house where the Arringtons lived contained six rooms, the family occupied only one side, or three rooms, of the building—a living room, a bedroom, and a kitchen. On the front and back porches, a wooden bannister divided the building for the two families that resided there.

Memories of the small dwelling are yet vivid for the Arringtons. In the kitchen a small table and a handcrafted cabinet built by the father added to the aesthetics of the room, but the large wood-burn-

21

ing stove with a warmer on top dominated the entire area. The middle room of the house was the bedroom for Richard's parents, and a small cot, or "roll-a-way" bed, made its appearance when needed. Young Richard and brother James slept in the living room, which contained a couch and a high, narrow chest of drawers for clothing. Here the boys not only lived but also bathed in a large metal tub with water that had been heated on top of the kitchen stove. An aunt who stayed with the Arringtons for a time also resided in this small room.

Other relatives sometimes lived with the Arringtons, but despite the increased numbers in the household, the boys did not consider their home crowded. Only in retrospect did they ponder how those who lived in the small dwelling on Avenue "H" endured without "violating someone else's space." Perhaps the key to the absence of great friction lies in the respect the Arringtons and their kindrēd had for the idea of the extended family, an important feature in black southern life that had its roots deep within African soil. Assistance to family members in "getting ahead" and in providing them with the mechanisms that made possible self-reliance were features of the black community almost as old as black freedom itself in the United States. Ernestine Arrington felt a special obligation "to look out for the others," since she was the oldest child in the Bell family.

The outside appearance of the Arrington home reflected its location within this Fairfield working-class community. A modern sewage system had not yet been installed in the part of the city where young Richard and his family lived. As in Livingston, an outhouse stood some distance away from the dwelling, but a major difference was the visit of a city worker to collect the contents of the "sanitation cans" for disposal. The backyard served as a convenient place for James and Richard to play, and it also provided space for stacking wood for the fireplace and the stove. During the winter season a large coal pile broke the landscape when the family purchased the hot-burning fuel for use in the fireplace. Coal, James has recalled, had its advantages and disadvantages. It burned with intensity and heated the house well, but "it was hard to get started on very cold mornings." Moreover, the boys did not have the pleasure of baking sweet potatoes in the fireplace when the family burned coal, for the ashes stuck to the potatoes' outer peeling. Wood ashes produced a different result. Both James and Richard remember many pleasurable moments in the winter season, when they ate baked potatoes and good bread cooked in the family's fireplace.

Part of the backyard served as a garden in the summer, and for many years the boys' mother grew peas, onions, tomatoes, and other vegetables. Collard greens were a virtual staple in the family's diet; no garden of Ernestine's existed without the green, leafy vegetable. "Mom," James once noted, "could eat collard greens every day of the week if she really had her way." Growing a garden for the Arringtons was more than a mere pastime in the city; it was part of surviving on a tight budget. The canning of food had been common in rural Livingston, and after the move to Fairfield, Ernestine Arrington continued to preserve fruits and vegetables.

TCI owned a commissary where many of the workers shopped for food and other items. Richard remembers going there a few times with his father, but the Arringtons bought much of their food from a community grocery store owned by a black man. Most items were purchased on credit and paid for on payday, a system of buying that prevailed in many black communities across the South. And not until the proliferation of large supermarkets and chain stores did this practice end. Although some local stores often charged high prices because of their inability to buy in large volume, many of the establishments owned by black entrepreneurs deliberately lowered their profit margin in deference to the community they served. The Arringtons never had any reason to believe their black merchant overcharged them for the things purchased on credit.

The senior Arrington could have easily driven to the commissary to shop, or he could have gone elsewhere in the Birmingham area after he purchased a car. But convenience, his view of black business, and his attachment to the owner of the store caused him to support black enterprises whenever possible. That choice was sometimes difficult, of course, when buying certain types of clothing and durable household goods. Black business experienced great limitations in those days of segregation, and only a few owners could accumulate enough capital to establish competitive enterprises, especially ones that competed with the large stores in the Birmingham area. Understandably, most of the black businesses in the vicinity sold food or provided entertainment, for whites excluded blacks from their places or, in the case of food, offered it to them "to carry out."

Adjustment to a new home and a new environment came slowly for the Arringtons. For the young Arrington boys the early days in Fairfield challenged their youthful ingenuity and their nerves. Timid and highly sensitive to exclusion, Richard experienced problems from community youngsters who felt the need to "test the new kid on the block." The entire first year in his new home was a very painful experience for him. When other children harassed him, he would cry, which sometimes only provoked further intimidation. Fights bothered the lad, and he desperately struggled to stay away from any rough encounters, if for no other reason than that they scared him. James, the younger of the two boys, came to display much more physical aggressiveness, and he encouraged his older brother to "duke it out," a street expression for a fistfight. And at least on one occasion, young Richard did exactly that. After playmates had made fun of him, he had come home with tears in his eyes. Tired of his timid behavior, his mother admonished him to defend himself if attacked. If he did not, she warned, a whipping would await him. The next time a friend provoked the boy, "Richard was all over the little fellow like a hornet." He had earned respect, had become one of the established boys on the block. Although he continued to remain quiet and somewhat withdrawn, he had clearly carved out his spot in a new order. *"Their* turf" was now *"his* turf," too. He felt much more comfortable, and so did his family.

The move to Fairfield did not force the Arringtons to abandon deeply held values. For Richard's parents, instilling religious and educational values in their sons remained a central concern. They had brought with them a social philosophy of life that clearly delineated right and wrong. And they also had strong ideas about the worth of a good education, which were as old as the Bell family itself and as intense as the Arringtons' appreciation for hard work and their spirit of optimism.

Participation in church activities continued to assume high priority in the family. In Fairfield the mother joined First Missionary Baptist, but later she moved to Crumbey Bethel Primitive Baptist Church, her husband's congregation. Primitive Baptists believed in the literal interpretation of the Bible, and their worship services reflected an intensity that had long characterized the history of the black church in the American South. Founded in 1926, Crumbey had a very small membership of fifty persons when the Arringtons joined the church, and this number grew slowly until by 1986 it had two hundred in the congregation. Historically, Crumbey demonstrated a humanitarian concern for its members and its community that transcended a narrow religious orthodoxy and preoccupation with heaven and hell. The church's mission brought it into contact with the trials and tribulations of both members and nonmembers, who daily faced the difficulties of a harsh and demanding world made even more trying by the dehumanizing effect of racial discrimination. In many ways Crumbey provided a remarkable exception to the stereotyped view of the black church as a highly emotionalized institution that turned its head skyward as God's children suffered on this earth under the brutality that came with southern white supremacy. Four decades after the Arringtons joined Crumbey, the church had bought land to establish a community center, and it had further broadened its programs to address the pressing needs that both young and old faced in an area that continued to grow more impersonal with urbanization.

Richard's mother insisted on his involvement in a range of church programs. He usually attended eleven o'clock worship service with her, since his father, who suffered from a hearing defect, attended church only on special occasions. As a young man he did not have to attend regular midweek prayer services, but he joined the church at one of these Wednesday night meetings. While still in his teens, he became secretary of Crumbey's Sunday school, and later he served as its superintendent. He also took part in vacation Bible classes, sang in the choir, and as a young adult sat on the Deacon Board, a position he continued to hold even after he became one of the best-known names in Alabama.

Sunday had a special meaning for the Arringtons. Not only did the boys dress up and "put on their best behavior," but it was a time when they looked forward to chicken and dressing and, of course, collard greens. It was a day to abstain from certain kinds of unacceptable activities "that the Lord frowned upon," although the Arrington parents may have demonstrated greater leniency than many southern families of the 1940s and the 1950s. A certain satisfaction came from having the head of the household at home for Sunday dinner, away from the labors of TCI and his other job as an occasional carpenter. Father Arrington did very little on the Sabbath except relax and read the paper when he did not attend church. He had a keen interest in discovering the outside world through reading, and that habit had a profound influence on Richard and James. While the father held to the sacredness of Sunday, he did not invoke the usual prohibitions of some parents against playing baseball, shooting marbles, or going to the movies, but he did have one particular dislike, which family members carefully honored. "If you were going to iron clothes or press the wrinkles out of them," James remembers, "then you had to do that on Saturday night, not on Sunday."

The early religious development of Richard Arrington, Jr., mirrored that of many other southern leaders who grew up in the region, especially in the era when the church occupied a much more dominant position in the community than it does now. As an institution that relied principally upon black support for its existence, it allowed a freedom of expression and action not possible in other places. That the church served as a training ground for leadership was a natural development that grew from the rigid system of southern segregation. And it ultimately became the institution that provided money, energy, and spiritual reinforcement that helped topple the old social order, built on white supremacy. The church provided security in numbers, it strengthened a feeling of racial identity, and it gave children like Richard Arrington a sense of self-worth. At a practical level it favorably affected lives by providing a wholesome outlet for the creative talents of blacks, and it

26

challenged their intellectual and decision-making abilities. Church activities taught the meaning of discipline and the benefit of planning and organization to many young blacks. Preparing for Sunday school or "preaching" required a quality of thought not remarkably different from other kinds of intellectual activity. Except for the public school, few institutions had as much impact on the lives of "Dick" and "Joe" Arrington as the church.

Fairfield offered much better educational facilities than did Livingston. While black schools throughout Alabama did not receive funding equal to that of whites, institutions in more urbanized areas had broader programs than those in rural parts of the state. Thus, when Ernestine Arrington thought of "making a better life for my children" by moving from Livingston, she had in mind, among other things, the education of her young boys. And it was Ernestine who forcefully impressed upon her children the need for soldierlike discipline in the pursuit of knowledge and excellence in academic performance. "I attribute my thirst for knowledge and discipline to my mother," Richard Arrington recalls. He had already experienced something about learning early in life when he attended school in Livingston with his aunt, and once he had adjusted to the new environment of Fairfield, he found the educational process a challenge and, most of the time, enjoyable.

Young Richard Arrington's sense of importance among his peers came with the recognition of his intellectual abilities. As a student at Sixty-First Street (later renamed Robinson) Elementary School he excelled in most of his subjects, despite an occasional distraction from a student who ridiculed him because of his dedication and his mother's absolute insistence upon study in late afternoon and early evenings. His commitment and his mother's watchful eye enabled him to master most of his courses without great difficulty. Of all his subjects mathematics posed a special problem, although he did not dislike the subject. One of his third-grade teachers, Mittye Woodruff, a tall, strong woman with a personality to match, "made sense of math to me for the first time," Arrington once fondly recalled. His promotion from the third to the fifth grade, however, may not have represented an advantage. "The fifth grade was hard for me," he said years later. "I was advanced when it came to reading and the like, but again I had a very difficult time with math." Indeed, it was at this period in his life that one of his teachers discovered the young boy's insufficient mastery of the multiplication tables, a problem the school had him hurriedly address through continuous practice. Arrington remained at Robinson for seven years, since Fairfield did not have a junior high school, but his mother's strict discipline and that of his instructors prepared him well for Fairfield Industrial High, a school then known in the state for its strong curriculum.

Fairfield High did much with limited financial resources. While Arrington would become one of its star graduates, its history is the story of many young blacks who later contributed significantly to American culture. Established in 1927 as the Interurban Heights High School, the institution changed its name to Fairfield Industrial High in 1940 with the erection of a new, three-story building that contained twenty-five classrooms and vocational shops. The center of the community's educational life, it also became an important part of the social life of Fairfield's black citizens. Along with the church, it constituted the hub of community activities, and its leadership conditioned attitudes toward many social issues.

For more than four decades one forceful man guided the mission of Fairfield Industrial High, and he profoundly influenced the life of Richard Arrington. In many ways E. J. Oliver represented the prototype of the progressive black principal in the American South, who had to struggle under the restraints of a segregated social and educational system. Born in Wilcox County, Oliver attended public school in Birmingham and later studied at Tuskegee Institute, Alabama State College, and Miles. He taught in the Jasper city schools, but when opportunity beckoned, he accepted the principalship of the Sixty-First Street Elementary School, which in 1924 had eight grades and eight teachers. While at Jasper, Oliver had decided not to live in the midst of the community he served. Therefore, when he went to Fairfield, he moved to the Woodlawn area of Birmingham, which required him to travel some thirty-two miles a day to work. With his residency outside the city, Oliver carefully avoided many of the entanglements that plagued the life in Jasper, and he also escaped weak, belabored explanations from parents who, after school hours, tried to explain their children's absence from school or their violation of rules. By distancing himself from certain kinds of social contacts, he avoided the danger a principal faced when pressure existed to bend regulations to suit a few.

Oliver had a clearly articulated educational philosophy. He had brought much of it with him from Tuskegee Institute, and his approach to learning reflected the work-study philosophy that had characterized the institution since the days of its noted founder, Booker T. Washington. Not surprisingly, then, the early years of Industrial High stressed vocational training, but Oliver did not ignore college-preparatory courses.

Oliver combined stern discipline with moral training in the operation of Industrial High. Although he reluctantly administered punishment to students, he had refused to accept his job in Fairfield until the superintendent agreed not to interfere with his "proven method" of correcting wayward behavior. Some students may have exaggerated Oliver's means of achieving conformity with the rules, but few ever denied the authoritarian control of his institution. "Everyone knew who operated the school," Arrington commented years after he had graduated from the institution. The principal left no doubt about his role when he wrote in a semiautobiographical work, "Authority means that the person . . . vested with it is responsible for the success or failure of that over which he or she has [control]." A leader of an educational institution, he noted, had to create a vigorous academic climate, although that responsibility sometimes involved punishment or condemnation of a particular kind of behavior. Seldom did Oliver administer whippings, primarily because he succeeded in inculcating a spirit of loyalty, social values, and Christian morality through twice-a-week assembly-hall programs. During his forty-three-year tenure at Fairfield, Oliver expelled only about twenty pupils for violation of the rules. He encouraged students to admit their guilt if expelled and to apologize during an assembly to the entire student body for their transgressions upon their return to school.

Richard Arrington respected Oliver's fairness and even-handed treatment of students. But the principal did not claim infallibility. Occasionally he himself had to offer an apology in assembly for punishment administered to an innocent soul. But he firmly defended his method of operation, and he adhered firmly to the philosophy that the teacher stood in place of the parent while the student was in school. Oliver's faculty members felt confident of his support and his sensible discipline of students. They had no fear of reprisals for punishment of children, and they were certain of his defense, even when it involved disciplining children of the community's power structure.

Oliver saw no basic conflict between a strong vocational program and an academic curriculum. When he discovered that the federal government would assume part of a teacher's salary for teaching shoe repair, Oliver organized the first course at Fairfield. Among the most popular programs in the curriculum was that of dry cleaning, dyeing, and pressing. Taught for many years by a highly efficient and business-oriented teacher named C. B. Slaughter, this course attracted large numbers of students, including Richard Arrington, who found temporary work while attending school. Facing an intense curriculum, students spent three hours a day in class for a period of two years before graduating with a diploma in the trade. Fairfield also offered other courses, including tailoring, auto mechanics, upholstering, carpentry, and bricklaying.

An emphasis on academic competition and a strong faculty made E. J. Oliver's school one of the most respected in the state of Alabama. Unlike many other black principals across the South, Oliver played a leading role in choosing personnel for his institution. The board of education apparently trusted his judgment, for he received expenses for recruitment trips as far away as Nashville and Atlanta to interview teaching prospects and to arrange for visits to Fairfield. His many contacts throughout the region and his careful study of applicants greatly reduced the number of weak teachers. The school profited, too, from an Oliver policy that guided instruction at every grade: teachers usually taught in their special fields. Only on rare occasions did instructors handle courses outside their specialty, and then only until the school could find a trained person. No matter what a teacher's area of interest, Oliver demanded allegiance to the school's philosophy of creating a healthy attitude toward scholarship and a respect for athletic competition.

Racial pride and an informed citizenship assumed importance among the students who attended Fairfield Industrial High. Before the demand of black history during the era of the 1960s, Oliver had such a course in his curriculum. A strong believer in the Association for the Study of Negro Life and History, founded in 1915, he strongly supported the objectives of its founder, Dr. Carter G. Woodson, the "Father of Black History." Oliver accepted the premise that the education of any people remained incomplete unless it embodied their ideals, and he argued that black schools should foster racial solidarity and achievement by exploring the black past.

Black children, Oliver emphasized repeatedly, needed heroes they could use as models. "Races of men," he once wrote, "cannot appreciate each other unless they know each other's past accomplishments." Oliver taught his students at Industrial High that the easiest way to prevent a race of people from progressing was to deny them a knowledge of their past. If a group could not look back and see something valuable in its past, it had not accepted the challenge to move forward. Whites' ignorance of black history, on the other hand, helped to reinforce a narrow view of black life. In 1928, Oliver established a *required* course in black history. Not only did Fairfield adopt Carter Woodson's book *The Negro in Our History* as a text, but the library subscribed to the major publications of the association—the *Journal of Negro History* and the *Negro History Bulletin*. Oliver believed that the *Bulletin*, tailored especially for young readers, instilled courage and creativity in them. The black principal's ideas contained much merit, but this dynamic educator, who had such an impact on Richard Arrington, may have invested too much faith in the power of history to bring about effective reform, especially in a society such as the American South. That faith, however, grew from a fundamental belief that quality education could alter people's behavior, even their racial attitudes.

Critics argued that Oliver's emphasis on black history could result in a kind of racial chauvinism, but little evidence surfaced to document this contention. In fact, the reverse seemed true. Cultural pluralism appeared to have gained strength among black students because of Oliver's teaching, and that attitude probably mitigated against the narrowness that undergirds racial chauvinism. Undoubtedly the study of black history strengthened the idea of a cohesive black community, and it provided a kind of psychological shield from the white supremacists' contention that blacks were inferior and culturally depraved. In Oliver's hands black history was not antithetical to the idea of a composite American nationality.

Oliver did not allow the abuse of black history. He refused to let black students employ it as an escape from intellectual rigor or as a diversion into a provincial world of race. As taught at Fairfield, black history enabled students to look at the experience of humankind through the eyes of blacks, provided an opportunity for the critical assessment of democracy in the United States, and probed the meaning of ethnicity in a complex society such as America. The course also addressed the issue of national unity. The destinies of blacks and whites, Oliver believed, were inextricably bound together, although whites may not have conceded that point at that time.

While Oliver's philosophy of life and his strong character made him an excellent role model for Richard Arrington, others at Industrial High also made a deep impression upon the shy, young man. Angelina Roe and Ruth Cook did much to channel his intellectual curiosity. Roe accepted no feeble substitutes for good communicative skills, and no doubt she would have cringed at the assault on standard English that came roughly a generation later. Conventional in her approach to teaching, she drilled her students in the fundamentals of writing and speaking, always insisting that they properly conjugate verbs, recognize parts of speech and sentence fragments, and apply logic to the thought process. Cook provided the spark that ignited Richard's serious interest in history and spurred him toward debate, an exercise that gave him valuable experience in thinking on his feet. There was little in his high school years, however, to suggest young Arrington's later fascination with the sciences, which became the heart of his professional career before he entered into college administration and politics.

The lack of a formal counseling program at Fairfield Industrial High adversely affected Richard Arrington. Two years after his graduation an evaluation committee of the Association of Secondary

Schools criticized the academic guidance program at the school. It stated a need for "much improvement in that area," and it called for more counselors to direct students. Arrington observed some years later that "poor counseling got me off track, and my parents did not have the background to guide me." He had the choice at Fairfield, of course, of pursuing a straight academic program or a vocational curriculum. Although he wanted to specialize in tailoring, the large number of students who requested the class forced the administration to draw names from a hat for places in the course.

Chance did not smile favorably upon Arrington. The school did not select him for tailoring, and he had to choose another subject. With little guidance, he followed the lead of a friend and took dry cleaning. For two years the quiet-spoken student spent half a day studying this trade. While he learned from this experience, to be sure, he later lamented that he had actually taken no tests to determine his real academic strengths. "I was recognized as having some scholarly abilities, but no one knew exactly what they were," he said thirty years after the experience. His study of dry cleaning, however, did not represent a complete waste of time, since a local establishment eventually hired him as a ringer boy. His job at Howard's Cleaners helped him defray much of the cost of his college education and some family expenses.

A commitment to academic excellence did not make Arrington a social hermit. At Fairfield other students accepted him as "one of the gang," although a few of his peers may have viewed his scholarly prowess with some suspicion. While he never participated in varsity basketball or football, he had an excellent relationship with the school's athletes, and they regarded him as "a regular fellow." During his senior year he did try out for the football squad, but the coach rejected him, "since the team was in a *rebuilding* year." Eventually he settled for serving as team manager. Even if he had played for the Fairfield Eleven, some believed that his lack of aggressiveness and his small size would have limited his success—and his playing time. Athletic greatness had not been preordained. He probably would not have been to football what his schoolmate Willie Mays later became to baseball and the New York Giants. He was, however, a good debater and actor, and he served with distinction in the student government association. His shyness perhaps kept him from aspiring to become a notable campus socialite, but he ranked high on his own popularity register, modestly giving himself seven on a scale of a possible ten! He avoided the easy way to social recognition, carefully restraining from the use of tobacco or alcohol until his college days. Even then, he drank only moderately, and never developed a taste for tobacco.

The black public school provided a kind of protective shield for Richard Arrington and other black youngsters in Fairfield and the American South. But a very different world existed beyond the black community and the school, and contact with that world was inescapable. That world was white, and few blacks could assume its essential friendliness or goodness at all times, although both qualities existed within it. A threat to the established order—even a *perceived* threat—could excite open hostility from white southerners, including violent emotional behavior toward those who only indirectly challenged the "southern way of life." But even a passive acceptance of the system did not necessarily assure exemption from physical harm or abuse when it came to protecting white society in Alabama.

Without conscious effort or labored thought, both black children and white children in the South grew to understand the structure of society, and they honored it, albeit for different reasons. Whites paid deference to it because it offered advantages, blacks because they had little choice, although time eventually wrought significant changes in their behavior. Most blacks had neither the resources nor the financial support to battle the system openly in the American South during the period of Arrington's youth, yet dissenters always existed. Truly, the idea of accommodation never became an integral part of the thinking of black people in the region. An actual threat to white supremacy sometimes brought economic reprisals and, in some cases, outright death, but resistance constituted a part of the history of the region. What kind of psychological and physical problems arose from living in a society that severely limited mobility and that created great stress may never be completely known, but some authors have already written of the emotional and social maladjustments that could have developed from growing up black in an oppressive society.

Richard Arrington, Jr., experienced the harshness of the other world that produced anxiety in the lives of black folk. Hardly any black youths in the South in the 1950s could escape direct contact with a system not designed to accommodate two races on equal terms. Black parents feared their children would say or do things in the presence of whites that would evoke hostility or a possible beating. "A lot of things scared you in those days," James Arrington said in speaking of his youth in Fairfield. The police brought particular fear to the Arrington boys. Policemen symbolized the law and enforcement—and white supremacy! James remembers walking nervously from the movie through white neighborhoods with his brother, hoping the police would not stop them as they hurried home. Policemen could react cruelly, especially toward black children whose parents had no political or social clout. It was not at all unusual for officers to enter a home without a search warrant or without knocking. When James observed a student stealing an automobile from the school parking lot, he thought it his duty to report the crime. He did. Instead of congratulating the boy for performing a civic duty, the police rigorously interrogated him about his possible involvement. The incident left a negative impression on James that took much time to erase.

Memories of contact with the police revealed much about the application of the law and race relations during the period. Despite the existence of laws that supposedly kept blacks and whites distant from each other, the two groups did sometimes mingle. On one occasion policemen discovered Richard and several black boys engaged in a football game with a group of white youngsters. The officers firmly cautioned them not to make that mistake again, or to prepare themselves for jail. At another time he and his cousins stopped at a park to survey leisurely the peaceful surroundings, but the police chased them out. "I was always conscious of the police," he recalls, "for stories abounded about their harsh treatment of black citizens."

Arrington knew of the rigidly segregated society that engulfed him, but he never indulged in any profound abstraction about the southern way of life. His heightened sense of social and economic justice came with his gradual development. "I think I accepted things as they were, and I probably suppressed any strong resentment . . . I had against the system," he related three decades after his departure from Fairfield. While blacks in the Alabama of Arrington's youth did not readily confront the system, their acceptance did not imply approval of the social structure, as many white politicians maintained when they spoke to other whites or to northern audiences. Richard recognized the potential for violence when blacks pressed legitimate claims against the system of inequality, for racial incidents had already marred life in Birmingham and other places. "I was aware of the Ku Klux Klan," he stated quietly in 1982, "and all that that group stood for."

When he went to register to vote, Richard encountered no harassment or threats from violent groups. He knew not only that registrars had denied some blacks the opportunity to vote but that some blacks trying to register had been victims of intimidation and outright physical violence. He was apprehensive, realizing that registrars had turned away blacks with college degrees. He studied hard to pass the examination required to vote under Alabama law. When he presented himself for the test, a female registrar appeared to ask him a "few questions about my background." She then looked up at him and said without any facial expression, "You pass the test." Puzzled by the entire proceeding, he then gladly raised his right hand to take a loyalty oath administered to all registered voters. Still stunned by the quickness of the event, Richard Arrington walked out of the Jefferson County Court House a registered voter, ten years before the historic Voting Rights act of 1965! At age twenty-one he could not have foreseen that many blacks and whites would have to make great sacrifices before the ballot became available to other black citizens in the state. Clearly, his voting status had made him one of a small percentage of blacks that had acquired the franchise in a state widely known for its political repression of black folk.

Richard's years as a student at Miles College sharpened his awareness of citizenship in a democratic society and acquainted

The Erskine Ramsey Library (1955) at Miles college where Richard Arrington, Jr., spent many hours of study. (Courtesy, Mayor Richard Arrington, Jr.)

him more keenly with the essence of race in America. His choice of Miles had not been difficult. He and his family—his mother, in particular—had always assumed that he would continue his studies beyond high school. Oddly enough, however, the Arringtons had made no special financial preparation for their son's college career. Upon graduation from Fairfield Industrial High in May 1951, Richard chose Miles because a good friend of his, Thomas Harden, had decided to enroll at the institution. Moreover, since he had little money, staying at home had some real advantages. He had also acquired the job at Howard's Cleaners, which he could keep while in school. Without employment his matriculation at Miles would have been impossible, since no federal or state scholarship grants existed. Although aware of the institution's solid academic reputation, Richard made no profound, critical assessment of its faculty or its curriculum before he entered college.

When he enrolled at Miles, Richard Arrington affiliated with a school that had miraculously survived hard times. The college had begun in 1898, when the Colored Methodist Episcopal Church in Alabama established an institution for the higher education of black youth. In fact, the denomination created two separate campuses in 1902—at Booker City (now Docena) and at Thomasville, Alabama. Miles developed from the merger of the two campuses. The church exchanged the Booker site for the present location in Fairfield, only a short distance from the Arrington home, and work on the new Miles campus started in 1907. The following year the church charted the school under the laws of Alabama as Miles Memorial College, a name retained until 1941, when the trustees dropped the word Memorial. Significantly, for half a century blacks could attend no other college in the Birmingham area except Miles.

At Miles Richard Arrington found other black students with similar backgrounds. Most of them came from the black working class, from families involved in the ceaseless struggle to make ends meet. The student body, however, did contain some sons and daughters of a few professional blacks, notably teachers and ministers. The college expected—indeed, required—a level of scholarly competence from all those that enrolled, and it insisted that each student pass a battery of tests in English, Mathematics, and Reading. While Richard Arrington had prepared himself well to enter Miles by graduating cum laude from his high school, Miles had a surprising number of very good students, many of them from Fairfield.

Arrington did not wander in the academic wilderness at Miles in search of a legitimate scholarly goal. At Miles he came into contact with a good teaching faculty sensitive to the plight of young, struggling black students. "By the time I got to Miles," he recounted in an interview, "I was already conditioned to do well, competitive almost by nature." He had grown to dislike mediocrity, and from the beginning he set his sights on academic excellence and the honor roll. His scholarly objective, however, greatly taxed his discipline, since he worked thirty to forty hours a week at the cleaners. Despite his desire for a good education and his quest for superior achievement, the young student did not choose a specific course of study in his freshman year. Not until a psychology professor, Verdelle Martin, inquired about his major did he seriously ponder the question. Martin suggested diplomatically that he pursue the sciences, and she then referred him to Emmett Jones, head of the biology department. His contact with Jones made a significant imprint on his life, for that particular professor pointed him toward advanced study after Miles and also reinforced the meaning of superior scholarship. By his sophomore year Richard Arrington had resolved to become a scientist, a good scientist.

If E. J. Oliver had served as a healthy role model for Arrington during his high school years, so did William A. Bell at Miles. Bell, who twice served as the president of Miles, 1912–13 and 1936–61, ran his institution much like Oliver had run Industrial High. He, too, was in control, and no one doubted his authority, at least not openly. Bell viewed the black college as a training ground for leaders with sound moral values who could serve as role models within the black community. So closely did he link scholastic activities and moral training that some students had to struggle desperately to determine the difference. Bell prided himself in his leadership capacity, and it was a serious mistake for faculty or students to misunderstand his position.

Miles's leader took seriously student attendance at what some termed "vital nonacademic functions." But practically everything that happened at Miles was academic to the president. "Chapel," or "assembly," was a very special event for the institution's chief executive. During this period "everything came to a halt," and professors searched buildings and grounds for clever students with enough nerve to cut a Bell assembly. Three times a week the student body gathered in Brown Hall to hear the institution's president or a noted invited guest. Anyone with excessive unexcused absences faced suspension from the school and a trip home. Chapel services, in Bell's mind, had an important effect on a student's life. Richard Arrington noted in a reflective moment that these assemblies helped to shape his aspirations for a better life and gave him a view of the world that may have otherwise escaped him. Black students had an opportunity to see and meet some of the most distinguished black leaders in the country: college presidents, businessmen, lawyers, doctors, and others of the race who, by herculean effort, had prevailed over the system of discrimination in the

United States. Many years after he had graduated from Miles College, Richard found himself using phrases from speeches he had heard in assemblies that Bell had defied students to miss.

At Miles a rigorous schedule and a demanding academic program forced the young college student into a strict, regimented life. With the careful use of his time, however, Richard Arrington "struck a happy balance" between academic life and extracurricular activity. Gradually, Arrington displayed more extrovertedness as he matured and ventured out on his own and as he slowly broke away from the driving influence of his mother. His fellow students detected leadership qualities in him and sought him out for participation in a variety of activities. In 1952, he joined the Alpha Phi Alpha Fraternity because of that group's strong emphasis on scholarship and achievement. Founded in 1906 at Cornell University, the Alphas had produced many distinguished Americans, including a long list of black college presidents and professional men. The accomplishments of Alpha men impressed Arrington, and so did the persuasion of Professor Iva Williams, director of the college band, who ultimately convinced the young man to join the fraternity. In affiliating with Alpha, he broke with most of his friends from Fairfield, who joined the Omega Psi Phi Fraternity, a historically strong group in the Birmingham area. After his induction into Alpha, Richard became president of the group, and he also held office in the Honor Society and in the Thespian Club.

Involvement in college activities and learning did not forestall a serious romance that had blossomed brightly before he entered Miles. A reserved Richard Arrington had met Barbara Jean Watts during his senior year at Fairfield Industrial High. A native of Westfield, Barbara was an attractive, energetic, junior cheerleader at the time Richard went to college. A star basketball player, she contributed to the dominance of Industrial High in girls' basketball in the state of Alabama. Upon graduation from high school Barbara received a scholarship in band and basketball and chose to attend Alabama State College in Montgomery. At the conclusion of her first year, however, the eighteen-year-old Richard took Barbara's hand in marriage, a decision that prompted many changes in their lives. Richard anticipated continuing his studies at Miles, and his

Eighteen-year-old Richard Arrington, Jr., as a college student in 1952. (Courtesy Mayor Richard Arrington, Jr.)

parents encouraged him to remain at the institution, since he was already well into his program. They also offered the young couple the opportunity to live with them until Richard's graduation from Miles, an offer the newlyweds accepted.

The Arringtons happily accepted their new daughter-in-law into their home, but some inevitable tensions surfaced. The Arringtons' rented house, of course, contained only three small rooms, and with James still in high school, space was limited. "It was crowded there after the marriage," James commented years later. An aunt also resided with the Arringtons for a time, and occasionally an uncle came to visit. More troubling for James was a feeling of Barbara's imposition, a feeling produced by the closeness between the two brothers. He and "Rick" had been together alone "for all those years, and now someone had stepped in to take him away." As a youngster he found it difficult to adjust to the new arrangement; and he had a terrible sense of invasion of his territory from the outside. He did not like it, but civility and peace generally prevailed. "The whole thing," James noted in recapturing memories of years in Fairfield, "required tremendous adjustments, and, admittedly, we had some rough spots."

Normal family stresses never unduly affected Richard's academic performance. By his senior year at Miles he had already decided to pursue graduate study. Several of his professors had discussed his career with him, but Jones did the most to encourage him. In the spring of 1955, he graduated cum laude from Miles College and headed north to the University of Detroit, which had offered him a graduate assistantship. This was Barbara's first contact with a large sprawling urban area, with all of its impersonality. Never before had she or Richard experienced a close relationship with whites, and that prospect produced some understandable anxieties for both of them.

Tensions had developed within Richard from the self-doubt that came from living in a southern system that had nothing to gain from producing confident blacks. Whites in Detroit, however, had their own brand of racial conservatism, for, after all, they had inherited a social and legal tradition that exalted the idea of white dominance. And that legacy had a profound impact on race relations in the North as well as in the American South. Yet, whites in Detroit did not have the preoccupation with race that seemed to characterize white Alabamians. Adjustment to the region, nevertheless, was difficult for the Arringtons.

The segregated life in the South had not conditioned the black student for an integrated campus life. The emotional strain that sometimes resulted from racial contacts had very visible effects. "I recall sitting in a class in Detroit, and knowing the answer to, say, four questions, but not the answer to a fifth . . . and feeling that I had let the black race down," Arrington confessed after he left school. In time, however, he not only learned to compete successfully with white students without stress, but he also discovered they "did not know all the answers to questions." In 1957, he finished his master's degree in zoology, near the top of his class.

Upon graduation from Detroit, Miles College offered Arrington an assistant professorship in its science department. From the time he accepted the position, he had anticipated returning to graduate school for his doctorate, but that hope remained distant until the president of Miles offered him an opportunity to return to his studies. He had now gotten valuable teaching experience and had learned to work diplomatically within the committee structure and to maintain his poise under pressure. It was now time to pull up stakes and travel west to the University of Oklahoma. In September 1963, Richard and Barbara said a temporary good-bye to Fairfield.

Located in the small town of Norman, the University of Oklahoma (OU) had an enrollment of twelve thousand students. The predominantly white city, situated some twenty-five miles from sprawling Oklahoma City, had never attracted a large number of blacks. When Arrington enrolled at OU in 1963, Norman had approximately twenty-five thousand people and only one permanent black resident. Although the Sooner State had a western flavor, it also had a racial history remarkably similar to that of the Deep South. Segregation and discrimination had been important parts of life in the state until the system began to crumble in the latter part of the 1940s. In 1948, a federal court had compelled the University of Oklahoma to admit its first black student, and the following year the United States Supreme Court shattered segregation in higher education in Oklahoma in the famous *Sipuel* case, which forced the institution to grant black students all the rights of whites.

Not more than one hundred blacks matriculated at OU when Arrington arrived on campus of the school that had an enviable national reputation for winning football teams. A large percentage of those blacks were graduate students from the American South who, like Arrington, had been denied the right to study in their home states. During the age of segregation southern states (including Oklahoma for many years) gave modest scholarship grants to black graduate and professional students who enrolled in out-of-state schools that accepted them. These states paid a price to maintain segregation, but the money students received did not compensate for the inconvenience of leaving home and the basic denial of civil rights. Arrington received an out-of-state award from Alabama, and he chose Oklahoma because of its proximity to Alabama and its generally good reputation in such fields as education, petroleum engineering, and the sciences.

The University of Oklahoma necessitated little academic adjustment for the ambitious Arrington. He had already confronted many of the social problems that came with integration. The fears and reservations he had encountered at the University of Detroit no longer greatly frustrated or disoriented him. Time had made a difference. More than six years had now passed, and he had gained considerable confidence in his abilities. He seemed certain of his capacity to compete, believing that the old southern system had not irreparably damaged him by trying to make him think that he was inferior. Also, he could rely on Barbara. His drive and his tenacious will to succeed made Arrington as determined to excel at Oklahoma as he had been at the University of Detroit. He would mold himself into the best zoologist his abilities would permit. The quicker he completed his course at Oklahoma, the sooner he could return to Miles to get on with his career.

Professors at the University of Oklahoma found their new student a bright prospect for a doctorate. Richard Goff fondly recalled meeting his eager advisee from the South shortly after his arrival on campus. "Dick came to us on his own merits," said Goff, anxious to stress that his department had not devised any special admissions program to accommodate the Miles College black. The faculty liked Arrington's businesslike manner. Indeed, the university had already registered its confidence by awarding him a graduate assistantship, an action not taken lightly by a school that had a heavy southern orientation. "He had a sense of direction, and he knew exactly what he wanted to do, what he came to achieve," Goff related with the proud sense of a former adviser. Keen competition characterized student life within the zoology department, and Arrington's entrance scores and his grades compared well with those of his peers. Professor Harley P. Brown predicted a brilliant career in education, if not research, for the black student. At Oklahoma he never repeated any exams or asked any favors. Said one of Arrington's professors emphatically: "He did not need any [special treatment]! He just zipped right through."

The energetic student made a profound impression upon those around him at the University of Oklahoma. He had a natural ability to elicit a positive response from others, and he could relate to people in a genuine way, said one of his former instructors. Cluff Hopla, chairman of the zoology department at the time Arrington attended Oklahoma, occasionally invited graduate students to his home for a "rare moment of relaxation" from their studies. He noticed the black student's affability and the ease with which he mingled with his peers. "But he always remained his own person," Hopla said of the quiet Arrington. The greatest testimony to his individuality and to the respect others had for him came from his fellow zoology students, all of whom were white. In 1966, they chose him to receive the coveted Ortenburger Award, given to a graduate student who showed unselfish interest in the welfare of other students, had a good relationship with peers, and maintained high academic standards. Although he often appeared shy to those who did not know him well, students sought him out for timely advice and were willing to take him into their confidence. "He was so smooth," said Brown, who kept a diary during those years, and that quality "just put people at ease." "He was a good diplomat," the professor remembered, and it surprised him little that one of his star students entered politics.

Professors in zoology at Oklahoma believed that Miles was grooming Arrington for an administrative post. His specific goal, however, had nothing to do with administration. When he completed his doctoral thesis "Comparative Morphology of Some Dryopoid Beetles," he looked forward to a life as a scientist. He had overcome great odds, and he had given real meaning to the idea of self-reliance. In addition, his successful experience at the University of Oklahoma had symbolized the triumph of a value system that prided discipline and belief in the ethic of hard work. By his own personal achievement, Richard Arrington had defied a racial system in the South that endeavored to restrict severely the talents of black people.

If Miles College officials had anticipated long service from Arrington following his return from Oklahoma in 1966, they met disappointment. Anxious to make use of his leadership abilities, President Lucius Pitts asked him to serve as acting dean and director of summer school. The following year he acted in the dual capacity as chairman of the Department of Natural Sciences and dean of the college, a job he retained until 1970. New challenges beyond Miles, however, beckoned. Less than five years after returning to his alma mater, Richard Arrington left the institution to become the executive director of the Alabama Center for Higher Education (ACHE). The move had implications for the future, for had he remained at Miles it is doubtful if he would have become so intimately involved in the political life of Birmingham.

The job at ACHE removed the former teacher from the practice of science, but it suited the expanding interest of a man who had a strong commitment to the survival of black education. Organized in 1968 by presidents of eight predominantly black colleges in Alabama, the center had as its central purpose the promotion of interinstitutional cooperation among its members. ACHE had developed from a proposal funded by the Ford Foundation that made possible a seminar at Tuscaloosa's Stillman College. Officials at Ford believed that cooperation among colleges, especially small black schools, was necessary if many of them had any chance of survival. Consequently, the foundation gave grants to schools in southern states to explore collective educational endeavors. At Stillman Col-

46

lege, representatives of black Alabama institutions—Miles, Alabama State, Talladega, Stillman, Tuskegee, Alabama A & M, Oakwood College, and Daniel Payne—composed a document that set forth possible areas of cooperation between them.

Arrington had initially rejected an offer to serve as the center's director because he was "not ready to move." However, he did accept a second invitation from the presidents of the consortium. An opportunity to work with both private and public colleges, a better income, and a chance to establish quality programs that would help ensure the survival of black institutions contributed to his decision to leave the school he had known for nearly two decades as a student and faculty member. When he joined the center, he had only a secretary, Jessie Huff who had studied at Miles, and a shoestring budget of forty thousand dollars. Nine years later under his leadership ACHE had a staff of some thirty people and a budget in excess of a million dollars. Because of the shortage of staff during his early years at the center, Arrington wrote many grant proposals for funding programs himself. While most people could have predicted his success at this endeavor because of his educational background and his experience at Miles, few could have anticipated the favorable results he realized at personal fund-raising. "I knew I had to get out and find money," he said in reflecting on his years at ACHE. And with practice he became "very good working the streets of New York."

The center never had a large operating budget, compared with those of some other regional educational organizations, but by the judicious use of funds Arrington achieved "a lot with a little." Undoubtedly, some of the center's most successful cooperative programs were those in highly specialized professional areas, such as veterinary medicine at Tuskegee Institute. Because of the center's existence, many black students had an opportunity to achieve their educational goals by completing part of their study on their local campus and the remainder at Tuskegee. The program that perhaps received the most enthusiastic support from the public was ACHE's Summer Internship Program, which assisted predominately black Alabama counties in preventing the out-migration of young people. The center's Oral History Project also enjoyed some success, with Tuskegee Institute, which had some familiarity in that area, the chief beneficiary. Arrington also administered successful programs in the cultural arena. Under Talmadge Foster, an employee at the consortium and later a strong Arrington political supporter, the center sponsored one of its most popular cultural events, "The Festival of Choirs." It attracted hundreds of listeners who came great distances to hear talented youths earn the honor as "the best singers anywhere in Alabama."

Arrington considers the failure to expand and enrich faculty research at center institutions his greatest disappointment. He found himself trapped by a tradition at member schools that gave low priority to scholarly investigation. Some administrators believed only in a mission of teaching. Even when he offered to pay the salaries of some faculty members to conduct research, some presidents at member institutions refused to approve their programs, and others insisted that faculty members subsidized by the center carry a full teaching load! Only at schools that had a tradition of research did Arrington make any progress in promoting the idea of scholarly research—principally at Tuskegee and Alabama A & M.

The directorship of ACHE brought Arrington valuable experiences. As the person responsible for raising money for consortium activities, he learned to manage a budget prudently and to take pride in the effective use of every penny that came to him. His contacts at ACHE were not limited to a select group of leaders, and he reached out to maintain an association with people. Indeed, he had a sensitivity toward "the man on the street" and to those who were "down and out." His religious background and his close association with Lucius Pitts at Miles helped produce a consciousness that fostered a desire for change. But Arrington could not escape history— it reached out and siezed him and made him its servant.

3

Shape of the Old Order: The Black Community and the City-Council Years

.

The eventual ascendancy of Richard Arrington in Birmingham politics owed much to the successful fight for black equality in the American South in the post–World War II era. The decade before Arrington returned from Oklahoma to Birmingham witnessed dramatic advances in civil rights that stunned many southerners who vowed not to change "their way of life." The South did not easily accept reform, especially Arrington's Alabama; not surprisingly, Alabama came to occupy an important place in the history of black civil rights. Here the struggle assumed the nature of a cause célèbre among those anxious to redress grievances, and it was here also that a national black leader came forth who would take his followers toward freedom.

The dramatic movement for black equality in the South gathered momentum in 1955 with the arrest of Rosa Parks in Montgomery, Alabama. This determined black woman refused to give up her seat on a local bus to a white man when the driver ordered her to move. Parks chose to defy the city's segregation laws. To lead their fight, Montgomery blacks drafted the young pastor of the Dexter Avenue Baptist Church, Martin Luther King, Jr. After a boycott that lasted a year, King and his followers achieved success with a United States

Supreme Court decision that overturned the Montgomery ordinance that required segregation aboard the city's buses.

The entire system of segregation did not end in Alabama or throughout American society with the court decree. Even though the 1954 *Brown* school-desegregation decision weakened the props that supported restrictive racial laws, reformers still had much to do. Success in Montgomery, then, was just another step in the march toward social change in the American South. In the years following the bus boycott, the drive for black equality quickened, and across the country blacks organized and strengthened protest groups that carried out massive demonstrations against racial injustice. The National Association for the Advancement of Colored People (NAACP), the Congress of Racial Equality (CORE), and the Southern Christian Leadership Conference (SCLC) were among the most important active organizations in the 1950s and 1960s.

King held unquestioned leadership of the civil-rights movement in the years before his death. He stood at the center of the crusade and so dominated it that the period 1955–68 has been justifiably called "the Age of King." It is impossible to comprehend what transpired in Birmingham and other places in America without some understanding of King's philosophy. Like his preacher-father, young King placed faith in nonviolence and direct action as a reform technique. A follower of Mahatma Gandhi, the Indian leader for national independence, King believed that the liberation of his black brethren in the United States would come through strict adherence to Gandhian principles. The Atlanta-born minister had charismatic appeal, and with his powerful oratory, he seemed destined to lead his people out of the valley of racial injustice. At the heart of his philosophy stood love of humankind, even of one's enemies, and the belief in the brotherhood of all people. King gathered around him young, idealistic crusaders willing to fill the jails for justice and to change those who oppressed blacks.

King and his followers struck hard at Birmingham, the "most thoroughly segregated city in the United States," in the spring of 1963. With hundreds of followers willing to suffer arrest, King carried out protest demonstrations that, because of white violence, attracted attention around the world. Birmingham officials fought back with a brutality that indicated their commitment to "the southern way of life." Eugene "Bull" Connor, the city's talkative and bombastic Public Safety Commissioner, tried to preserve "law and order" with methods that shocked even some white southerners. When King and his young disciples marched in Birmingham, Connor sent his policemen against the defenseless group, ordering his men to use dogs and powerful fire hoses to stop the demonstration. Law officers arrested scores, King among them. Later the black leader published from a jail cell his now-famous "Letter from a Birmingham Jail," which stands as one of the notable documents in the struggle for black civil rights.

America and the world watched closely as television showed the ugly picture of life in Birmingham. The brutality of Connor and his police crew aroused many citizens, and it also disturbed President John Fitzgerald Kennedy, who had moved slowly on civil rights after he took office in 1961. The hideous events of Birmingham forced the president toward stronger political action. He went on national television to condemn vigorously the unlawful use of violence against citizens, and he proclaimed more forcefully than any other American chief executive the immorality of segregation and discrimination. Every American, he said, had the right to equal service in places of public accommodation, the right to the ballot, and the right to a full and free life "without being forced to resort to demonstrations in the street."

Pious words were no substitute for action. Kennedy did offer blacks something more concrete than verbiage. The president called upon Congress to enact legislation to remedy the racial ills that had long plagued American society. That body, however, mirrored conservative public opinion on racial questions, and the civil-rights bill the president requested became hopelessly bogged down in the Congress. Black leaders moved to unearth an old idea of A. Philip Randolph's, then the grand old man of the civil-rights movement, that called for a massive "March on Washington." Much of America held its breath as churches, labor groups, civil-rights organizations, and others joined to make their voices known to lawmakers in Washington. Kennedy moved cautiously, ever worried about the possibility of violence that could do irreparable harm to his civil-rights plans. Moreover, he had been elected by a very slim majority of popular votes, and he could hardly afford negative political fallout.

In August 1963, some 250,000 blacks and whites came to Washington from every corner of America to demonstrate their support for civil-rights legislation and for better job opportunities. In many ways, however, the march represented not only the hopes of black America but the changing consciousness of white Americans. It was, too, a reflection of what had already been happening in many southern communities. Above all, it constituted a dramatic plea for justice and common decency that supposedly went with citizenship in a free society. And although the march itself ultimately proved nonviolent, its very size suggested the possible tragic consequences that could flow from continued protest against injustice in America. During this march, Martin Luther King, Jr., successfully captured the spirit of the movement, sounded its rhythm, and provided inspiration for its devoted followers in his now-famous "I Have a Dream" speech. Although a masterpiece of American oratory, King's speech did not sway diehard southerners in the Congress, who filibustered the Civil Rights Bill for seventy-five days. But growing public opinion did not favor them. In 1964, Congress passed the measure, a fitting memorial to President Kennedy, who lost his life by assassination the previous year in Dallas, Texas.

Richard Arrington watched closely the unfolding civil-rights events from the quiet campus of the University of Oklahoma. Black leaders and their people were not "Free by '63," and even with the historic Civil Rights Act, black Americans still suffered from disfranchisement in many parts of the South. After the passage of the measure, blacks turned their attention to other pressing concerns, especially voting rights. Violence again showed its face as hostile southerners vented their aggression upon their oppressed brethren. In Arrington's Birmingham a bomb blast tore away a part of Sixteenth Street Baptist Church, killing four black children. So much bombing occurred in the city during this era that some people referred to it derisively as "Bombingham." Violence and brutality, however, could not stop social progress or silence the strident voices that had come to demand the vote and "Freedom—NOW!"

The historic Sixteenth Street Baptist Church. (From the Photographic Collection, Department of Archives and Manuscripts, Birmingham Public Library, Birmingham, Alabama)

Frustrated by continued opposition to voting in the South, King led a march in 1965 from Selma to Montgomery, the state capital, to dramatize blacks' fight for the ballot. State troopers brutally assaulted demonstrators, but their action could not deter the "train destined for freedom." Thousands of both black and white demonstrators came to join King in Governor George C. Wallace's Alabama, and when they arrived at the capital, the segregationist governor watched angrily from a window a short distance from King's former pastorate, Dexter Avenue Baptist Church.

Civil-rights activists received strong support from President Lyndon Baines Johnson, who took office following the tragic death of Kennedy. Although a Texan, Johnson did not fit the description of a classic racial demagogue, but many doubted that he was liberal on race issues. The nation, however, was ripe for change—and for Johnson, who abetted it. The president clearly articulated his views on voting, and he told Americans unequivocally of his support for legislation that guaranteed the ballot to all citizens. He confidently declared, "We shall overcome."

Congress heeded the president's wishes by passing the Voting Rights Act in the summer of 1965. Richard Arrington had returned to Birmingham about a year after the enactment of this historic piece of legislation. Sweeping political reforms had taken place at the national level during his relatively short time in Oklahoma, and the winds of change had now created giant political swirls that would unsettle the old order.

The political and social changes that took place in Birmingham while Arrington studied in Oklahoma would have a direct effect upon his life and later career. The horrible racial incidents that had taken place in the city had shaken him and had driven him to write letters of protest against the ugly violence that characterized the Birmingham demonstrations. Yet, he had never abandoned the hope of returning home, for he envisioned a role as an educator and citizen in bringing about constructive changes in the city. The King crusade in Birmingham, of course, had not suddenly changed racial attitudes, but Arrington was aware that it had altered behavior and that federal laws were slowly undermining the racist props that supported segregation.

Only time would reveal the revolutionary character the Voting Rights Act would have on the political life of Birmingham and the American South and upon the personal life of Richard Arrington. But the 1965 voting measure and the black revolution of the sixties had already produced a new mood and a "New Negro." Although some years would pass before black people would become accustomed to participating comfortably in the political process, institutional structures already existed to mobilize them for action. Indeed, three decades before Arrington would enter politics in the city, black leaders had already formed the Progressive Democratic Council, which preached political unity and self-help. The NAACP had also stressed the value of the ballot and active political involvement.

A change in the form of Birmingham city government that took place while Arrington pursued a doctorate in Oklahoma also had a dramatic effect on social and political life. Before 1963, the city had a commission form of government that some people contended had become the symbol of a social order whose time had passed. Led by David Vann, a young attorney, and other progressive citizens, a movement developed to install a new system of government. Although the fight to abolish the commission structure had no direct connection with racial policies per se, those who favored its continuation did interject the issue of race into the debate. Bull Connor, one the three commissioners under the system, attacked racially liberal Vann and his allies, accusing them of trying to desegregate Birmingham. His tactic failed. When the city held an election on the adoption of a new kind of government, a proposal for a mayor-council structure gained some 52 percent of the vote.

Black ballots played an important role in overthrowing the commission form of government in Birmingham. It also helped to defeat Bull Connor, who ran against "moderate" segregationist Albert Boutwell in the spring 1963 mayoral election. Blacks had shown the possibility of more widespread reform through the vote. The old political and social order seemed sure to pass with the registration of more voters under the 1965 voting law. And black leaders in Birmingham now worked harder politically to ensure the demise of an outmoded system that had survived too long.

The Birmingham that approved a new form of city government was not one of democracy's brilliant showcases. Located in Alabama's Jefferson County, the metropolitan area had a population of about 600,000 people at the time Arrington finished his Ph.D. degree and returned home to join Miles College. With an economy that had been built around the steel industry, Birmingham represented the social and political heartbeat of the region. Although urban, the city's white racial attitudes, however, were more akin to those of rural Mississippi towns than, say, to the attitudes in Atlanta of the 1960s.

In 1960, blacks represented about 35 percent of the population of Jefferson County. They moved in a restricted world, but they had created a vibrant culture within the "veil of segregation." Few whites really knew of life behind the veil, but cultural forms (music, for example) leaped over the walls of segregation to win adoption from white America. As in other southern communities, poverty characterized the life of blacks in Birmingham, and it showed in practically every facet of their existence.

Leadership within the black community in Birmingham came under increasing pressure as activist activity mounted in the 1960s and early 1970s. Older black leaders such as millionaire A. G. Gaston, John Drew, and Arthur Shores heard insistent demands for direct action. More militant leaders, such as the Reverend Fred Shuttlesworth, challenged the old guard by their uncompromising stand on equality. When King came to Birmingham, people such as Shuttlesworth and others had already attracted the attention of the white power structure. And they had also thrown down the gauntlet to a black leadership that had grown too cautious for the times. The brilliance of King, Shuttlesworth, and other leaders resided in their ability to mobilize the masses and to limit friction and frustration in the Birmingham movement.

In the years after King's death blacks across America turned more and more toward the ballot as a viable instrument for social change. Despite increased voter registration and participation in the electoral process, they had made few advances by 1971 in sharing real political power in Birmingham and Jefferson County. Many whites anticipated that the drive for greater power would soon abate, but as the black population grew along with the number of registered black voters, that hope became increasingly remote. The "threat" now was not the acquisition of minor offices but the possibility of winning powerful decision-making positions in local and county government. Black domination had long been an obsession with many white southerners, and to those in Birmingham it seemed all too real in the 1960s as the demographics of the city changed.

The first major black political appointment in Birmingham came with the selection of attorney Arthur Shores in 1968 to fill an unexpired term on the city council. A longtime resident of the city, Shores had attended Talladega and Daniel Payne colleges. He taught school at Bessemer, Alabama, and later became the principal at Dunbar High School in Birmingham. With an interest in law, he took a correspondence course and was admitted to the Alabama bar. Struck by the injustice toward black people who lived in his city and in the South, he involved himself in the struggle for civil rights; and for a time his name became virtually synonymous with the legal assault upon inequality, especially in education in the state of Alabama. For his persistent efforts, he paid dearly. White bigots harassed him, and they bombed his home to curtail his civil-rights activities. Yet, the quiet-spoken, genteel lawyer did not let fear deter him. Never radical in his approach to social reform, Shores mirrored the strategy of the NAACP, with which he was closely associated. But to whites of Birmingham any attack upon racial segregation was radical, a real threat to a way of life that southerners had known for generations. Shores's bravery won him admiration from the black community, and he became a heroic symbol that gave young people such as Richard Arrington pride and courage. By the seventies, however, his posture on civil rights appeared too moderate for more activist blacks in the city.

For racially conservative whites who remembered his career, Shores was the enemy, the very caricature of a black radical that troubled their minds even after he had ended his more energetic period in civil rights. Understandably, when his name surfaced as a replacement for the late councilman R. W. Douglas, heated debate raged in some quarters over his qualifications. The Birmingham City Council and Mayor George Seibels, who had won office in 1967 with black support, received pressure to appoint the noted civil-rights attorney. In November 1968, a group of black leaders, including Lucius Pitts, president of Miles; S. J. Bennett, grandmaster of the Prince Hall Masons; the Reverend John Porter, of Sixth Avenue Baptist Church; and A. G. Gaston petitioned the city to name a black to the council. Cognizant of the growing political power of blacks in the city, leaders in the community warned of their intention to use their votes wisely for those who wanted to give them representation in government. If results did not follow from their efforts, they told the city fathers, their followers would know that "your system is a foul thing and not worthy of the energy expended in such an apparently foolhardy endeavor." They pointed to the possibility of racial unrest and to the danger that came with it if a black did not receive a seat on the council. Black leaders had urged restraint and support "for the orderly process of effecting change," but they were clear in demanding the appointment of Shores.

Some liberal whites joined blacks in articulating the urgent need for a new racial makeup on the council. Mrs. James Ross Forman, Jr., expressed her strong feelings to Seibels in supporting a black appointee. Echoing the contention of some black leaders, she maintained "that unless the Negro . . . can become a legitimate part of our economic and political power structure our city is doomed to endless riots and civil disorder." A telling letter came from a white citizen in Perry County whose father had fought for the Confederacy and had served in a Union prison camp during the Civil War. "If anyone should be against the Negro," he wrote Mayor Seibels, "it is I. But I am not." Whites had not given blacks opportunity, "and I feel that we should make amends for it." He proposed the selection of some responsible black "like Dr. [A. G.] Gaston or Arthur Shores."

Blacks expected some heated opposition from whites. It came. Jessie T. Todd deplored how black groups had been "turning up the heat" for the selection of one of their own to the council. Completely ignoring the accomplishments of Shores, who had emerged as the consensus candidate among blacks for the position at city hall, Todd tried to exempt herself from any charges of racism by calling for appointment to the council based on "qualifications." It was "disgusting to the average citizen to see how some of our communities give in to [blacks'] threats, whims and fancies." Others echoed Todd's opinion—but time had caught up with Birmingham.

The Birmingham City Council did not heed voices that looked to the past. It appointed Arthur Shores. No political scientist had to ponder what had transpired. Mayor Seibels and the council had deferred to the growing political strength of the black community, the argument that political injustice existed, and the fact that the denial of a seat on the council to a black could mean demonstrations. Seibels, who still enjoyed great popularity in the black community, highly praised Shores as a booster of the city. He wrote to a citizen that the council had made the best possible decision for a city that had such a large black population. One enthusiastic white citizen who agreed saw the appointment as a symbol of a "new attitude and spirit in . . . Birmingham." That, however, was not the opinion of S. Patrick Ballard, who, unable "to keep my cool," wrote that the council's choice of Shores "constitutes in my opinion the most obnoxious, underhanded, backdoor affront to the majority of citizens in this community." Seibels knew "damn well the city electorate would not have . . . [chosen] such a substitute." Ballard turned heatedly to Shores's past. The black lawyer had gone from "social trouble maker" to city council in a few short years. His appointment clearly revealed that white citizens had mistakingly elected "liberals" to city government rather than "progressive conservatives."

Birmingham had taken a giant first step away from its past. Richard Arrington applauded the council's efforts as he methodically went about his work at Miles, quietly watching the unfolding social revolution taking place in the city and across the nation. He had known Shores for many years, admired him, and like other blacks, applauded his appointment to the council. But he knew that the selection of a single black would not appreciably alter life in Birmingham. The appointment, however, did give hope to blacks, who had been closed out of the system; and now that time had shattered tradition, it seemed probable that the increased political consciousness of the black community in Birmingham could score greater victories.

Arrington had not seriously contemplated a life of politics upon his return to Birmingham. He preferred a life of the mind. Despite his administrative duties at Miles, teaching and intellectual exchange had a special attraction for him. Changing conditions in Birmingham, however, drew him involuntarily to the center of political activity in this town struggling to reshape its image. As he sat quietly in his ACHE office in the summer of 1971, he received a telephone call from three black young men who had met to discuss prospective black mayoral candidates. They had seen Arrington's work with a number of civic groups, and they knew of his community interests, especially his concern for the advancement of blacks. They put the question to him without equivocation: "Do you want to run?" The answer came back an unqualified "No!" Before the call he had not considered public office, and after reflecting upon politics, he reached the conclusion that "the time was not politically right" for such a move. He believed that a sufficient black political base was absolutely necessary for victory in a mayoral campaign, and such a foundation did not yet exist in Birmingham. He did not want to run simply "for the sake of running."

Arrington's friends persisted in their efforts to get him involved in the political process. They accepted his decision not to enter the mayoral race in 1971, but they asked him to seek a position on the city council. Arrington agreed to give it some thought, and he scheduled a meeting at his office to discuss the details of a contest. Following that meeting, he decided to throw his hat into the ring. Ironically, Arrington had always taken a serious interest in the growth and development of his city, but he had never attended a city-council meeting. Like so many other blacks who had been distant from the political process during the years of segregation, he recognized by 1971 that the reality of social change resided in the decision-making that took place in court houses, city halls, and legislative bodies. Although Arrington's black supporters did not choose him because of ideology, they did believe he would demonstrate more aggressiveness than the quiet Shores, now regarded as a symbol of the "old Negro leadership."

To comprehend adequately the Arrington candidacy is to understand in greater detail the nature of black leadership (and dissatisfaction with it) in Birmingham during the 1970s. Many of the younger blacks in the city wanted to continue to build on the advances of the 1960s. They conceded that the old guard had helped to create progress in a violent period that challenged their courage, their fortunes, and sometimes their lives. They appreciated the sacrifices of this leadership, but it was now dated. To a few it had become selfish, consumed with protecting its own power and influence, and determined to hold on to it at all cost. The old black leadership, they argued, accepted the slow pace of change too willingly and concentrated too much upon not offending the white power structure. Birmingham needed a new generation of leaders with more energy and a different view of progress. "A lull had existed in reform," Arrington commented in 1982, despite minor concessions by whites in power. Black leaders, he said, exerted little real power without the sufferance of the white power structure.

They had to go to whites, who greatly determined what the black community could and could not do and what it received in the end.

To secure their position and the continuation of their ideology, black leaders tried to isolate, or totally exclude, youthful "upstarts" who appeared threatening or too radical. Arrington's most striking example of the old leadership's tactics is the case of Clarence Woods, an outspoken and articulate young man "who sometimes threatened to rock the boat." Woods had many talents, but he found himself virtually excluded from any influence within the black power structure. Older black leaders "tended to take leadership to the grave with them," and reluctantly did they agree to share their power with others.

Throughout the 1960s, blacks forcefully emphasized control of their own communities and the right to choose their own leaders. A dramatic development that illustrated this changed direction in black thought in Birmingham took place while Arrington still served on the faculty at Miles. Both he and Lucius Pitts had raised questions about employment discrimination and police brutality in the city, and in 1969 they called a meeting of blacks at Gaston's restaurant to air opinions. The group adopted a document written by Arrington and later presented it to white leaders. As a result, a biracial committee came into being, the Community Affairs Committee (CAC), which today remains part of the structure of a larger body called Operation New Birmingham (ONB).

White leaders named ten blacks and ten whites to the CAC. A new spirit, however, now prevailed, and many blacks felt affronted with the attempt to "handpick our leaders." Blacks sent two representatives, Dr. James Montgomery and Calvin Woods, to a meeting with whites, Arrington related, "to tell them we were going to appoint our own leaders." They picked nine of the ten persons chosen by the white group! But that was hardly the point of crucial significance—blacks themselves had chosen their own representatives! This particular episode graphically depicted the rise in a new kind of black leadership in Birmingham, not radical in the traditional sense of the word, but insistent that the black community determine its own direction. Outsiders—those of the white power structure—would no longer unilaterally write the agenda for the black community; nor would whites have to "anoint" its leaders. Blacks demanded access to a better life and respectful treatment for public servants, and they would not beg for the common decency that rightfully belonged to them. Their ballots would speak for them.

This was the prevailing political attitude in the black community when Arrington officially announced his candidacy for a council seat in September 1971. He spoke of "progress" in the city and a willingness to face the demanding challenges of problem solving. "I have always had an interest in the development of this city, in seeing it become a city of which all of her people can be proud," he told a predominantly black audience at the Fourth Avenue YMCA. He did not address the issue of race directly, but few could mistake his pledge to help build a Birmingham where all citizens could feel a sense of belonging and could have a stake in the future. He had the mental ability and the energy to match the perplexing problems the city faced. Economic growth, urban blight, and the effective use of human resources, Arrington said, constituted the central concerns of a modern, progressive Birmingham.

The candidate chose his longtime friend Lewis White to head his campaign. The two had met at Miles as students and had known each other for twenty years. An excellent writer and a good speaker, White studied biology at Miles along with Arrington, but he had gone into communications after college. Sometimes disheveled and disorganized, the extroverted White had enormous talents that seemed to eclipse his more obvious weaknesses. He knew the city, especially the black community, and he had a "certain way, a kind of charm with people." He also knew "the streets," and he could disarm the unsuspecting person with his "down home, folksy" demeanor and speech. He moved in and out of social classes with great ease, and only his chain-smoking and his rapid speech gave away any possible anxiety.

Arrington could raise only limited funds to aid him in the 1971 campaign. Thus, he faced severe limitations in building a political organization and in advertising his campaign. "I had almost no money . . . and only a few workers," Arrington commented about his beginning in politics. Much of the funds he succeeded in raising came from people connected with Miles. With few resources the candidate relied heavily upon past contacts, principally the black community and a select number of whites. Despite some of his criticism of black leadership, Arrington touched base with long-time community leaders such as Arthur Shores and got their support.

The nonpartisan city-council election drew a large field of hopeful candidates. Three incumbents—Don Hawkins, Tom Woods, and Russell Yarbrough—were among the twenty-nine persons who vied for the five seats at stake in the election. Besides Arrington, four other blacks joined the political battle—Rev. A. A. Smith, a Baptist minister; Eddie Bryant, an industrial employee; Thomas E. Wrenn, a dental technician; and Jessie Stewart, a staff member of the Jefferson County Committee for Economic Opportunity. Smith and Bryant, lesser known for their civic activities, dropped from the race before election day.

For the black community the central issue in the 1971 city-council election was greater political representation. Arrington repeatedly stressed that blacks in Birmingham composed 42 percent of the population but had only a single voice in the nine-member council. Other issues, however, such as revamping the local civil-service system, the appointment of blacks to various city boards, the practice of closed-door public meetings, unpaved streets, and poor services, attracted attention from the aggressive Arrington. One citizen, struck by Arrington's appeal, expressed the belief that his leadership would recognize the plight of the needy, the disadvantaged, "the socially scorned," and those that had no voice. Discussion in the campaign, nevertheless, invariably returned to the sharing of power and participation in decision making at city hall.

Political endorsements are vital to success in a large city, where direct personal contact is limited. A boost came from the powerful *Birmingham Post-Herald*, which had shown a willingness to support some social and political changes in the city and in Alabama. The paper urged its readers to "balance" membership on the city council. The *Post-Herald*'s 6 October 1971 endorsement of Arrington addressed the issue of adequate black representation at city hall and the candidate's ability to serve effectively: "While black citi-

zens are more than 40 percent of the total population of Birmingham, only one present councilman is black. Dr. Arrington is not
campaigning as a 'black candidate' nor asking for a seat on the basis
of race. He is, however, superbly equipped to provide the city government with increased understanding of the black community
and in turn [he can] transmit [a] better understanding of city government to the black community."

As the 12 October election approached, Arrington sensed victory.
Nothing had surfaced to derail his campaign. He had hoped to avoid
a runoff by winning an overwhelming mandate in the primary, but
"the numbers were not right." The results of the contest left six
contestants in the field for a runoff for the three remaining council
seats. Arrington had received overwhelming support in the black
community, and he had placed third in the overall field with 19,893
votes. The election had not only catapulted him into a runoff, but it
had also seen the selection of two political moderates for the final
contest, the attorney David Vann and the attractive Angi Proctor, a
former Miss Alabama. The voters again returned Mayor George Seibels to office with a majority of the black vote in his favor.

While the failure to win a seat on the council in the primary
greatly disappointed Arrington, he welcomed increased black involvement in the political process. The large black turnout encouraged him, for it signaled the potential power of the black ballot,
especially if the city ever voted by districts for council positions
and if reapportionment gave blacks more seats in the state legislature. The primary had shown a solid black base of political support,
which constituted the basis for his optimism before the runoff. In
the period between the primary and runoff, he tried to broaden his
base and to win white votes by emphasizing the need to improve
Birmingham's image and the necessity of attracting more jobs to
the city.

If the primary showed unity within the black community, it also
revealed some divisiveness, and it raised again the gnawing question of "the old leadership." The Jefferson County Progressive Democratic Council came under attack from the *Birmingham World* for
not designing a mechanism for testing the allegiance of politicians
that ran for office. The absence of a yardstick for measuring can-

didates, wrote one black editor, did not represent a good approach to hard-nosed politics. That kind of behavior in the past had accounted for the "unsatisfactory situation of the Negro group which represents 42 percent of the Birmingham population." The *World* sounded Arrington's theme: black people had to insist that whites share political power, but in the past the old leadership had not demanded that. The paper's editor blamed blacks who participated in "closed door leadership" meetings (in the CAC) for the relative absence of political power that existed. The 16 October 1971 *World* called for the election of candidates who promoted unity in the community and who favored the distribution of the benefits of government to all segments of the population.

The runoff excited unusual interest within the black community. The opportunity existed to select another black to the council, but enthusiasm developed for other reasons. The equally divided field of white and black candidates in the race, including some white moderates, also had much significance. Proctor and Vann enjoyed a favorable reception in the black community. Besides electing more blacks, then, the challenge was to defeat the one white conservative, Tom Woods. Since voters had to cast a ballot for *three* candidates, it was possible for blacks to vote a "straight black ticket" or to "cross over" to aid a particular white candidate.

An Arrington victory in the runoff rested with a good voter turnout, continued cohesion within his black base, and support from the media that had previously backed him. To encourage voter participation, the Jefferson County Progressive Democratic Council and the Alabama Christian Movement for Human Rights sponsored rallies to get voters to the polls. W. C. Patton, then associate director of the NAACP Voter Education Project, strongly urged blacks not to surrender their chances for effective decision making at city hall by staying at home.

The *Birmingham Post-Herald* tried to reduce fears of political doom among whites if Arrington, Proctor, and Vann arrived at city hall. The paper stood solidly behind them. The new council persons, said the 1 November 1971 *Post-Herald*, "will by no means have the capacity for carrying out a revolution," since they would compose only one-third of Birmingham's city council. Turning to

Arrington, the journal strongly urged voter support for him declaring that "all the circumstances of his life and career have shaped him for service" and that his "dignified and introspective" personality would well serve the city. The newspaper showed a sensitivity to the candidate's past and prevailing political currents when it told readers that Arrington could communicate effectively with a wide range of citizens and that he understood the conditions that restricted the lives of the poor.

By a whopping vote, the citizens of Birmingham chose Richard Arrington, Jr., to his first political office. His selection to the council took on added meaning with the triumph of both Proctor and Vann, who later joined him in support of several crucial issues. One observer of the election noted with only slight exaggeration that voters had had a choice primarily "between liberal and liberal," except for candidate Tom Woods. Arrington's impressive showing of 29,415 votes had brought him in second behind front-runner Vann, who garnered 32,710 ballots. Proctor had beaten Woods by nearly 1,400 votes. Although black candidates Jessie Stewart and A. A. Smith had entertained high hopes for victory, their 20,321 and 11,901 votes, respectively, failed to win them a seat on the council. Both Vann and Arrington earned a four-year stint at city hall, but Proctor had to accept a two-year term for her third-place finish. Arrington's election, of course, made him the second black to sit on the Birmingham City Council. In Vann the contest had brought to office a man who had played such a vital role in the creation of the mayor-council system, and it had dramatically created a council where two blacks served along with two white women (Proctor and Nina Miglionico). Surely, change was in the air in Birmingham, the Magic City.

Those who thought the election of Arrington would stifle the voices that called for greater black political representation were mistaken. Had all black candidates enjoyed victory in the 1971 contest, blacks would have had a total of four of the nine council slots. In the opinion of some, the black community rightly deserved that many. The time for tokenism had passed. The challenge to black leadership, wrote one black editor, was to commence a search for other good black candidates to run for office. Pressure for political participation and power sharing had to continue.

Arrington joined a council with a moderately conservative political bent. Among the white councilpersons, Vann most closely fit the description of liberal. Proctor, however, did reflect a new social attitude among more progressive Alabamians, but time later tempered her political posture. Don Hawkins, president of the council when Arrington came aboard, carried a heavy baggage of political conservatism, but he ably pulled together divergent personalities and factions. Nina Miglionico, affectionately referred to as "Miss Nina" by her friends who knew her well, had a keen mind, was intellectually tough, and usually dealt objectively with issues. She was an attorney, and her mild liberalism probably outweighed any conservatism that occasionally showed on public matters. Miss Nina had a sense of the city, where she wanted it to go, and how it would get there. A member of the original council elected to replace the old commission, she brought experience and determination to her job. Liston Corcoran represented the eastern section of the city, and his politics mirrored the area he served. He was "a very, very, conservative man," Arrington said in profiling the city politician. Upon his untimely death the moderately liberal David Herring replaced him. Councilman E. C. "Doc" Overton had very little "political backbone," and Arrington remembers him as a vacillator who "hardly ever took a firm stand on anything." In an earlier period, "he had been one of the strongest segregationists on the council, although he moved some as the times changed."

The greatest ideological distance separated Arrington and Councilman Russell Yarbrough, who carried unchallenged conservative credentials. Blunt and often verbally colorful—even rustic—Yarbrough could disarm an opponent with his direct, down-home approach to complex matters, a trait that led some erroneously to believe he had little capacity for creative thought or politics. But Yarbrough was a master politico, in a class by himself. A Georgian who grew up in Birmingham, he spent most of his life in sales in the northern part of the city. He possessed a verbal ability to "rip apart an adversary" with language that sometimes belied his association with the Deacon Board of the Woodlawn Baptist Church. While he never fit the classic definition of a political demagogue, the press and opponents did accuse him of shifting positions to suit his political advantage and of playing to the crowd, habits not uncommon to some other politicians.

Yarbrough's conservatism and his years at city hall before the 1980s produced doubt in the black community. His steadfast support of the Birmingham police on practically all matters of controversy, especially in cases of alleged police brutality, frustrated black citizens. Considered the darling of the Fraternal Order of Police (FOP), he seldom called the department to task for alleged misdoings. And at one point in his career, he even suggested that the city not remove policemen from the force for breaking regulations. His ardent defense of the police raised questions about his motives, in a town where black people often felt the crushing blows of policemen's clubs. As black people became more of a force in Birmingham politics, Yarbrough tempered his political ideology, especially at election time. Ultimately, he would win the support of the most powerful black political group in the city—an organization, ironically enough, created by Richard Arrington.

An ideological difference should not have separated Arthur Shores and Richard Arrington. And it did not, but time had greatly cooled Shores's driving passion for social change. A veteran of the civil-rights movement, Shores did not have to apologize for his fight to achieve equality for black folk. His performance on the council, however, disturbed some citizens within the black community. Extremely harsh editorials critical of him appeared in the black press, and they must have stung the old civil-rights leader. Arrington respected Shores's work to elevate his people, but he believed the attorney had not kept pace with the changing mood in civil rights and prevailing attitudes within the black community. Whether it was increasing age or "civil-rights burnout," the once-dynamic black lawyer now projected a conservative image in the black community. Shores, of course, had never occupied radical positions on civil rights, and his approach to social problems had always mirrored his quiet personality. Yet, he had once displayed a fire that more openly burned against racial injustice and inequality.

68

Arrington applauded Shores's strength, but he critically assessed his weakness as a member of the city council. Shores did not want to "rock the boat." Low-key, he was never vocal on the council, and never controversial. As restrained as Arrington seemed to most people, "Shores's presence on the council" made him look "more radical, or at least more progressive," and that factor had a lot to do with Arrington's standing within the black community and his political fortunes. Shores plowed no new ground during his tenure in office, and his critics maintained that he rarely insisted upon meaningful changes that benefited blacks. Yet, Shores's presence on the council had a distinct advantage. Arrington could ask him to seek support of some conservative whites "who did not like my posture, but . . . who liked Arthur." While the younger councilman explained the basic difference between Shores and himself as a matter of style, there was clearly a difference in the way the two viewed racial changes and the pace of social reform.

As a councilman, Arrington was disappointed with Mayor George Seibels's position on major black issues. Seibels had a passion for politics, and he "loved to be mayor." He delighted in moving around the city cutting ribbons, giving speeches, greeting visitors, opening new businesses, and performing other duties as the city's chief executive. A conservative man with a healthy ego, Seibels basked in popularity. More than any other previous mayoral candidate, he took time to visit black institutions and to woo the black vote. "I remember when George Seibels used to just pop into a club during election time, start shaking hands and talking like he was part of the community," said a longtime city resident who had witnessed the politician in action. Seibels left behind good will, but "that was about the extent of George's commitment, for he was not going to take any [constructive] action," Arrington critically commented in an appraisal of the mayor. That assessment had much to do with Seibels's stand on two issues closely associated with Arrington's political success—affirmative action and police brutality.

As chairman of the Communication and Transportation Committee and the Public Safety Committee, Arrington dealt with a variety of nonracial issues. However, he could hardly escape those matters that heavily impinged upon race and equality. The federal government had established affirmative-action guidelines, for example, to give blacks, other minorities, and women greater economic opportunities. President Lyndon Baines Johnson had established affirmative action in 1964 with Executive Order 11246, which required hiring goals by certain public and private institutions and government. At the time no loud outcry came from the American public, probably because of the prevailing mood in the country, Johnson's strong leadership, and the relative weakness of conservative political forces. President Johnson concluded that to announce equality without making a serious effort to redress past economic wrongs through constructive programs would leave undone an important task of the civil-rights movement.

Equality, Johnson believed, involved more than the removal of the legal balls and chains from the legs of black Americans. That act alone would not place them in a fair, competitive position with white Americans, who had enjoyed opportunities without the burdens that attended racial discrimination. The black condition, then, required "corrective therapy" to compensate for many years of economic oppression. During those years of denial, the argument ran, whites had enjoyed their own kind of "special treatment" ("affirmative action") by closing out blacks from opportunities that existed in the American economy.

Arrington accepted the logic and the morality of affirmative action, and he became its champion on the Birmingham City Council. Disappointed that Shores had not already pressed the case for a program, he set out to make meaningful the spirit of Executive Order 11246. Nearly seven years had passed since the institution of the program at the national level, yet Birmingham had made no progress toward adopting an affirmative-action plan.

The black community applauded Arrington's efforts, for there had long existed a desire for greater participation in the city's work force. In the midsixties black leaders had petitioned the mayor and the city council for a meeting to discuss a list of demands that called for the hiring of black policemen and firemen and for greater representation on committees and commissions. The heart of their petition addressed the idea of fair employment in all city positions. Blacks, of course, recognized the limited influence the city had over private businesses, but they urged white leaders to start conversations with business and industry, particularly those receiving government contracts, to win approval of nondiscriminatory employment.

The possible hiring of blacks by the city, especially police officers, met stern opposition from local whites. Many of them argued that the employment of blacks would "destroy the morale of the . . . police force" and that white policemen would eventually have to serve under black officers. "Should Negro policemen be hired," wrote one irate citizen, "this would increase demand for jobs such as secretary, clerks, firemen, engineers [and others]." The city should not hire black policemen to serve 40 percent of the population. In a line of reasoning that characterized the era of segregation, someone suggested that the city put the hiring of blacks to a vote, "to let the white majority once more rule." The West End Civitan Club passed a resolution that opposed the employment of blacks, because white policemen had performed their jobs admirably and hiring blacks would represent an injustice.

Arrington had recognized the ineffectiveness of Birmingham's voluntary hiring plan for blacks. Therefore, he had introduced a council resolution reaffirming the city's commitment to fair employment. When Siebels's administration continued to drag its feet on the hiring of blacks for city jobs, the young councilman wrote the mayor in July 1972, requesting information on employment. Arrington applauded the appointment of a few blacks to important positions, such as attorney Peter Hall, the first black to serve in a city judgeship. But he lamented that the honor arrived belatedly. The selection of Ossie W. Mitchell by the city council to a five-year term on the Birmingham school board—the first black woman to serve in that position—also drew praise from Arrington. As significant as these appointments may have been, they had not seriously addressed the fundamental question of affirmative action in employment for a city fast approaching 50 percent black population. Only a few blacks had acquired positions in the classified service, and the city had no black department heads. Evidence abounded, wrote one black leader, that Birmingham had not lived up to the spirit and requirements of affirmative action. Disappointed with the slow pace of progress in employment, Arrington searched for a better way to open up job opportunities in the Magic City.

In November 1973, Arrington introduced his affirmative-action proposal. The city needed guidelines, he said, to ensure equality of opportunity. Nearly a year and a half had passed since he first sponsored his resolution on equal opportunity, but Mayor Seibels had taken only minimal action in this area. In support of his ordinance, Arrington turned to a report of the Federal Aviation Administration, which had reviewed the city-owned airport to determine if Birmingham had complied with civil-rights laws and regulations. It found that the city had failed to meet nondiscrimination mandates and that no affirmative-action plan existed to remedy the negative effects of discrimination. Following the submission of Arrington's proposal, cosponsored by Shores, the progressive Community Affairs Committee adopted a resolution sponsored by W. C. Patton that called for affirmative action.

Patton, the ever-present civil-rights advocate, gave Arrington consistent support. He wrote the city council of Birmingham's progress, but he reminded its members that it had not yet reached utopia. He cited the lag in economic opportunity for blacks, and he urged the passage of an effective ordinance to provide for employment. Patton appealed to the good will and fair play of the council, but he also armed himself with the law and the threat of direct action. He pointed to the amended Equal Employment Act of 1964, for example, which required local governments to institute fair-employment programs and plans to overcome discrimination.

Patton characteristically rejected a "sledge hammer" approach to the resolution of problems, but he made clear his message. The NAACP official, a member of Operation New Birmingham, urged the creation of a department of compliance to monitor vendors that did business with the city to determine whether they adhered to equal opportunity in employment. In his letter to the city council, Patton also tried to dispel the fear that blacks would replace whites under affirmative-action guidelines. That idea was abhorrent to him. "This would be wrong," he contended, and "the last thing I would request." Arrington shared this view, although he fully recognized that whites had often acquired positions at the expense of blacks who were closed out of the system. Statistics strongly supported Arrington's quest for equal-opportunity legislation, for at the time he introduced his measure, only 62 of the city's 1,200 police officers and fire fighters were black!

Arrington's affirmative-action proposal resembled similar plans adopted by other cities across the country in the 1960s. The measure seemed mild to most blacks, and in their opinion, it contained little that was radical. Naturally, it tried to eliminate discriminatory practices based on race, religion, or sex, and it addressed economic problems that persisted from years of racial oppression. The ordinance sought results through the expansion of economic opportunity, not punishment for white wrongs against blacks. As Patton had stated, it had no provision for eliminating jobs already held by whites to accommodate black people. Because of past discrimination, however, a certain number of blacks approved for jobs by the Jefferson County Personnel Board did receive priority over others who qualified for employment.

The proposed ordinance required city departments and agencies to adopt hiring plans and goals and to submit them to the mayor, who had responsibility for forwarding them to the council. The legislation called for the employment of minorities and women based on their percentage in the city's total work force. A separate proposal also required private companies that did business with the city to adopt affirmative-action goals. Arrington contended that only a remedy such as his proposals would help solve a difficult, historic racial problem. But many white groups had a different view. When affirmative-action recommendations came before the council in December 1973, representatives from private groups appeared to oppose them. City department heads also spoke against them. Significantly, city attorney J. M. "Mac" Breckenridge attempted to shatter the legal props that supported the measures. The long, tough battle had begun.

Arrington's strongest support on the council for affirmative action came from David Vann. Vann had faced other rough battles, especially in 1963, when he had worked against the old commission form of government. He had an excellent knowledge of Birmingham's racial history and what had happened to blacks in his city.

He knew the stifling impact of racial exclusion, and no one had to tell him about the advantages that came with being white in the South. Attorney Vann recognized that law could, and did, condition people's behavior, even if it did not alter their attitudes. "Liberal guilt" did not prompt his strong support for Arrington and affirmative action, but his strong belief in the ideal of social progress and his sense of fair play, however, did move him. Although the council failed to adopt a measure that would have prohibited the city from doing business with firms that discriminated, it did approve the city's first affirmative-action ordinance, which established hiring goals for minorities and women.

Mayor George Seibels strongly opposed affirmative action. His veto of the council action came as a disappointment, but no surprise, to Arrington. Seibels's action reflected his philosophical opposition, and that of many other whites in Birmingham, to measures that redressed economic grievances of blacks. The mayor's position seemed to suggest that black folk now had equality, and that was enough. In his veto message, he skillfully moved the issue away from the central concern, and he cleverly attempted to paint the proposed law itself as unfair, even though affirmative-action programs were in place in other cities. He wanted to continue the voluntary approach to hiring, and he reaffirmed his intention to crush discrimination. A fundamental assumption that guided the mayor was that affirmative action would lead to the employment of individuals who lacked the ability to perform their jobs.

The mayor struggled to defend his record, as he alluded to past evils that no longer plagued the city. In a public statement following his veto, he declared:

> There has been discrimination and unfairness in years gone by, but I have made my stand extremely clear in trying to correct it. I do not think it is fair to black people or any other minority group to give preferential treatment to them over others who are better qualified. The day of hoodwinking or saying something about fairness in hiring and not meaning it is gone and I think the record speaks for itself. We have made *substantial*

74

efforts to recruit blacks for the Fire Department and have had good results in the Police Department going from 24 in November of 1972 to 70 [in December 1973]. . . . The coined phrase "Affirmative Action" to me is totally misleading. There has been Affirmative Action with regard to hiring of minority groups in City Hall and there will be more of it.

Clearly Seibels and city attorney Breckenridge, who provided much of the legal ammunition for the mayor's veto, did not understand the intent of affirmative action. Both of them completely ignored the city's responsibility under the Equal Employment Opportunity Act and Executive Order 11246. The mayor and his legal aide also conveniently overlooked the actions of other cities in establishing affirmative action. Had Breckenridge's legal arguments come one or two years *after* the creation of the program, his contentions may have had some merit. But by the time he raised his legal questions, affirmative action had received sanction from the courts in various parts of the land. Seibels and Breckenridge refused to acknowledge that federal affirmative-action decrees had clearly provided for "excepted" or "protected" classes of persons—victims of discrimination—who could receive preference in fulfilling stated hiring goals. Affirmative action, then, meant more than declaring for simple equality. Breckenridge surely was in a position to know this fact, but he apparently did not, or chose to ignore it. It is arguable, of course, that his duty demanded continued questioning of legislation and programs that seemingly affronted the Constitution, even though the courts had already spoken.

Arrington's disappointment with Seibels showed in increasingly sharp attacks against the mayor's position. The councilman was disturbed that the city's leader had misled the public and had unduly praised himself for only minimal accomplishments in black employment. Seibels, he said, had shown a kind of defiance of the black community in its bid to remedy discrimination. Arrington pointed out that the mayor had alluded to black employment in the police and fire departments without mentioning other city departments. In a telling rebuttal to the mayor's statement, he stressed that the partly successful effort in recruiting those city employees to which the mayor alluded resulted from the efforts of the CAC of Operation New Birmingham.

Again the city's employment record buttressed Arrington's argument that Birmingham had taken no great leap forward in hiring blacks. As of June 1973, the total employment of blacks at all levels came to only 721 persons. Figures showed that 70 blacks received appointment to the 473 available jobs in classified positions from January to November 1973. Almost half of those went to the police department, while the majority of the remainder were clerical positions. Arrington was confident that the facts supported his case for affirmative action. "I submit," he said in alluding to a study of black employment by the city, "that these facts and others borne out by my study of the city's hiring practices over the past two years do not support the mayor's claim about his policy on equal employment opportunity." Had Seibels exercised truly effective leadership, Arrington criticized, the city council would have had no need to pass affirmative-action measures. With the precision of a surgeon, Arrington cut away neatly at the ordinance's assumed unconstitutionality that Seibels had borrowed from Breckenridge, emphasizing again that the courts had repeatedly upheld affirmative-action legislation.

The intensity of Arrington's fight with Seibels produced even greater cohesion among black groups in Birmingham. Affirmative action became a celebrated issue among those who viewed it as another necessary step toward group progress. David Hood's Jefferson County Progressive Democratic Council broke its silence in support of affirmative action. Hood proclaimed it the "best minimum" effort to overcome the debilitating effects of discrimination, and a "moderate first step" in the continuing drive to compensate for racial oppression. W. C. Patton's Greater Birmingham Emancipation Association acted predictably. It cited statistics on employment, and it castigated Seibels for not granting an audience to black leaders before his veto of affirmative action. The mayor's refusal represented a bitter pill indeed for those who had steadfastly backed him in two previous elections.

Patton had supported Seibels in 1971, and he had enjoyed a good relationship with him, but the mayor dealt a shattering blow to the civil-rights official with his veto. Patton deplored the decision to kill the measure. That Seibels had slighted black leaders represented a personal affront that cut deeply. He struck even harder at the mayor when he practically demanded that he stop trying to sidestep affirmative action by talking of his contributions to black progress in Birmingham. "At this point," said Patton, "our concern is . . . only one issue . . . [and] that is an affirmative action program with teeth." He lashed out at Seibels for alluding to his past help in solving the city's problems and for invoking his name when the mayor declared against Arrington's affirmative-action legislation. His correspondence became more cutting, for Patton saw the hand of race in Seibels's action. He had been "fed some advice from sources which have racial prejudices," and unfortunately the mayor had "fallen for that line of thinking."

Arrington's leadership at city hall on affirmative action further fueled a burning political spirit within the black community. Old black leaders came to life, younger ones became more emboldened. Arrington prodded the white community, and despite his quiet, gentle manner, he inspired in others a will to "take on the fight." The outcome of affirmative action, he believed, could make a significant difference in the lives of blacks. He knew the value of strong offensive action, and when it was apparent that Seibels had neither history nor legalism on his side, he moved forcefully to dismantle an old structure that had stifled black folk in employment in Birmingham for most of the city's one-hundred-year history.

Arrington had invested much time and energy in affirmative action, and he would not abandon it. After considerable discussion, the Birmingham City Council considered a compromise proposal palatable to Hawkins, Yarbrough, and Overton, those members who voted to sustain Seibels's veto of the initial ordinance. The new measure passed without a dissenting vote. Now faced with enormous political pressure from the black community, the mayor signed it. The compromise ordinance required city departments to develop hiring plans approved by the mayor that called for increased numbers of minorities and women. It also mandated the establishment of recruitment programs and provided a yardstick to measure their effectiveness. If a city department failed to meet its hiring goal, it had to justify the rejection of those persons certified by the Jefferson County Personnel Board. The council passed a related ordinance that forbade the city from doing business with firms or persons that engaged in illegal discrimination. After months of concentrated effort, Arrington had finally achieved part of his objective.

Despite the historic nature of the affirmative-action ordinance, some believed the new measure did not sufficiently address past economic wrongs. The American Civil Liberties Union of Birmingham greeted the passage of the new law unenthusiastically, describing it as a weak effort to remedy massive wrongs in an imperfect way. Sallie Gaines, the organization's president, proposed to strengthen the legislation by having the mayor appoint an advisory committee of women and minorities that would review the various affirmative-action plans from city departments, monitor the program, and investigate complaints.

On the other hand, the Jefferson County Employees Association, led by David Dunn, protested that the new law had gone too far. On the day the council adopted the measure, the association passed a motion opposing "preferential hiring of any minority group for classified positions." Although Arrington had explained the law's intent on several occasions, the association fought to protect its interest; it reflected little appreciation for the history of racial oppression that made affirmative action necessary. The program would take jobs from whites, or it would discriminate against them, Dunn maintained. Eventually preferential hiring would destroy the merit system. But the city council had spoken. And so had the United States Department of Justice, which had accused Birmingham of past discrimination and which had encouraged the city to take corrective measures.

Arrington had achieved a major goal with the acceptance of an affirmative-action plan. Birmingham had taken another small, restrained step toward racial equality, although it had not made a "quantum leap forward." The passage of affirmative action by the city council had forced whites to come to grips with their own history, to take an introspective view of themselves and the institutions that had sustained their economic way of life. The examination proved painful, and it created anxieties, even oppressive fears, for white southerners had not been trained to accept black competition for jobs. They had sown the winds of racial oppression, but they unwillingly faced the whirlwinds of change that led to economic justice. Arrington believed in the morality of his fight; in the end, he contended, greater progress would come to Birmingham, and its quality of life would also improve. The city had moved closer to being a fair society.

Arrington had high expectations for the new affirmative-action law. The major responsibility for the success of the ordinance, of course, rested with the mayor. Although he had appointed a black woman, Sherold Lockhart, to his own staff in August 1974, the city continued to move slowly in the hiring of blacks. Arrington wrote critically in December 1974 that nearly a year had passed since the passage of the new law, but there existed "little evidence . . . the affirmative action ordinance has been implemented." City departments had not established recruitment programs, and black employment showed no significant increase.

Seibels remained on the defensive. While the mayor could count on substantial white support, black political strength made it impossible for him to ignore, or offend again, his black constituency, one that had given him strong support in previous elections. In a statement to the CAC following Arrington's complaints in December 1974, he reported on the progress in implementing affirmative action. He cited an increase of twenty-five blacks in city jobs, without specifying whether their employment came in the classified ranks (that is, jobs covered under civil service). During 1974, Seibels had been able to increase minority employment from only 6 to 7 percent—and that in a city over 40 percent black. In defending his record, the mayor spoke of an austere budget that permitted little hiring, and he placed blame on the Jefferson County Personnel Board, which had the responsibility of certifying applicants. The board, he said, had to change some of its policies to accommodate affirmative action if the city was to realize any progress.

Arrington remained unimpressed with the mayor's lack of achievement, although he admitted the need for a change in personnel-board rules to get more blacks into the system. The major problern, however, was Seibels. The mayor had neglected a program he basically opposed, and he was trying to shift the blame for its failure. Moreover, the councilman noted, Seibels had given out misleading statistics. Arrington pointed out that the percentage of black employment in some areas had actually declined, and that fact constituted "part of the dreary picture" of the city's employment of blacks. By the summer of 1975, Arrington was convinced that only court action, or a new mayor, would get strong affirmative-action enforcement at city hall. A hiring-discrimination suit filed by the United States Department of Justice did shake up some city officials, but not until the mayoral administrations of David Vann and Richard Arrington himself did affirmative action enjoy any great success.

Economic advancement for blacks and other minorities had stood at the heart of Arrington's drive for a strong, workable affirmative-action policy. It also inspired his efforts for a television-cable franchise system in Birmingham that permitted participation and partial ownership by blacks. Although the discussion over cable and affirmative action occurred about the same time, they were, in fact, two separate issues. Both, however, mirrored an existing political and social attitude in the black community that surfaced through Arrington, its chief spokesperson. The fight that took place over cable television went beyond dollars and cents; it had much to do with the role blacks would play in influencing the city's culture and general outlook.

The Birmingham City Council began serious consideration of a cable franchise in 1972. From the beginning Arrington clearly articulated his position—he wanted some minority participation. Following the council's call for proposals, it received a total of thirteen applications by January 1973, which included only one black group, Freedom Cable Television Incorporated. Led by attorney Oscar Adams, Jr., Freedom represented a number of the city's black leaders. It wanted black control of television in the black community, and it desired an end to the isolation of blacks in the communications media in Birmingham. A city with such a large black population, Freedom maintained, should gain from the benefits of radio and television. Profits from the media, said its spokesperson, "can be used to train our young people for jobs in the communications industry" and to improve the quality of life for black people. "If you do not own the broadcast station," a black leader remarked, "you do not have the power to determine how that station will be used and what the programs will be."

As chairman of the council's Communication and Transportation Committee, Arrington occupied a strategic position during the debate on cable. His influence became evident when the council passed an ordinance establishing a Cable Commission, which included two black citizens. It was much harder, however, to get a franchise award for an all-black group, or one with significant black representation. In September 1973, the council announced its *intention* to award the city franchise to Teleprompter, an action that disappointed Arrington and angered blacks. The company did have, as some described it, "token black ownership of about 4 percent of its stock, listing among members of its board David H. Hood of Brighton and Robert Washington of Collegeville. But that level of minority participation did not please most blacks, and the issue became heated. While some blacks spoke of demonstrations to protest the council's decision, the more restrained suggested a political or legal solution to the problem.

Arrington eventually supported the awarding of more than one cable franchise. The possibility of a black company's acquiring the right to service the entire city, he recognized as extremely remote. But if the council did not grant a monopoly to one company, then a black company would have a much better chance for an award. Arrington, however, faced a politically touchy situation. He saw merit in the Teleprompter agreement and believed it contained a few advantages for minorities. His major objection was that the company had no meaningful black ownership of its local stock. Thus, Arrington really proposed his two franchise idea as a solution to a very difficult problem. He pointed to other cities that had awarded multiple franchises, and he stressed again the importance of black involvement in the communication field. "I believe that significant ownership of local cable television stock," he wrote during the debate over the issue, "provides the last opportunity for black [input into] the media industry."

In a dramatic turn of events, the Securities and Exchange Commission suspended Teleprompter's stock from the New York Stock Exchange. With the company's financial status in question, the Birmingham City Council postponed any action on the proposed agreement. The decision sent the matter back to Arrington's committee. Although the committee did not automatically remove Teleprompter from further consideration, realistically, the SEC action irreparably damaged its chances. Two other companies now remained effectively in competition for the franchise—Freedom and Birmingham Cable Communications—and later a third, Warner Cablevision, entered the field. While Warner appeared to have a good chance for the award, the franchise eventually went to Birmingham Cable. Arrington worked hard to give blacks a share of the economic benefits from the arrangement. While the cable company had no black shareholders, the councilman did insist that some black institutions in the city have the right to acquire a percentage of company stock. Black organizations eventually held roughly 4 percent of Birmingham Cable stock. The long, hard fight for a black share of cable television in Birmingham had not yielded the results Arrington desired, and it was difficult for him to hide his disappointment.

The struggle over cable television and affirmative action had revealed to the black community the tenacious character of its leader. And it had also shown whites the creative abilities Arrington possessed. He had become the most persuasive voice in the black community—the quiet, deliberative figure that signaled the forces of racial justice to unite in dismantling the remaining restrictive walls of discrimination. Some liberal whites in Birmingham could accept his kind of leadership. To them he was a calm voice issuing a reasonable call for needed change, an articulate councilman who fought battles in an open, democratic manner, and one who knew the responsibility of good citizenship. He had not simply craved and enjoyed power. He had used it in the broad interest of social change to involve those who had been outside government.

With his record of achievement Arrington's reelection to office seemed certain. No longer a neophyte, and with some potential for raising funds, he could concentrate on establishing a stronger organization. To lead his campaign he chose the owner of an independent insurance agency and former student at Miles College, Lamorie "Tony" Carter. A neat, extroverted figure, Carter had a businessman's mind that contained a healthy knowledge of the city. His personality, ready "how ya'll doing" greeting, and friendly smile had an obvious advantage to a politician who wanted to win votes. He also had a rapport with youth, attracting them to Arrington's campaign as volunteers. He succeeded in doing what his boss had mastered so well—giving people a sense of personal involvement. Tony Carter needed to rally people, for such motivation was crucial in a community where black people often responded only to crisis. The psychology of involvement probably constituted one of the truly important lessons that the Arrington campaign gave to the black community in Birmingham. With Carter and his corps of young workers, and with more money than before, Arrington set out to win his council seat without a runoff. But in the process he wanted to get white voters accustomed to voting consistently for qualified black candidates.

Arrington emphasized a number of broad issues, most of which did not impinge on race. Blacks already knew his record on issues that most concerned them—economic development of the black community, affirmative action, cable television, police brutality, and human rights. While he did not ignore these matters in the campaign, he addressed issues important to all citizens, regardless of race. He wanted to stabilize neighborhoods, and he favored a congressional measure that made money available to cities for more housing. He supported the enforcement of zoning laws to maintain the integrity of neighborhoods. And he tried to ease fears in a city that had a relatively high crime rate by his pledge to provide a stronger police force. Contrary to the belief of some whites, Arrington did not support a citizens' review board to examine the actions of police officers in critical cases of alleged abuses, but he did support "a process which included citizens *and* police." Where the city had to engage in economic belt-tightening, he told voters, the police would get cut last, a statement that must have pleased those persons who viewed the black councilman as "soft on crime" because of his attacks on officers who abused their position. He preferred reducing public works, street and sanitation crews, if financial stringency absolutely dictated cuts. On the touchy issue of collective bargaining for city employees, which popped up during the campaign, Arrington favored it, but he opposed binding arbitration. He also supported the election of councilpersons by districts, but he allowed for the election of some at-large seats.

Arrington placed his reelection hopes on a secure black political base, especially Birmingham's powerful black clergy. He needed to demonstrate to blacks the wisdom of going to the polls, to show that votes translated into policies that could aid individual citizens and the community. Carter sent young volunteers into housing projects, put them on the phone, organized rallies, and scheduled community events to create that vital sense of participation. The local press aided the campaign by giving Arrington strong backing. The 8 October 1975 *Birmingham Post-Herald* wrote of Arrington's record in glowing terms. He was one of those public officials, said the paper, "who has remembered that government is for the people." The *Post-Herald* conceded that the black councilman took some unpopular stands, but "more often than not, he is right." The paper's editor admired his courage in facing up to controversy rather than trying to sweep it under a rug. The newspaper endeavored to turn its readers away from Arrington's race: "A resident of West End [a predominantly black section of Birmingham], Arrington happens to be black and is often viewed as a spokesman for black causes, [but this view] misses the whole point. . . . His interest is in people and seeing that government and its representatives treat all individuals with respect." While he had earned praise for his work on the affirmativie-action ordinance and the cable franchise, the advancement of human relations, the *Post-Herald* believed, stood as his invaluable contribution to the city.

Arrington scored an impressive victory at the polls in his second run for office. He won reelection without a runoff, a feat that had escaped him in 1971. His campaign had gotten out the vote, and the elecorate had heeded Tony Carter's admonition to "do it right the first time around." Arrington picked up 16,155 ballots, trailing only incumbent candidate Don Hawkins, who received 31,297 votes.

The 1975 council runoff would virtually assure another historic first for Birmingham, since one more black would join the nine-member council. In the primary the voters had chosen Arrington along with Don Hawkins and David Herring for three of the five seats up for reelection. Four other candidates advanced to the run-off, three of whom were black—Demetrius Newton, a lawyer; William Hamilton, a minister; and Bessie Estelle, a retired school principal. The fourth candidate, Russell Yarbrough, had barely missed reelection by a few hundred votes, but hardly anyone doubted his chances for victory in the forthcoming contest.

The mayoral race of 1975 also had a far-reaching impact on the city and upon Arrington's political future, but only a soothsayer could have predicted future developments. Dissatisfaction with incumbent George Seibels had mounted in the black community as the mayor continued to frustrate Arrington at almost every turn. The black community had once believed in Seibels, who had said "nice things," had visited black areas, and had declared against discrimination. But he had also vetoed affirmative action, and in the judgment of blacks he had no serious desire to enforce the ordinance the council had passed. More than Seibels's stand on race, however, bothered Arrington. The black councilman maintained that the mayor had become inefficient, partly because of health problems.

Arrington's ally on the council, David Vann, shared a similar view of George Seibels. Dissatisfied with the drift in government, Vann decided to run against the two-term chief executive. He already had name recognition, since many citizens knew him from the 1963 fight to kill the commission form of government. He had also been very active on the council. Though by southern standards David Vann may have leaned slightly left of center in his politics, placing a label on him was extremely difficult, for the lawyer refused to become trapped in any tight ideological straitjacket. A talkative politician, he held to ideas and pushed them with such intensity that he sometimes irritated his opponents, and even some of his friends. One political belief, however, had emerged by 1975 of which Vann was certain—Seibels must go!

Vann recognized Seibels's vulnerability, but in opening his intense five-week campaign for mayor in September, Vann did not launch a direct frontal assault upon the incumbent. "Birmingham needs a new mayor," Vann exclaimed. Two terms were enough for Seibels. Vann wisely avoided projecting an image of a candidate that engaged in negatives, and he tried to stress the positive aspects of change. Although he praised the successful programs Seibels had instituted, criticism did show through in some of his statements. For example, when he pledged to work with the council to adopt the city's budget thirty days before the beginning of the new fiscal year, city-hall insiders recognized that statement as a hard slap at the tardy mayor. Vann also wanted to give citizens more involvement in citizens' participation groups—a system that gave residents some control over projects and activities in their communities. Under the arrangement citizens also had a voice in budgetary matters, and they could help in setting priorities for their neighborhoods. Vann's allusion to the increasing crime rate and the day-to-day management of the city from the mayor's office again turned attention to the question of Seibels's alleged inefficiency.

As expected, the 1975 mayor's race boiled down to a two-man contest, although other minor candidates entered the field. Ostensibly a nonpartisan affair, the election saw Seibels receive support from the Republican party, while Vann got some aid from the Democrats. A former insurance man and city councilman, the mayor shared no illusions about the difficulty of trying to turn back his opponent's stern challenge. Vann's attacks on his efficiency struck close to home, and Seibels made a determined effort to refute these charges. He cited pay raises for city employees, and he talked of public improvements and a successful $50-million bond issue as concrete examples of his ability to get things accomplished. Turning directly to Vann's allegations, Seibels stated repeatedly that "you couldn't have all this without good administration at City Hall. We have better administration than we've ever had." He endeavored to eradicate the image of a "ribbon cutter" that Vann had tried to paint in the minds of the voters. It was harder for him, however, to deny the submission of late budgets or the point that the city's schools badly needed improvement to help stabilize neighborhoods.

For Vann to win the 1975 mayoral election, he would have to capture a significant share of the black vote. Although Seibels had antagonized many blacks, he still had some support. After all, he had been the first major politician in the city to address some of their needs seriously. The Republican-oriented *Birmingham World*—part of the chain of black Republican newspapers founded by W. A. Scott—endorsed Seibels. The paper endeavored to deflect some of the political heat from the mayor, arguing that the council had to take blame for some of Birmingham's ills. "Things have changed," wrote the editor of the *World* on 11 October 1975, "in spite of the fact that there is room for improvement." And the city leader most responsible for that change over the years was, of course, George Seibels, Jr. The *World* conveniently ignored Arrington's fight with the mayor over police misuse of power. Instead, it looked to a past era when the heads of black folk in Birmingham were "fair game" for the clubs of law-enforcement officials. The Republican paper contended that "in the past eight years, there have been only isolated cases of alleged 'police brutality.' " The journal did not say that Mayor Seibels had done little to address the problem, despite Arrington's requests to act. Arrington, whom the *World* also supported, strongly disagreed with the journal's assessment of Seibels and worked energetically to defeat him.

Arrington's backing of Vann proved decisive by tearing away much of Seibels's black vote. Previously the mayor had received in excess of 80 percent of the black community's ballots. The two candidates ended up in a runoff after three other contestants siphoned off enough votes to prevent either from gaining a majority. Because of Arrington and such people as "Tall" Paul White, a popular black disc jockey, Seibels had correctly anticipated some black defection to Vann. Therefore, he campaigned heavily in the conservative white eastern section of the city, which he had lost in the 1971 mayor's race.

That Seibels continued to impress some blacks surprised Arrington, who knew that a rising political consciousness existed within the black community. But apparently he had failed to communicate effectively to black voters the gravity of the mayor's negative actions. Thus, he and other black leaders moved to educate them further. They did so by reprinting a strong, anti-Seibels editorial on affirmative action by the late Emory O. Jackson of the *Birmingham World*. On 1 November 1975, Jackson's commentary "Seibels Is Not Our Friend" appeared in the paper that still supported the mayor—the *Birmingham World*!

The unkind veto by Birmimgham Mayor George G. Seibels, Jr. of the Proposed Affirmative Action Ordinance reveals that Seibels is not our Friend. His nearly six year record as Head . . . of Alabama's chief city is a sad story of skillful public relations, adroit use of the public media to hide his failure of bringing Negro persons into City Hall employment and his penchant for using pious prayers to conceal his lack of conviction that Black persons are equal citizens.

For over 100 years Birmingham City Hall has practiced the preferential hiring of white persons. Until a few years ago "white only" was the policy . . . . Certainly if Mayor Seibels has researched the subject, or lived as an informed Birmingham resident, he would know this. *Birmingham World* does not believe Mayor Seibels is so far off or so unlearned that he does not know this. If he does not know this, he would seem to lack the material to be mayor. If he does know, in light of his veto, it further reveals him to be the number one economic enemy of the black man.

Mayor Seibels['s] veto of the proposed Affirmative Action Ordinance is an act that will live in infamy. It is an act which has insulted the total Negro community which represents over forty-two percent of the city population. What mayor Seibels['s] veto has also done is challenged the total black leadership to fight his veto and his record at the ballot box, in courts, on the street corners, in the pulpits, and everywhere else that commitment to the American credo required that a man fight for the right to live. *Birmingham World* believes that the total Birmingham Black Leadership will accept Mayor Seibels['s] challenge.

For too long Mayor Seibels has fooled the Negro group and gotten away with it. He has not been a job-opener; nor does he work to have the employment doors of Birmingham City Hall hang out the welcome sign to Black persons with it written into city law.

It would seem to be all right with Mayor Seibels and the trade union leaders to champion Blacks as garbage collectors but not as a member of the Mayor's top level staff which is presently all white. Mayor Seibels['s] top level staff is a good mirror of the Mayor's employment attitude toward Black persons, it seems to us. It is reasonable to conclude that Mayor Seibels['s] veto places the Negro group upon the Mayor's job opportunity enemy's list.

Jackson had issued an urgent call to "sound the freedom bugle" in the days that saw Arrington pitted against the mayor. He wanted the "trumpets of employment opportunity" to blast from every corner of Birmingham. He had challenged every "good soldier of righteousness" to join the battle. And now in 1975, Arrington and his pro-Vann followers spoke in the language of the late editor when they recalled his admonition to summon "even the ghosts of those who died to rid Birmingham of the ugly spirit manifested by Mayor Seibels." But Arrington and Vann needed votes more than ghosts from the past. Just how much impact the reprint of this article had upon the electorate is impossible to determine, but Arrington hinted at its significance when he stated in 1983, "We took Emory O. Jackson from his grave to defeat Seibels."

The mayor felt the heavy pressure applied by Arrington and black supporters of David Vann, and it directly affected his political stance on race. During the latter part of October 1975, the racial issue moved from the political shadows into the full light of the heated battle. At that time Vann claimed his opponent had turned the campaign into one of "slander, inneundo and racism." The sharp attack came after Seibels charged that Vann had created a "bloc vote by distoring the facts" and that he threatened to destroy the progress that had been achieved in the city of Birmingham. Moreover, the incumbent instituted a telephone campaign heavily directed toward white areas of the city. When faced with the allegation of igniting the racial issue, Seibels attacked Vann, accusing him of using fear tactics and of trying to intimidate voters. Seibels's campaign showed signs of desperation. "Vann supporters," the mayor raged, were "trying to wreck my credibility." He would have experienced clear sailing in the black community a few months ago, had Vann not made unfounded attacks upon him, and had not there been the work of Richard Arrington. But Seibels, not Vann, had raised the issue of "bloc" (that is, black) voting. And the mayor, of course, not Vann, had vetoed affirmative action.

For Seibels to mention "bloc voting" struck Arrington as ironic in the extreme. Indeed, that very same bloc vote had given him staunch support in previous years and had kept him from defeat in 1971, when many whites on the city's Eastside deserted him for his opponent in the mayoral race. With the tables now turned in 1975 and with blacks leaning toward Vann, Seibels had to shore up declining black numbers with white support. The charge of bloc voting, Seibels may have reasoned, could highlight Vann's liberalism, in a town with a history of political and racial conservatism. The bloc-vote charge, wrote one white editor of a large newspaper, needed no interpreter to voters of Birmingham. Bloc meant black. Seibels, he said, had engaged in an "obvious effort to frighten white voters into his camp." But the electorate would not yield to such "an old and discredited . . . bit of political trickery." Seibels's charge disturbed his old friends in the black community. And on the eve of the election, it seemed readily apparent that a sharpened political consciousness and the education of the black community that Arrington had worked to achieve had become a reality.

In the November election Vann barely nosed out Seibels by 1,300 votes. The elated Vann, turning away from his personal political triumph, interpreted the victory as a great step forward for the city. He optimistically (and erroneously) proclaimed that voters had shown that race represented a dead issue in city politics. It is possible to attach some racial significance to the Vann victory, but the election involved too many issues to measure precisely the impact of race upon the voters. It does appear, however, that a heavy vote in predominantly white areas kept Seibels close to his competitor, and that the black vote spelled the margin of difference for Vann. Without Arrington's help, that black vote would not have materialized. While Seibels did retain some black support, returns from the larger black districts in the city showed a two-to-one margin for Vann. It is reasonable to assume that the race issue probably encouraged the large turnout in the 1975 election, as some 63,000 of the city's 112,000 registered voters went to the polls.

The city-council runoff election gave the city the first black woman on the city council, Bessie Estelle, who profited from the heavy turnout. Estelle came in second behind Yarbrough, trailing the popular veteran councilman by only 2,700 votes, a remarkable showing for a first-time candidate. Black candidates Demetrius Newton and Rev. William Hamilton failed in their bid for office. Both ran good races, but Yarbrough's incumbency and Estelle's name recognition and long service in the city proved too much to overcome.

If Arrington had received plaudits from the white press because of his hard-working, deliberate approach to the city's problems, the white vote he received in 1975, although small, told a more important story of Birmingham's continuing struggle with political and social change. His real encouragement came with the reality of the growing solidarity of the black vote, a vote that could be used not just in the interest of narrow political goals but for the benefit of a new Birmingham responsive to the needs of both black and white citizens. The greatest challenges still lay ahead.

4

Do Not Abuse the Citizens: Assault on Police Brutality

•

Much of Richard Arrington's conflict with Mayor George Seibels had arisen over the issue of police brutality. The black councilman's effort to spotlight police abuse of power had contributed to the incumbent's insurmountable political woes in the city election of 1975. If affirmative action, cable television, and his efforts to ensure efficient city services for the black community had made him a recognized name in Birmingham, his fight against police brutality stood out as the most important issue with which many citizens readily identified Arrington. The misuse of power by law officials struck a sensitive nerve in the black community, and it also said much about the state of black-white relations in Birmingham and much of the Deep South. It also provided a commentary on the use of force and fear to maintain the status quo.

Blacks in Birmingham disliked the police because collectively they represented a cruel symbol of a political and social order that had no desire to share power and that utilized harsh methods to maintain privilege. One forty-five-year-old native of the city put it simply in 1983, when he spoke of the pre-Arrington era in Birmingham. Policemen were "mean as hell," he said, "and they could take your life, and nothing could be done about it." The legacy of fear created by the Birmingham police had real meaning for blacks who walked the city streets, for an unwitting provocation of a white or an inadvertent confrontation with the system could lead to police brutality.

Until the 1960s, law enforcement in Birmingham remained in the hands of white officials. For blacks, policemen *were the law*. "If a policeman said you were wrong or that you had done something, that was it," Arrington recalled of early years in the Birmingham area. In an effort to temper the behavior of white policemen and to provide job opportunities, black leaders after the 1940s had repeatedly called for the hiring of black officers. The city could also reduce crime, the leaders argued, by having black police officers and detectives operate in the black community. "It is a sad reflection upon our present City Commission," wrote one of the city's black editors in those days of rigid segregation, "that they have made no steps to employ and use Negro law enforcers." Change came slowly. But by the time of the civil-rights demonstrations of 1963, black leaders had greatly intensified their demands for black policemen.

The issue of police brutality, of course, involved much more than the mere presence of black police officers on the force. In fact, the physical abuse of blacks continued in some cities long after the employment of blacks, but their appearance in the department did make fellow officers look over their shoulders when they contemplated unlawful violence against citizens. At its very core, police brutality and the willingness to tolerate it revealed an attitude about race and the perceived role of blacks in a society built upon Jim Crow. A young black Birmingham teenager perceptively dealt with the question of the police and racial attitudes when he wrote the mayor of Birmingham about the time Arrington and Lucius Pitts of Miles were calling for an end to police violence. Barry Jones's ungrammatical letter of 13 March 1968 is a penetrating commentary on the state of affairs that existed in Birmingham at the time. It addressed a local matter and a southern problem, and it captured what became the heart of Arrington's fight against the disrespect and inhumanity that made fear and police abuse a reality for many black folk. Jones told Mayor Seibels:

I have heard about you. How you are a determine person and how you are going to try your best to make Birmingham a better place for its people. I would like too suggest an idea that I know will make Birmingham a better place for its people. First of all I am a teenage Negro and I would like to see Birmingham solve its own problems. The problem is the way the police treat Negroes. I am not [only] talking about police brutality or a physical treatment against the Negroes but respect toward the Negro. I have seen and heard policemans call grown Negroes boys. I have passed by their cars and motorcycles and heard them describe a Negro as a black Nig[g]er. . . . I pass policemans on the street daily. I smile at them [and] sometimes I say hi! to them but I have not yet got a reply or smile from not one policeman yet. My suggestion to make their jobs easier is too smile at a Negro. I know if they do this that the Negro will surely respect them a lot more. And when they report a robbery or an accident that [the police] use the word Negro. Another thing that I would like to suggest if it hasn't been done or suggested is that the police (white) department maybe play basketball or baseball or something with Negroes at least once or two times a month. I know my suggestions are hard for the white policeman to conduct or do but I think if they do it that they would get alot more respect from the Negro and their jobs may be easier.

By the time Arrington joined the city council, Birmingham had taken some halting steps to address some of the larger issues implicit in young Jones's letter. It had moved to hire black officers, and the police department had established a small community relations program. Enormous problems, however, remained between the police and the black community. Deeply ingrained attitudes die hard, and long-standing institutional behavior is not quickly reconditioned. Under the watchful eye of the federal government and the relentless pressure of civil-rights leaders such as the Reverend T. M. McKinney of the Alabama Christian Movement for Human Rights, the city had made some feeble efforts to moderate the attitudes of emotionally immature and racially intolerant officers.

Arrington wanted to push the city and its leaders to recognize the problem of police brutality by placing it in the public forum. At the same time, he continued to preach political awareness within the black community to provide the necessary leverage for change. Arrington reasoned that most of his colleagues would not attack his position on police brutality outright, although they may have actually disliked his public moves. Councilman Liston A. Corcoran told Arrington privately that he was right in his stand on police abuse of citizens, but Corcoran never took a strong public position on the issue. Only Russell Yarbrough consistently opposed Arrington on police brutality, and sometimes Yarbrough took vehement stands in favor of the police that bordered on the extreme.

Within six months after he came to office, Arrington had received eighteen charges of police brutality, all but two of which came from blacks. Part of the built-in problem with the police in Birmingham, Arrington quickly discovered, was the method of investigation of complaints and the system of discipline that characterized the department. Under departmental policy, charges of police misconduct led first to an in-house investigation through the Internal Security Division. "The difficulty with the entire concept [of in-house investigation]," Arrington once noted, "is that the chance of the Birmingham Police Department finding one of its own members guilty of brutality charges is indeed, based on my experience, remote." Despite strong evidence that seemed to substantiate brutality in the cases he filed, nothing happened in most of them. When the police department failed to discipline errant officers for wrongdoing, Arrington argued, then the mayor had to take action against those policemen. Frustrated by continuing problems with Seibels over police abuse of citizens, Arrington took his message to the people. A decent public would recognize the truth about those officers who misused their power, and they would demand an end to brutality—that was Arrington's hope.

The case of Willis "Bugs" Chambers, Jr., received much attention from Arrington, and it gave him the opportunity to spotlight the issue of police brutality. The case contained elements of high drama, with suspense, much speculation, and tragedy. A black man who often served as an informant for the police, Chambers met death on 21 February 1972, when a Birmingham policeman shot and killed him after he had been arrested. As the sketchy details of the shooting leaked to an already-suspicious black community, concerned citizens requested a full-scale inquiry by a body outside the Birmingham Police Department. Outraged by the death of Chambers, a group called the Black Youth Caucus, led by Walter F. Jackson of Miles College, requested Mayor Seibels to suspend the officer responsible for the killing until the city had held a complete investigation. Jackson further demanded that Seibels take steps to establish a citizens' review board "representative of the grass roots electorate in the black community to ensure the swift and immediate review of all such cases involving [the] citizenry and police officers." The mayor denied the request.

Arrington had moved quickly to have the city council establish its own investigation of the case. His insistence upon an inquiry reflected his obvious distrust of the police department's normal procedures and the importance of the Chambers case. In an unprecedented action, the council adopted a motion calling for its Public Safety Committee to investigate the case. Composed of Yarbrough, Shores, and Arrington, the committee had authority to hire two attorneys to assist in its work. Significantly, Arrington had already begun his own investigation of the circumstances surrounding the affair shortly after he learned of the shooting, and he had questioned residents at the apartment complex where Chambers lived.

For roughly three weeks the city council's Public Safety Committee organized for the investigation. Selecting a black attorney and a white attorney took time, but by mid-March the committee had chosen James Baker and Douglas Corretti to aid in the inquiry. Baker, a graduate of Cornell and a member of the firm of Adams, Baker, and Clemon, had impeccable credentials, as did Corretti, who had a partnership with Donald Newsom. The seemingly slow pace disturbed some black citizens, and Arrington had to reassure them of a "thorough and impartial investigation." He also dismissed the contention of some white critics that the incident had already been adequately investigated by the police department and that elected officials should not hear any new facts.

As the council committee busied itself with the Chambers killing, allegations of police brutality continued to take place. One of

96

them in particular provoked a strong letter from Arrington to Mayor Seibels, who generally left investigations to the police department and then rubber-stamped its findings. Ronnie Hill, a North Birmingham resident, complained that, at the time of his arrest, Birmingham officers handcuffed him and then "slapped him around." Hill also contended that the police beat him with a rifle butt and that law officers also brutalized his brother-in-law, James White, who had voluntarily given himself up for arrest. According to Hill, White sustained injuries that hardly left him recognizable, but when Arrington corresponded with Seibels the day following the alleged beating of White, the victim had not been taken to the hospital.

Arrington wrote angrily to Seibels that the mayor had the responsibility for discipling policemen who abused citizens. "I am appealing to you again as the mayor of the city," the black councilman said, "to see that police officers in Birmingham bring a halt to this kind of conduct." He cited the Hill case and the unfortunate circumstance of Willie J. Mitchell, a young black man who had experienced a beating approximately two weeks earlier at the hands of the Birmingham police. In Mitchell's case, however, officers had arrested and beaten the wrong man! "To date nothing has been done about Mitchell's case," Arrington complained, "even though he was released with no charges against him and filed a complaint with Internal Security." The city should have acted decisively, Arrington contended, since the facts appeared clear and indisputable. Arrington challenged the mayor to demonstrate that the police department could discipline itself, and that Internal Security was not a place where citizens let off steam without getting positive results.

The Public Safety Committee's investigation of the Chambers killing took seven weeks. A total of thirty-seven witnesses appeared before the committee, which assembled a massive 1,300 pages of testimony. The final report pleased neither the black community nor Arrington, and it contributed further to the controversy. It showed that Chambers had no involvement in an earlier disturbance with the police on the day of the shooting, as some believed. A drunken male acting under police orders, the report said, had enticed Chambers to leave his apartment to point out dope houses to the officers. Once in the hallway of his building, they arrested Chambers for public drunkenness. They then took him to a nearby parking lot, where an officer named James Howell shot him.

The police contended that Howell killed Chambers when the prisoner pulled a knife. Unfortunately, conflicting testimony by the police did not resolve the question whether or not Chambers had been searched after his arrest but before police took him to the squad car. Howell had supposedly "searched him good," but other officers testified they had not frisked him for weapons. Arrington later informed his constituents that, "as officers at the shooting scene were searching Chambers whose hands had been placed on the [police] wagon and feet spread apart, officer Howell yelled that he had a knife, pulled his pistol, and shot Chambers, whom he testified was coming toward him with a knife."

Confusion had also surrounded the question of where Howell's bullet actually entered Chambers's body. The coroner's report had clearly stated that Chambers had been shot through the stomach, but three medical doctors and the embalmer testified that the victim had entrance wounds "in the middle of the back." To Arrington much of the testimony indicated the use of force beyond that necessary to subdue a criminal, but Russell Yarbrough did not accept this interpretation. According to Arrington, Yarbrough actually created a scenario that made it possible for Howell to shoot Chambers in the back without murdering him. With so many disagreements between Yarbrough and Arrington, who conducted most of the hearing, the committee settled for issuing a "report of the facts."

Arrington held strong views about the Chambers killing, and a decade after it took place, he still maintained it had been unprovoked. Yarbrough steadfastly refused to talk about the case or any other developments during his council years. A widespread belief prevailed in the black community that Chambers had been "set up" because of his knowledge of the police department and criminal activity among officers. Two nagging questions gnawed at Arrington. Why, he asked, had Howell gone to Chambers's house looking for him several days before the shooting? And why did the person who had called Chambers out into the hallway of the apartment building disappear during the hearing? Only two weeks after the committee completed its work and issued its report, however, the mystery man surfaced! More perplexing was that "the person who found [this man] was Russell Yarbrough, because [his] son-in-law, an attorney, had him as his client." Only then did the committee call him in for interrogation. "This guy admitted he was drunk [on the night of the shooting]," said an excited Arrington, still disturbed about the case years after it had taken place. Of all the incidents of alleged police brutality that Arrington handled during his council career, the case of Willis "Bugs" Chambers still stands out as one of the most intriguing, even bizarre.

The black community's acceptance of Arrington's views of the Chambers killing had spelled more pressure for Seibels. The Reverend T. M. McKinney, who led marches protesting police abuse, sharply criticized the mayor for not moving to clear up the matter. He agreed with Arrington that the most effective way to combat police brutality was "to rid the police department of those guilty of such conduct." Seibels remained unmoved except to comment that the city and federal officials were involved in investigating the case. Slowly, the Chambers death, like others before it, slipped into the archives of Birmingham's history, rarely again noticed except by historians anxious to retrace the path of the city's troubled history that eventually gave way to a new day and a new spirit that spelled the end to police brutality.

Police abuse of citizens troubled Arrington, and he again troubled Seibels. He sounded McKinney's theme that the city could maintain the integrity of the Birmingham Police Department by weeding out those policemen who misused their position. Seibels, of course, chose to rely on his Internal Security Division, but abuse had continued. Arrington emphatically reemphasized that point to Seibels when he complained about several cases, one of which involved a beating of a black citizen in his home by a "mob of officers." Not only had they entered the man's house, fired a shot while there, and manhandled his wife, but they had allegedly taken his wristwatch. Police arrested the man for speeding! Arrington wrote Seibels that the officer responsible for the shooting, who allegedly took the watch, was Ed Cousins, "whom you must know has a shameful record as an officer." He asked the mayor, "How long will we continue to condone this kind of behavior and to keep men like Cousins on the force?"

The strain of the fight over police brutality showed on Arrington. He now began to question his own wisdom in directing citizens to channel complaints through Internal Security. "I wonder . . . if I am doing them an injustice?" he once asked the mayor rhetorically. Arrington contended that a clear, unmistakable pattern had emerged from the brutality cases: police beat a victim and then charged the person with a number of violations, including assault on an officer. The black politician threatened to use every resource at his command to call public attention to the deplorable situation of police brutality. He did not play loosely with words.

While wisdom dictated that he keep the issue of police brutality in the public forum, Arrington had to avoid the appearance of "restless agitator." Despite opposition by the Fraternal Order of Police and Seibels's nonsupport, the councilman persisted. In a column written on 5 July 1972 for the *Birmingham Times*, he focused on a Vietnam veteran who now walked with a cane, the victim of a beating by police in a men's room of the local Trailways bus station. Again law officers had reacted without much caution. Four policemen had brutally assaulted and arrested the wrong man! Arrington vigorously protested. The city did nothing.

The city did act in a case that involved a young, black robbery suspect, but that action did not please Arrington. After arresting a Charles Williams, police handcuffed him and allegedly pistol-whipped him and broke his jaw. The police department responded. It suspended the two policemen involved—for not taking the victim to the hospital in accordance with standard procedures, but not for brutality! Arrington wrote Seibels that "I would still like to know why the officers struck him in the first place or how his jaw was broken." Although Williams remained free for two months without charges, police arrested him after embarrassing publicity about the case. By that time, Williams had turned sixteen years of age, and the city could try him as an adult. In a similar but not so tragic a case, a black woman filed a charge in behalf of her husband, whom police supposedly abused. Two policemen received reprimands *for failing to have the victim checked by a physician*, although visible injuries appeared on his body.

Arrington's stance on police brutality drew harsh criticism from many white citizens. To them "law and order" was the important glue that held society together, and the police had to protect the social order from those who would destroy it. Arrington, of course, had no argument with this contention, and he had never contested that fundamental premise. Time and again, his critics attempted to redirect attention from those officers who damaged the idea of "law and order" by their own lawlessness and by their violation of the public's trust. There existed among some citizens the belief that the victims of brutality "asked for it," deserved it because "the police had to be right." Ironically, an elderly black man articulated this view when he told Arrington that the councilman had been misled in his crusade against police brutality. Most of the people abused by the police, he said subjectively, worked for the police and "had gotten out of their places," or they had cheated someone out of money. John Hill, a local attorney, also sharply disagreed with Arrington on the issue of police brutality, but he did support the councilman's suggestion for an impartial investigating committee to hear complaints of police abuse. That particular idea, however, had little chance of success.

The FOP vigorously rejected Arrington's charges as unfounded and injurious to the Birmingham Police Department and to the city. James Cousins, president of the organization, stated his case clearly in July 1972, charging that the morale of the police had slipped with Arrington's attacks and that law enforcement had become more difficult to carry out. The safety of citizens stood in jeopardy. These sweeping and outlandish charges brought a swift rebuttal, even from Seibels, who wanted to squash any notion of an ineffective police force being paralyzed by the opposition of a single black man.

Seibels pointed to the improvements in the police department compared to previous years. About the time Cousins blasted Arrington in July, the mayor wrote the councilman that "there are still problems and lack of understanding between blacks and policemen." Allegations of police brutality arose from this conflict. Acting Chief of Police Jack Warren agreed with Seibels that friction existed between the black community and law officers, but he proved much more sensitive to the problem than was his boss. The charges of police brutality disturbed Warren, and he pledged not to defend any officer for misconduct, "be it rudeness, incompetence, neglect, discourteousness, or brutality."

Arrington and his supporters argued that both conservative white and weak black leadership helped to sustain police brutality. Emory O. Jackson of the *Birmingham World* lamented during the summer of 1972 that Arrington had become frustrated, and the editor tried to rally public support to his cause. He again placed blame upon the shoulders of the mayor, but he also criticized the Community Affairs Committee of Operation New Birmingham. But Jackson went even further when he hinted at a possible boycott of business leaders that did not speak out against police brutality. The black editor also argued that the local NAACP leadership and that of the Alabama Christian Movement for Human Rights had become too closely identified with the Community Affairs Committee to achieve any meaningful corrective action. The committee, wrote Jackson, had done what he called a "public relations varnish" on police misconduct. Unfortunately, he said, Arrington "must do work alone, that the NAACP and the [Alabama Christian Movement for Human Rights] ought to be doing." And he asked, "Are NAACP leaders in such debt to the downtown power structure that they no longer can speak out against wrongs committed against black citizens?" Jackson's comments about the two black groups may have been too harsh, but they did further arouse the community.

Comments in Arrington's notes about police brutality graphically reveal the depths of his despair and disappointment with some of the old black leadership. At a meeting with friends during the height of the police controversy, Arrington proposed calling a summit conference of black leaders to discuss developments in the battle against brutality. In arranging for the assembly, he decided to talk with A. G. Gaston, the rich black businessman, about a meeting at one of his facilities. What transpired between the two men provided a rare look inside black Birmingham and some of the differences that existed over methods of social and political change. Arrington wrote:

> When I arrived at Mr. Gaston's home, he was very gracious and asked it I wanted to join him in eating a steak which he was preparing. He was very kind and listened to me; but I was somewhat disappointed in his response. Dr. Gaston explained to me . . . [several] things: He recognized that my concern was genuine, and that he agreed with me in that something needed to be done. He reminded me, however, that we [had] made much progress here on this matter [of police brutality] and that things are not nearly as bad as they once were. I explained my concern about the fact that Mayor Seibels was not responding to my complaints, and of course, Mr. Gaston reminded me that Mayor Seibels was the best Mayor we have had. He thought that I should not try to call a meeting of community leaders because it would appear that I was trying to step into the forefront and declare myself . . . a community leader, and that many people would say that I am still wet behind the ears, and that I should not put myself out in that position. . . . I could end up being isolated with no support at all. He suggested that I let him arrange for me to meet with some of the community leaders . . . and he assured me that we could get some action. I explained to Mr. Gaston that I didn't necessarily agree with him, but that I respected his opinion and I agreed that if he [would] arrange a meeting with people like Mr. [Vincent] Townsend [the newspaper publisher] that I would attend the meeting and say to Mr. Townsend what I had to say to him.

Gaston admitted to Arrington in this meeting that he had not heard of many of the cases of police brutality until the latter provided detailed information on them. But he seriously questioned the marches against brutality being conducted by T. M. McKinney. More revealing to Arrington than anything else was the shocking revelation of how Seibels worked with some black leaders. Arrington learned that, before McKinney had received a city permit to carry out one of his marches against police brutality, the mayor had called Gaston about the advisability of issuing it. Gaston gave his approval. The black businessman also related to Arrington confidentially that persons had come to him to determine "what could be done about Rev. McKinney." Arrington left Gaston without the response he desired, since he "dashed cold water on the idea of calling black leaders together." Yet, the youthful black leader remained unmoved by the businessman's admonition to "take it slow," since he did not want to see a "good man get hurt." Birmingham, Gaston told Arrington, was a southern city and would not change overnight.

Following his meeting with Gaston, Arrington learned that Justice Department officials had been in Birmingham and had consulted a list of leaders about allegations of police abuse of citizens. Reportedly, several of them claimed no awareness of brutality or admitted "that some abuse probably existed but that it was not nearly as bad as it had been . . . and that claims are exaggerated." Arrington was disappointed at the leaders' reply, since "not a single one of [them] . . . probably had anyone come to them and say anything . . . about being brutalized by police." The fact was, he contended, that people abused by the police did not go "to so-called community leaders like Mr. Gaston or Dr. [John] Nixon or Mr. [Edward] Gardner." They went to elected officials like Arrington. It distressed him that the so-called leaders the Justice Department contacted did not check to determine if a factual foundation for charges of police brutality existed in the city of Birmingham. Again Arrington arrived at a harsh conclusion, and one shared increasingly by younger blacks during that period in the city's history:

> The failure of so-called black leaders in this community to speak out about police brutality simply reconfirms my belief that there is really no such thing as black leaders in this community—they are people who are used by the white power structure in this community who take an ego trip because they are called upon by some powerful white citizens to fit black folk into an agenda that has been set up by the white community, particularly the business structure here.

Some validity may be attached to Arrington's assessment of

black leadership, but undoubtedly the heat of battle against police brutality and his preoccupation with other major issues at the time produced a hypercritical attitude that less stressful times eventually softened. As already demonstrated, however, Arrington did not stand alone in his assessment of black leadership. Indeed, public criticism of that leadership led to growing support for the black councilman and greater pressure on the city. A group that called itself the Committee Against Police Brutality applauded his stand and decried the leaders, churches, and civic organizations that had yielded to the comforts of silence and inactivity. Blacks, it said, had to tell the city unequivocally that Arrington spoke the truth and that they would persist until police abuse ended.

The Walter Crook case gave Arrington an opportunity to focus not only on the issue of brutality per se but upon police use of firearms in the apprehension of suspects. While the facts of the 1974 Crook case may not have seemed as clear as those in other such cases (notably the Chambers affair), it created anger in the black community because of the police department's refusal to release results of its investigation into Crook's killing. In mid-June 1974, a policeman shot and killed a black man who, according to the officer's testimony, attacked him with a stick and a file. Eyewitnesses refuted the policeman's claim, with one of them testifying that Crook had no file. When the police department failed to make available the facts of its investigation, one of Crook's relatives asked the city council to conduct its own inquiry. Councilman Russell Yarbrough's Public Safety Committee, however, did not recommend any action beyond that already taken by the police department. But Arrington requested the city to make available the complete file and all statements from witnesses. Police Chief James Parsons argued the confidentiality of the investigation, and Yarbrough strongly agreed with him. Mayor George Seibels, of course, had the final word.

Yarbrough's unwavering defense of the police generated great friction with Arrington. In the latter's opinion, the white councilman had been able to prevent the exposure of policemen who held bigoted attitudes and who should not have served on the city's force. Tempers flared between the two men when after the Birmingham

Police Department suspended four officers for the beating of blacks, that decision was overturned by the Jefferson County Personnel Board. (The board, incidentally, had recently reinstated a police officer who had taken a bribe and had actually been caught with marked money!) The decision to reinstate the officers accused of brutality disturbed even the conservative Seibels, who now supported Arrington. Yarbrough defended the policemen and the personnel board. He disagreed with the police department's decision to suspend the men in the first place, and he claimed they were being "crucified." Finally Yarbrough, who once alluded to black civil rights as "freedom crap," asserted that the same people who supported the movement for equality in Birmingham wanted to destroy the personnel board.

Arrington's persistence bore fruit. An important case that aided his cause and had some political impact occurred in the summer of 1975. The beating of John Sullivan had neither the controversy of the Crook case nor the drama of the "Bugs" Chambers killing. And that fact, strangely enough, was probably why it made such an emotional impact on Councilman Arrington. It provided a classic picture of the outright use of force and a deliberate attempt by the police to maim a helpless black citizen. The hideousness of the case created such emotionalism in the black community that, in the words of one person who carefully followed the affair, it threatened "a breach of the general calm and tranquility" in Birmingham.

Arrington spelled out painstakingly the history of the relationship between young Sullivan and the police when he asked Mayor Seibels to investigate this case of alleged brutality. A twenty-six-year-old employee of Stockham Pipe and Valve Company in North Birmingham, Sullivan had stopped with his brother and two friends at a service station on 18 July 1975 to purchase cigarettes. The occupants of Sullivan's vehicle became engaged in a heated verbal exchange with two white males and a white female who sat in a car at the station. Although the three persons wore civilian clothes, they identified themselves as law officers after getting out of their vehicle. According to witnesses, the policemen placed a gun to Sullivan's head, pulled him from the car, and arrested him. One of the males then began to jab him in the ribs with a nightstick, which

Sullivan angrily jerked from the officer's hand and threw to the ground. A skirmish developed. The officers subdued Sullivan and held his hands behind him as the woman officer made several unsuccessful efforts to strike the prisoner with her nightstick. When she approached closer to hit Sullivan, he kicked her to the ground. Officers now handcuffed him and his brother and threw them into a patrol car. They had no apparent bodily injury at this time.

The policemen requested everyone to leave the service station. Unknown to them, some persons remained on the premises and witnessed what subsequently transpired. Officers angrily jerked Sullivan from the patrol car and threw him to the ground, Arrington related to Seibels in his summary of the event. An officer, he said, "placed his knee on [Sullivan's head] and another . . . jabbed him in the eye with a blunt object," which splattered his eye. "The circumstances surrounding the loss of Sullivan's eye," Arrington wrote the mayor, "suggest a deliberate attempt by officers to maim [him]." When the police learned of the severity of the black's injury, a captain on the force went to the local hospital, found Sullivan, and then changed the charges against him from disorderly conduct and insulting an officer to assault on an officer with a deadly weapon. But witnesses at the scene testified that Sullivan had no weapon.

The emphasis the mayor had given to the kicking of the policewoman introduced an important factor into the case. Arrington knew the emotionalism connected with a black's striking a white male policeman; and he knew the extent of white male anger when a black man struck a white woman, especially a policewoman. Arrington, however, stuck to the point of broader significance. "I trust that you will agree," he told the mayor, "that it is not the job of officers to deliberately maim a prisoner or to determine his punishment once he has been arrested."

Seibels denied Arrington's request for a special investigation of the Sullivan beating. Such an action, said the mayor, would only imply a lack of faith in the police department's Internal Security Division. Arrington found support in Councilman Arthur Shores, who expressed his disappointment in not having a committee study the facts of the case. To remedy the long-term problems between the police and the black community, Shores now belatedly echoed a demand of his black colleague on the council—the need for citizen participation in police-brutality investigations, an idea strongly opposed by Chief James Parsons. Parsons had once declared that "policing is rough business, and people are going to find out that if they mess with the police they are going to get killed." The issue, of course, was the death and maiming of citizens who allegedly did not "mess with the police." The opposition of Parsons and Seibels to a citizens' review board or to citizen participation in an investigation raised an inevitable question in the minds of some: "If the police had nothing to hide, then why the strong objection to a review board or citizen involvement?"

Arrington believed that David Vann as mayor would demonstrate more sensitivity toward the issue of police brutality than Seibels had. The attorney's past told an eloquent story of his fight against injustice and his belief in fair play and civilized behavior in an orderly society. On the council he had supported Arrington on major black issues, and he had stood up against those forces that would, if possible, take Birmingham back to a past era. As a lawyer he exalted the idea of accused persons having their day in court, rather than the authoritarian belief that apparently prompted some police officers to take the law into their own hands and to act as judge and jury. Arrington trusted Vann's history, and he hoped it would not betray his loyalty. To end police abuse, the mayor would have to stand up to the police bureaucracy, especially the FOP; and such a stance would mean taking a terrible political risk, since the police had a strong constituency in a southern city like Birmingham.

Unfortunately, a Vann decision in a police-abuse case foreshadowed a later action that tumbled him from power. When Officer John Cousins killed Vernon Lee Burroughs in December 1977, then-mayor Vann faced a stern test. Witnesses testified that Burroughs attempted to flee the scene of a robbery he had allegedly committed, but Officer Cousins and his partner successfully apprehended the suspect, who offered no resistance to arrest. Police ordered the black man to raise his hands and to place them against the wall while they searched him. He complied. But the police contended that Burroughs then made "a sudden movement," interpreted by

Cousins as an effort to reach for a weapon to use against the officer. Vann resolved any doubt in favor of Cousins, but he expressed some reservation about the degree of professionalism he displayed on the night Burroughs died.

The case had a negative impact on Vann's image within the black community. But the tragic slaying of Bonita Carter by the police near the end of Vann's term spelled his political doom. As a result of this young woman's death, the city would undergo a political transformation of profound consequences. Arrington was the essential catalyst for change, successfully galvanizing opinion in the black community, which eventually said, "There has been enough suffering, enough killing by the police; brutality will stop here." As is often true in history, an event that triggers historic change is unplanned and can appear when people least expect it. Whether such an event becomes a tool for social or political action is determined by the readiness of a people to act concertedly, and the quality of leadership. Because of the history of police brutality and Arrington's work, black Birmingham had developed the resolve to stop police abuse of blacks. Ironically, Vann, who had done much to shape the city's history, would find himself in the midst of a volatile current of social action that politically pushed him aside but eventually swept in a new day in the history of Birmingham.

History will ultimately assign David Vann good grades for his performance as mayor of Birmingham. But in the summer of 1979, a tragic chance development made it virtually impossible for him to earn high marks from both blacks and whites. A twenty-year-old black girl named Bonita Carter was the reason. Her death in a "police incident" that hot, summer season brought the city of Birmingham to its bitterest racial crisis since the "Movement" days of civil rights. Vann's inaction during those terrible times tarnished his image as a racial liberal and champion of fair play. Whatever historians may say about Vann, they cannot avoid the conclusion that Richard Arrington's political career and political change in Birmingham were inextricably tied to the untimely death of this young woman.

Jerry's Seven-Eleven convenience store at 4500 Tenth Avenue North seemed an unlikely place for the beginning of a new era in

Birmingham's history. This little "quick stop" business greatly resembled a score of similar stores that dotted Birmingham's urban landscape, but on the night of 22 June 1979, it took on special meaning. A small place with a parking lot, located in an area of the city generally referred to as Kingston, the store drew customers from nearby housing projects and residences. Both children and young adults met frequently outside Jerry's to socialize and to dash in for a quick purchase. Most of the people who lived in the area were working folk who struggled to earn a marginal existence in a city that, economically, appeared somewhat other than its nickname of the Magic City. A majority of the families had either a lower-class or lower-middle-class income, but a considerable number of them hovered near or below the poverty level. But their view of life and their vision of Birmingham bore a remarkable similarity to that of other citizens. They worked, played, served their God, and lived with anticipation that opportunity and fate would somehow suddenly smile on them. Some, like others elsewhere, displayed a disregard for the public peace; and they could hate or even excite the wrath of those responsible for keeping order and ensuring a stable, law-abiding society.

Bonita Carter lived in this community, only a short distance from Jerry's. So did Alger Pickett, who quickly moved center stage in that shocking mid-June drama that so forcefully compelled Birmingham's rapt attention. Indeed, he commenced the gripping historic production on that steamy, summer day when he and wife Helen Charles drove into the convenience store to purchase gasoline for their 1971 Buick Electra. Action moved swiftly. Upon discovering that Jerry's now required payment for fuel before customers pumped it, Pickett, a black man, became angry. Tempers flared as Pickett protested to Michael James Avery, a white employee at the establishment. Words multiplied. Violent argument developed as Pickett warned Avery not to reach for a pistol if he wanted to stay alive.

The tragic story now unfolded more rapidly. Agitated with Pickett's aggressive action and convinced that he did not need a pistol to handle him, Avery moved from behind the counter and rushed toward the front door of the store, where he and the black man "stood . . . arguing and shaking . . . hands in each other's faces." Fists flew. Only the intervention of a black worker at Jerry's, Wayne Crusoe, who had witnessed the entire affair, prevented further trouble at that time. Pickett then went hurriedly to his car, took the gas nozzle from his tank where he had left it, and placed it in its proper place on the pump. He left. Avery then quietly returned to the store, while Crusoe replaced a door torn from its hinges during the altercation.

Passions had only temporarily subsided, at least for Alger Pickett. A few minutes after Crusoe had replaced the door at Jerry's and had gone into the back for rest, he heard a loud sound that he casually dismissed as noise from a closing cooler door. Crusoe was wrong. Alger Pickett had returned to Jerry's with a rifle! Couched outside Jerry's, Pickett aimed his gun toward the small store and proceeded to shoot as customers and employees scrambled for safety. By the time Crusoe emerged from the back of the building, Pickett had accomplished at least part of his assumed mission—he had shot Michael Avery, in the left shoulder. Crusoe, unaware of Pickett's presence outside, moved cautiously from the back of the store, pistol in hand. Heeding Avery's warning that Pickett had returned, Crusoe crawled on his hands and knees, trying to determine the actual number of people shooting into the store. Pickett was by himself.

Jerry's manager, Ray Jenkins, had no way of knowing that Pickett had chosen to act alone. When the black man made his dramatic reappearance and began blasting away at the store, Jenkins had been sleeping in a back room. Assuming that a robbery was in progress, he pulled the burglar alarm attached to a twenty-dollar bill inside the cash register. Seconds later, Crusoe and Jenkins peeped cautiously from their shelter to hear someone say, "He is getting away in the car." Ignoring Crusoe's words of caution, Jenkins dashed toward the door of Jerry's. Act two of the ugly drama was about to begin.

Bonita Carter awoke on the morning of 22 June unaware of the unfortunate role fate had assigned her. But history is chance; and chance often deals up tragedy. An attractive black woman, Bonita stood five feet seven inches and weighed 160 pounds, a physical description that had some bearing on the high drama that played in the Magic City. Several hours before Pickett had argued with Avery, the twenty-year-old woman had visited with her mother, Ethel Carter. The two had spent much of Friday afternoon together, passing the time laughing and talking. Bonita had been upbeat, full of spirit and vitality. "She was a happy person [who] liked the best in people," her mother later recalled; and that extroverted proclivity, perhaps, contributed to her death. Her unknown journey toward death had begun after she left her parents' home and joined friends at Kingston park. When she left that location on a bicycle, bound for Jerry's with close friend Louise Daniels, she rode fast to center stage in a violent episode that soon caught the city's attention.

About the moment Ray Jenkins rushed toward the door of Jerry's convenience store, Bonita was making her way to the Seven-Eleven quick stop. When the two young women arrived, Pickett had already fled across Tenth Avenue, a major east-west street that ran directly in front of Jerry's. Pickett's green Buick remained in the store's lot, where he had stopped it to remove his rifle. Bonita and Louise Daniels, now aware of what had taken place, stood nervously talking to each other at the edge of Jerry's when Pickett called for someone to bring his car across Tenth Avenue. Turning to her friend Louise, whom she affectionately called "Tina," Bonita said, "I am going to get his car and take it home, because they will pull it in." She smiled, approached the vehicle, then backed away in a playful, indecisive manner. The fatal decision then came. She went to the car and, with her tall body slightly bent, opened the door and entered the eight-year-old green Buick. Louise Daniels recalled what took place: "She got in the car . . . and by the time she could get it . . . straightened up in the lane [of Tenth Avenue], this blue car came up, and two white men [policemen] got out."

Roughly sixteen short seconds passed between the time a dispatch came out over the police radio that a robbery (designated 16-A in police code) was in progress and the time policemen made a request from Jerry's for emergency medical aid. When Ray Jenkins rushed out of Jerry's and ordered Bonita Carter to stop the green Buick, his action triggered a chain reaction of staggering events that figuratively turned Birmingham upside down. Bonita heeded Jen-

Bonita Carter, 1979. (Courtesy of the *Birmingham News*)

kins's demand, and brought the automobile to a halt about the time the two plainclothes policemen arrived. Although it is unclear where the officers actually were at the time the robbery signal came over the radio, it is certain they were near Jerry's, or actually on the premises. They had started there to "get soft drinks and [to] take a short break." Upon arrival, Officers Richard Hollingsworth and George M. "Mike" Sands jumped from their unmarked police car, guns drawn. They heard the voice of Ray Jenkins, who shouted to them, "They're in that car—that is the car—they shot Mike Avery." Jenkins also yelled, "There they go," although the lone person in the vehicle had now stopped the car on Tenth Avenue.

In those few short seconds after their arrival, Sands and Hollingsworth received more information than that given by Jenkins. Willie Wilson saw both police officers with their guns and ran toward them as they approached Tenth Avenue. He came close enough to the two policemen for them to hear him yell, "A man with a gun is across the street. He has a rifle in his hand. That isn't a dude in the car. She is a chick. She has nothing to do with this." Louise Daniels, too, had observed the police as they got out of their car "in a mad passion." Bonita's friend also tried to warn them that a girl occupied the vehicle in the middle of Tenth Avenue. She later testified that the officers were "practically in my face" and had to hear her cries that "it's a girl in the car—the man gone with the gun." Hollingsworth and Sands said nothing to her. The city claimed later that the officers, their attention riveted on the car, did not hear, or failed to understand, the shouts from bystanders. But they did hear Jenkins.

Bonita Carter remained quietly in the front seat of the automobile. If the vehicle had indeed been a getaway car, it had ceased to serve its function. Bonita had "stopped the car on a dime," said one witness. Hollingsworth and Sands carefully approached the vehicle from the rear, one officer on each side of the automobile. Hollingsworth testified that he and Sands called out, "Police officers—y'all hold it, come on out." Some witnesses to the affair questioned whether such a command ever came from the two officers, but Hollingsworth contended that "we didn't get any response at all to that command." Even Mayor David Vann unintentionally cast some doubt on the testimony after the shooting when he hinted that the policemen may not have called to the occupants "to come out . . . with . . . hands up prior to approaching the car so closely."

The next-to-the-last episode in this drama now flashed quickly on Tenth Avenue. Louise Daniels and Willie Wilson provided testimony on what took place. "They [the police] didn't even ask her to get out of the car," Daniels related; she said that "they went up—up to Bonita and shot her." Wilson saw one officer go to the driver's side of the Buick, arriving near the front door of the vehicle before his fellow officer reached the opposite door on the passenger side. Wilson's shouts to Sands that Pickett had fled went unheeded as the veteran of the Birmingham police force continued his mission.

As the officers moved alongside the car, closing in on Bonita with every step, the black girl suddenly raised up from the front seat where she had been lying. With a body now in sight, George W. Sands, who had approached the car from the passenger's side, rapidly drilled three bullets into the frame that had risen from the car seat. A fourth bullet missed its mark. Sands's fellow officer on the driver's side of the car never fired a single shot, although he came closer to Bonita than his buddy. By the time an ambulance arrived at Carraway Methodist Hospital with its twenty-year-old victim, no life remained in her tall, dark frame. The end came violently to Bonita, but the trauma that rang down the curtain on this hideous drama wrote a new play and brought forth different actors on Birmingham's political and social stage.

The killing of Bonita Carter stirred the black community, and it erased any lethargy that remained after Arrington's persistent attacks against police violence. As eyewitness accounts and information filled with both truth and rumor swept through North Birmingham and the rest of the black community, hatreds and old antagonisms built to a feverish pitch. To a large number of black folk, the young black woman had been callously murdered. Had not blacks witnessed police killings at other times? Restraint had characterized their actions in previous cases, but a different mood now filled the air. John Streeter of the *Birmingham Times* caught the prevailing sentiment in the black community when he wrote on 26 June 1979 that almost no one could misunderstand the feelings of

115

Kingston citizens "or black residents anywhere who were knowledgeable of the incident."

Birmingham now stood at the edge of real violence and even more bloodshed. Bonita's shooting had brought several hundred angry black protesters to Jerry's. Rocks flew at vehicles that had white occupants, and bottles crashed through the windows of some businesses. Continuing racial disturbances and a picket line forced the convenience-store owner, Jerry Huff, to close his business following the shooting. Soon it was obvious that this particular police killing would not pass as others had. Long-standing black wounds and the immediate sorrow that came with Bonita's death did not fade when Chief of Police William "Bill" Myers proclaimed that Hollingsworth and Sands did not know Bonita was in the car. Nor did his sensitivity in describing the event as a "tragic thing" impress them. The chief pledged a full-scale departmental investigation, and he placed George M. Sands on administrative leave. But it took three days after the shooting for a representative from the police department to pay an official visit to John and Ethel Carter, the young woman's parents.

Tension and racial conflicts disturbed the Kingston community in the weeks following Bonita Carter's death. Chief Myers reinforced police units in the area immediately after the shooting to prevent escalating violence and other criminal activity. On 24 June he ordered two teams of tactical officers to break up black gatherings following an outbreak of rock throwing in the community. Police shot out lights near Jerry's to help protect officers who came under attack from objects hurled at them. Myers reaffirmed his intention to keep peace and to prevent confrontation between Kingston blacks and the Ku Klux Klan, which had threatened to demonstrate in the area. Fear of the Klan and other hate groups no longer gripped blacks, and they readied themselves to "walk through the valley of the shadow of death for justice." Austin Thomas, a Kingston neighborhood leader, mirrored existing sentiment in the black community when he called upon the city to rid the police of "trigger happy" officers. "We would just as soon die in Kingston over this matter," he exclaimed, "as to die in other countries fighting for this country's freedom."

Richard Arrington understood the anger in the black community that came with the death of Bonita Carter. He had witnessed up-close other cases that had taken lives, and for nearly eight years he had fought at city hall to change the behavior and the attitudes of the police toward blacks. Here was a continuing episode in an ugly, sordid tale. And now he had to face the bitterness and the deep hatred that followed the killing of Bonita. Arrington did not try to escape his responsibility when Myers called the night of the shooting to ask him to go to Kingston with him, where blacks were throwing rocks and displaying anger over the death. Although Myers outlined the problem the police were encountering in the Kingston community that night, Arrington had few details at that time about the shooting. Significantly, he did not know the name of the officer who had done the killing before he drove to city hall to meet the chief and his assistant.

A hostile black crowd greeted the men upon their arrival near Jerry's. The presence of a large number of policemen only fueled the bitterness that existed among black residents, who had entered the streets to demand that the city dismiss Sands from the police department. Most of the demonstrators stood opposite the police on the south side of Tenth Avenue across from the small convenience store. Profane screams, a product of deep hurt and much frustration, broke the southern night air. Some persons aimlessly milled around, while others stood silently. When the people saw Arrington they rushed from across the street, an action that brought them into closer contact with one of their objects of momentary hate— the police. The councilman instantly realized that this particular crowd had little interest in abstractions or belabored commentaries on law and order. He comprehended their anger, their hurt. Most of them were "serious, sober, but very much outraged."

Arrington had difficulty persuading the crowd to disperse. Although not unruly, the gathering clearly manifested impatience. Arrington carried on a conversation with persons in the group, several of whom he personally knew, and he spoke to the crowd with a bullhorn, expressing his own sorrow. He cautioned them against further violence, which would only complicate the problem at hand and damage the objective they all sought. He tried to convince the protesters to return to their homes. They refused. The councilman now saw the real depths of the crowd's anger. With the assistance of a minister, Rev. Tony Cooper, he decided to edge the crowd away from Jerry's to separate blacks from the police, "toward whom they were becoming very, very hostile." Arrington stayed in the area for more than twenty minutes without any success in getting people to leave. The beginning of a long summer's night that finally led to daylight of political change had just begun.

Arrington returned to city hall with Myers, where the two met Mayor Vann. The brief encounter between the three men provided Arrington with more crucial details on what had taken place—and it also forecast difficulties. In his discussion with Vann, Myers mentioned the name of the officer who shot Bonita Carter, and it struck Arrington like a thunderbolt. He knew it well—George W. Sands, or Mike Sands, as some referred to him. Over the years Arrington had filed brutality complaints against this officer, and he had also spoken directly to the mayor about Sands's performance. When Myers mentioned Sands, the mayor and Arrington said almost simultaneously, "uh-oh," a clear indication that Vann, too, remembered the policeman who had now killed unarmed Bonita Carter in a car stopped in the middle of a Birmingham street. The news of Sands's involvement shocked Arrington, for the councilman believed the police department had transferred him to a less visible position because of complaints from citizens in North Birmingham.

Sands had experienced a troubled personal life, and he had not been a "model cop." The thirty-two-year-old son of a former army sergeant joined the Birmingham police force in 1971 after serving with the city's fire department. A profile of Sands by two specialists in November 1979 painted a picture of a man with considerable self-doubt. In their psychological report, Richard Crews and C. J. Rosecrans showed that the policeman had a sensitivity to criticism and possessed "feelings of inadequacy." He was also "moody, unsociable and easily agitated." At age twenty, Sands had married and later became the father of two children before divorcing his wife of eight years. Another marriage also ended in failure.

When blacks initially called for Sands's dismissal, they had no

118

complete knowledge of his professional record. Through Arrington they learned of his role in other, although less tragic, cases of alleged police brutality. In his eight years on the Birmingham police force, citizens had filed over a dozen complaints of abuse against him. In almost every case the victim was black, although a 1978 incident did involve a local white male. The department's Internal Affairs Division investigated the charges against Sands, but only once did he receive a verbal reprimand.

The public revelation of Sands's performance made it more imperative for blacks to seek his dismissal before a reoccurrence of 22 June took place. In a column on 26 June 1979, John Streeter of the *Birmingham Times* raised the question Arrington had posed for nearly eight years at city hall. Why did the police department continue to send officers into the community who consistently received complaints and whose actions aroused concern about their professionalism? Sands, said the reporter, should have been "blackballed years ago from patrolling, if not kicked off the force." Previous complaints should have warned the top brass at city hall that the man did not belong in police work. The black community, said one black leader, had no place for "trigger-happy officers who became judge, jury and executioner."

Events moved fast as Arrington carefully digested every development. With the involvement of the Southern Christian Leadership Conference in the growing controversy, blacks could better coordinate their efforts. Led by Abraham Woods, a clergyman, SCLC had experience in performing the role it delegated to itself—directing blacks toward positive, long-range, humanitarian and civil-rights goals. Woods had grown accustomed to activism and accepted it almost as a way of life. Although he had earned distinction in the civil-rights movement, Woods's role in Birmingham had not previously received the notice of some other leaders.

Abraham Woods graduated from Parker High School in Birmingham and then attended Morehouse College. He later switched to Miles College where he completed his undergraduate degree. The minister began doctorate studies at the University of Alabama, but he humorously remarked in 1983 that he had been "too busy trying to run . . . business in the community" to get any work done on his degree. Whites in Birmingham may not have liked this short, heavy-set, sharp-eyed reformer, who had worked with his idol, Martin Luther King, Jr., but they could not easily ignore him or fail to take him seriously. Woods meant business. "Some people consider me an agitator or trouble maker, somebody that rocks the boat," he once told a southern historian, "and they are absolutely right!" Confident of his religious and social mission, Woods projected an image in 1979 of a man out to defeat injustice and the remaining remnants of white oppression. He had seen the lifeless body of Bonita Carter as it rested at his St. Joseph's Baptist Church. All along, he had known the strength of Arrington's fight against police brutality, and he and other ministers had supported the councilman. Now it was time to "speak in unmistakable language" to end police abuse in Birmingham. He would do that for the benefit of generations yet unborn. That was his moral mission.

An apostle of nonviolence, Woods had seen black people's anger reach a fever pitch in the past and then subside. That must not happen in the case of Bonita Carter, for it would dampen the possibility of long-range reform. Yet, Woods wanted to avoid violence. Therefore, he and other ministers in Birmingham met in a series of meetings to discuss protest strategy and to coordinate citywide activities. They fully recognized the potential that violence could engulf Birmingham, which posed a continuing problem for black leadership. But now was not the time for excessive conservatism. A black person lay dead! When blacks held a meeting at Hopewell Baptist Church, their mood became clear when they shouted down State Representative Jerome Tucker because of his appeal for nonviolence. But Woods did not want *actual* violence to become the central concern of white leadership. He did desire that the establishment worry about the *possibility* of its occurrence. After Arrington gave Woods and the other ministers Sands's dismal performance record, they became unyielding in their demand for the officer's dismissal. And they now called for a permanent civilian police-review board.

Arrington's longtime political ally David Vann had to act decisively. The councilman and other black leaders had tried not to box him in, but the details of the shooting, Sands's record, and the prevailing mood in the community made concrete action necessary. Blacks had lost faith in white city-hall leadership, and they virtually ignored the city council's routine call for an investigation of Bonita Carter's shooting. Sensitive to this sentiment, the astute Vann decided to make a historic move in a serious game of political chess. He announced the formation of a blue-ribbon citizens' committee to probe the shooting of Bonita Carter. The committee could hold public hearings and had the power to call witnesses and to make recommendations. "When you've got testimony taken behind closed doors . . . you leave the community open to all kinds of rumors," Vann said in creating the committee.

The eight-person citizens' committee had an equal number of blacks and whites. The black members had years of distinguished service to the community and to the city. Dr. James Montgomery, a civic-minded physician, had long practiced in the city and had vigilantly fought for human rights. At the time of his appointment he served as cochairman of the Community Affairs Committee. Rev. Edward Gardner presided over the Alabama Christian Movement for Human Rights, and Rev. Sam Davis pastored Saint Paul AME Church. The fourth black, Emmett Lockett, was from Kingston and served as president of that community's neighborhood association.

Whites on the committee also enjoyed notable backgrounds. Rabbi Milton Grafman, the committee's chair, served at Temple Emanu-El; Dr. Wilmer Cody was superintendent of the Birmingham school system. Dr. Blaine Brownell came to the committee from the administrative ranks at the University of Alabama-Birmingham (UAB). Mrs. Julia Anderson had served as a neighborhood president, and she enjoyed the respect of many blacks, despite her basic conservatism and her general support of the police department. Whether she viewed herself as "the police department's person" on the committee remained a speculative question, although some regarded her in that light. Indeed, years after the investigation, one black confided, "I don't believe she would ever have voted against the police."

Vann's blue-ribbon committee elicited mixed reaction from the black community. Some saw it as a lamentable waste of time, a lightning rod to take the heat off the city's leader and the police department. Others saw it as a political device to ease Vann's reelection in the forthcoming mayoral contest. In a sharp-edged editorial, a reporter for one black newspaper wrote impatiently of the procrastination over the cut-and-dry matter of police brutality and the dismissal of Sands. The 5 July 1979 article showed signs of the frustration and the accompanying emotionalism that permeated the black community:

> Birmingham Mayor David Vann . . . will probably seek reelection this year. He is playing politics on the emotions of black people in order to secure votes he needs desperately. The latest polls show Vann behind [his opponents] in popularity. Therefore, with the murder of Ms. Carter gaining city-wide and even nationwide attention, Vann sets up a Citizen's Review Board to look into the situation and make a recommendation to him. Vann's so-called blue-ribbon panel is a waste of money and time to the citizens of Birmingham. And furthermore, it infringes on the intelligence of black people. This case is cut and dry. And anyone who can justify the murder of Ms. Carter has rocks in his head. This is only a political move by Vann to get votes and it's wasting time [when] Sands could be locked up behind bars. A Review Board was needed in the Chambers murder and some others. But Ms. Carter's loss of life was self explanatory.

Arrington had called for a civilian review board in the past, and Woods and others had echoed his demand. When black leaders met with the mayor on 27 June to discuss the Carter killing, some of them expressed displeasure with the investigation, since it would, as one newspaper reporter had noted, only delay Sands's removal from the police force. However, Woods eventually saw some advantage in the blue-ribbon committee. Perhaps, he reasoned, the city had made a beginning toward a genuine change in how it would investigate officers in cases of alleged police misconduct. While he had initially disliked the idea of an inquiry board, since the facts of the Bonita Carter case seemed clear to him, he admitted upon reflection, "I'm beginning to see something."

Arrington remained in close touch with black leaders. It was crucial not only to attend community meetings but to gauge prevailing sentiment in the city. Like other blacks, he wanted Sands off the police force, and he had worked toward that end. The councilman, however, had not expressed the open hostility of some persons toward the creation of the blue-ribbon committee. Obviously the committee was not a civilian review board in a strict sense, but like Woods, he knew its establishment represented a historic step. He had argued consistently that the victims of police brutality stood a better chance of having their cases resolved successfully before such a board than through existing police-department procedure. At least Vann's special committee conceded the important principle that an outside body could discover the essential facts of a controversial police shooting. Arrington strongly rejected the contention, advanced mostly by the FOP and its supporters, that the committee threatened to violate Sands's constitutional rights.

The FOP had vigorously attacked Arrington and his crusade against police brutality, and the group's opposition to Vann's civilian investigation of the Bonita Carter killing came as no surprise to anyone who followed developments in the city. The organization's leader, Ted McCoy, flippantly denounced it as a "kangaroo court." A lawyer for the group pledged to protect Sands's rights, and he lamented that the mayor had not left the matter to the Internal Affairs Division. He, too, hinted that Vann had a political motive for his action. Supporters of the FOP had appeared at city hall to protest the creation of the committee.

Other citizens wrote stinging letters to local newspapers. Mrs. A. M. McDonald applauded Birmingham's policemen for their tough job, and John Kiker asked rhetorically if the citizens committee would seek justice when shots ripped through the men in blue that protected the city. Jack Pilley missed the central point of the raging controversy, but his correspondence doubtless drew applause from those who shared similar views. Alluding to an unrelated case of rape and murder in Birmingham, he declared "against our mayor giving in to all these demands," although it was not clear what Vann had conceded, since blacks only wanted Sands fired. A twenty-year-old woman, Pilley wrote, "is old enough to know what

123

she is doing or certainly should be." He turned away from the shooting itself to focus on the aftermath. Police had the authority to enforce the law, and anyone, black or white, who resisted that authority, "should be restrained by whatever force is necessary." Resistance to authority, of course, had never been at issue in the Bonita Carter case.

Sporadic violence and confrontation between blacks and whites took place in Kingston as the committee began its work. Snipers sometimes fired at police, and blacks accused law officers of violence against them. Members of the Ku Klux Klan made occasional trips into the community but succeeded in frightening no one. Eight of them eventually got themselves arrested. Klansmen found blacks willing to confront them openly and, if necessary, shoot back. A new day had indeed arrived.

The citizens' committee encountered problems in compiling its report. One of the many frustrations arose from Vann's refusal to order release of the police report of Bonita's killing and the personnel file of Sands. After consultation with his legal counsel, Vann decided that none of the records contained any evidence that "would be legally admissible in these proceedings." To turn over Sands's files, he said, would invade the officer's privacy. His refusal to surrender documents, he told the committee, should not pose an obstacle to its work. Whatever the legal merit of his decision, Vann did significantly limit the committee, and he kept it from acting as fully as some had hoped.

The panel confronted other difficulties. Three of the key actors in the hideous Magic City drama never testified before the body. George Sands did not appear, and his partner on the night of the shooting contributed little of substance to the investigation. Alger Pickett, who triggered the peace-shattering developments on the night of 22 June and who still remained subject to criminal prosecution for assault with intent to murder, did not testify. And since the committee could not compel Helen Charles, Pickett's wife, to come forward, part of the story that led to the shooting itself never reached the hearing. Arthur Hanes, Sr., Pickett's attorney, had advised Charles not to testify, since her husband had "a trial or two down the road." Ray Jenkins eventually testified, although reluctantly. Questions of committee procedure also arose on more than one occasion, and, unfortunately, there was little time to recall some key witnesses to resolve inconsistencies in testimony.

If the thousand pages of committee hearings did not resolve every question of Bonita Carter's killing, they did help many readers fix in their mind a picture of what took place on the night of 22 June. Whether police knew that a young woman actually occupied the car and not a man will probably remain an open question unless history forces a change in the testimony of the two officers. The committee wrestled hard with whether or not the victim of the shooting posed a threat to the officers. This question really seemed most crucial of all. The interrogation by Dr. James T. Montgomery clearly fixed attention on specifics that helped the committee deal with this difficult issue. His exchange with Dr. Ronald Rivers, Jefferson County coroner, was highly significant, not only because it represented the most probing part of the entire investigation, but because it involved the expert commentary between two professionals in a position to draw sound conclusions based on evidence in their specialized fields. The exchange between the two men, one black, the other white, went to the core of the controversy.

[DR. MONTGOMERY]: I am trying to decide whether or not this lady's [Bonita's] movement threatened anybody. I am not asking you [Rivers] to make that judgment. I am trying to make it for myself. . . . When you look at these wounds . . . [on the back of the deceased] and you are talking about the position of them and you see [the] car [the woman was in] and that car has a high seat, even in the center, and from the position of the . . . entry wounds . . . it appears to me . . . that from that position it would be difficult for . . . [bullets] to enter the body if her body was straight up from the rear unless [they] went through the seat, is that your testimony?

A. [DR. RIVERS]: Yes, sir.

DR. MONTGOMERY: It seems to me that the only way these wounds could have been made, three entry wounds and one exit wound, is that if a patient [person] apparently some time had laid down in the car or attempted to lay down in the car . . .

and was getting up in this direction [toward the passenger side with the back partially turned] and the shots coming through the window of the car. . . . I don't see any [other] way [these wounds] could have been made. Do you. . . ?

A. [DR. RIVERS]: If the lady was sitting in the passenger's side of the [car]. . . .

DR. MONTGOMERY: I am assuming she was not sitting [on the passenger's side]—if she was sitting on the passenger['s] side, she would have to be almost sitting with her legs in the seat. . . . She couldn't have been sitting straight in the seat at the time [she was shot].

A. [DR. RIVERS]: We are assuming that the shots came from the right side of the car?

DR. MONTGOMERY: Right side of the car, that's right. We know that.

A. [DR. RIVERS]: If she was sitting—if she was sitting in the middle of the car and raised up and was turning toward the other—

DR. MONTGOMERY: Toward the left.

A. [DR. RIVERS]: Toward the left?

DR. MONTGOMERY: Yeah.

A. [DR. RIVERS]: These shots would be consistent with that position.

DR. MONTGOMERY: If she was shot through the front window [from the passenger[s]] side.

A. [DR. RIVERS]: She would have to be completely—the shots are traveling from the right [side of the car] to the left.

DR. MONTGOMERY: Yeah, right to left.

A. [DR. RIVERS]: So, the back window would be a better window [from which the shots came.]

DR. MONTGOMERY: I think they are too low to [have] come from there.

A. [DR. RIVERS]: That's right.

DR. MONTGOMERY: [The entry wounds are] too low [for shots] to come from the back window.

A. [DR. RIVERS]: That is a good point.

DR. MONTGOMERY: [The shots have] to come from the front window.

A. [DR. RIVERS]: They would have been too low [from the back window.]

DR. MONTGOMERY: That's correct. That is the way I see it, at least. [W]hat I am trying to find out in my own thinking, and that is all, is what threats could this young lady have been . . . to the officer who shot her in the back, getting up from this position (demonstrating), apparently like this, and this is the back window behind me, how could she have been a threat to his life.

MR. WYATT [an attorney]: Let me object to that.

DR. MONTGOMERY: I don't mind you objecting. I am saying I can't see in my own mind what threat she could have offered. I still don't see in my own mind what threat she could have offered.

MR. BAKER [committee attorney]: I think the committee members ought to ask questions of the witnesses and not testify. . . .

DR. MONTGOMERY: We know pretty much where the young lady was when she got shot. She was in the front seat of the car. So, the two things have to be put together, where the assailant was and where the victim was. Where could she have been really and got shot in all of these [three] positions without any bullets going through the seat other than the fact that she was getting up with her back toward the right window and the shots coming from the right window. Where else could she have been?

Dr. Rivers's testimony, coupled with Officer Hollingsworth's difficulty in explaining why he had not shot into the car, since he stood near the door with Bonita close to him, had a dramatic effect on those who followed the proceedings. If Sands had stood directly in Hollingsworth's line of fire, as the latter testified, then why did Sands have far less regard for his partner, who could have also been killed by a stray shot from his gun?

127

The committee's decision gave David Vann greater woes. The panel noted the existence of conflicting evidence, but its major conclusion came without equivocation. No threatening actions occurred to Hollingsworth and Sands as they approached the car that held the black woman. "Even assuming that Officer Sands believed an armed person was in the car, and had shot Mike Avery," the report said, sufficient justification did not exist for the shooting of Bonita Carter. The eight-member committee approved the report by a 7–0 vote with Anderson abstaining.

If Vann had established the blue-ribbon committee as a lightning rod, as some had speculated, he now had to deal with the electricity generated by its report. Dissatisfaction and political problems had already followed the mayor's creation of the panel, and now its findings had put Vann in a no-win situation. Any action on his part would surely produce hard feelings and enemies in parts of the community. "Vann had miscalculated," Arrington stated five years after the mayor had faced the most difficult decision of his political career. "In my opinion," he said, "Vann did not believe the committee would come back with the findings that it did, and certainly not by such a large vote." His virtually handpicked committee had declared the shooting unjustified. And Arrington asked rhetorically: "What can you do in such a case?"

The question had more than rhetorical significance in the summer of 1979. Arrington then argued more forcefully than ever that fairness and justice dictated Sands's dismissal from the Birmingham police force. To the mayor the case did not appear as clear-cut. He huddled with his police chief immediately after the committee's report to discuss his dilemma. Before he rendered a final decision, however, Vann wrote the Jefferson County district attorney, Earl Morgan, about the case. He asked Morgan to review the evidence against Sands to see if probable cause existed for a grand-jury case. With the FOP threatening a possible work stoppage if an adverse decision came down against a fellow officer, and with black leaders hinting at a boycott if the policeman remained on the force, Vann found himself in a precarious position. A sharp attack on the use of a citizens' panel in the 10 July 1979 *Birmingham News* doubtless aggravated the problem that faced the mayor, for the paper's commentary may have lessened the possible acceptance of the committee's findings.

Ten days passed after the citizens' committee report before Vann made a decision on Sands. On 17 July he issued a seventeen-page statement that recounted the essential facts of the case and gave his decision. Even the best literary talent and diplomacy would not have been able to extricate Vann from the political hole the circumstances had created. The mayor often used phrases and combinations of words laden with sentiment—the "tragic death," the "tragic mistakes," and the "tragic unjustifiable mistake"; he appealed to "courage," "prayer," "cool heads," what was "just and fair and right" to all concerned, and the "painful loss" suffered by the Carter family. David Vann had produced a masterful literary document. But it was not good enough.

Vann's decision displeased many whites and thoroughly enraged blacks. He refused to fire Sands. He cited the report of the police department's Firearm Discharge Review Committee, which ruled 5–1 that the shooting of Bonita Carter came within the department's policy. In short, Vann had now rejected the report of his blue-ribbon committee for that of the police department. To Arrington, Vann's approach to the matter of the Bonita Carter shooting became increasingly obvious. The mayor would divert responsibility from George Sands and blame departmental policy and training.

The logic of Vann's decision strengthened the case for Sands and the position of those who wanted to keep him on the police force. In reviewing the evidence in the case, Vann argued that, on the night of the shooting, Sands had other alternatives open to him, "such as holding back and calling for the occupant of the car to rise slowly and get out of the car with both hands in sight." And why had Sands failed to use this approach? Vann's answer led him to the heart of the argument. "I find," he wrote, "that such alternatives have not been adequately taught by the Birmingham Police Department." The city had trained its officers "to be bold and aggressive and to protect themselves with rapid fire of their weapons when *threatened*" (my italics). Other officers probably would have handled the situation the same as Sands did. Given Vann's logic, how could the mayor possibly punish a Birmingham police officer for a job performance consistent with his training? Obviously, he could not. The mayor was convinced that Sands "honestly thought that either his life, or that of his partner, was in danger and that it was a case of shoot or be shot." Delay in similar incidents had caused the lives of policemen.

The mayor assumed that the Bonita Carter killing and subsequent controversy had shaken Sands's confidence. Therefore, he removed the officer from street duty and reassigned him to a "noncontact position." His decision now behind him, Vann offered a program of change within the police department, a logical outcome, of course, of Vann's explanation of Bonita Carter's shooting. He made a commitment to revamp the department's shooting and firearm policies and to revise the training program for officers. Those policemen with a substantial number of complaints would have their records examined regularly to determine possible incompatibility with the community they patrolled. Finally, the mayor vowed to continue to work for improved recruitment of minority policemen and to review city services and improvements in Kingston.

Vann's determination not to fire Sands now tore Arrington away from his old friend. "David handled the whole thing badly," Arrington said in reflecting on the event that partly resulted from a lack of advice from blacks. A real problem for the mayor, too, other than white public opinion, was his police chief. Bill Myers had the reputation as a "tough cop," but in a critical assessment of the man Arrington noted that he "was never going to take any strong disciplinary action against police officers unless he absolutely could not avoid it." To Arrington, Vann had now become a tragic symbol of one of the city's greatest ills. "If anyone ever wondered how Birmingham could go on with a long history of police brutality, the reaction to that incident answered it," he said as he sadly relived the case.

Black leaders now turned to direct protest and political mobilization. "Sands or Vann" became the rallying cry that reverberated throughout the black community. On the Monday before Mayor Vann's monumental decision, the SCLC had held an assembly at St. Paul Methodist Church, where the Reverend Joseph Lowery, national president of the organization, had discussed plans for a pos-

sible march on city hall. "We will not stand idly by," he told an emotionally charged audience, "and let black life be snuffed out while
those responsible are let off scot-free." Abraham Woods, in his pat-
ented deliberate oratory, thundered that black Birmingham had
"leaned way, way, way, way, way over backward" in waiting for Vann
to act.

The day following the mayor's announcement about Sands's retention, Woods had asked local businessmen and black leaders to
apply political and economic pressure on Vann. And he threatened
a boycott ("blackout") against those who failed to cooperate. The
moderate James T. Montgomery, who had been a valuable member of
the blue-ribbon committee, labeled Vann's decision a shameful re-
treat. Black councilman Larry Langford termed Vann's decision a
mistake, and Councilwoman Bessie Estelle called for disciplinary
action against Sands. Former Vann supporter W. C. Patton bitterly
deplored the action. All agreed with Arrington, who told the press
after a meeting of community leaders that, following the killing of
a black, there was usually a proposal to change police policy and
hire more blacks. But "nothing is solved," he said. The city's chief
executive had to enforce rules against police officers who violated
them. He took strong exception to the local newspapers' contention
that the mayor's decision had been reasonable, just, and fair. He did
not agree that Sands had simply made a "mistake."

Pressure on Vann and the city did not abate. On 20 July 1979, led
by SCLC, blacks held one of the largest protest marches in the city
since the 1960s. To older civil-rights veterans, Kelly Ingram Park,
the starting point of the march, brought back memories when the
fight for justice and black rights occupied center stage in Birmingham and claimed national attention. With city hall their destina-
tion, protesters sang freedom songs and chanted repeatedly, "Sands,
Vann, and the Klan must go." This was "D-day," declared the Reverend E. W. Jarrett; and it would deliver a knockout punch to any
misguided hope of retaining Sands on the police force. But if the
mayor stubbornly continued to resist black demands to fire the officer, then blacks would prepare to "dig in" for a long, hard fight. Despite a heavy rain, an estimated three thousand demonstrators
gathered at city hall. The young, the old, and the feeble joined the

131

folk from the street and the black middle class to express their outrage and to call for Sands's immediate dismissal.

Vann's attendance at the gathering at city hall took courage. It required even more strength for him to remain poised as Abraham Woods blistered the mayor for a decision his audience deemed insensitive, if not downright unforgivably cruel. "We thought you were going to be one of the outstanding mayors of Birmingham," the SCLC leader told Vann and the crowd, "but you have turned on your black folk." "Dismiss Sands," Woods shouted in a political warning, or "it's going to be Vann." The audience began to echo the chant already popular in the black community: "Sands and Vann must go." To one speaker Vann symbolized a new-style Bull Connor. In a dramatic gesture Lowery removed from his neck a key to the city that Vann had given him the previous year, and he pledged not to wear it again until "justice ran down like water, and righteousness like a mighty stream."

The march may have been D-day for the black protesters but it dealt no destructive blow to Vann's decision. Talk of an economic boycott again surfaced, but that suggestion met with considerable negative reaction from within the black community. Such talk disturbed whites. In a long 22 July 1979 editorial, the *Birmingham News* opposed the boycott and called for a different kind of strategy. Disruptive activities and boycotts, it said, "would not be welcome under any circumstance." The black community would lose most in case of a selective-buying campaign. The counterthreat was not easily disguised. A boycott would damage the economic welfare of blacks, for it would adversely affect businesses that had opened up job opportunities. "Would it not now be appropriate," the *News* asked, "for other leaders in both black and white communities to step forward and make the case for reason and reconciliation?"

A rapprochement with what blacks considered injustice did not constitute part of their agenda for Birmingham, that hot summer of 1979. By August it had become clear to Arrington that an extended boycott would require considerable effort and resources. As a punitive measure it may have had some merit, but punishment was not the most important goal of the black community. If the boycott failed, that would damage the chance of police reform. Not surprisingly, blacks began to think again of politics as a viable instrument to achieve their objective, not just to punish Vann but to reorder a power relationship between the races that could reshape institutions and how they operated. The black community had a renewed mission, and it had a champion for its cause—Richard Arrington, Jr. It was time to make him mayor.

5

Bottom Rails and Ballots: The 1979 Election

·

Although Richard Arrington had played an important role in the Bonita Carter affair, he had abstained from political demagoguery or the exploitation of the tragedy for his own self-serving political purposes. He did not "beat the drum" of violent protest or issue clarion calls for all the faithful to stand at Armageddon and declare to the opposition, like Marshall Henri Petain at Verdun, "You shall not pass!" He had made every effort to assist the city in bringing about a resolution to the problem following the dastardly affair of 22 June. He had urged patience, and he had counseled against violence. When Vann had finally administered the coup de grace to the black community's "wait and see" policy with his decision to keep George W. Sands on the police force, Arrington seethed with anger and disappointment, but he continued to work for a solution short of violence. His attacks on the decision, however, and upon the climate of opinion that made the shooting possible became sharper. All along, Arrington had clearly in mind what stood at the bottom of the matter—race. The city of Birmingham, he wrote during the heat of the controversy, "will continue to [tread] the same old course of racial injustice" until it admitted that bigotry was still a factor in police treatment of blacks. Until that time whites would continue to line up on one side and blacks on the other.

Arrington's political stock in the black community hardly needed a boost from the tragedy that visited Birmingham in the summer of 1979. Knowledgeable blacks recognized his role and applauded his actions. Significantly, he had not tried to dictate every move of the black community. Arrington had been deliberate in his approach to the problem, but no less intense than others who hated conditions in Birmingham that helped make possible Bonita Carter's death. "He has done everything expected of him," said the reporter of one newspaper column in the city during the controversy. The black politician had provided details of the killing, and he had released information on Sands when the city refused to release it. "He's marched," wrote John Streeter in the 26 July 1979 *Birmingham Times* in high praise of the councilman. Arrington had "been vocal to the point that his views were heard and he has . . . let the community . . . know the kind of Mayor Birmingham has and the kind of police officers we are dealing with." Streeter had less kind words for other black councilpersons. They had stood on the sidelines hoping to avoid questions or a firm stand. The reporter reserved his bitterest remarks for Councilman Larry Langford, who had used the Bonita Carter killing to talk of black-on-black crime, an issue that had received attention in several of Streeter's past columns.

The pressure generated by Arrington and others revealed the continuing influence of Birmingham's past and indicated that some of its ugliest features had not "gone with the wind." The Bonita Carter shooting had brought about some revamping in the police shooting policy, and the city had addressed some community problems, but Arrington, Woods, and the Southern Christian Leadership Conference considered these reforms relatively small steps, given the gravity of what had transpired. Sands's dismissal would have indicated a fundamental new direction in the attitude of the city. When Birmingham continued to refuse to settle a suit filed by the attorney U. W. Clemon for the death of Bonita Carter, Arrington took the action as evidence that the city really had not changed much.

Blacks again turned to the political process for remedy. If the mayor had failed to "stand up for right" and had helped to abort justice, then why not elect a different executive? The idea was not novel. When Arrington ran for the council in 1971, it will be recalled, a group of young blacks had first asked him to seek the mayor's office, and the black press had occasionally spoken of the possible election of a black chief executive. As the city became increasingly black and as citizens noticed the election of black mayors in Atlanta and New Orleans, a black leader in the Magic City seemed a real possibility. Moreover, with a good candidate who had political experience in public office, victory was not as remote as it appeared in 1971.

Before the shooting of Bonita Carter, Arrington had dismissed the idea of running for the city's top position, but the death of the young woman helped change his mind. He had already been asked to run by several people during his council years, but he had continued to decline any invitation to enter the mayor's race. In January 1979, five months before the Bonita Carter affair, Arrington had told the press that if he entered the race he had "an excellent chance" of victory, regardless of his opponent. Speculation on his candidacy continued, and political guessers believed that Arrington would make a move when "the time was right," unlike 1971, when the chance of victory for a black candidate appeared less hopeful. Even as Mayor David Vann encountered increasing political problems with such things as a strike by some city employees and his decision to drop the city's insurance policy with Blue Cross/Blue Shield because of the company's decision to move from Birmingham, Arrington remained noncommittal. The black councilman shied away from a full-time political life; and, moreover, the mayor's job paid less than his salary as director of the Alabama Center for Higher Education.

The outrage over the Carter killing, nevertheless, did not prompt Arrington to enter the race for mayor immediately, and nearly two months elapsed before he joined the mayoral contest. He had enjoyed his council years, and before June 1979 he had little ambition to seek office beyond his council seat. Pressure, however, had mounted during the hot summer of 1979 as blacks sought a nonviolent solution to their problem with the city. What they needed most, one important leader noted, was strong leadership in city hall that could address political realities. A little over a month after the 22 June death of Bonita Carter, a group composed of about fifty influential black leaders met with Arrington to discuss his possible mayoral candidacy. Following the meeting, the councilman left town, but he pledged to make a decision upon his return to Birmingham.

Suspense mounted as black leaders laid plans to make it impossible for Arrington to reject an offer to run for mayor. For two politicians, Mayor David Vann and Councilman Larry Langford, who had already declared their candidacy, much of the future rested with Arrington's decision. "Pretty soon now," Bill Crowe of the *Birmingham News* wrote on 21 August 1979 with his customary literary flair, "Richard Arrington will smooth down his close-cropped moustache with the tips of his fingers, clear his throat and put a lot of people out of their misery by saying whether or not he's a candidate for mayor of Birmingham." If Arrington entered the race, said Crowe, black councilman Langford could "hang it up." Withdrawal from the race, while holding to his council seat that he had won in 1977, would be his best course. But Crowe obviously did not understand Langford. Although he incorrectly predicted on 21 August that Arrington would not enter the race, his implied contention that the black councilman's candidacy would fragment the black-liberal vote proved accurate. The rest of Crowe's scenario made for amusing reading to everyone except, perhaps, David Vann. The journalist painted a picture of Arrington's leaning on Vann to get results and then throwing the mayor his support after key concessions, especially on police matters. Then he and Vann could "kiss and make up." If that happened, Vann could happily walk away with the election, although it would still be "a tough row to hoe."

Arrington decided to run. After his return to Birmingham in August 1979, he found that black community leaders had already taken a bold political step. "When I got back in town," Arrington said sometime later, "they had called a news conference . . . at Trinity Baptist Church with the intention of drafting me." After he had talked with one of the leaders of the movement and discovered plans to draft him for mayor, he "just didn't think that was a good way to proceed." At that point Arrington consented to declare his candidacy. He went to Trinity, and in Rev. E. W. Jarrett's study, he hurriedly wrote out a statement of his candidacy. Arrington had now answered the question whether the time was right for a black candidate, and he had resolved doubts (temporarily at least) about the possible success of a grass-roots campaign based essentially in the black community.

The Bonita Carter death and all that it meant within the context of race in Birmingham had continued to disturb Arrington, and that terrible event had pushed him toward his decision. To be sure, Arrington, as a powerful and very astute politician, would have been a potent force without the tragedy, but few events since 1963 had so ignited the black community or produced the mobilization for political and social action as the dastardly killing of 22 June. "The import of that incident," Tony Carter, Arrington's 1979 campaign manager, told an interviewer, "kept the black community so enraged that [blacks] said there . . . must be . . . political change." Had the brutal killing not taken place, Arrington, in all likelihood, would not have been able to amass the black community's energy and support that made victory a real probability.

Arrington's candidacy gave an entirely new political complexion to the forthcoming mayor's race in early October. Crowe had been right about one thing: David Vann had found himself in an "absolute pickle." Larry Langford, however, did not "hang it up," by immediately withdrawing from the race. Although some observers had expected Councilman Russell Yarbrough to enter the race, Arrington's entrance into the campaign did not prompt the conservative politician to take the plunge. How Arrington's decision would affect another candidate in the race, Councilman John Katopodis, was not clear, but with Katopodis's strong opposition to the blue-ribbon committee, any significant support for him from Arrington's political core, the black community, seemed nil. Katopodis had argued that the committee's investigation threatened to infringe upon Sands's rights.

Arrington's decision to run irritated Langford, for it administered a virtual deathblow to his candidacy. But Langford, an energetic and talkative former television reporter who had been elected to the council in 1977, claimed boastfully that he would win without a runoff. Langford placed his reliance in "the people on the street." With Arrington in the race, however, the political landscape looked very different. Langford charged that his colleague on the council had promised to stay out of the race. "He told me after I had already declared my candidacy," Langford said to a reporter a few days after Arrington's announcement, "that he was 99 per cent sure he still would not get in the race." But Arrington claimed he never made such a pledge when he met with Langford and his campaign manager. Once he began planning to run, Arrington asserted, the Langford camp contended "that if people wanted me to run, then my campaign should repay . . . all the money they [the Langford people] had spent." Langford may have assumed optimistically that the black vote would naturally go to him with Arrington out of the race. That assumption, however, never had the chance to be tested.

Because of Langford's colorful style and forceful rhetoric, the media had made him a popular figure. He had enjoyed the exposure that came with television, and as a councilman the press delighted in quoting him. But Langford had sometimes refused to take a strong stand on key racial issues and programs to aid the black community; and he had been cool toward Birmingham's minority business plan, created to give 15 percent of the city's contract money to black firms. What really disturbed blacks was Langford's failure to take a forthright position on the Bonita Carter shooting, once the blue-ribbon committee had made its report. In fact, Langford said very little about the affair and was one of the least vocal of Birmingham's visible black leaders. Even though he stated long after the event that the city should have removed the officer who shot the young woman, he angered many people when he wondered "what she was doing in the car in the first place." While Langford had an appeal to the common person because of his devotion to the small things that affected the everyday life of the average citizen, he had become identified in the minds of many blacks as a friend of the Fraternal Order of Police, and that perceived relationship inflamed many of them. Langford now needed more than the FOP's support and the tough rhetoric that had become his trademark.

The presence of two well-known blacks in the Birmingham mayoral contest raised problems for the black community. With seven candidates in the field (Vann, Langford, Arrington, Katopodis, Don

Black, Frank Parsons, and Mohammed Oliver), a win for either Langford or Arrington appeared a slim possibility. And serious questions arose over whether either could make it to the runoff. Clearly, Langford lacked Arrington's broad-based support, although the news media often tended to exaggerate Langford's strength as a mayoral candidate. Arrington, however, did face a serious problem. He could not accurately gauge his black opponent's backing, but he knew that a win in the primary would come easier with Langford's withdrawal from the campaign. The black press quickly saw the terrible ordeal. "The drama is beginning to unfold," wrote one black journalist. "Any rational thinking political observer can see," he said, "that there is a chance for Birmingham to have its first black mayor if Larry Langford or Dr. Richard Arrington pulls out of the race." If both remained, he predicted failure for them and for the black community.

Pressure developed for one of the two candidates to withdraw from the race. Realizing that Langford could play the role of political spoiler, Arrington's campaign manager went to Langford and asked him to drop out of the race, but "he was too far gone." Langford believed he could win the election, and he probably took some delight in challenging the man who for nearly eight years had been a powerful voice in the black community. An outright Arrington victory in the primary with Langford in the political fray would be a tough struggle.

Arrington's choice of Lemorie "Tony" Carter to manage his mayoral campaign did not surprise those close to the councilman. Carter had done a credible job in the 1975 council race as a political neophyte, and now he had more experience in the workings of politics. It remained somewhat of a mystery to Carter, however, why Arrington chose him, since there really was no close, continuing social contact between the two men. Carter had first met Arrington at Miles College when the latter taught on the faculty at the black school and served as dean of the college. He regarded "the dean" as a "tough cookie" who told him not to create any problems as he had at Morehouse before transferring to Miles. Arrington bluntly said to his future campaign manager, "Now look, I will not stand for any silly stuff here at my school." Following that encounter, Carter felt at ease around the dean. Students could approach Arrington without reservation, Carter said of his former professor, but they knew not to engage in any extended nonsense. He found Arrington intellectually provocative as an instructor and an extraordinarily good teacher. "Not too many people skipped his classes," Carter remembers, because his conduct and the atmosphere he created "demanded your presence there." Despite the enormous respect students had for their mentor, they still could regard him "as just another brother from Fairfield" who had done well by overcoming many hurdles.

Tony Carter did have occasion to witness the "other side" of his dean's normally restrained temperament. At Miles, Carter did well as a student, but at one point competition forced him to seek "special advantage." Despite having a B average, he reasoned that a forthcoming final examination in a French course would unduly keep him away from his outside job. Therefore, "almost without thinking," Carter decided during the test "to go ahead and get this thing over as quickly as possible" so he could "get on to my work." He then opened his book, finished his test, and left! Later, he received a call from a fellow student who had also cheated. Ironically, the young woman had an A average, but apparently under great pressure she had also tried to make her grade secure. When she informed Carter, "We're in trouble," he immediately readied himself for the confrontation with "the dean," whose wrath toward an offending party could strike with crushing force.

Carter knew he had clearly broken the rules. "I felt . . . terrible!" he recounted. But he felt even worse after Arrington "had bawled us out," lecturing to them on "the fundamental issue of right and wrong." He explained to the two frightened and embarrassed students how they had cheated themselves. Indeed, the tongue-lashing that Arrington gave Carter and his fellow classmate "was worse than putting an 'F' on my record." The dean graciously gave the two students an incomplete, then made them retake the examination the following semester. Carter had come close to failure, and he never tested Arrington again. He had left the man with an appreciation for his principles, to say nothing of his boundless compassion.

Carter had only limited contact with Arrington until the former dean took control of the ACHE. The two met from time to time, however, at civic and social functions. When ACHE accepted a proposal from Carter's insurance agency for group life insurance, the two men developed a closer association, and both had an opportunity again to assess each other. In following Arrington's public life, Carter became more attuned to politics and politicians. Undoubtedly, the insurance executive's love of Birmingham, his broad personal contacts, and political and social ideas similar to Arrington's convinced the mayoral candidate to choose Carter to coordinate his efforts to win the mayor's office.

Arrington anticipated a low-budget campaign of roughly nineteen thousand dollars. Without an unparalleled grass-roots effort of monumental proportions, he could not possibly overtake his major competitors, especially Vann and Parsons, who could spend large sums of money in their quest for office. Therefore, Arrington wasted little time in organizing after his decision to run. He found a large building in downtown Birmingham at a very reasonable rate. It was not a showcase of modern architecture, but with the help of building contractors who gave materials and labor, the old structure became a functional center buzzing with political activity. The black "grapevine," long a survival tool for transmitting community news and gossip in southern towns, now became a powerful political instrument. Word of Arrington's efforts spread daily through the streets of Birmingham with lightninglike quickness.

The key to Arrington's hopes rested not with hundreds of campaign workers alone but with careful organization. Volunteers consisted of the young and the old, and they cut across racial and class lines. Most came from the black community, but some progressive whites also lent their support. As he had always done, Arrington "went to the churches" to seek help and money, and some black preachers became recruiters for the campaign. A few ministers began and ended their sermons with a plea for support. While the campaign had a few full-time people such as Alice Jones and Gussie Harris, who managed the office, little money existed for a large, highly trained staff. Many young volunteers regarded their effort as part of one large community affair to turn back a threat from the outside. People made their way to Arrington's downtown headquarters from all over the city of Birmingham. Some elderly citizens who could do nothing else brought food or money, or just sat around giving encouragement to younger people determined to change Birmingham. One elderly woman came to headquarters from one of the city's projects and told Tony Carter, "Maybe I can just sweep up." Arrington's army had swung into action.

Arrington gave priority to the effective mobilization of his core black support. Limited funds precluded the possibility of trying to woo the entire white community with an intensified campaign. Therefore, the candidate decided to concentrate upon selected pockets of white voters. Structurally, the campaign relied heavily upon much direct contact with the leadership of neighborhood groups that were a part of the city's Citizens Participation Program. So, when the candidate and his campaign manager went to the neighborhood officers and asked them to "take the ball and run for Arrington," they met with a generally warm reception. Many delighted in their new role, for never before had many of them taken on such an important responsibility. They wanted to be effective agents for change. Faced with little time to achieve his objective, Arrington also concentrated on a rather uncomplicated committee structure, and he worked hard to find partisans in certain key areas who had a "sensitive outlook" and who wanted to join the campaign.

The number of workers that eventually joined the ranks of the campaign surprised even Arrington. Since it was impossible to recruit directly the large number of volunteers needed for political success, Arrington selected neighborhood coordinators, who in turn encouraged others to work in specific sections of a community. In fact, Arrington organized down to the block level with the creation of block captains, who had their homes identified by a sign that read "Block Headquarters for Arrington for Mayor." The movement reminded one of an army preparing for combat. These new soldiers in political battle were willing to struggle for Richard Arrington, Jr., whom they hoped would redress past grievances and deliver them from the kind of police abuse that had led to the death of Bonita Carter. They would stand as their champion Arrington had stood and say with their feet, their hands, and their votes, "We are men and women—citizens—who deserve respect."

While racial crises had aided political participation in the black community, Arrington did not rely upon the emotionalism of Bonita Carter's death for success. In the past the NAACP had played a vital role in Birmingham and other cities in urging blacks to vote. A nonprofit organization, the association could not engage in partisan politics, but its efforts, in reality, were consistent with those of the Arrington camp. Churches again sustained their efforts in acquainting their members with the voter-registration process and in impressing upon them the need to "vote right to prevent further racial discrimination." To spur voter interest, Arrington's "Get Out the Vote Committee" enlisted well-known personalities to make announcements encouraging registration and voter participation; and Arrington's staff also drew up detailed plans for coordinating free transportation to the polls. Here was democracy at work at the grass-roots level. The city had never seen such a movement among blacks, nor had it experienced the intensity of such a massive number of people, especially among the young, since the movement days of civil rights. Indeed, the very reason for the deep interest in the campaign was its perception by many blacks as a part of the continuing civil-rights struggle.

With such a large field of candidates in the primary race, a runoff appeared almost a certainty. Publicly, Arrington stated he could win "the first time around." That was a "realistic objective," Carter said in an interview after the election, "because we had the momentum." Actually, only three other candidates besides Arrington (Vann, Katopodis, and Parsons) stood any possible chance of winning the mayor's office outright in the primary or of gaining a place in the runoff. Vann had the advantage (or disadvantage) of incumbency, powerful friends, thorough knowledge of the city, and adequate financing. Katopodis possessed a quick mind and a good Harvard education, and he could appeal to several classes of voters. Parsons, an attorney who was politically the most conservative of any of the major candidates in the race, had never held elective office, but he had considerable personal wealth and a great number of individual contacts that he hoped to use to develop a political base within the white community.

Arrington and other candidates assumed that David Vann posed the greatest obstacle to victory. Even with the burden of Bonita Carter, Vann still had support among liberal whites, and some people assumed he would pick up some conservative voters antagonized by the black reaction to the killing. Vann, of course, counted on some black backing, although he could not possibly anticipate the turnout of 1975 for him with Arrington and Langford now in the race. As much as blacks cursed Vann for his Bonita Carter decision, many of them probably would have voted for the mayor over more conservative white candidates, or for Langford, had Arrington not entered the race.

During the primary the candidates shadowboxed with a number of questions that had little real meaning to most citizens. The contest really focused on three major issues—crime, the economy, and race. Vann in particular found himself extremely vulnerable on the issue of law enforcement. When the mayor told citizens they did not have to consider idle promises because of his past performances, he left himself open to serious attack on the crime issue. Since the city had proposed the reduction in the number of police officers, Parsons found it easy to attack Vann for not providing adequate protection for citizens. Katopodis competed with Parsons in his attacks on Vann and in his praise of the police. "It is time," he said, taking a swipe at the incumbent and at Arrington, "that we have a mayor that supports the police department . . . that would provide the means by which businesses are protected." He also criticized Vann for his support of a new shooting policy that required more restraint by officers before firing at suspects.

As Arrington had predicted, law and order became a heated issue that excited emotions and that exposed the ugly element of race. "Some candidates," he wrote in a newspaper column, "are going all out to fan . . . citizens' [fears] and frustration[s] about crime." Arrington believed that other candidates had few concrete proposals to deal with crime except for the single solution of having more police officers. "The public needed more than hot air, political gymnastics and hysteria"; and voters had a responsibility to look beyond scare tactics and to demand that politicians spell out specifically what they planned to do about crime. But fear is a powerful force in people's lives that can have a decided political effect. To those in the Arrington camp, Vann, Katopodis, and Parsons were deliberately trying to generate fear among white citizens over the issue of crime.

Arrington's competition must have recognized the possible political gain if they could successfully paint him as soft on crime. Certainly his fight against police brutality and his forthright stand on the Bonita Carter affair had not endeared him to many white citizens, who saw him as a "radical," even a racist, determined to punish white folks if elected. Both Vann and Katopodis knew Arrington personally and could hardly make such a direct charge, but by implication they did hint that his election would leave the city open to more criminal activity. In the past Katopodis had acknowledged a relationship between black unemployment and crime, and Vann had criticized police behavior toward blacks, especially during the Bull Connor era of the 1960s. But in 1979, their allusion to race in discussing crime brought into question their professed liberalism and their sense of fair play. When Mayor Vann cited three cities with black mayors that had experienced a rise in the crime rate under their leadership, the statement badly stung Arrington and produced unusually critical language from the normally mild-mannered black candidate. Katopodis ran television commercials on crime that Arrington said contained a racist message that subtly warned citizens to avoid the "tragedy" of Atlanta. Vann's decision to use the tactic of race, however, proved far more painful to Arrington, for the mayor's approach appeared out of step with his past behavior. But the times were not normal, and Vann, Katopodis, and Parsons found themselves in a position where they had to pick up additional votes in the only available place—the white community.

Arrington struck back sharply at his opponents who tried to tie black leadership to the rising crime rate. He hit hard at Vann, whose own administration had faced an escalating crime rate, and he castigated him for overlooking cities with white mayors that had a high incidence of crime. Arrington recognized, of course, that political leadership represented only one factor in the fight on crime. Since John Katopodis had support from the FOP, Arrington expected a strong statement from him on crime, but he challenged his fellow councilman to propose measures to combat crime in Birmingham without reference to Atlanta or other cities. At a news conference at the city's Bethel Baptist Church, he charged that his opponents wanted to deliver a "coded message of racism" that whites understood; and he asserted that not a single one of the candidates for mayor had mentioned the significant reduction in crime in Detroit under black mayor Coleman Young. Holding a copy of a full-page newspaper advertisement that Vann had run in his mayoral campaign four years earlier, Arrington challenged his old friend to tell voters why he had not fulfilled his promise to stop crime. Realistically, Arrington did not expect Vann to respond, but he also did not expect the mayor to continue to play on the racial fears of citizens. In an apparent effort to woo white voters, Vann had fanned the fires of racial discord and bitterness, and he had further polarized Birmingham's black and white communities.

Arrington did not content himself with harshly criticizing his white opponents, who had endeavored to draw a connection between black mayors and crime. He advanced his own program for effective law enforcement that would make Birmingham streets safe and the city's property secure. Strong leadership, he said, was central to any progress. Aware that his opponents had tried to picture him as an antagonist of the police who consistently worked against their interests, Arrington tried to reassure voters that he had as much at stake in a safe city as anyone else did. He was aware of the results of a lawless society where the strong preyed on the weak and where fear daily stalked the lives of decent citizens. Ignoring crime would ultimately lead to anarchy and the crumbling of institutions that formed the cornerstone of a civilized social order. Citizens of Birmingham had the right to live free of the fear of crime, and he pledged to eliminate what he called "a spreading disease" that threatened the city's life.

Arrington made no attempt to cover up his past problems with the police. He would work against police misconduct, but he stressed that only a small percentage of the police force committed most abuses. Taxpayers should not pay police officers to brutalize citizens, and any mayor who failed to address that problem would be guilty of unforgivable negligence. Unwillingness to tackle the issue, Arrington maintained, would demonstrate the breakdown in law, and it would indicate that some people—in this case, police officers—stood above the law. For the city to attack crime more effectively with the aid of the community, then, officers had to adhere to professional conduct. Once mutual respect was obtained between the citizens and the police, said the candidate, the city could create an effective law-enforcement program.

Arrington pledged himself to maintain sufficient police manpower. He pointed out, nevertheless, that on the basis of recent data from other police departments, Birmingham's force did not suffer from limited personnel. While he did not rule out having more officers, he first committed himself to study how the police department utilized its present force. "While I will provide adequate manpower," he told a group of reporters, "I do not suggest a program of wall-to-wall police officers to fight crime." Arrington reasoned that citizens could play a much more active role in the prevention of crime, and he proposed an organized program of community involvement similar to that established in some other American cities. He also would devote funds to upgrade street lighting in the city's neighborhoods and in business areas.

Arrington also addressed black crime. He claimed near the end of the campaign, "I am the only candidate to speak directly to halting the rising crime rate in [the] black community." As he had in his council years and in his newspaper column for the *Birmingham Times*, the candidate sharply condemned black-on-black crime, which plagued the black community. Rape, robbery, and murder were hardly expressions of true brotherhood! Arrington recognized the social and economic reasons for crime within the black community, but he refused to excuse the reprehensible behavior of those who disregarded the law. At the heart of much of the crime in many black neighborhoods, he contended, was the large amount of illegal dope and whiskey and the many gambling houses. He promised to create a special task force after his election to work with neighborhoods to identify "shot houses" (places that sold illegal liquor) so that the city could close these "crime cesspools." Such places had harmed the black community and the city, and they had created an atmosphere where violence often flared, and death sometimes visited. "For too long," Arrington noted, "officials have tried to explain away these illegal operations by saying that they are friendly neighborhood gathering places, when in reality they breed crime and contempt for law."

Race could not stay hidden throughout the primary, and when it failed to appear openly it always lurked just beneath the surface of the campaign. Even racially neutral economic issues became clouded sometimes by the issue of race. Arrington's opponents, for example, hinted that a black mayor would not be able to attract business and industry successfully but they did not point to black mayors who had gained new enterprises and had kept other businesses in their cities. Refusing to become sidetracked by negative racial arguments, Arrington set forth a plan to bring about economic stability and growth. His program called for assistance to small business, among other things, and the establishment of a committee of leading businessmen to advise the mayor on economic matters. Birmingham's image had long been an obstacle in wooing both industry and tourism and to address this problem Arrington proposed creating a professional force led by the mayor to promote the city and to start aggressive recruitment of business. Taking clear aim at Vann, he said that city government could improve its own economic condition by better management and accountability and by reducing unneeded bureaucracy. Arrington believed Vann was vulnerable on the issue of management, and he successfully joined the question of governmental efficiency and economics in an effective frontal assault upon the incumbent.

Despite the debate over crime and the charges of racism, the major white candidates emphasized their fairness and belief in equality. Katopodis alluded to his battles against racism when he had worked for the school board of Sumter County, Georgia. He also pledged to work aggressively to help blacks acquire jobs, for true freedom, he argued, came with economic power. As earlier indicated, Mayor Vann had built a plausible record in support of programs aimed at helping the black community. Indeed, he had championed the city's minority contractors' program to give minority firms 15 percent of the city's contracts. Although some of the money that should have gone to blacks under this plan apparently got diverted to white firms, no one could question Vann's commitment to the program. Parsons, of course, had been outside government, but he pointed to his close association with some of Birmingham's blacks and his work to strengthen the community at large.

Arrington's opponents experienced difficulty competing with him for black votes. Blacks had begun to question Vann after the Bonita Carter case, and Katopodis had never openly condemned the police after the shooting or called for reform within the police department. Frank Parsons simply struck blacks as too far right of political center to address black problems constructively. When Arrington declared that he had taken the lead and the abuse in the fight against police brutality, blacks not only understood him, they shared the pain that had come with white criticism of him. And when he said on the campaign trail, "There is no affirmative action law, no minority economic development law on the books in the City of Birmingham that I did not take the lead in [creating]," he preempted any statement his opponents may have made on those issues.

Candidates laid out their position on neighborhood stability, revitalization of downtown Birmingham, city services, accountability in government, taxes, and other issues. But Tony Carter isolated the central concern in the primary contest when he said that "there was really only one major issue in the campaign, and that was race and who would control this city." Even John Katopodis admitted that the campaign became bogged down in racial politics, but he did not view himself as one of the persons responsible for that dubious state of political affairs. "I think it's . . . unfortunate," he said, "that people would exploit race for the sake of their own election." Only those candidates who could attract both blacks and whites to their side, said Katopodis, should run for the mayor's office. The harsh truth is that, with the shooting of Bonita Carter, the city could not escape the issue of race. What shocked some people is that it appeared so openly in politics, as evidenced by the labored comments on crime in Atlanta, black mayors in others cities, and the emphasis on support for the police.

For many black citizens Birmingham stood at a crossroads in 1979. Enthusiastic voters who had fervently worked to defeat incumbent George Seibels fours years earlier now expended themselves to topple Mayor Vann. Partisans of Arrington now exclaimed that Birmingham had suffered from a leadership that managed ineffectively and that had actually contributed to the city's racial problems and unrest. Birmingham could find a positive, aggressive leadership in Richard Arrington that could bring social harmony, attract industry and federal programs, and in turn would lift the city. The 20 September 1979 *Birmingham Times* spoke best for those in the black community who favored Arrington. Race relations, it said, had deteriorated, unemployment in the city stood above the national average, downtown was decaying, population was dwindling, and police-community relations stood at a low point. "This is the best time in the history of Birmingham for a black mayor to come in and strengthen [the city]," wrote the *Times* editor.

As election week neared, Tony Carter and the Arrington camp intensified their efforts to get voters to the polls. Block captains canvassed their neighborhoods and headquarters, carefully rechecking voter lists to find those they may have overlooked. Anxious to get out a large vote, the NAACP also focused more keenly on areas in the city that had large numbers of nonvoters such as Avondale, Collegeville, Kingston, Powderly, Ensley, and West End. Arrington volunteers phoned unregistered persons and stressed the importance of their votes. Roy Woods, who wrote for a local newspaper, urged black people to vote, but in a veiled reference (probably to Larry Langford), he warned against "choosing that will-of-the-wisp called popularity." Richard Arrington, he said, "is far and away the best qualified among the black candidates." The Reverend N. H. Smith of the New Pilgrim Baptist Church spoke for a group of concerned clergymen when he alluded to Arrington's "proven track record" in education, in the religious community, and in politics. People could vote without speculating on his accomplishments.

Peter Moss, a reporter for the *Birmingham Times*, captured the prevailing spirit in the black community in the days before the election. Too much blood had been lost and too many tears had been shed, he said in a 4 October 1979 editorial, to throw away the opportunity to decide the outcome of the mayoral contest. Blacks had to flock to the polls "in substantial numbers" and to vote intelligently. He wrote: "We must appear at the polls October 9th regardless of the weather. Should God send rain, snow, sleet, or hail we must be visible October 9th. Not only should we vote . . . but we must appear again if a runoff warrants our votes the second time. . . . We are involved in the movement for equality, justice and economic opportunity."

Arrington went to bed the night before the election confident he had conducted a good, hard campaign. Voters trooped to the polls on Tuesday, 9 October, aware that they had a vital role in shaping Birmingham's future. They would either assist in defeating a black candidate or contribute to his success. It was that simple. The crucial question for Arrington was whether enough black voters would turn out to vote, and if he could get enough crossover white votes, particularly from the Southside of the city, to win 51 percent of the ballots and avoid a runoff. Had Langford not been in the race, Arrington could have realistically counted on more black votes, but the former stayed in the race to the very end. Whether Langford actually believed he could achieve a victory in the primary or whether he had some other motive in the campaign must be left to conjecture. Before the election, however, polls clearly showed the impossibility of his triumph.

The heated campaign had generated widespread enthusiasm and much emotionalism. Race, law and order, and the fear of social and political change in Birmingham led to a large turnout, with some 55 percent of the city's voters going to the polls. Arrington, of course, had worked for an outright victory without a runoff. When the returns came in, he had outdistanced the field, garnering 31,521 votes, or more than 44 percent of the vote. Mayor Vann had hoped for at least a runoff spot, but his 11,450 votes were not sufficient to catapult him into a showdown with Arrington. With the loss of blacks, Vann had to share white voters with Parsons and Katopodis. The black shift from Vann, with his past years of support for civil rights and progressivism, left him without a win in a single black voting box in the city. The mayor also experienced difficulty in getting slightly more than half of the 30 percent white vote he had received in defeating Seibels in 1975. Clearly, the bullets that had killed Bonita Carter had also politically destroyed Vann.

In a surprising showing, neophyte Frank Parsons received 12,135 votes and thus won the runoff spot with Arrington. By less than 100 votes, John Katopodis failed to make the runoff, which surprised many observers. Both candidates had catered to the law-and-order constituency, and neither had conducted an all-out campaign to win black voters, virtually conceding them to Arrington. Because of his two-year service on the city council, Katopodis had more initial public recognition than Parsons, but his flippancy and his occasional arrogance may have caused those that knew him well to shy away from him. He was at his best in one-on-one situations and in small gatherings, where he could more easily display an affability that usually remained hidden. Katopodis usually showed his worst side in larger audiences when heated controversy appeared. While he conducted a basically conservative campaign and received strong FOP support, he was not as far to the political right as Frank Parsons.

As stated earlier, Arrington had viewed David Vann as the most difficult candidate to beat. The day following the primary election he told the *Birmingham News*:

I thought David Vann would be the toughest man as an opponent for me. [I was] very confident that I'd beat anybody else. I felt if Vann were able to make the runoff, it would be a dog fight. And that's simply because my strategy called upon picking up some white support. Most of the places I've gotten white support from in the past have been in areas where David has had support. And I feel that with David out of the race, I'm going to pick up some of that, and that's going to make the difference in the campaign. I think I can defeat . . . Frank [Parsons]. I feel very comfortable of that . . . [but with] David [in], it would have been 50-50. We would have just gone out and it would have been a bare knuckle, knock down drag-out.

Arrington had handily won the primary over Vann and his other contestants on a "pauper's budget," but disturbing signs surfaced during the contest. The black councilman had not expected large financial contributions from the city's business community or a large number of endorsements from white groups. His relatively small white vote in the primary, however, greatly disappointed him. Some white citizens did look upon Arrington's efforts sympathetically, but very few of them joined up to work in the campaign. While Arrington wanted the mayor's job, he stressed the importance of winning with some white votes. "I've said to people that [it is] awfully important for anybody going into office to say they've got support from everywhere." Despite his hopeful anticipation Arrington received only about 3.5 percent of the white vote in the primary election.

Following the primary battle, Arrington theorized that Langford's withdrawal from the race and the support of the Jefferson County Progressive Democratic Council would have led to an all-out victory. Analysis of the results, nevertheless, does not support that contention. Langford had made a very poor showing with his 2,856 votes, and even if Arrington had won all of his ballots, the total would not have gained him victory. Arrington may have received the majority of the black votes that went to Langford, had that candidate not been in the race, but it is questionable how many of his white votes would have gone to Arrington, since some of them surely came from conservative persons who liked the black candidate's support of the police and his stand on other issues. Assuming that Arrington had won *all* of Langford's votes, he still would have needed Vann's black ballots for outright victory in the primary.

The failure of David Hood's Jefferson County Progressive Democratic Council to endorse Arrington officially did not significantly affect the outcome of the election. It is impossible to determine precisely how much influence the council had on black voters, but in all probability Arrington overestimated its influence. There is little evidence that any large number of the council's members worked for Mayor David Vann. Whatever the allegiance of the council in the primary, little doubt existed that the organization would support Arrington in the runoff against conservative Frank Parsons.

The Arrington camp had little time for rejoicing before its last crucial test. Birmingham had already experienced change in its most historic primary contest, and Arrington's followers had enjoyed the moment when hundreds of them had assembled on election night at his downtown Holiday Inn headquarters to herald the beginning of a new day. Olivia Barton, a reporter for the *Birmingham News*, captured that dramatic moment. "Long after parties for mayoral candidates David Vann, Frank Parsons, John Katopodis, and Larry Langford had broken up for the evening," she wrote on 10 October 1979, "Richard Arrington's supporters were riding high on election night euphoria." They had come early and stayed late, crowding into a room that by ten o'clock had nearly filled to capacity. Perhaps one partisan expressed the sentiments of many campaign workers when he said, "Its sort of unbelievable that we did what we did."

Even in elation, hard-core realists recognized the challenge before them. Reporter John Streeter of the *Birmingham Times* wrote on 11 October 1979 that the celebration must wait for three more weeks. Ultimate victory, said one woman, depended on black folks' second trip to the polls. Rachel Arrington, the candidate's wife (whom he married in 1975, after he and Barbara were divorced a year earlier), expressed the hope and optimism that pervaded the Arrington camp when she said, "I think Birmingham is ready for a black mayor. No doubt about it." Two central questions, however, remained: Would blacks return to the polls in large numbers? And would any significant number of white voters support Arrington against a white candidate who had limited political experience? On those questions the election rested.

Success in the primary had brought joy, but it had also produced some apprehension for Arrington supporters. Tony Carter shared his fears nearly four years after the election when he confided, "For the first time I was afraid." It now struck him that the opponent, Frank Parsons, "had us one on one." Carter's concern, oddly enough, did not develop from any reservation about support in the white community, which Arrington sorely needed, but from the necessity of sustaining an emotional intensity in the black community that would translate into votes. If the percentage of black

155

Mayor-elect Richard Arrington, Jr., takes the oath of office as his wife Rachel looks on. (Courtesy of the *Birmingham News*)

voters fell in the runoff and if whites coalesced around Parsons, that would mean Arrington's political defeat. Despite some anxiety, however, the fears of Arrington's supporters were lessened somewhat, since the candidate entered the runoff securely in the driver's seat.

Arrington had bolstered his strength by hiring political consultant Cindy McCartney of Nashville, Tennessee, who had worked with Vann in the primary. Reared in Birmingham, McCartney brought greater professional experience to the Arrington camp, and her very presence in the campaign may have had some favorable effects upon the staff and even some white voters, particularly those of a liberal or moderate persuasion. McCartney believed that, next to a large black turnout at the polls, success required votes from the city's liberal Southside.

Arrington's opponent in the runoff also knew the prescription for victory. Much of Frank Parsons's strength rested with his political philosophy more than his articulate projection of issues and plans for the city. His outlook and his background provided a remarkable contrast to those of Richard Arrington. Both men had grown up in the Birmingham area, but each of them had shared different worlds shaped by a segregated society. Parsons had known the comfort of an upper-middle-class family steeped in the values of a society that prided home and the ethic of hard work. His father, a practicing attorney, had grown up in Columbus, Mississippi, and his mother came from a city with the same name in Georgia. The family sent young Frank to a private military institution in Chattanooga, Tennessee, after high school. He later attended the University of Alabama, where he completed his college education and obtained a law degree before settling in Birmingham in 1965.

Prior to entering the mayor's race, Parsons had led an active civic and professional life that gave him an economically secure existence and status within the community. As a young lawyer for United States Pipe and Foundry, he assisted the company in establishing a law department at that firm. His job gave him practical experience, and it offered him valuable contacts with the business world. Parsons had gone to US Pipe when it employed only one lawyer, but when he left, he was the aggressive leader of a vigorous staff. As the company's chief attorney, Parsons had responsibility for compliance with the 1964 Civil Rights Act, and he also handled some labor negotiations. His contact with persons in the labor movement proved valuable, for, despite his association with man-

157

agement, he made a number of friends who respected his professionalism and his rapport with workers. As a good corporate citizen, US Pipe encouraged community participation from its employees, especially those in management and supervisory roles, and Parsons took full advantage of this opportunity to cultivate friendships when he went to work for the company.

After leaving US Pipe, Arrington's runoff opponent took up private law practice and later bought a travel agency that developed into one of the most profitable in the Birmingham area. In fact, Parsons's financial freedom gave him time to engage in civic activities and to accept appointments from government. He had been involved with the city through his service on the Birmingham Housing Authority, and in 1976, Mayor David Vann, who later deeply angered Parsons during the run-off campaign because of Vann's support for Arrington, appointed him to chair the local Bicentennial Commission. During the national administration of Richard Nixon, the president appointed him to the White House Committee on Education. Perhaps his most enjoyable, yet most challenging involvement, came with his association with the United States Jaycees, an organization that drew from him an enormous commitment in time and energy. He ran for and won the presidency of the Alabama Jaycees and later competed for that same office in the national organization. Although he lost his bid to win the presidency of the Jaycees, his experience gave him some familiarity with political maneuvering; and it made him aware of the possible cost of a large-scale campaign.

By his own admission a conservative, Parsons became uneasy with the course of political and social developments within American society. Although he disliked—in fact; rejected—the tag *ultra-conservative*, some of his detractors placed him in that camp. Certainly, if one had to place him on a political spectrum, the registered Republican would have found himself on the right wing of the GOP. Parsons reminded one of a man caught in the grip of sweeping—and to him unacceptable—changes, over which he had little or no control. While no one could accurately register the impact of past events in molding his life, it was plausible to believe that the culture that nurtured Parsons made it more difficult for him to di-

158

gest the reform that came by civil disobedience, street demonstrations, and sometimes violence during a period of his early manhood. Significantly, the fundamental social and racial changes that Alabama witnessed took place *after* Parsons had formed most of his values and had already entered adulthood in a world controlled by white people.

Parsons projected an image of a highly religious person fully in control of his life. No matter what interpretation one gives to his past and the impact upon his political behavior, it must seriously take into account the man's deeply religious character. A member of McElwain Baptist Church, located in Birmingham's politically conservative Eastside, Parsons proudly wore his religious beliefs, but he never blindly adhered to a "born again" philosophy that saw the devil at work in every human misfortune. He recognized the presence of evil influences in society and not surprisingly spoke more than once during the mayoral campaign of morality and its relation to city government.

The decision to run for mayor posed few difficulties for Frank Parsons. Unlike his black opponent in the runoff, he never had to consider seriously personal financial factors in deciding to run. Parsons had watched the Vann administration as it unfolded, and he finally concluded that the city had reached a state of stagnation. Birmingham needed new leadership. He believed that "a young energetic fellow that had not been in politics could be effective." If, as Parsons alleged, the events surrounding the Bonita Carter killing had no impact upon his decision to run for office, it is also true that his growing dislike for Vann had a powerful effect upon him. In his own mind his candidacy represented the thousands of disenchanted persons in the city who believed they had not received their "fair share" of services and resources from a liberal Vann administration, especially those citizens in the predominately white eastern section of the city.

It is difficult, however, to discern any clear pattern of discrimination in the distribution of city services and resources that went to the Eastside during the Vann years. Parsons, however, accepted as truth the assertions of those who argued the relative neglect of his area of town. Strongly supported by a small group of members in his church, he decided to test the public waters and to turn the city around by unseating the man who had done so much to change the old Birmingham. Little did he recognize that Vann would not represent his greatest obstacle to success but, rather, a man who, at the time David Vann helped to change the city's form of government, could not dine at a downtown restaurant or drink water from the "whites only" fountains in the Magic City of Birmingham.

Parsons, like Arrington, attracted many people from the grass roots. But here much of the comparison between the two men ended. Although initial campaign contributions came from persons from within his church, funds eventually flowed from a variety of sources. To get into the runoff, Parsons expended fifty thousand dollars. "We spent a lot of money," he said, "to get identified, then we started working on specific issues." Along with the outlay of funds, volunteer workers assisted his effort, supported by a paid consultant, Jack Hatchett, the only real professional in the campaign. Essentially, Parsons acted as his own campaign manager, although he listed Robert Earl Branton in that capacity in his literature. A member of Parsons's Sunday school class, Branton had been active as a labor organizer for the economic engineers of the Southern Railroad.

From the beginning, Parsons and Branton had recognized their goal—beat Vann and get into the runoff. In part, success came in the primary because they had taken Parsons's status as an outsider and turned that into an advantageous underdog position. However, as the element of race and law enforcement emerged as powerful factors in the campaign, Parsons attracted a solid, conservative core of citizens. "[People] remember the bad things about government, they don't remember the good things," he said in commenting on Vann's demise and the defeat of John Katopodis. "I could say [to citizens] I was not a party to your not getting service on this end of town or your not getting this [or that]."

At the outset of the political fray, each candidate had tried to downplay publicly the touchy issue of race, and each had spoken of the need for unity. But the 11 October 1979 *Birmingham News* correctly gauged existing sentiment when it wrote two days after the primary that the "clear possibility exists for the election of a black mayor." And that possibility, said the *News*, could lead to a black-white cleavage. When a reporter asked Parsons after the primary if he foresaw race as an important element in the runoff, he said, "We do not anticipate nor do we have any intention of making it an issue." Professed hopes and disclaimers aside, history had already dictated much of the course of the campaign. It was obvious to any casual observer that each candidate's base was his own racial group, although success for Arrington could come only with some white support. Parsons, however, could win without blacks, since white voters slightly outnumbered them in the city in 1979; and some maintained that Parsons all along intended to focus only on the white vote.

Controversial statements on race from the primary followed Parsons into the runoff and constituted the basis for charges of racism. If he had vowed to work to heal the city's racial wounds, many of his comments appeared rather to have aggravated existing tensions in the black community and among some whites. In a press conference where he made race relations a central theme, Parsons pledged to set up a biracial citizens' advisory group to work with the mayor's office; and he promised to visit black and white neighborhoods to acquaint himself with their problems. But when he attacked the SCLC along with the Ku Klux Klan as "extremist groups," his statement contributed to the further polarization of the races, and he lost any advantage he may have gained among blacks. Parsons's leading black supporter, Rev. Richard Cunningham, pastor of St. John Baptist Church and a former president of the Ministerial Association of Greater Birmingham, disagreed with the candidate about the SCLC, but he continued his support of the white politician. Although Parsons had seemed unperturbed initially by possible assistance from the Ku Klux Klan before Klansman Don Black entered the mayoral race, political wisdom later dictated his rejection of that group's support.

Parsons's emphasis on racial matters and his comments on black political involvement did more to convince blacks and liberal whites of his conservative posture than his verbal disavowal of racism. During the primary the candidate from the Eastside had said to an all-white group, "We're going to lose by default. We're going to have a black mayor, and I guarantee you I'm not for any of those blacks. Then we're going to have a black police chief." When quizzed about his comments, the attorney explained feebly that he "didn't support any of the black candidates *running for mayor.*" David Vann had been so disappointed with Parsons's comments that he accused him of waving "the bloody shirt of racism." In a press release following his talk, Parsons noted, apparently without any awareness of the meaning normally assigned to such a statement, "Some of my best friends and colaborers are black people." Blacks, nevertheless, remained unimpressed with his explanation and with his promise to appoint some of their race to key positions in his administration.

Perhaps Parsons had foreclosed any possible breakthrough in the black community early in the campaign when he expressed his views on the shooting of Bonita Carter and its aftermath. He openly favored placing the policeman who killed her, George "Mike" Sands, back on the beat. And at a meeting with the officer present, Parsons won the enthusiastic support of a local law-and-order group. He had stated his distrust of the blue-ribbon committee that Vann had established to study the Bonita Carter shooting, preferring instead to leave police matters to the "professionals." More disturbing to many blacks and to some whites was Parsons's use of misinformation about Bonita Carter. During an appearance at a Birmingham elementary school, he told a group of sixth graders that the twenty-year-old black woman who had lost her life in the shooting had a "seven page rap sheet," and he sharply criticized the media for not reporting all the facts. Police records did not support his comment, and he had to make a retraction. But even had the facts supported Parsons, his statement would not have addressed the issue of the shooting itself or undo the conclusions of the special committee appointed by Mayor Vann.

The Arrington camp viewed Parsons's attempt to discredit Bonita Carter as a deliberate effort to win white voters. Others called it purely racist. When asked in 1983 if he had consciously exploited the Carter shooting and the race issue, Parsons heatedly denied the contention, and he again exclaimed that he had "worked with blacks for a long, long time," including Chris McNair, a former legislator and the father of one of four black girls killed in the 1963 bombing of the Sixteenth Street Baptist Church.

Predictably, law enforcement also became entangled in the web of race. During the primary, it will be recalled, Parsons had not consistently harped on Atlanta's crime problems, as had Vann and Katopodis, who talked about the cities with black mayors, but the issue of race surfaced in other ways, appearing implicitly in campaign statements on law enforcement. Police shooting policy provided an excellent example of how the issue of race forcefully emerged. Following the death of Bonita Carter, the city had adopted a shooting policy that imposed greater restraints upon a police officer's use of personal firearms. Proponents of the rules, such as Arrington, argued that the new policy did not endanger the safety of officers, while opponents bitterly disagreed. Parsons strongly favored a much less restrictive policy rather than the new shooting code adopted by the city of Birmingham. Blacks had contended that the old regulations had led to the untimely death of citizens, notably Bonita Carter, and that a disproportionate number of their people, compared to whites, had died at the hands of officers who abused their authority.

For Parsons and many other whites "law and order," not injustice or police brutality, had been at the heart of the policy debate. The differing perspective of black and white groups on the shooting policy said much about the distance between them and the impact that the relatively recent killing of Bonita Carter had had upon their attitudes. The endorsement and strong support of Parsons by the FOP, which had opposed a change in policy, made blacks even more suspicious of the white candidate. The organization had no love for Arrington, and it had so ardently defended George Sands at the time of the Bonita Carter shooting that it alarmed even some supporters of the police.

Parsons's law-and-order stand, coupled with the issue of race in the campaign, made it more difficult for Arrington to push his crime proposals among whites. The white candidate cleverly tried to keep his campaign focused on support for the police and concern about the high crime rate in Birmingham. "I certainly feel that at a time when the crime rate is going through the ceiling," he told a group of reporters during the runoff, "the last thing we need is a mayor who can't get along with the police department." He urged more support and less criticism for Birmingham's officers, an obvious reference to Arrington's long-standing fight with the police department.

Arrington defended his record of support for the police during his tenure on the council. He again stressed that his complaints had always been directed toward a small group of men who brutalized citizens, not against the entire police department. He spoke frankly and without apology for his sustained attack upon those officers who abused power. To deny the existence of problems among the department's seven hundred men, he said, amounted to "sticking our heads in the sand." As mayor, he would not declare war on the police, but he would demand an end to improper conduct. He had made that position clear the day following the primary campaign when he remarked, "I will expect their professionalism to be commensurate with the kind of authority that the people of this city invest in them." No need would exist for him to discipline officers if they did their jobs effectively and within the rules. He pledged his strong backing of hard-working policemen, for they had a "tough, dirty job." He would give them the benefit of the doubt in cases where the facts were in question. Although he had no plans to dismiss officers for past offenses, he did note his intentions to examine closely the record of officers and their performance over a period of time. All men and women on the police force would start with a clean slate when his administration took office.

Parsons's charges of bloc voting also heated up the campaign. The candidate, of course, had grown up in a Birmingham where blacks had very little political voice. Almost without exception, blacks had held no political offices in Alabama, and not until the Voting Rights Act of 1965 did the government enact meaningful legislation to curtail restrictions against them, especially in the southern states. Three more years passed, it will be recalled, before Birmingham got its first black councilman. (Election of black representatives and senators from the area to the state legislature did not come until later.) Southern politics in the pre-1960s period, then, had been reserved "for whites only," and politicians had won election to office by a bloc of voters religiously devoted to white supremacy.

Frank Parsons viewed the black community as a political monolith that blindly took its cue from its leader, Arrington, and his political organization, the Jefferson County Citizens Coalition. Ironically, the lawyer-businessman had implied that, unless whites voted in large numbers, they would lose their historic hold on the mayor's office, thus surrendering years of white power. When pressed about his dislike for bloc voting by blacks, Parsons defended a position from which he never totally retreated. He told reporter Richard Friedman of the *Birmingham News* on 11 October 1979:

> One of the things that bothers me tremendously is the manner in which the black community has selected their candidates. This was a way in which a small group of people made selections and then handed the ballots to the people. And my concern then, and my concern now [as the runoff approaches] is over the process. I don't think that's very healthy for a community to have a person that is selected by one small group of people and then they tell other folks [how] to vote.

Parsons's statement on bloc voting and the black community in a 1983 interview more clearly expressed his views. He again rejected the notion of having voters told how they should vote. It was offensive to the democratic process. But in a more biting (and perhaps unintended) criticism, Parsons expressed the hope that eventually people "will be intelligent enough to make their own decision based on what they have read or heard or seen." He also hit hard the perceived power of the black church in political campaigns. "It is no secret," he said, "that [sample] ballots are drawn up . . . names are marked . . . and they are handed out in a church meeting, . . . predominately in the black community." To his knowledge, that procedure had never taken place in the white community. Robotlike voters, he continued his criticism, were transported to the polls by an efficiently functioning political machine; and that fact greatly disturbed the man who in 1979 faced an opponent who had masterfully mobilized the black community beyond the expectations of practically all political observers. Parsons seemed eager, even after the election, to stress that black people "ought to make up their own minds."

Arrington could gain little by using time to rebut every single one of Parsons's comments on race during the campaign. His opponent stood to gain little in the black community because of his stand on Sands, and that issue alone had already doomed him before his comments on other racial issues. More important, Arrington knew where he had to concentrate his energy to win votes, and the issues he emphasized in the last days of the campaign demonstrated that awareness. He spoke often of economic concerns and of streamlining government to ensure more effective services. He also stressed the linkage between an effective mass-transit system and the city's progressive economic development. A proponent of self-help, Arrington also spoke of assistance for small businesses. "I don't believe the city of Birmingham," he said during the closing days of the campaign, "will ever recognize its full potential economically, unless the minority business community can contribute more now [than] it is . . . contributing." He also pledged to pursue a more aggressive policy in the competition for international trade, and he sought to encourage businesspeople to explore possibilities abroad so that Birmingham would progress in the quest for economic growth and additional dollars.

Parsons pointed to his own personal economic accomplishments as a test of leadership in his bid for the city's top job. He attributed his success in the travel business to "astute and thorough business planning," and he criticized Arrington as one of the leaders at city hall who had contributed to poor management and a dismal business climate in Birmingham. His association with the national Jaycees organization had given him broad exposure to many businessmen, and he asserted that those contacts would prove valuable as mayor. He managed to tie his strongest issue, law enforcement, to that of economic development, stressing repeatedly the disadvantage to businesses in a city gripped by fear and rampant lawlessness.

The racially focused campaign brought heated language from citizens. Phil Joiner wrote to a local paper that "race has been the very springboard of Richard Arrington's candidacy and has characterized his background." He criticized the black candidate for his role in the Bonita Carter affair, accusing him of encouraging the demonstrations and exciting the tensions during that hideous episode of the city's history. Arrington had "unfairly" raised racial issues during the administrations of George Seibels and David Vann, "though both did much for the black community." Joiner warned that, if Arrington, along with black city-council candidates, won office through racially oriented politics, "such a general takeover will bring an unwholesome reaction from whites." Significantly, he said that Birmingham would experience white flight beyond the city limits and such a development would mean a reduced tax base and fewer services.

Carl Presner wrote in a similar vein. The tenure of Arrington on the city council, he said, "will long be remembered because of the tirades and tantrums he used against the police department." Presner sarcastically attacked one white Arrington supporter by urging her to move from her peaceful Mountain Brook home to the black community in Birmingham "so she could have her yard littered with debris like everyone else's over there." Oley Kelley damned the endorsement of Arrington by the *Birmingham News* as "absolute garbage." Barry Rich did not think that policemen's rights would receive protection from a man like Arrington. The tenor of all these letters revealed the deep racial division in Birmingham and the powerful influence of history.

Some white citizens did openly support Richard Arrington. Marie Stokes Jemison placed herself squarely in the Arrington camp. The election of Arrington, in her judgment, would assist in shattering an ugly image of Birmingham, and it would indirectly attract businesses and industry to the city. The argument reversed the logic of some supporters of Parsons who used an opposite line of reasoning that said a black mayor would hinder economic development. Karl B. Friedman subtly rejected the emphasis on race employed by Parsons's backers when he asked, "Aren't the man . . . and his qualities and experience the proper test of what a citizen should seek from his representatives?" Friedman accused Parsons of attempting to highlight personality rather than the real issues that mattered to Birmingham.

The endorsement of Arrington by the city's two major white newspapers came as a shocking surprise to many citizens, both blacks and whites. Two days before the election the *News* applauded Arrington's veteran service on the city council, his work with the Alabama Center for Higher Education, and his diligent efforts to foster better race relations. Experience in government, the newspaper said, was the essential quality for a mayor in search of solutions to difficult problems facing the city. In glowing language the 28 October 1979 *News* commented:

Of unimpeachable integrity, Dr. Arrington's record shows great promise that he will be effective in leading the fight against rising crime, which bedevils the city as it does the country generally. He has knowledge of city government that will enable him to get the highest return on the taxpayers' dollar. With a balanced view toward race, he should be able to unify the city by establishing goals and policies that will benefit all persons.

Major black organizations lined up in support of Arrington. In the primary the Jefferson County Progressive Democratic Council had backed David Vann, but it endorsed Arrington in the runoff. The NAACP, of course, could not make partisan political endorsements, but W. C. Patton, for years a leader in the organization, emerged from retirement to support Arrington, whom he believed could bring about constructive change in Alabama's largest city. Social groups such as Jack and Jill and black fraternities and sororities declared for Arrington.

Mayor David Vann's decision to vote for Arrington gave his former colleague and friend on the council a considerable boost. But it greatly disappointed Frank Parsons. Immediately after his defeat the mayor had avoided taking sides and merely indicated a desire to support whomever the people selected to lead them. Whatever Vann's public posture toward Arrington, he must have experienced some regret that history had pitted him against a longtime friend who had forcefully condemned his judgment on the Bonita Carter affair, and who had accused him of sending up racial smoke signals on the crime issue during the primary. The mayor believed that Birmingham had fragile race relations and that Arrington could best provide harmony between the races and promote mutual under-standing. While he tried to soften the blow of his decision by de-claring that either candidate "would grace this office," he emphatically proclaimed Arrington the more qualified person for the job.

On 30 October 1979, citizens of Birmingham went to the polls and expressed their agreement with David Vann's assessment of Arrington. Shattering tradition, the son of a former Sumter County tenant farmer beat back the determined effort by Frank Parsons. Ar-rington's time had come; and now it was also time for Birmingham to join southern cities like Atlanta, New Orleans, and Richmond that had elected black mayors. Birmingham had always been slow to change, almost riveted to the past by forces that continually con-spired to defeat progress and reform. Time, however, had now caught up to the city once dubbed "Bombingham" and "the most segregated large city in the South." In the final tally Arrington scored a narrow victory over his Eastside opponent, 44,798 to 42,814, a slim margin of 2.2 percent.

Arrington had recognized the need to attract additional blacks to the polls after the runoff and that he had to get some white support, especially from the liberal Vann camp. He did both. In the primary, with the death of Bonita Carter still a powerful issue, some 63 per-cent of the registered black voters had cast their ballots, but in the runoff the figure jumped to 73 percent. Given his margin in the pri-mary, the large number of voters who again went to the polls gave testimony to Arrington's hard work and superb organization. Sig-nificantly, he zeroed in on the city's Southside in search of crucial white votes, which eventually helped turn the contest in his favor. When one looks at select election boxes in respective black and white areas, it is clear how racially lopsided this historic election really was. At Center Street School, for example, where a large black community voted, Arrington decidedly crushed his opponent, 2,389 to 27. At Eastwood Mall, on the other hand, a white area, Par-sons eclipsed his black opponent, 2,285 to 234. This pattern, al-though less extreme in other areas, appeared all over the city. Arrington's strongest white support came from the old Vann area of Forest Park and other sections of the Southside. But even here his vote was not staggering, given his investment in time and the qualifications he brought to the campaign.

Parsons had pinned his hopes on a large white turnout, since he could not count on any considerable black defection from Arrington's black base. Whites did vote in increased numbers in the runoff, and they helped to cut into the large victory Arrington had anticipated. Understandably, the narrow defeat stunned Parsons and left his supporters at a loss to explain their failure. Referring to whites who failed to go out and vote, one dejected partisan commented, "I can show you what happened, but I can't tell you why." Several years later a more reflective Parsons honed in on the reason for his defeat. "We lost the election," he said, "in our own area." When asked to explain exactly what he meant, he answered more directly and thus revealed much about the entire campaign. "We did not lose by not getting black support . . . but we lost because we did not get enough white turnout." He could have won, he said, given the demographics of the city. But Parsons strongly denied that he had not sought the black vote. He had attended black meetings, but many times he "felt like it was a waste of time."

From his plush Birmingham office in 1983, Parsons advanced other reasons for his defeat. He believed that a number of whites, uninformed of developing political events, did not think a black could get elected, or that Arrington's corps of youthful, neophyte, grass-root volunteers could ever mount the kind of campaign necessary to defeat a white candidate. Parsons also contended that some white voters chose his black opponent because "it was the thing to do" and that it was simply time for a change. "Dick picked up some of that kind of vote," and Parsons predicted that the black politician would get it again if he ran in the October 1983 election. The defeated candidate had fought a long, tough, expensive campaign, and political failure had now robbed him of any chance to "witness for the Lord" through service as mayor of Birmingham. The people had spoken, and history had now enshrined the name of the son of a black farmer who had assisted the swift-moving tide of political and social change.

Arrington and his followers rejoiced in triumph as acclaim poured in from across the nation. The last Tuesday in October 1979 would never again represent just another day in the history of Birmingham. With victory if had become the bright symbol of a new era. For many blacks success was stunning, even for those who knew all along that "the numbers [votes] were there *if* people went to the polls." The day of Jubilee, however, had not yet arrived in this Deep South city, once better known for steel and its football than for healthy race relations. In spite of antiprogressive forces, nevertheless, Birmingham had reached a crucial watershed in its long history.

When Arrington's supporters arrived at the downtown Holiday Inn in Birmingham, they reflected all the excitement, joy, and hope that came with victory after a tough struggle. They had won! Little bitterness surfaced to spoil the glorious moment. Bonita Carter's death, however, was no forgotten memory, for truly it had been a central feature of the campaign and bound blacks together. But sorrow, agony, and bitterness now took a brief respite. The moment called for revelry. Local reporters caught the flavor of the occasion in describing the setting at the Holiday Inn on election night. "The floor shook and wall-to-wall people reveled in Arrington's victory." "The day following the election," journalist Olivia Barton wrote, that "Arrington's place was filled. People drove blocks looking for parking places. They squeezed into the party room to be part of an historic moment." When the wining black candidate showed up at his headquarters, the crowd went wild as partisans gathered around him to witness history in the making. Chris McNair, who had suffered much after the death of his daughter in 1963 in the Sixteenth Street Baptist Church bombing, could hardly disguise his pride when he said that "anybody with two ounces of emotion has to know it's a plus for the community." Admittedly much doubt and more than a little fear existed among many nonblacks in Birmingham, but one of the black celebrants remarked optimistically that whites would come around, once Arrington had begun to govern.

The Birmingham election had drawn regional and national attention as eyes turned toward the city that had once typified southern racial tensions. President Jimmy Carter, a native of Georgia, called Arrington after his victory to congratulate his fellow southerner and to send best wishes. "All the eyes of the nation," Carter told him, "were on the city of Birmingham." Arrington, who rarely shows emotion, talked so calmly with the president that someone supposedly remarked that he appeared as "cool as a cucumber." While his election was enough to prompt a call from the White House, Carter must have recognized the political significance of developments in Birmingham. Indeed, the president had won the South in 1976 because blacks had given overwhelming support in his contest against Republican Gerald Ford. As the representative of a party that had not carried the white south since the 1964 election of Lyndon B. Johnson, Carter, in calling Arrington, a registered Democrat, showed great courtesy but even more political wisdom.

The news media hailed Arrington's victory as a significant personal triumph and as a step forward for Birmingham. Southern writers, however, proved cautious in their assessment. Many of them noted Arrington's success in winning 10 percent of the white vote, but they realistically outlined the imposing challenge that faced the new black leader. "Birmingham's first black mayor," said one writer, "faces a monumental but delicate task of bringing a substantially polarized electorate back together." He believed that Arrington's background had inspired confidence among many blacks and that he had helped some whites overcome many racially inspired fears.

Birmingham voters had not risen above race in October 1979. When one white woman proposed draping city hall in black, few could fail to comprehend her symbolism or the apprehensions and frustrations that still possessed some whites. Naturally, white Birmingham was bound by law to accept the workings of democracy, regardless of the outcome of the election. In the past, that process had often kept blacks out of office, but now it had aided them; and it had produced some disarray among those who had sworn time and again to defend the old southern order with their lives.

Whites worried not so much about Richard Arrington, Jr., but about blacks, the group they believed he represented. Had that day now come when "the last shall be first, and the first shall be last?" There could be no progress, no balm in the Magic City, if this electoral twist of history threatened to turn society upside down. Much of the problem, of course, lay in whites' perception of Ar-

Mayor Richard Arrington, Jr., meets President Jimmy Carter at the White House in 1979. (Courtesy Mayor Richard Arrington, Jr.)

rington. It is highly possible that he never appeared to them as a living, breathing, human being, or as an American who possessed the same values, hopes, and dreams as white people. It is also possible that some whites, cognizant of the despicable state of education during the era of segregation, could not regard Arrington as a highly trained person, the intellectual equal of any comparable white man.

Whatever voters' motives, both blacks and whites had brought their past, a vision of the future, and some of their particular racial beliefs to the election. Despite Arrington's quiet, low-key personality, some whites believed that the man simply hated whites, that he was a racist. Those who had already adopted the immovable position that the Birmingham police did not brutalize black people could only see in the election a police department restrained by a black mayor with criminals freely roaming the city. After the election Parsons expressed another concern that lurked in the minds of more than one white citizen. Pressure would mount, he contended, to compensate blacks for past wrongs. "Whites may be left out in the cold," another dejected white citizen lamented as he echoed the defeated candidate's beliefs.

Arrington did not have to assume a new posture or a new image as he readied himself to lead Birmingham. His election to office demanded no fundamental political or personal changes. Besides the issues of the economy, city services, rising costs, deficits, and crime, Arrington's greatest challenge was to move from candidate and councilman to leader of all the people of this "New South City." The real test of uniting blacks and whites, or at least getting them to work together for a common good, awaited him.

6

Neither Black nor White: The New Administration Takes Shape

.

The planning of Richard Arrington's inaugural activities reflected his desire for unity and his determination to preside over a government too absorbed in the future to look back. The mayor-elect left many of the details to his wife, Rachel, but they agreed that a well-orchestrated biracial ceremony would characterize the event, which was destined for national and international attention. The program would make clear, Arrington stressed, that his election did not symbolize "a new period of racial cleavage or polarization in Birmingham." Like her husband, Rachel Arrington saw the need for a united Birmingham, and she sought to create a program that favored neither blacks nor whites. She approached the planning for her husband's inauguration with the same optimism that she had demonstrated during the campaign. He was now the mayor-elect of Birmingham, and his challenges were those that went beyond narrow racialism and provincialism, although the majority of whites had rejected his candidacy. The inauguration had to send a powerful message to those who wanted to continue the controversy of the campaign and to those who said "Never!" to the idea of sharing power with blacks.

In structuring the inaugural event, Rachel Arrington collected opinions from a committee that included both men and women, blacks and whites. The Arringtons had already devised a general format for the ceremony, but they wanted to get a range of ideas to mirror sharply the philosophy of the mayor-elect and the desires of the people. Since the inaugural committee favored a public reception, no problem developed over invited guests, but as a matter of protocol, invitations went to elected officials. To reinforce the unity theme, the group suggested asking former mayors George Seibels and David Vann to stand with the mayor-elect during the administration of the oath of office. That decision, indeed, reflected Richard Arrington's desire to heal old wounds, for Seibels had been a devout Parsons supporter, and he had shown nothing but political disdain for Arrington since 1975, when the black councilman joined hands with the opposition to drive him from office. Vann and Arrington, on the other hand, had remained friendly toward each other, despite the tensions that grew from the Bonita Carter affair and a heated political campaign.

A sense of expectation grasped the city as it awaited the inauguration, scheduled for Tuesday, 13 November 1979. Unlike the excitement of a few weeks earlier, anxieties developed from the importance of the forthcoming historic event. Even whites who had opposed Arrington recognized that a revolutionary change had taken place, and some of his bitterest political opponents willingly conceded the moment to him and history by their civil behavior. George Seibels, for example, skillfully rebuked a reporter on inauguration day who wanted to unearth past differences between Arrington and the former mayor. The atmosphere that prevailed at Birmingham's Boutwell Auditorium, site of inaugural activities, temporarily eclipsed the serious problems the city faced. For blacks and most of the whites who came, the day was one of rejoicing, for simply watching history in the making. To a few it was a day for quiet political posturing, knowing that some new power arrangements had taken shape in the old Birmingham.

For blacks Arrington's inauguration spelled jubilation, a dream come true, born of years of denial, repression, and heartache. Arrington became political man and symbol of a race that had prevailed over great odds a century after the founding of the Magic City. But reporters who covered the Boutwell affair observed neither arrogance among blacks nor any desire for retribution. In fact, some of them had no exact notion how Arrington would change the city or deal with white folks. But they did know things had *already* changed and that Arrington had not betrayed their trust. They had demanded no encompassing "game plan" for altering the political and economic alignments in Birmingham. Nor had the black clergy structured a "black agenda" one bright, Sunday morning and handed it on a tablet to the black politician. Arrington had worked tirelessly for objectives familiar to both blacks and whites. These goals had been nonrevolutionary and were not ideologically obtuse. The person on the street, whether he or she agreed with Arrington, could understand him: The black politician was in the classic sense a reformer, moderate in tone, gentle in approach—yet a reformer. Although a staunch believer in democratic government, he knew that "the people" could, and did, make mistakes.

The dignitaries who came to honor the quiet, unassuming Arrington spanned the political and social spectrum. Bishop Philip R. Cousins of the African Methodist Episcopal Church opened the program, and Rabbi David J. Zucker of Temple Emanu-El was there to end the ceremonies. Arrington's own minister, Rev. John Cox of Crumbey Bethel Primitive Baptist Church, agreed to give the invocation. Jack Watson, an aide to President Jimmy Carter, came to represent the White House, and Ethel Kennedy, wife of the late Senator Robert Kennedy, attended with her son Robert, Jr., to pay their respects for Massachusetts's Senator Edward Kennedy. Both of Alabama's United States senators, Howell Heflin and Donald Stewart, came, along with Republican congressman John Buchanan, to pay their tribute to the man who had reversed political history in Birmingham. Local and state celebrities also joined national politicians and others in attendance. Alabama's governor, Fob James, former Republican turned Democrat, took time away from Montgomery to visit Birmingham, and so did Democratic lieutenant governor George McMillan, who had strongly supported Arrington and early identified himself with his runoff campaign. Defeated mayoral candidates Larry Langford and Frank Parsons buried their hostility and joined public officials and representatives from private groups that took part in this moment in southern history.

Most of the speeches touched on the theme of unity, but they also took cognizance of Arrington's personal triumph and the growth of a city that had struggled to overcome a past many wanted to forget. The president of the Birmingham City Council, Nina Miglionico, administered the personal touch of a woman who knew the Magic City intimately and who had lived through much of its troubled history. Miss Nina had avoided the conservatism that characterized her city and her region. She declared that "truly there is opportunity in Birmingham for . . . men of every color." But her unrestrained praise for her former fellow councilman told of her satisfaction with his accomplishment. "This day," she proudly exclaimed, "I will cherish for every day of my life." She knew of no person, "man or woman of any color that is more qualified to be the mayor in this city than Dr. Richard Arrington." United States Senator Donald Stewart said optimistically that Arrington's election signaled to the country that "fine things . . . have been happening in the City of Birmingham."

The comments that poured from some of the politicians at Boutwell seemed like an effort to rewrite a history that had conspired to defeat their very presence at a racially integrated Boutwell Auditorium. Senator Howell Heflin rightfully acknowledged the "beginning of a new era in the history of Birmingham," but he dismissed past race relations with the comment that Arrington's election "is the harvest of many plantings." The future, more than history, mattered to Heflin. "I believe," he told the large audience at Boutwell, "that Dr. Arrington's term in office will mark the continuation of a period of harmony between all races in Birmingham as each group comes to appreciate the hope[s] and [aspirations] of the other." In the spirit of the inaugural's unity theme, he encouraged blacks and whites to cooperate for a better Birmingham. This theme also resounded in the remarks of presidential assistant Jack Watson, who recalled notable lines from Martin Luther King, Jr., during his fight for southern justice. King had once said that blacks and whites were bound together in an "inescapable web of mutuality" and that they faced a common future. That truth was irrefutable, said Watson. There must be a "capacity as a people to unite around a common cause." Strong leaders were needed "who will not talk nonsense to our people." Richard Arrington was such a leader. Governor Fob James echoed that theme.

The day and the hour, however, belonged to Richard Arrington. Forty years and many miles separated his small, native Livingston from the large, industrial Birmingham. But his early childhood and his youthful days in Fairfield occupied Arrington's attention as he contemplated the challenges of the mayor's office. He had triumphed over great odds since he left Sumter County. He had survived a school system designed to train blacks for a segregated world, not for political office. Only black suffering, much sacrifice, and loss of life had enabled him to ascend the ladder of political power and influence. Privately, Arrington experienced a sense of triumph and pride at this special moment in his life, a joy at having conquered forces that conspired to keep him and other blacks "in their place." But victors can afford magnanimity. It was not part of Arrington's character to parade success or glory, but as a keen student of history he knew why blacks who came to Boutwell walked with backs straight and with a renewed dignity.

On that special day in November some blacks who had seen life snuffed from their children or friends proudly waved small American flags. "Americanism" no longer implied "for whites only" in the operation of government. The Alabama Symphony Orchestra's rendition of Martin Gould's "American Salute" had notable meaning for those who said "good-bye and good riddance" to a past era. The singing of the National Anthem and the presence of the black color guard from Phillips High School ROTC lent the feeling to some older black citizens that they were finally being "inducted into America." If justice had once been denied them, some blacks now saw it near at hand.

Arrington spoke little of power and influence in his inaugural address. And neither did the signs of the bitter campaign show through the lines of his prepared speech. He tried to reduce racial division further by noting the rejection by citizens of a campaign based on fear and intolerance. As the leader of all the people, he pledged to live beyond pettiness and the anger that an oppressive past sometimes conspired to dictate. History would eventually measure him against the best leadership qualities and would pay little deference to color. In his address Arrington remembered his past, praised his city, and invited all citizens to accept the task of creating a stronger community. A relatively short document, he had given his speech to his secretary for typing the morning before he left for Boutwell. He told his audience in part:

> My election is a clear indication of our progress in human re-
> lations. As a resident of this city and one privileged to serve in
> city government for the past eight years, I know that the Bir-
> mingham of today is very different from the Birmingham of
> yesteryear which was wracked by racial strife. Although there
> is still work to be done to improve race relations and to bring
> about full racial justice, we no longer deserve the image of the
> Birmingham of the early 60's. Our record of hard work for bi-
> racial communication and cooperation has earned for us a new
> image which this occasion today underscores. For 10 years in
> Birmingham blacks have served with whites in city govern-
> ment and today blacks sit on . . . decision-making boards of the
> city government. A significant number have been chosen to
> provide leadership for these boards. Even though I am aware of
> the racial pattern of voting in the mayor's election [and] the
> uneasiness which this political transition creates in many of
> our people . . . this is but another significant chapter in our
> history of progress. I want to make it clear that I do not view
> this election or its results as the onset of a new period of racial
> cleavage or polarization.

Moderation had characterized Arrington's remarks, and those who feared him as a radical could breathe easier. Many citizens had resigned themselves to his victory and said, much like the young student Arrington quoted in his speech, "I'm glad that you won. I wish Parsons would have won, but you'll do. I wish you luck." How-ever, as J. V. Jenkins sang the soul-stirring song "Here I Am Lord, Send Me," there surely must have been those who still asked what Arrington would do once he arrived at city hall across the street.

Despite the spirit of unity that prevailed at Boutwell, when the ordinary folk and the politicians filed out of the auditorium, they stepped into a world that often defied the idea of unity. And when Arrington left the building, he encountered much of the same Birmingham that existed the day before he defeated Frank Parsons, but with one important difference—he was now at the head of the city!

Arrington confronted a herculean challenge. After the election and again at his inaugural, he had tried to allay the kind of racial fears that could frustrate his administration, even disrupt the city. But a number of whites still contended that Birmingham was about to embark upon a course to "turn the city over to Blacks," with an administration that gave social programs priority over business and industry. Blacks, of course, had a stake in the entire city, but they did not want some city programs such as downtown development to take place at their expense or without some benefits to them. One writer captured the black mayor's tough dilemma when he wrote that "Arrington finds himself having to tread a narrow middle ground, knowing that almost any official act sensitive to the concerns of black people might be termed anti-white, and that any action he takes to implement other concerns might be construed [as] anti-black." But Arrington had an approach to such a seeming dilemma. Not only would he verbally reassure citizens of his evenhanded approach, but he would make direct contact with civic and political groups to encourage social harmony and their cooperation in community development.

Arrington had pledged to appoint a staff that would indicate his willingness to work with all segments of the population. Under Birmingham's mayor-council plan of government, the chief executive inherited department heads protected by a civil-service system. However, the mayor had seven political appointments that he could make without restrictions, and he had the responsibility of filling vacancies of department heads, although the selection process, as history later showed, sometimes proved troubling. Arrington had begun to give some thought to possible appointments about a week before the runoff, but he did not seriously focus on the matter until his victory over Frank Parsons. The possibility of defeat, however, had not kept him from dealing with the issue; rather, it was his lateness in entering the mayoral race and his hectic pace. Moreover, Arrington's grass-roots campaign had required more time than would have been the case with a politician who already had in place an organizational structure. Fund-raising, in particular, required much time.

Competency and the obvious consideration of reputation guided Arrington in fulfilling his promise to include both blacks and whites within the administration. Shortly after the election the mayor-elect turned his attention to his two top political positions—executive secretary and chief administrative assistant. City government was a big business that moved at a hurried pace, and it was imperative for a mayor to choose persons who could gauge its pulse and fully comprehend its functions. Little time existed for any extensive experimentation in an administration that would undergo perhaps the closest scrutiny in the city's history. Arrington wanted to find persons for his top jobs who had exposure to government, preferably someone already familiar with the structure at city hall and with some of the people who headed various departments. In his search he consulted with two longtime friends and political allies on the city council, Miglionico and David Herring, who strongly recommended Willie Davis for one of Arrington's major appointments. Davis, a black, possessed a good knowledge of the city and had served on the city-council staff as an administrative assistant for about three years.

Arrington's decision to hire Davis as executive secretary, the top position on the mayor's staff, raised questions among devout Arrington supporters. Even some of those who agreed with the mayor that a black should occupy a top-level, decision-making job had problems accepting Davis. To Arrington, however, the choice of Davis was natural, given his background at the council and his experience in accounting. The opposition to Davis, however, was political. He had not worked for Arrington and, in fact, had initially opposed the latter's candidacy. The mayor knew that Davis had attended a meeting in the summer of 1979 where he had expressed reservations about his candidacy. He had argued rather convincingly that good economic times had passed in Birmingham and that the city faced a recession. Money, said Davis, was "going to be tight," and a black mayor would find it difficult to operate successfully under such austere conditions. Moreover, the city faced a deficit. Arrington later admitted that Davis "knew what was happening at city hall" and that "Willie was absolutely right" in his assessment, for a recession in fact had begun to set in during Vann's last term. The years of plenty had indeed passed.

But much more than Davis's view of the city's economy bothered the appointee's detractors. They regarded an alleged offer to him to serve in the Vann administration as an effort to advance the white politician's reelection in 1979. Arrington gave Davis "the benefit of the doubt" in selecting him, and subsequently he "never had any reason to doubt his loyalty to the administration." The mayor took seriously the strengths Davis possessed in making his choice. Davis had broad contacts in the black community, had done a good job at the council, and was "an . . . old style politician, that understood basic politics." Although he did not possess the verbal skills of some more gifted speakers, he had a good mind, and he related well to the person on the street. Throughout his tenure Davis proved generally effective, but his occasional lack of organization and good judgment brought pressures upon the mayor for his dismissal. By midway into the mayor's first term, the belief prevailed in some quarters that "Willie tends to move on his own" and that he "abuses his authority."

The mayor's appreciation for experience and knowledge of government also led him to Tom Fletcher. While he was on the council, Arrington had interviewed Fletcher for a position on the council staff. Young, energetic, and bright, Fletcher had a penchant for research and organization, and after his employment by the city he had helped to strengthen the council office. Arrington believed the young man had a brilliant future either in government or in the private sector. Herring and Miglionico had not recommended Fletcher to Arrington, since, with Davis gone from the council, another mayoral appointment would further deplete the council staff. Arrington, however, "knew it would be pretty good politics to choose the young man." Herring in particular had reservations about taking two strong persons from the council staff, but Miss Nina encouraged him to go along with the mayor's' decision to appoint the white council assistant. Fletcher had never disguised his ambitions, and when Arrington offered him a job, it became clear that he desired the position of chief administrator, second highest on the staff. Although newspapers had discussed possible appointments and had attempted to slot candidates, Arrington had never indicated what position Fletcher would hold prior to his actual hiring.

Arrington's search for a third major staff appointment caused considerable misunderstanding and ultimately led to Fletcher's hurried departure from the staff. At the time the mayor chose Fletcher, he had also contacted other persons about candidates for positions at city hall, one of whom was Edward S. Lamonte, director of the Center for Urban Affairs at the University of Alabama at Birmingham. Lamonte had met Arrington at Miles College and worked closely with him on a number of projects, where he developed "more than just a superficial understanding of his way of going about business." Lamonte left Miles in 1966 to work on a Ph.D. degree at the University of Chicago, and upon completion of his program he accepted a job at UAB's Center for Urban Affairs. During Arrington's tenure on the Birmingham City Council, the two men had contact with each other, and Lamonte ultimately became one of Arrington's supporters during the mayoral campaign.

The soft-spoken UAB professor had welcomed Arrington's entrance into the 1979 race for mayor, but during the primary he had made only a modest contribution to the campaign. His wife, Ruth, was even more fired by Arrington's political possibilities, and after he advanced to the runoff, the Lamontes discussed ways beyond a modest financial contribution to further his campaign. Since Arrington needed support from the white community, especially from the Forest Park area, the Lamontes approached Tony Carter, who agreed that a reception at their home would help to attract potential white backers. Although new to direct political involvement, the Lamontes optimistically went about telephoning people, especially in the university community, with the hope of getting "fifty or sixty" people to their home. Over one hundred came! "Dick," Ed Lamonte recalls, "had a real impact" at that meeting, impressing people with his knowledge of city government and his ability to field questions.

Lamonte had no reason to give serious thought to a job at city hall. He had a good position at UAB and, like his future boss, seemed destined for a bright future in teaching or university administration. Time, however, wrought a change. When Arrington turned to Lamonte for advice on possible candidates for his staff, he discovered his interest in taking a leave to work at city hall. The mayor had found his man. Shortly before the inauguration the mayor-elect offered the job of chief administrative assistant to Lamonte.

Controversy born of misunderstanding ensued following Lamonte's appointment. After he filled the position of chief administrator, Arrington informed Tom Fletcher of his decision, and he asked Fletcher to remain on the staff as an administrative aide. If Fletcher accepted the appointment, the mayor would try to get the legislature to upgrade one of the appointive posts so that Fletcher could earn about thirty-five thousand dollars. The young man expressed disappointment. Fletcher contended that the mayor had really offered him the job of chief administrator. The misunderstanding that developed resulted from the role played by Willie Davis. After his appointment as executive secretary, Davis talked to Fletcher at the mayor's request about joining the staff. The black aide apparently left the impression with Fletcher that he could have the chief administrator's job if he desired it. But the mayor later noted, "I had never told Tom that [he could have that title]." A breakdown in communication had occurred. In reflecting on the event five years later, Arrington said that "there were similar cases when persons had complained of misunderstanding where Willie had been involved."

The mayor's decision disappointed the hard-driving, ambitious Fletcher. He had pinned his hopes on the chief administrator's slot, and the very fact that rumors circulated around city hall of his appointment may have created some pressure, even some embarrassment. "It was painful for him," said the mayor, in discussing the affair. Unable to live with a lesser spot within the administration,

Fletcher resigned after four days on the job to return to the council staff. He expressed doubt that the legislature would pass a bill that permitted the city to raise his salary as the mayor proposed. Fletcher told the press that the position offered him was "not the same" one promised him earlier and that it did not offer the kind of career advancement he had discussed with representatives of the mayor.

The mayor genuinely regretted Fletcher's departure and the adverse publicity that came so early in his administration. Reports in the media that his resignation reflected political power plays taking place in the new mayor's office, however, had no real basis in fact. A misunderstanding existed, and certainly the incident had no racial overtones. The mayor genuinely respected Fletcher's energy and the unusual quality of his mind, and so did Willie Davis, who had worked closely with him on the council staff. Arrington had tried to make clear to Fletcher his plan for a three-man team approach to decision making at city hall involving Davis, Lamonte, and Fletcher, and initially the young, white aide had accepted that arrangement. But it became clear to him "within a couple of days" that the team approach would be impossible to implement. Whatever damage may have resulted from the difficulties surrounding Tom Fletcher, however, was probably offset by the strength of Lamonte's appointment.

Fletcher's departure still left open a top position. Arrington finally decided to make a nonpolitical appointment from within the ranks of city-hall civil service, thereby putting to rest speculation that he had forced Fletcher out only to get another black adviser. The mayor chose a veteran civil servant, Leonard Gedgoudas, a seasoned city employee who had worked under two previous mayors. An analyst, Gedgoudas represented the classic picture of the systematic bureaucrat who, while realizing that people lived in the city, had an abiding concern for the mechanisms and the nuts-and-bolts details that made the city function. Obviously Gedgoudas had not participated in Arrington's campaign, a fact of little concern to the mayor in selecting him. Gedgoudas had seen mayors come and go, and he felt confident the city would survive, and he with it, if declining budgets did not take his job. For this reason, perhaps,

Gedgoudas assumed a kind of detachment about some issues and developments that disturbed other city-hall insiders. His distance from politics occasionally troubled some close supporters of the mayor who believed he should occupy a more aggressive political posture in defense of the mayor's policies, but Gedgoudas's position was *not a political appointment*. The mayor had simply elevated him to an administrative position, but he had kept his civil-service rank.

The many strengths of Lamonte and some weaknesses of Willie Davis prompted the mayor eventually to reorganize his top-level staff. The genesis of the change from the team approach took place about a year into Arrington's tenure, and it involved salaries paid Arrington's top staff, although that was only part of a story that involved job performance and personal styles of operation. Lamonte had left his university post to join Arrington at a reduced salary of $31,990. Significantly, the ceiling set by the state of Alabama for his position was $32,000, a figure the mayor had endeavored unsuccessfully to raise through legislative efforts. The executive secretary's position had no limits, and Willie Davis, who held the job at the time, made $32,968. In late October 1980, the mayor announced that Lamonte and Davis would exchange positions, a decision that brought a "mild objection from Davis" and produced some uneasiness for Lamonte, who expressed a willingness to remain in his present position if the change brought conflict. With the shift, Lamonte's annual salary went to $39,000, a competitive figure compared to the university salary he would have received at UAB.

But the question of salary was only one reason for the position change on the mayor's staff. After a year in office Arrington had had sufficient time to assess critically the key people around him. Mindful that the mistakes of his aides were his own, he stated in a 1984 interview, "I felt I had made an error in judgment in my assessment of personnel." While the mayor regarded Willie Davis as a valued member of his staff, he also recognized that Lamonte had extensive formal training, spoke and wrote well, and demonstrated remarkable balance and organization in his professional performance. Pressures had continued to mount in the administration to

187

"dump Willie," not because of inefficiency or any inability to think creatively but because of his sometimes poor judgment and lack of reflection. "People came to me to complain about what Willie had done," the mayor recalled, "and they accused him of mishandling authority, of wanting to do favors for people."

Curtailing the spirit of Willie Davis proved no easy task. His loyalty, his knowledge of government, his political savvy, and his genuine interest in the city were powerful factors that kept the mayor from firing him during the first term. Unfortunately, an insider at city hall confided in 1984, "Willie had a reputation of a wheeler dealer, an image he has not yet completely shaken." That description may have resulted in part from Davis's extroverted personality and his own perception of how a real politician should act. "Willie," said one of Davis's partisans objectively, "does sometimes overstep his bounds, goes at more power." When pressed on the matter of Davis's authority, the mayor admitted that occasionally his assistant "had hired folk, who had been on the payroll for several days before anyone really knew about them." Indeed, some significant friction arose when Davis employed a person for a job in an area over which he had minimal control. Fortunately, his demeanor and his willingness to admit error saved him from the blistering hostility that would have greeted a more abrasive personality.

The incident that created considerable problems for Arrington and that threatened to place Davis's job in jeopardy came in the administration's first year. In September 1980, the police took into custody a truck that carried gasoline. Though absolute proof did not exist at the time, rumors that the fuel was stolen filled the air. After a background check of the vehicle and its driver, who for a short time was a suspect in a gasoline-theft ring, Davis signed the necessary documents to release the truck. Controversy ensued when a local newspaper charged that the mayor's assistant had violated police-department policy and that he had interfered with an investigation. The heat generated by this affair prompted Arrington to write a detailed explanation of the event to neighborhood leaders. And he also sent a letter to the supervisor of the reporter at the *Birmingham News* who covered the story. Arrington strongly defended Davis's action, and he rejected the contention that his aide overrode police orders. The paper, he said, had misrepresented Davis and the administration.

Much more was involved in the affair than appeared on the surface. The press may have dealt Davis an unfair blow in its reporting, and Arrington was probably correct in asserting that the controversy resulted partly from politics and the antagonism that some policemen had toward the administration. But Davis had released the gasoline truck only after it had been cleared by Acting Police Chief Jack Warren, who later defended him. The controversy per se did not disturb the mayor, but what did bother him was Davis's occasional failure to follow instructions. "Willie had released some cars before, and I had told him not to do it," the mayor recounted intensely in discussing the case. But he noted that the newspapers "never treated him fairly." Davis's judgment, however, had clearly created some problems and increasing concern for the administration. But the zealous effort by some of the press to force the mayor to dismiss him backfired and, rather than alienating him from his aide, brought Arrington to his defense. The real issue for the mayor, however, went beyond the narrow affair and addressed the broader issue not of Davis's competence but of his ability to act responsibly in judgmental matters.

The mayor's problems with his team approach did not affect appointment of lower-level political appointees and his desire for a racially balanced staff. Naturally, he felt comfortable choosing people he had known or who had worked with him, but as the mayor discovered, such connections were both a strength and a weakness. Upon taking office, Arrington recommended the abolition of the Office of Public Information, and he left the position out of the annual budget. However, to serve as a press aide and to handle public relations, the mayor brought in Lewis White, an old college friend, former campaign manager, and one-time staff member at the Alabama Center for Higher Education. White wrote well, and he had a mind that easily grasped ideas. "If I had his brains and his talents, I could do so much more," the mayor said in appraising his strengths. White had abilities the mayor could not ignore, and despite some objections from close advisors, Arrington hired his longtime friend. His tendency not to hold a job for long periods concerned some of the mayor's friends, and the contention that he did not follow through on assignments caused some concern. The media, nevertheless, came to like White, and through his writing he effectively projected the administration's message. A writer with some literary flair, White handled much of the mayor's correspondence; and a close examination of the aide's letters reflects his keen awareness of the issues at city hall. His ability to organize his time, however, did not improve much from his days at ACHE. "A good secretary," a friend close to him commented, "would make him a superior press officer."

Lemorie Tony Carter, like White, helped to form the "Miles College connection" at city hall. Carter had worked diligently in the mayoral campaign, but he had expected nothing from his former professor and friend. Arrington hired Carter as an aide to handle citizens' complaints that came to the mayor's office, a tough job that could challenge the nerves of even the most patient soul. Carter owned a thriving insurance agency, which he never relinquished, and his occasional absence from his desk gave rise to rumors among some workers at city hall. "The mayor must have lived in fear that he would pick up a local newspaper to find a story about the [alleged] misuse of the city's time," one of them said after Carter eventually left the administration. That, of course, never occurred.

At Carter's urging, the mayor also hired Ocie Pastard. Although he had worked in the mayoral campaign, Arrington had no great enthusiasm for Pastard. Some controversy had surrounded his earlier career in California, but Carter insisted that the mayor bring him into the administration after a favorable background check. The mayor employed him. Clearly, Pastard did not have the experience of some staff members, and that lack concerned a few Arrington followers who believed that anyone who worked in the first black administration in Birmingham should have impeccable credentials and a good public image. Arrington concluded that Pastard's background would enable him to work in the community with people at the grass roots. He guessed wrong. Pastard was "an absolute disaster," and the mayor quietly eased him out, the first person Arrington removed from city hall.

Anxious not to discard Pastard totally, the mayor arranged a pro-visional position for him as assistant director of Boutwell Audito-rium. In his employment Pastard had the opportunity to learn his job thoroughly, thus making him a second choice for a full-time po-sition if he mastered his responsibilities. Arrington's decision to aid Pastard did not come solely from friendship but was part of an overall philosophy related to city government and affirmative ac-tion. The mayor wanted to put minorities and women in jobs where, with initiative and commitment, they could move up the income and occupational ladder. "All kinds of problems developed" with Pastard, the mayor lamented years later. With an apparent exagger-ated sense of his power, the former staff member dramatically an-nounced his intention to seek office, challenging the personnel board's rule against such a move. He did both and lost.

One other political appointment rounded out the mayor's official staff. In the past some mayors had brought their secretaries with them to city hall. Arrington continued this practice by his selection of Jessie Huff to manage his office staff, but she also took on much broader responsibilities. Although she had less formal academic training than some on the mayor's staff, she had a gift for quiet di-plomacy, for simplifying complex issues, and for recognizing the po-litical significance of events. Religiously devoted to Arrington, Huff strongly defended his interests, and as one of the insiders who knew him best and who possessed a ready entrée to his office, she was in a special position to voice her opinion about matters that con-cerned her.

The Arrington administration faced its historic mission with a politically moderate city council. Nine members sat on the Bir-mingham City Council, which exercised power defined in the 1963 Mayor-Council Act. At the time Arrington took office, five persons on that body were also sworn into office. Incumbents Pete Clifford, David Herring, and Russell Yarbrough had prevailed in the 1979 election. John Katopodis, E. C. "Doc" Overton, Bessie Estelle, and Nina Miglionico did not have to stand for reelection. Joining them were William A. Bell and Jeff Germany, who, along with Estelle, pushed the number of blacks on the council to three. Bell, a nor-mally quiet-spoken, thirty-year-old sales executive, worked for Xerox Corporation and he also had a small business of his own. A native who grew up and was educated in the city, he possessed a good knowledge of Birmingham, yet his triumph in the 1979 election clearly surprised many people.

Germany was better known than Bell because of his position as an administrative assistant in the Vann administration. A graduate of Miles and a strong supporter of Arrington, he liked the exposure that politics gave him. Although he had a firm grasp of city affairs, he was perhaps less probing than his colleague Bell. His real strength derived from the understanding of the political process, his contact with the black masses *and* the middle class, and his loyalty to Arrington.

Bessie Estelle was the lone black woman on the city council. She had come with her family to Birmingham at an early age from Greene County, Alabama, and she had made her way with distinction through the public schools of Birmingham and Alabama State College. The daughter of a minister, Estelle taught in the city's school system, won a "Teacher of the Year" award, and later became principal of Butler and West Center Street Elementary schools. A gifted woman of incredible stamina, she participated in a wide range of professional, religious, and civic activities at the state and local level, and for her many outstanding achievements the city of Birmingham gave her its "Woman of the Year" award in 1975. Although an advocate of self-help, Estelle knew first-hand the economic and social prohibitions of black life in southern society.

Arrington's most pressing problems in November 1979 were neither partisan politics nor race. From his council experience the mayor had learned that citizens most desired personal safety, secure property, and the effective delivery of city services. Since he already had a familiarity with the operation of the council and with most city department heads, Arrington lost little time in addressing the issues that faced him. As historic as his election had been, the city demands did not stand still for any extended celebration. Nor did Arrington desire that, for he was anxious to prove through example that the people had chosen wisely, to demonstrate that an administration run by blacks could function successfully. There would be no need, as one white citizen had lamented, to "drape city hall in black."

Arrington had pledged to continue major programs of the Vann administration. During the campaign he had steered clear of promises that required additional outlays of money and personnel, for such a direction would have ignored the general state of the economy, now reeling from the triple blows of high inflation, high interest rates, and high unemployment. As city businesses went into a slump or even failed and as people lost their jobs, further strains appeared upon local government as it tried to maintain essential services at an acceptable level. With declining revenues and a steel industry in the doldrums, Birmingham confronted serious problems that threatened some of the basic functions of government and the very quality of life of the ordinary citizen. Arrington had a keen awareness of these problems, and it may be recalled, he had rejected the notion that he stay out of the mayor's race because of a possible budget deficit from the Vann years. Although he recognized the precarious state of the city's economic condition, a projected \$2.5 million shortfall in the city's income for the last quarter of 1979 did not dishearten him.

Unfortunately, both sales and occupational tax revenues had declined, a problem aggravated to some degree by the movement of some white citizens to suburbia. White flight, however, did not result from Arrington's election. It was a development already in evidence, and it had left behind an increasingly black city. Many suburbanites, of course, returned to work in Birmingham, but they took their paychecks and their business back to their outlying communities. These employees spent relatively small amounts of money in Birmingham during the day, and only a few of them returned at night for special functions in downtown Birmingham. The city suffered. By offering occupational opportunities, of course, Birmingham helped support outlying municipalities.

The economic situation that confronted Arrington did leave him with options. Some unencumbered federal funds existed for his use, and he could make adjustments to conserve revenue. "We must learn," the new mayor told writer Miller C. Jordan, "to do more with existing revenues." Predictably, then, Arrington tackled his budget problem by emphasizing increased efficiency and more effective management of the city budget. He moved cautiously but confidently, and he achieved favorable results. He proudly proclaimed to *Future Magazine* in September 1980:

> I indicated that my major thrust would be to have greater efficiency to get some of the waste out of government. I have undertaken steps that people have talked about for a long time in city hall, but never implemented. We brought about savings in curbing the use of city automobiles at night. We've talked about that in City Hall . . . for eight years and never did anything about it. This administration has parked them.
>
> We have started to reorganize some of the departments, including consolidating efforts, for instance, in our personnel department. We also [have] started coordinating efforts between our economic development and community development department [in order to increase efficiency and to save resources].

The Arrington administration also employed a more sophisticated data-processing system to administer federal grants, thus realizing a gain in indirect and administrative costs. Savings also resulted from the city's self-insurance system for buildings, equipment, and employees. Indeed, Arrington's aggressive approach to the problems of the city's budget and his success virtually precluded successful attack from any opponent in the 1983 mayoral election.

A healthy business climate and a vibrant industrialism could help increase the tax base and produce the revenue Birmingham so badly needed. Initially, much of the city's white business leadership had shied away from Arrington, assuming that Birmingham's credit rating would fall and that the city would be unable to attract capital and the investment necessary for growth. Some businessmen believed the former educator did not understand the workings of the private business sector, despite his contact with the leaders of some of the country's most progressive enterprises. Others assumed Arrington's ability to comprehend the economic system but reasoned that social concerns would blind him to business or that pressure from his black constituency would turn his attention from the pressing requirements of economic growth.

Arrington's response to the demands of business must have surprised those who doubted his potential for strong leadership. Some of the people who had followed him and who had confidence in his abilities revealed an important reason for the mayor's determined efforts to aid business. Black councilman William A. Bell, who chaired the council's Municipal Development Committee, captured one of those important reasons when he said, "He wants it to be said that Richard Arrington, a black mayor, had a tremendous positive effect on white business." Bell praised Arrington's efforts, as did some of those who earlier had opposed the mayor. "The business community as a whole," wrote one observer, "feels the mayor has been responsive to them." Perhaps the highest accolade came in 1980 from Don Newton, an official of the Birmingham Chamber of Commerce, when he complimented Arrington for developing a means of bringing additional businesses to Birmingham and for his aid to those already in the city. An official of Parisians, one of the city's largest department stores, applauded Arrington for his sensitivity to downtown and outlying businesses. In the summer of 1983 (only a few months before Arrington ran for reelection), even Arrington's runoff opponent, Frank Parsons, privately praised the black mayor for his successful economic strides, especially for the large amount of building then taking place in downtown Birmingham. The business community had begun to take seriously Arrington's economic intentions to turn the city around.

Some of the projects of the administration provided an economic boost and created jobs. Such was the case with the city's housing program and community and commercial revitalization projects. And when Arrington gave his approval to a $27-million bond issue, he ensured not only the building of a high-school sports facility, a jail, and commercial revitalization projects but some eight thousand additional jobs for the city's citizens. The millions of dollars spent on public construction such as the central library also gave work to some who otherwise would have experienced unemployment. Likewise, the establishment of a downtown farmer's market in 1981 provided an emphasis on folk life, a place for the casual meandering of people, and an opportunity for small business.

The streamlining of government and retrenchment produced some understandable problems. Careful management, however, avoided extreme hardships for city employees. While attrition lessened the administrative burden of laying off some workers, it also enabled Arrington to reduce some unneeded supervisory personnel. In the case of the police department, the mayor decided to downgrade some officers, a move that generated considerable controversy and further inflamed already-strained relations between him and his old enemy, the FOP. The continuing challenge throughout Arrington's first term was "to do more with less."

Despite enduring economic austerity, Arrington believed that citizens' complaints demanded prompt attention. Therefore, he established the Office of Citizens Assistance within Gedgoudas's area, headed by Jackie Belcher, who had studied law at Miles College. Occasionally, complaints came from citizens who misunderstood the responsibilities of local government or from people who could have easily done a job themselves but who were determined to get their "tax-dollars' worth" of governmental service. Although some of them may have regarded Arrington as a liberal on many issues, his view on the responsibility of citizens to themselves and to their city bore a strain of old-fashioned common-sense conservatism. That outlook, however, was exhibited best in the administration by Gedgoudas, who, according to his colleagues, was as thrifty as his boss. Government, said Gedgoudas, within a kind of neo-Jeffersonian philosophy, should "do for people those things they can not normally be expected to do for themselves." The failure of citizens to interact with each other in a highly impersonalized urban atmosphere, however, often mitigated against the cooperation needed to solve city problems. Gedgoudas's view had some merit. The reasonable success of Birmingham's Citizens Participation Program, created to bring about cooperation between the city and its residents in the development of projects and policies, proved that urbanites could combine to promote their common interests, as in the Neighborhood Crime Watch programs.

When Arrington took office, Birmingham had begun to take

steps to diversify its economy, but unemployment remained troubling. The mayor argued that a successful future for Birmingham lay in the city's ability to attract its share of high-tech jobs, and his strong support for the acquisition of land for research and development parks reflected his view of future economic growth. It was apparent to him and to those who knew Birmingham that the city's "Age of Steel" had passed and that economic progress would have a direct connection with the UAB Medical Center and the technology associated with medicine, engineering, and related fields. Indeed, by the 1970s, the university, with the medical school as its core, had become the largest employer in the city. Arrington addressed this reality in 1983, when he wrote that "the city recognizes the central importance of UAB in developing economic opportunities and leadership for the future." While other institutions—Birmingham Southern College, Samford, Miles, and Jefferson State and Lawson State community colleges—could play an important role in providing technical and specialized training and leadership, UAB's size, its budget, and its faculty made it an important part of the city's changing economy.

The revitalization of downtown Birmingham constituted a significant part of an overall program for economic development. Unless the city could attract people to it to live, business—and, therefore tax revenues—would continue to suffer. A "Master Plan for the Redevelopment of Downtown Birmingham" had taken shape during Arrington's last year on the city council. The comprehensive plan drawn by local architect Pedro Costa and his associates was created as a guide to development in the city for the next twenty to twenty-five years. It envisioned both public and private investment, with the assumption that government would need to act as a partner in rebuilding the city. The detailed document contained massive amounts of data, and its proposals ultimately invited some controversy. When the city council held a public hearing on the plan in the summer of 1979, the Costa team spent three hours explaining it, but surprisingly little debate took place. According to one source, only "a scant ten minutes" of questions followed the explanation from master-plan consultants, although a large crowd nearly filled the council chambers. With the adoption of Costa's work, it appeared that city government had made a fundamental commitment to revitalization and that it had also endeavored to bolster its economic posture. Time and personal interests, however, altered the seeming tranquility that prevailed in the summer of 1979.

The heart of the city's downtown plan called for the development of a section called "Block 60." The proposal envisioned the construction of a major office-building complex, a large convention-quality hotel, and 130 units of residential housing. It would have created additional jobs, and it would have added to the office space so essential to Birmingham if the city wanted to become a regional center for large corporations. The project would have attracted more people downtown to live and work, which would have helped revitalize social life in the area. If Block 60 was successful, it would reaffirm Arrington's belief in a renascence of the central city and it would be a political plus for his administration.

Insurmountable difficulties surfaced to frustrate the hopes of Block 60. As earlier noted, little hard-core resistance appeared initially to the city's master plan, but when Block 60 neared the actual starting stage, opposition became readily evident. Since the project was essentially a private undertaking, many small merchants, both black and white, "probably thought it was kind of silly for the mayor to concern himself with a rich man's private development when sewers, streets and other city facilities needed repair," according to one proponent of Block 60.

The success of Block 60, of course, depended on the acquisition of the land for the proposed project. To acquire the site the city chose Metropolitan Properties, Incorporated (MPI), a local development firm that had a solid track record in the property-management field. Neither Arrington nor Metropolitan, however, could have anticipated the frustrations each eventually faced. When some owners of businesses along Block 60 balked at selling their properties at a fair-market value, the city turned to other means to aid MPI in acquiring the vitally needed land. Ordinarily, a city such as Birmingham could acquire property through eminent domain to carry out a vital project that affected the public interests. Block 60, however, was a delicate public-private undertaking.

Property condemnation by the city provided the answer to the problem of land acquisition. Loud cries of opposition came immediately from some Block 60 merchants, who detested the "strongarm tactics" employed by local government to take their property. Businessmen reacted bitterly to the city's contention that their block constituted a "blighted" area subject to condemnation for purposes of renewal. Lawyers for the entrepreneurs came before the city council in August 1981, armed with arguments that must have provoked serious thought from the most ardent booster of Birmingham. Douglas Corretti, who represented one of the businesses on Block 60, declared that the idea of taking private property "and turning it over to a private developer is very repugnant." Block 60, he suggested, already stood as one of the best business areas in the city.

Corretti's argument did not raise the more important—and to some the more frightening—question to the person on the street, who feared "the long strong hand of ever-present government." But Donald Brockway surely did when he warned, "If word gets out to the business community that you can come to the determination that an area [like block 60] is blighted . . . then you can do it in any city block in Birmingham." The city council's proposed condemnation resolution, said another business spokesperson, indicted all property owners along Block 60, some of whom had businesses far superior to those found in other parts of the city. Block 60, of course, occupied a strategic location, and the council recognized that the inconvenience experienced by the owners would ultimately result in enormous progress for the city. Mayor Arrington was never blind to the sacrifices of owners along Block 60, and from the beginning he had worked to ensure a fair price for the property in the area.

Arguments against condemnation did not sway the city. In early September 1981, the Birmingham City Council, by a 6-2 vote, declared Block 60 (an area bounded by Fourth and Fifth avenues North and Nineteenth and Twentieth streets North) a blighted area. The approved resolution gave the city the right to condemn land within the area if owners refused to sell to a developer named by the city (i.e., Metropolitan). It also pledged help in relocating displaced tenants. Councilmen Pete Clifford and Russell Yarbrough opposed the resolution, but to the surprise of some, Councilman John Katopodis, increasingly antagonistic to Arrington and friend of one of the largest property owners along the blighted block, supported the measure. Katopodis argued that some owners actually wanted the threat of condemnation "because of the tax benefits."

Condemnation had required the city to demonstrate an overriding public purpose and to show that it was a tool of last resort. Ed Lamonte, who handled the details of Block 60 for the mayor, rebutted the contention of those persons who saw condemnation as a step toward reckless government action that oppressed the individual citizen. "The mayor," Lamonte later stated in defense of his boss, "is a very conservative man in his regard for private property." Block 60 did not bring out the "latent socialist leanings in Richard Arrington." Whatever the arguments for or against his support of Block 60, the mayor kept his course, confident that the development, as well as other parts of the master plan, would bring profit to the Magic City. He remained acutely aware that other cities had legally acquired private property for urban renewal and then reconveyed it to private business. While both the mayor and Lamonte had been reluctant to consider condemnation, the administration had worked carefully to protect the rights of owners, while at the same time addressing the long-range interests of the city. The mayor's position drew indirect support from most city politicians who ran for office in 1981, since the overwhelming majority of council candidates approved the city's master plan.

In early 1982, Mayor Arrington reported enthusiastically on Metropolitan's progress in getting sale agreements from Block 60 property owners. Unless the project encountered delay from litigation, he noted in his "State of the City" address, construction on Block 60 would begin around April. At the very time the mayor delivered his optimistic statement, Metropolitan had obtained purchase-option agreements from only roughly half the property owners on Block 60. Therefore, the city extended Metropolitan's contract, and when it again expired, the city agreed to another adjustment, with the provision that the city's two consulting attorneys handle negotiations with Block 60 property owners. With purchase options on all property finally achieved, only one more major hurdle stood in the way of a project that would enhance the city's image and give it a further boost toward becoming a more attractive convention center. And that hurdle was money to pay for the valuable land.

On 27 December 1982, Metropolitan had to turn to Mayor Arrington for assistance in acquiring the $11 million necessary to purchase Block 60. Arrington moved with dispatch. Working furiously to "get the money in place" before the expiration of sell agreements with businesses, he successfully arranged a deal between Metropolitan and the Southtrust Corporation to pay for Block 60. The developer argued that it had been able to get all documents in place and to assemble the money to purchase the property within its contract period. A different opinion, however, eventually prevailed, which brought the $125-million Block 60 project tumbling to the ground before builders turned a single spade of earth.

How did a multimillion-dollar project that involved hundreds of hours disintegrate, when success stood so near? Researchers may spend years trying to unravel the details that led to the failure of Block 60 and to the defeat of the city's most ambitious downtown-development project during the Arrington years. Certain facts, however, are clear. The initial deadline for closing property settlements for the required area had been set for Friday, 31 December 1982. But two days before the stipulated deadline, the city's legal representatives informed Arrington that Gusty Yearout, the attorney who represented the largest owner on the block, Cameron Grammas, would be away from Birmingham until 31 December. Yearout's impending absence forced the city to request an extension of purchase options from other Block 60 owners. A new closing date now became 3 January, 1983—at least, *that was the city's assumption*. With the money now in place and with options to purchase accomplished, everything seemed ready for the actual signing of contracts for property that would catapult downtown Birmingham into a new era.

Frustration now became a terrible heartache for Richard Arrington. Cameron Grammas maintained that Metropolitan had not lived up to its legal obligation to close on property before the expiration date. He would not sell! Yearout, on the defensive for alleg-

201

edly torpedoing the project by his absence from the city, heatedly exclaimed that he had told Alton Parker, Jr., one of the city's legal consultants, of his forthcoming trip out of the city and that Parker had responded by saying the closing on Grammas's property could take place *without Yearout's presence.* Moreover, he maintained that his partner, Jerry Lorant, had been prepared to conclude the deal on 31 December but that the city's representatives did not show up.

Reasons other than the technicality of a closing date also apparently shaped Grammas's decision not to part with his property. Three days after the failure of Block 60, Yearout spoke of the factors that compelled his client's action. Grammas, he said, felt betrayed. The Block 60 owner had earlier signed a contract to sell his property at one hundred dollars a square foot, but he discovered later that another owner had been offered twenty-five dollars more per square foot. Grammas had not received equal treatment! Why his client waited until the last minute to raise the issue, however, remains a puzzling question. Rather than the $3.2 million originally agreed upon, Grammas now requested $4.8 million for his property; and he also made another demand Arrington could hardly honor. He wanted to become the owner and developer of one-half of Block 60! A concession to Grammas on the selling price of his property, however, would have surely meant renegotiation with other owners.

Yearout also spoke of his client's dissatisfaction with Metropolitan. In the attorney's judgment it was not a good developer. "To let Metropolitan try and develop it . . . would have been a disservice to the city," he said. Nor did he and Grammas like the role of Southtrust Bank, which they viewed as a potential developer because of its loan to Metropolitan. He and Grammas had the city's best interest at heart. "We weren't . . . greedy," Yearout noted in responding to charges that he and his businessman client were trying to maximize profits. Cameron Grammas, said the attorney, "cared least about the money." Greed may not have been the chief factor that motivated Grammas, but it is hard to ignore the last-minute 50 percent increase in the asking price for his property, or the potential for profit if the city had honored his request to develop half of Block 60.

Failure of Block 60 dealt a hard blow to the mayor. He had long believed in the necessity of developing downtown, and he had carefully followed Block 60, meeting with Ed Lamonte on a regular basis to discuss the details of the multimillion-dollar project. If the completion of Block 60 had not been *the* major goal of the Arrington administration, it surely was a project close to the mayor's heart. The day after the failure of Block 60, Arrington appeared withdrawn and depressed, and it was difficult for him to disguise "a hostility toward the circumstances." But disappointment did not lead him to assign blame recklessly for the collapse of Block 60. In fact, he did not readily concede the death of the project, and for a short time Arrington thought the plan salvageable. When the dust cleared from the Block 60 ashes, irreparable damage to the downtown development idea lay clearly before the mayor and those who had worked so hard and so long for its fulfillment. No one could adequately gauge the political fallout.

There was, nevertheless, an ill-disguised bitterness among many within the Arrington administration over the destruction of Block 60. The urbane and scholarly Lamonte could soberly discuss the project months after its demise, but underneath his quiet, deliberate, and measured tone, there existed disappointment and some suspicion about what may have taken place. He found little consolation in the reality that the "flagship of the master plan didn't move forward." The administration had paid a price, had encountered a terrible setback. While Lamonte praised the efforts of Metropolitan, he did not exempt the developers from criticism, admitting that "they created some antagonisms." Yet, he never questioned their desire to succeed at the project.

Arrington and Lamonte spoke more cautiously of other chief players in the Block 60 game, especially of Pedro Costa and Councilman John Katopodis. Costa, a handsome, debonair architect, looked the part of a confident Hollywood celebrity who seemed to have the world in the palm of his hand, or who wanted to shape it to his own vision. The Uruguayan-born creator of the city's master

plan had won high praise for his work, but Costa's later actions
raised suspicions from some persons unable to explain satisfactor-
ily the disastrous collapse of Block 60. Following the completion of
the master plan, the architect and another developer, Nelson Head,
bought large shares of downtown properties, some in an area south
of Block 60. No impropriety apparently existed, since both the master plan and the purchase of this land were public knowledge. Indeed, as Ed Lamonte objectively pointed out after the Block 60
failure, other investors also had the chance to acquire downtown
properties. "It was," said Arrington's aide, "not as though Costa . . .
acquired property, and then developed a plan that would benefit
him." The man had been "darn smart."

Privately the mayor and his aide Lamonte did have complaints
about Costa's transactions that violated unwritten agreements.
While Costa and the mayor had indeed enjoyed a close relationship,
Arrington later contended that Costa and Head "did not live up to
their commitment to inform him of [their] Block 60 involvement."
At one point the architect of Birmingham's master plan had supposedly assured the mayor that Costa and Head "would not have
any interest on Block 60 unless the mayor was comfortable with
their approach and involvement." Yet, Costa "turned around and
announced he had acquired property on Block 60." Naturally some
of the suspicions that engulfed city hall had much to do with developments that involved the Costa-Head maneuvers. A fact of crucial significance in considering Block 60 is the intense competition
between developers interested in establishing themselves in the
downtown area. Indeed, it may be recalled that Grammas himself,
although not a developer, had proposed his involvement in Block 60.
Even before Metropolitan failed, friends had warned Arrington that
"certain things would happen, that . . . agreements would be
reached by certain parties," and that "ultimately we would have
certain parties stepping in and asking to work with the city on
Block 60."

An intricate set of events and personal relationships, however,
may have contributed to the collapse of Block 60 and to the continuing puzzle over what really happened. While nothing pointed directly to a conspiracy to defeat Arrington's downtown project,

Costa's association with Head, John Katopodis's 1979 campaign manager, drew many comments from Arrington partisans. More troubling to the mayor and his aide Lamonte was the revelation that Grammas had become an investor in a Costa-Head project to develop another block in the city. Costa quickly defended himself from allegations of betrayal and conspiracy. He had had a good relationship with the mayor, and he had contributed to his campaign. "If I'm the creator of the downtown plan, I don't want to see a development fall through," Costa said in appealing to logic and to his allegiance to the city's goals. Block 60 would not have hurt his business venture. Besides, had he not encouraged the city to choose Metropolitan Properties instead of another developer?

John Katopodis's role was even more unclear to Arrington. A booster of Birmingham, only Katopodis's self-confidence and ego exceeded his love for his city. He had supported the master plan, but he could not have completely ignored the possible negative political results for Arrington from a Block 60 disaster. With Metropolitan experiencing difficulty in raising the money for Block 60 land and with Grammas requesting more money for his property, it is arguable that Katopodis visualized real political advantage in the collapse of Arrington's efforts. Katopodis, however, thought it "ludicrous" to believe that Grammas "would give up $3.2 million to see me elected mayor." Framed in those terms, the issue seemed simple enough, but Katopodis oversimplified the situation. Grammas's property was no less valuable after the Block 60 failure, and moreover, he stood to gain from any other developments that took place on the block that involved his holdings.

Some critics contended that part of the sticky problem resulted from the very nature of public-private cooperation in the redevelopment of cities. With all the handicaps inherent in such alliances, wrote Mitch Mendelson of the *Birmingham Post-Herald* on 6 January 1983, "it is not surprising that such partnerships fail. It is surprising that they work at all." Although Mendelson concentrated his comments on the broad question of the cooperation between cities and private property, he expressed his opposition to such ventures when he wrote that "private property is best acquired privately." Doubtless his philosophical view had many supporters, but it did not push him toward a narrow consideration of the causes for the death of Block 60. The public-private partnership, he said, did not mean

> the city's involvement killed Block 60, anymore than Cameron Grammas killed Block 60. It could be argued that Block 60 was dead on [December] 27 when Metropolitan President Raymond Gotlieb told Mayor Richard Arrington he didn't have $11 million to buy the block. Even with South Trust riding to the rescue, $11 million speculative land deals don't usually get done in seven days, the time between . . . [December] 27 and [January] 3. Perhaps in Texas, but not in Birmingham.

The city's involvement in the Block 60 project, Mendelson contended, may have damaged its possible success, since its participation encouraged too large an undertaking.

The destruction of Block 60 did not bring Arrington's troubles to an immediate end. The designation of the block as a blighted area by the city had never pleased many merchants. Disturbed by the term *blighted* and its legal implications, William S. Gibbs, owner of Tutwiler Drug, charged in a suit that the city had voted capriciously in characterizing the area. The case lingered in the courts for months, but in June 1983, Circuit Court Judge Jack Carl rendered a decision that further added to the rubble left by the Block 60 catastrophe. Carl ruled that the city had no legal foundation for the condemnation of commercial property for development by a private developer, and he removed Block 60's designation as blighted. Existing law that bore on condemnation, said the judge, related specifically to housing, not to business developments. It troubled Arrington and other officials that Carl accused the city's community-development staff of intentionally misleading the city council about the supposedly blighted condition of Block 60. The factual data collected by the department, wrote Carl, "is either false or so out of context . . . as to be materially . . . misleading."

Judge Carl's legal pronouncement came as a sharp blow to Arrington. Not only did he believe Carl had ignored relevant precedents in cases from other American cities where urban renewal had gone apace, but he was aware of the decision's possible impact upon the city's master plan for downtown development. Clearly, Birmingham needed condemnation powers if the city wanted to acquire large enough parcels of land to carry out redevelopment plans similar to Block 60, as well as smaller projects. Therefore, Arrington appealed Carl's ruling. A definitive ruling from the Alabama Supreme Court on the legal authority to undertake redevelopment in both residential and commercial areas, the mayor argued, was in the best interest not only of Birmingham but of other Alabama cities. On appeal the Alabama Supreme Court overturned the Carl decree.

Although Block 60 lay mortally wounded by a combination of deadly forces, the father of the city's master plan did not long mourn its death. Rumors of conspiracy and other charges did not keep the city council from approving a $7.5 million low-interest loan from federal funds to aid development projects of the Costa-Head company. Whatever Arrington may have concluded about the role of Costa, Grammas, Katopodis, and others in the defeat of his Block 60 project his overriding interest in downtown prompted him to support a Costa-Head development project called the Magic Place. When Costa-Head ran an advertisement that promoted the undertaking, it included supportive statements from five members of the city council, who labeled the project "a viable and attractive solution to the problems which existed downtown." The mayor himself applauded Costa-Head for showing confidence in Birmingham. Certainly any opposition to the Costa-Head proposal, or to any other reputable private development, would have appeared petty and may have cost Arrington support in some quarters.

No one could measure precisely the political damage the Block 60 collapse had upon Arrington. John Katopodis pledged not to make the issue a political question, and indeed he had avoided sharp attacks on the administration during the days immediately following the Block 60 failure. In great measure, of course, any criticism of the administration would have been self-criticism. But after the Carl ruling the politically ambitious Katopodis, with a mayoral election not far distant, tried to exploit the issue. He seized upon Carl's contention that the city's community-development department had misled the city council. That staff, he said, was "operating at the direction of the mayor, and Block 60 was the cornerstone of his [Arrington's] administration." The implication of Katopodis's statement was clear. Arrington would have to take full responsibility for failure of the project, even the alleged deception that had supposedly prompted the council to vote condemnation of Block 60. Whether Katopodis's strategy would bear fruit had to await a forthcoming election that pitted him against the man who had invested great faith in Birmingham and the city's downtown project.

7

The Spectre of Race:
A Police Chief and
a Council Race

.

More than any other issue, Richard Arrington's appointment of a police chief revealed the fears and frustrations associated with the election of a black mayor of Birmingham. From the beginning, many whites believed Arrington was "soft on crime," no matter what the actual record indicated. But they took some solace in the reality that the police force remained predominantly white and a symbol of control and white power in a town almost half black. Any change, or threat of change, in the police by a mayor with recognized liberal racial views raised fears among many whites, who imagined the unraveling of the social fabric and the demise of the old southern way of life. Would not black oppression of whites follow? And even if that did not take place, would not Birmingham become another Atlanta, with a high crime rate that threatened the safety of hardworking law-abiding citizens?

Arrington's past relationship with the police led to many of the assumptions that underlay the controversy surrounding the police-chief battle. Citizens who had followed city affairs knew of his fight against brutality, his insistence upon having more blacks in the police department, and his role in helping bring about a change in police shooting policy. In a city with high unemployment and a relatively high crime rate, what was there to protect the population if Arrington appointed a chief "soft on criminals" or, worse yet, a black chief? But the mayor was more interested in increasing the number of black police officers than he was in appointing a black police chief. When Arrington took office, Birmingham had approximately seven hundred officers, only sixty of them black. The black community believed that increased numbers of blacks on the police force would engender more respect for law and order. For too long, blacks contended, they had lived in a society that punished them for breaking the law but did not hire them to enforce it.

Arrington had moved aggressively to attack the troublesome issue of crime, but his antagonists dismissed or ignored his efforts. He had pledged to destroy the breeding place of illegal activity, especially the shothouses that infested some areas of the black community. He threw his personal reputation behind the move, and early in his administration the mayor symbolically oversaw the closing of one of the illegal houses. Sensitive to the strained relations between the police and black citizens, Arrington wanted to make sure that citizens understood that the mayor of the city had declared war on the shothouses and black-on-black crime. "We are going to have to deal with crime in the black community," he forthrightly told the press. He fired two policemen who had allegedly taken payoffs from shothouses, and he gave strong support to Police Chief Bill Myers, who established a special neighborhood task force that Arrington had supported during the campaign. The arrest of some sixty black people in mid-February 1980 showed the seriousness of the mayor's efforts. About the same time, Arrington and the city council were busily establishing a citywide lighting program to improve visibility within Birmingham neighborhoods, thereby, it was hoped, reducing the incidence of crime. Arrington also lifted the hiring freeze on police officers that former mayor David Vann had imposed as an economy move before he left office.

Arrington's approach to combating crime sent a clear message that he would give the police the resources and the backing necessary to make Birmingham a safe place. A part of his program, however, was a volunteer neighborhood-patrol system coordinated by the city's police department and structured to increase public awareness and participation in the fight against criminals. While Arrington's tough anticrime moves should have lessened the fears of white citizens, nagging doubts and ingrained attitudes did not suddenly disappear. And once the possibility of the appointment of a police chief by a black mayor became a real likelihood, old anxieties and new fears surfaced.

Mounting problems in the police department and conflicts with Chief Myers over policy greatly complicated Arrington's task and did not improve his image within the white community. Naturally he had not anticipated a passive response from the Fraternal Order of Police, which represented most of the white officers on the force, but he did expect them to acknowledge him as the city's legitimately elected leader, with ultimate power over the department. Represented by Officer Jimmy Williams, the FOP bitterly criticized actions of the mayor and even mildly chastised Myers for not forcefully supporting their position on key issues. The FOP attacked Arrington for overriding Myers's disciplinary decisions, especially those related to officers Bill Brown and Carl Harris. In Brown's case, the mayor rejected a departmental suspension for alleged involvement in a scandal at a local social club and, instead, fired him. Harris, a black officer, had killed a woman apparently justifiably, and Chief Myers had given him a written reprimand. Arrington, however, suspended the officer for having consumed more alcohol than he claimed before reporting for duty.

More than disputes over disciplinary actions invited police criticism of the mayor. A new shooting policy adopted by the city highly incensed FOP leaders, who said that it too narrowly restricted officers and, consequently, made it harder to enforce the law effectively. They also showed anger when Arrington charged that the FOP had engaged in disreputable tactics in misinforming the public about law enforcement and public safety. Arrington contended that the new shooting policy did not endanger the citizens of Birmingham. Antagonisms grew more inflamed when the mayor remarked that "the leadership of the FOP is still resentful of any authority which calls for fair, progressive, and even handed law enforcement" and that "police officers are servants of the public and not masters of the public who are themselves above the law."

The mayor's economic retrenchment program also triggered a skirmish with the police establishment. To reduce city expenditures and a deficit that stood near $3 million in 1980-81, Arrington called for a modest cutback in civilian personnel within the police department and a reduction in the rank of some officers, a proposal that emerged after much discussion at city hall. FOP leaders assailed the plan and painted a picture of gloom. They were disturbed that Arrington did not adopt a proposal submitted by Chief Myers that would have chopped a half million dollars from the budget by reducing or eliminating existing programs. The differences between Arrington and the FOP, however, went deeper than disciplinary actions and budgets. And they also involved more than race, although that was an important part of the clash.

The police force represented a powerful unit of city government, and it had a natural constituency, since every citizen had a stake in law and order. The degree to which the police won support from the black and white communities, however, differed. Police officers had an awareness of their strong backing and of the crucial role they played in the life of the community. They occupied a strong position from which they could press their objectives, and unlike some other city groups, they could easily draw attention to their demands. Police leaders remained mindful of their power; and that very power gave them an entrée to the mayor's office and compelled him to take seriously their requests.

Arrington refused to relinquish the responsibility given him by the electorate to make the final decisions that affected city departments. The FOP complained that the mayor had become too closely involved in departmental operations and policy, a charge the FOP had also made about Arrington's predecessors. Race aggravated tensions, but to interpret the relationship between Arrington and the police only in terms of race misses the mark. The FOP, wrote the 25 April 1980 *Birmingham Post-Herald*, "aspires to greater political influence than it is likely to achieve in the near future [and that is] a cause . . . of some frustration for the group." The paper also contended that many police officers found it hard to accept Arrington as the officially elected representative of the city.

Mounting problems also developed between the mayor and the

head of the police department. Myers had served on the Birmingham police force for nearly thirty years. Through his dedication he had risen steadily through the ranks, earning the respect of his fellow officers, his supervisors, and citizens. A deliberate man, he exuded a fundamental conservatism that reflected his years on the force and his place in the field of law enforcement in Alabama. While he had a good relationship with those around him, he did not fit the "hail-fellow-well-met" image that characterized the "good-ole-boy" syndrome. Years of service, attention to detail, and professional loyalty won him the police chief's position when James Parsons left for a similar position in New Orleans. By and large, Myers performed well under intense pressure, especially during the case of the Bonita Carter shooting, demonstrating a willingness to meet with the general public and with black leaders. After the mayoral election of 1979, rumors circulated of Arrington's desire to appoint a black chief. A meeting between the mayor and Myers, however, dispelled that notion, and most city-hall observers casually assumed that Myers would continue in his job, although he had expressed a willingness to resign if Arrington wanted someone else.

Myers found himself caught between the mayor and the FOP in disagreements over policy. A continuing source of friction was the chief's support of George Sands, a man the FOP continued to back. Arrington had suspended Bonita Carter's killer, but a favorable court decree eventually placed him back on the force. More troubling for Myers was his assumed lack of authority. There had been, Myers contended, "an accumulation of little things" that had helped to undermine his power in the department. A real problem for him was the pressure applied by the FOP, which disliked the mayor's policies and which regarded the chief as unwilling to take strong stands.

Myers must have known that previous mayors had overturned decisions of chiefs and other department heads. But he vowed to remain an active administrator rather than a figurehead who simply shuffled papers. In April 1980, with mounting pressure from police officers over Arrington's proposed cutbacks in the department, Myers again complained of the erosion of his influence and the decline in morale within the department, a condition that resulted, he implied, from his lack of decision-making power. "I will retire," he said after meeting with the mayor and Jimmy Williams of the FOP, "if I can not be the police chief this city needs—the police chief that is true to my nature and philosophy. . . . I have the professional ability, I believe. The question is the authority factor." If necessary, he would leave for the "good of the city." Myers bemoaned the lack of morale that allegedly existed in his department, but he shifted the blame away from himself and onto the mayor. Correcting departmental problems, he lamented, was difficult "when my decisions are not in fact regarded as decisions." The FOP and the chief implied that departmental morale would improve if the mayor let them handle personnel problems without interference from the mayor.

Arrington's resolute determination to carry out his delegated functions drew praise from the media. The 21 April 1980 *Birmingham News* recognized the problem of a police chief who became a figurehead, but a larger problem, in the paper's judgment, centered on the inability of some police officers to recognize the mayor's leadership and final authority. The city's other major paper took an even stronger position but praised Myer's record and the mayor's decision to retain the longtime veteran of police work. The *Birmingham Post-Herald* wrote that Myers and some policemen had improperly assigned wrong motives to the mayor. "There is no indication," the paper editorialized, "that Arrington wants to have a figurehead police chief," and it related the record of previous mayors in overturning disciplinary actions. In fact, said the 22 April 1980 *Post-Herald*, a new mayor should spend the early months of his administration "reviewing in greater detail than he will later, the decisions of his department heads." Reversal of decisions by a mayor did not necessarily reflect unfavorably upon a department head. The paper contended that "special racial perceptions" had created some of the problems. The FOP's distrust of Arrington and the question of race and police politics assured continuing controversy between the mayor and the men and women in blue.

By the summer of 1980, some of the conflict between the mayor and Myers had abated, or at least had become less public. The chief drew praise from the city council for his job, but pressures, nevertheless, did not quickly fade. Complaints continued from a few officers about Myers's stubbornness and his dictatorial manner in operating the department. Rumor circulated that the chief's resignation would pave the way for the possible appointment of Deputy Chief Tommy Rouse. Rouse, a strong-willed, self-assured, hard-driving veteran officer, had been the choice of some of his colleagues when Vann appointed Myers. Whatever the politics of the department and the intentions of FOP leadership, Arrington gave Myers a vote of confidence, and he expressed the belief that the two men could resolve their differences. Working through the mayor's aides (especially Willie Davis) had sometimes irritated the chief, and Arrington had agreed that he and Myers would communicate directly on "things of real substance."

The rapprochement between the mayor and the chief did not last. Only the sudden disappearance of the FOP would have brought peace between the two men. When Arrington proposed the creation of a police review committee to examine police shooting policy in the wake of a killing of a Birmingham burglary suspect, FOP leaders again went on the attack. A change in review policy, said representative Tommy Rouse, could hinder the fight against crime. Chief Myers agreed and defended the policy that gave officers the right to assume a suspect carried a weapon, although he expressed a willingness to discuss a change in procedure. When FOP leaders later blocked the adoption of a new shooting policy, Arrington harshly criticized them for distortions of that policy.

Chief Myers admitted to continuing pressure. It disappointed him that "every time we have a shooting we have a controversy." As a result, police morale remained low. The chief failed to stress, however, that the failure of the department to discipline severely some officers in the past had caused friction between the police and some segments of the community. A common view prevailed that policemen would protect each other, that loyalty demanded it, and that only in the most flagrant cases of wrongdoing would their department harshly discipline officers. History provided some support for this contention, although the city had made an effort under Vann and Arrington to encourage greater professionalism in carrying out law enforcement.

The police chief may have been able to resolve some of the problems with Arrington, but he found it difficult to survive the additional pressure generated by the FOP. Even if disciplinary and budgetary headaches had not existed, departmental irritations would have persisted. Myers found it hard to reject demands of the FOP, and he tried unsuccessfully to walk a tightrope between that organization and the mayor—an impossible task, given the FOP's opposition to the city's leader. To avoid recurring controversy and to enjoy "the peace of retirement," Myers resigned, effective January 1981.

The application and interpretation of the merit-system law produced conflict over Arrington's selection of Myers's replacement. Under state statute a county personnel board had the responsibility of administering rules and regulations of the civil-service system. The three-person board chose its own director from outside that body, who, incidentally, was not a civil servant; the director had no accountability to any elected governing body, a fact that disturbed Arrington. Of the three members who then sat on the board in 1981 (Henry P. Johnson, James Johnson, and Hiram Y. McKinney), only James Johnson was black. Before Arrington took office, heated controversy had occasionally followed board decisions, especially in cases where the board overturned police-department disciplinary action. Arrington argued that the merit-system law did not provide for adequate checks and balances that normally characterized government agencies that came under the control of elected officials.

Before Myers left office, Arrington and the personnel board director, Joseph Curtin, met to explore the guidelines for the selection of a police chief and to discuss the mayor's role in the process. Arrington expressed his desire for a wide-ranging search, but he did not exclude the hiring of a person already within the department. After his meeting with Curtin, Arrington disavowed any special effort to choose a black person for the job, but he stated plainly that color or sex would not serve as a disadvantage. The personnel director agreed to a national search, and he gave the mayor the opportunity to outline his qualifications for the job, although he could not make comments on the written portion of the police-chief examination.

The board's announcement for the chief's position specified entrance requirements and stipulated the kind of examination applicants had to take and the weight assigned each section of the test. The board also required some previous involvement in police work, but it made no absolute requirement of a college degree, a concession probably to the possible candidacy of Acting Chief Jack Warren, who did not finish college. However, he did have valuable years of experience in law enforcement. One of the most important sections of the job announcement provided that a candidate have the ability to manage a $19-million budget and an "innate sensitivity to social concerns and public relations." The rules provided that applicants receive examination results and that the board place those who passed on an eligibility list. The personnel office also had the responsibility of investigating the background of successful applicants.

In mid-January the mayor sent to Curtin further suggestions on recruitment and testing. Significantly, he gave much more weight to experience than did the board, and that input fueled the belief he had tailored his standards to fit Jack Warren. Had he been totally free to act, Arrington probably would have completely abandoned the written test, which put Warren in a much less competitive position. Warren had done poorest on the written examination when Birmingham had last chosen a chief of police. His long tenure on the police force was his greatest strength. And Arrington did not disguise his respect for him, a fact reflected in his choice of the police veteran to lead the department after Myers's departure. Warren had openly expressed his delight in working for Arrington. In fact, those who speculated that the mayor wanted to fashion standards for a black chief may have been more correct in contending that Arrington wanted to devise procedures that gave Warren a fighting chance at the chief's job. While his sixty-three years of age made no difference under law, his past drinking problem did bother some people. Arrington antagonist and city councilman John Katopodis wondered whether the position would cause additional stress for a recovering alcoholic. The mayor's favorable disposition toward Warren, however, became obscured by the controversy over the board's alleged discriminatory treatment of Arrington.

On 27 May the board sent the names of three eligible candidates to Arrington, although it had not made complete background checks on them. The top candidates comprised Arthur Deutsch, captain of detectives of the Brooklyn division of the New York City Police Department, Captain Tommy Rouse of Birmingham, and James Parsons, former chief of the Birmingham department. While the merit law placed no specific time limit on a selection, the board itself had allowed ten days for choosing one of the three top applicants for the job. By mid-June Arrington had made no pick, and rumblings developed over the delay, especially since Warren (who, incidentally, had not made the board's top five) had served as acting chief since December 1980. But no specific law governed the tenure of a temporary appointment, and authority remained with the Jefferson County Personnel Board to make a determination on the service of an acting official.

As June drew closer to an end, all signs indicated that choosing a chief would become a heated and involved process. Although Curtin and the mayor had reached an apparent understanding when the two met and when Arrington later announced his intention of appointing a chief within fifteen days, no one could have possibly anticipated the series of events that delayed the process for many weeks. A possible clue to serious problems between the board and Arrington came when the mayor unveiled a list of some thirteen requirements for the chief's job after he received the board's three names. He declined to comment on the applicants he had already received, and he strongly hinted at the rejection of candidates who did not fit the standards he had tailored. But the mayor had not decided to dismiss arbitrarily all board candidates to force an early showdown with Curtin. Press reports mistakenly gave rise to that idea, and some of Arrington's statements further strengthened that belief. Before his interviews with the candidates the mayor had said that, if Curtin did not permit rejection of *some* or *all* of the names, the process might grind to a halt. From the beginning, Curtin maintained that a "specific and valid reason" had to exist to oust a candidate and that the mayor could acquire new names only if a person dropped out of contention for the job or had been turned down three times.

Curtin soon discovered that the mayor took seriously the possibility of rejecting one or more of the board's top three candidates. In early July 1981, Arrington turned down James Parsons, and he asked for another name. Obviously disturbed by the dismissal of the board's top-ranked candidate, Curtin asked the mayor for specific reasons for his actions. The candidate, said the mayor, had expressed boredom with his job before leaving Birmingham as chief of police. More crucially, Parsons had faced serious racial problems in his tenure in New Orleans, where blacks had charged some of his officers with brutality. Parsons's most difficult moment had come after the shooting of four blacks, following the killing of a policeman. Although he expressed disappointment with the mayor's rejection, it did not surprise Parsons, who probably had anticipated the outcome.

The former chief had his supporters while in Birmingham, but he also had strong detractors who openly expressed their views. Jerris Leonard, the director of the Law Enforcement Assistance Administration (LEAA), praised Parsons highly for his "exceptional leadership" in leading the city's police department. "Some of the things going on in the Birmingham Police Department rank with programs of the finest Police Departments in the country," Leonard had told a city council meeting before Parson's departure. But police chiefs have a way of also encouraging a critical view of their work, and Parsons was no exception. "Birmingham deserves more," wrote one resident harshly critical of Parsons's public and personal behavior. A citizen of the city for forty-eight years threatened to move his business elsewhere if Arrington reappointed the former chief. He had no sense of fairness, a correspondent informed the mayor, and "the best thing that has happen[ed] to Birmingham was when he left our city." He should have "stayed down south," another person bitterly exclaimed. One concerned voter wrote that, if Arrington put Parsons back in as chief, the mayor could forget his vote. The strong letters against the former chief provided an indication of the public feeling against him. Parsons's lamentable failure in New Orleans and the knowledge Arrington acquired of the former chief from confidential sources had far more influence on his refusal to appoint him than any other factors.

The *Birmingham News* understood the board's request for more specific information about Parsons from the mayor, but the paper had an appreciation for the issues raised by Arrington. The editor of the *News* wrote on 11 July 1981:

> For the mayor's part—and despite what candidate Parsons says—he is not trying to hand pick a yes man or make a spoils appointment so much as he is trying to find the man he considers to be the most competent and one with whom he thinks he can get along. And, he has some legitimate concerns about Parsons. The former chief's New Orleans problems deserve close scrutiny and his statement upon retiring from the Birmingham post that he was "bored" with the job should cause anyone taking an objective look at the situation at the very least to question his enthusiasm.

The board dropped Parsons from the eligible list. The decision to scratch him, however, led a citizen to complain heatedly that Arrington now had "supreme power to accept or reject any policy regardless of precedent." And he asked rhetorically, "Does Birmingham now have a king to whom all must bow down?" Parsons's elimination now pushed Birmingham police captain Tommy Rouse to the top of the list, with Deutsch ranked second. The newcomer on the list was Michael O'Mara, chief administrator of the office of the Cook County State's Attorney. O'Mara later withdrew, and his replacement became Captain Richard Townes, a Birmingham officer, followed by a colleague with the same rank, George Howze.

The replacement of Parsons and the elevation of Tommy Rouse to the top position on the eligibility list did not end the stalemate between the mayor and the board. Rouse, a hardworking officer, had risen through the ranks. He projected a self-assured attitude which struck some of his colleagues and acquaintances as arrogance, an image created in part by the extent of his education and an apparent need to make people aware of it. Rouse took seriously his ambitions. At one point in his conflict with the city's black mayor over the chief's job, he proclaimed, "I perform. I'm a winner"; and he said, "I'd be doing a disservice to the citizens, the department, and the mayor if I dropped out of the race." Rouse had voiced displeasure when the city passed over him for the head police job at the time of Myers's appointment. Yet, he had done little to endear himself to the people at city hall that held appointive power. In fact, Rouse, along with FOP official Jimmy Williams, became sharp critics of Arrington, which could not have possibly commended him to the black politician.

Very compelling reasons also forced Arrington to reject Rouse and to request that the personnel board replace him with another person. Curtin, however, insisted that the mayor adhere to the ten-day appointment deadline and make his decision by 14 August 1981. Moreover, the board applied added pressure by threatening to stop Acting Chief Warren's pay if he continued to fill the post, a threat Arrington countered by raising the possibility of heading the department himself if Warren's salary was stopped.

The threat to remove Warren did not force acceptance of a man Arrington had no intention of appointing. The mayor viewed Rouse as immature and undiplomatic, a belief further reinforced when Rouse told the mayor in an interview that he had no objection to his children's playing with those of his black boss. But more serious professional reasons prompted intense opposition to Rouse. Arrington accused him of deliberately falsifying a question on his application. When asked if he had been suspended from duty on the Birmingham police force, the candidate had answered no. The truth was that, in 1967, Police Chief Jamie Moore had discharged Rouse, who, with his partner, had allegedly picked up two teenage girls while on duty, given them liquor, and then had sexual relations with them. When Rouse appealed his case, the Jefferson County Personnel Board overturned Moore's action. Instead, the young officer received a ninety-day suspension. Although the board had vetoed the original punishment, its subsequent action clearly specified Rouse's failure to adhere properly to procedures, even if it did not specifically address the alleged violations.

The revelation of Rouse's past problems brought an angry retort from the candidate, but his response did little to strengthen his case in the city or within the police department, where some fellow officers already disliked him or had reservations about his ability to work cooperatively with others. It was hard for Rouse to escape the criticism that he had been guilty of deliberate omission when he failed to inform the personnel board's interview panel of his discharge by Moore. Technically, Rouse had been disciplined by the board for conduct unbecoming a police officer. "It is the only blemish on my record," he told a news conference during the heat of the controversy. He had learned from the unfortunate experience. But Rouse confessed to nothing more than a mere "rules infraction," not to the more serious charges brought by Moore. He had served the city well, and the discussion surrounding his application had done "a great disservice" to his family and to his career. Ironically, Rouse and the FOP contended throughout the Arrington years that a chief should be allowed to discipline a police officer, but apparently they did not believe in this principle in 1967 when Rouse's supervisor, Moore, dismissed him, only to have that decision overturned by the board.

Curtin's insistence upon keeping Rouse's name on the eligibility list puzzled the mayor and brought the harshest words of the long, involved, and heated selection process. Although Arrington had been restrained in his public comments, the continuing recalcitrance of the personnel board forced him to adopt a more critical posture toward the board's shoddy work in investigating eligible candidates. He directed verbal fire at Curtin specifically, who had earlier made little effort to conceal his attitude toward Rouse. "When I received the initial [eligibility] list," said Arrington, Curtin stated that Rouse was "not a candidate I would want to appoint." Moreover, the mayor contended, the director informed him that he could reject a candidate for immaturity and that it could be done quickly under board rules that provided the right to remove a name from the eligible list after a three-time rejection.

Arrington ultimately rejected Rouse seven times, but Curtin and his colleagues proved intractable. The case eventually went to court. In a gesture to end the standoff over the selection process, Curtin agreed to remove Rouse's name if the mayor would choose a chief from the first four names on the eligible list. But Arrington would not consent to this arrangement. Nor would he pledge to appoint from the first six or seven names. The drama continued. The heart of Arrington's argument—the real challenge to the board— came in his comments about Rouse's rejection. "My position," he noted, "has always been, and remains, to select a Police Chief from the *three best qualified candidates on the eligible list.*" Obviously here was something different from the *top three candidates* chosen by the personnel board.

Amid rumors that Arrington might appoint himself as police chief, the personnel board went to court to force the mayor to meet a prescribed deadline. At the heart of the executive's argument for his actions was that he actually did not have three *acceptable* candidates, and that contention contained some truth, since Arrington had repeatedly rejected Rouse. On the other hand, the board maintained the eligibility of the Birmingham policeman. Determined to effect its will after Arrington had ignored a 14 August deadline, the board joined a suit brought by former candidate James Parsons to mandate Arrington's immediate selection of a chief. In presenting its case, the board accused the mayor of frustrating the civil-service process and of opposing standards established by the Jefferson County Personnel Board. The suit reasserted the board's right to establish eligibility requirements, and it termed Arrington's failure to appoint a chief an illegal act without foundation in law.

The mayor strongly defended his case when it came before Jefferson County Circuit Court Judge Jack Carl. In his testimony he criticized the personnel board for its incomplete background check of candidates. In the past, he said, his office had sometimes received names of persons who had criminal records. He had no intention of placing himself beyond the civil-service law. Arrington forcefully maintained, however, that a three-time rejection of a candidate removed him from further consideration. Despite Arrington's defense, Carl ruled that the board had authority to force an appointment from the mayor within ten days after sending him three certified names. The judge did not demand an immediate appointment from Arrington, since the board had not yet made complete background checks of candidates. Disappointed, Arrington continued to complain of his discriminatory treatment compared to other Birmingham mayors, but he pledged "not to be a hero . . . by letting a judge put me in jail." The conflict between the mayor and the board was as much a political power issue as a racial one.

While the legal skirmish took place, Arrington rejected another of the board's three choices. When Captain Michael O'Mara withdrew from the chief's race, his replacement became Birmingham police captain Richard Townes, who waived his candidacy for a period up to six months. Although considered by some as one of Arrington's favorites, Townes did not possess the experience of the other "favorite," Jack Warren, and the mayor never really seriously contemplated his appointment. Nor did he have any plans for choosing officer George Howze. When that candidate's name came to Arrington, he rejected it and gave his reasons in a letter to the personnel board. Experience, he told Curtin, showed that "Howze's behavior can be characterized as unpredictable and, at times, somewhat bizarre." He also had an attitude of superiority and insensitivity toward others and an intolerance toward opinions different from his own. The mayor also noted that two groups had come to city hall to request his veto of Howze because of his "questionable behavior."

When the board stood resolute in upholding the candidate's certification, the mayor provided more information on Howze in a personal appearance before the group. But even his testimony and that of three police officers with a combined service of more than twenty-six years did not prove persuasive enough for Curtin and the board. In the judgment of the officers, Howze often equivocated, made uninformed judgments, showed irrational tendencies, had a volatile temper, and engaged in intemperate outbursts. Most damaging was Howze's failure to communicate properly with those around him. Only one of the three board members, James Johnson, voted not to send Howze's name back to the mayor. Curtin wrote Arrington on 8 October 1981, "The Personnel Board and I . . . deem your reasons for removing George C. Howze from the certification list to be insufficient."

Stymied by the board, the mayor decided to take his case to the people. All along he felt that the press had concentrated too much on his decisions, while the actions of the personnel board had received little critical examination. After concluding that a press conference alone would not enable him to inform the public adequately about the behind-the-scenes dealings that had shaped the controversy, the mayor decided to issue an open letter to the citizens of Birmingham. Questions raised over the cost for newspaper space were resolved when the *Birmingham News* asked him to contribute an article to the paper. In a detailed three-thousand-word letter the mayor skillfully retraced events of the selection process on 18 October 1981, as he carefully defended his role in the affair. Essentially his task was twofold: to acquaint the citizens more fully with the facts surrounding his decisions and, politically, to lessen any unfavorable fallout that had resulted from delay in appointing a chief.

Although the mayor's letter reflected a low-key approach to the problem, it did contain some harsh criticism of the personnel board, which had conspired, in his opinion, to treat him differently from previous chief executives. He placed the blame for delay upon the board. "The truth is that in the past," he wrote in discussing the role of the personnel board, "it has been necessary to go beyond the top three names to find candidates suitable for . . . [an] appointment." Curtin's attitude and his actions during the selection process, Arrington alleged, blatantly indicated that he was treating the appointment differently than others. The mayor wanted an even-handed application of board rules.

Following a discussion of the creation of an eligibility list and of the candidacy of Rouse and Howze, the mayor focused his letter upon operating procedures of the board. How the board had weighed training and experience puzzled him, when only sketchy data existed from some candidates. And its testing program, although well intentioned, was "wholly inadequate." Delay in appointment of a chief, Arrington further criticized, had resulted from belated background checks of candidates and because of the board's refusal to accept the mayor's findings. The letter restated the criteria the mayor believed necessary for appointment of a police chief. He did not desire a yes-man, but an appointee had to feel comfortable as an integral part of a management team.

How much Arrington's letter helped to shape public opinion is difficult to assess. But it did contain several features of considerable merit. It was a readable document, easy for the citizen to grasp, and it had no condescending language or harsh tone. It also demonstrated a sensitivity toward the problems of the personnel director, despite sharp criticism of him. Curtin's integrity never came under attack, only his judgment and his application of board rules and regulations. But the mayor argued well his own position. He again advanced evidence, some of it new, to justify rejection of Rouse and Howze, and he played the role of historian in presenting facts to prove that the board had treated him differently from other mayors. He put the board on the defensive by exposing some of the weaknesses of the testing process and the casual way it had conducted background investigations. For the first time, he openly applied pressure upon Curtin by releasing previously withheld information about Captain Rouse. Although the mayor stated his adherence to the present merit law, his statement argued for new civil-service rules that gave appointing officials much greater latitude in appointments.

Pressure from many sources came upon Arrington to put the police-chief appointment behind him. In a 21 October 1981 letter to T. B. Sheehan of the Midland Division of the Dexter Corporation, the mayor explained what he had tried to do in deciding upon a chief. He again sounded the refrain of fair play and equal treatment. He wrote Sheehan:

> You must understand, sir, that for me to appoint a police chief under the circumstances would be similar to asking you or your company to accept a ruling by the Federal Government that all other companies of your kind could file . . . taxes under the current rules, but Midland must do so each night by sun down! That would be outrageous, would it not? Chances are your company would fight such an [unequal] application of the law with all of its resources. It's the principle that counts.

Arrington had complained that the media often misquoted him or failed to grant proper coverage to his actions. It must have been encouraging, then, when the 17 October 1981 *Birmingham Post-*

Herald carried an editorial about the police-chief controversy. Although the *Post-Herald* saw some stubbornness in the black executive, it placed greatest blame upon Joe Curtin and personnel board members who had "thwarted the mayor's efforts" in selecting the best candidate for the chief's position. And the editor of the paper criticized the board's "sham background investigation" of Rouse and Howze.

Whatever the merits of Arrington's arguments, they were not sufficient to prevent Judge Carl from ordering him to meet a deadline of 12 November 1981 for the appointment of a chief. Anxious not to delay the process further, the mayor chose the man who had been among the remaining candidates for the chief's job, Arthur V. Deutsch. The mayor had become more impressed with him compared to his other choices on the list, and the appointment caused him no great pains. In fact, given Arrington's strong feelings toward Rouse and Howze, Deutsch was the only possible selection among the top three candidates.

The New York City officer brought considerable strengths to the Birmingham police. The forty-nine-year-old native of Brooklyn had spent twenty-six years on the New York City police force, and at the time of his appointment he had recently been promoted to commander of a Brooklyn detective zone. His district had given him experience in working with people of various backgrounds, and he was no stranger to the concept of affirmative action, since he had introduced a plan when he commanded a New York City precinct. An occasional writer, Deutsch had authored a novel about a detective who worked off-duty as a hit man for the Mafia. But whether he could master the challenge of Birmingham's seven-hundred-member force in a city where race was still an important consideration, only time would tell.

Near the end of the police-chief controversy, Birmingham held city-council elections. In September 1981, Arrington had openly voiced his concern about the forthcoming contest. In tying the police-chief controversy to the upcoming political battle, he said that a move existed in the city to elect councillors opposed to him. Arrington charged that the Moral Majority, a conservative political movement with its base in fundamentalist white churches, had been trying to solidify public support and to organize a campaign for a conservative council.

The black mayor aggressively accepted the challenges of those who wanted to make the council race a referendum on his administration. Although he praised the present city council for its support, he naturally wanted a greater majority that reflected his philosophy of government. But he rejected color alone as a basis for election to office; and he steadfastly refused to predict whether the Jefferson County Citizens Coalition would endorse a mixed or an all-black slate. When asked about the advisability of having a black majority on the council, the mayor emphatically argued that that was neither good nor bad. The council had always had a white majority, and in 1981 that situation still existed in a city that had a population with a slim black majority.

In January 1981, Arrington had talked with several people who wanted his backing in the city elections. When Dr. Margaret B. Little wrote him belatedly about support for a council seat, the mayor sent her a letter that revealed his interest in trying to achieve greater racial balance on the council. He told Little in his correspondence of 29 July 1981:

> In the past few months I have made what I consider . . . firm commitments to five persons to support their candidacy, providing our organization, the Citizens Coalition, agrees to endorse them. Should either of these five persons . . . not be endorsed by the organization or not run for some reason, I would be more than happy to lend my active support to your race since I feel that you and these persons I've referred to represent the caliber of individuals who would make valuable contributions to our city as elected officials.

As his correspondence showed, Arrington did not casually assume the endorsement by the coalition of persons he personally supported. While the organization was his own creation, it contained men and women of great independence and critical judgment who did not operate in a political vacuum. Although highly revered, Arrington was no dictator to blacks, many of whom had fought "in the trenches of civil rights" to make possible social and political progress in the Magic City.

Arrington's coalition ultimately became the focus of the election, and for many whites an object of disdain. The "machine," as its enemies derisively called it, had a short history, but the group had grown into a powerful entity among blacks in Jefferson County. To comprehend the 1981 election, then, one must understand something about black political development in Birmingham. For many years before the appearance of the coalition, the only black political organization in the area was the Jefferson County Progressive Democratic Council, founded in the 1930s. Although loosely affiliated with the national party at its origin, it had little association with the segregated local party. Organized and supported by such leaders as Arthur Shores, W. C. Patton, and Odie Hancock, the council focused most of its attention on black voter registration and black political unity. Since only a few blacks in that era exercised the ballot or ran for public office, the organization worked for a unified black vote and for the election of racially moderate white candidates. Blacks, of course, had no choice but to pick from all-white slates that favored the continuation of segregation, but politicians did not openly court them, for fear of rejection by white voters.

The council's strength in the black community, much like that of the later coalition, belied the size of its actual membership. A loosely knit organization, it had units across the city and a central body composed of three representatives and three alternates from each individual group. The small number of members who participated in its monthly meetings never reflected the real interest in the organization, especially during an election period. For more than thirty years under the aggressive leadership of attorney Arthur Shores, the council sponsored rallies, brought in speakers, and distributed pamphlets to generate enthusiasm for its programs. Shores and his successor, David Hood, used the Democratic Council not only as a base for political action but as an important tool in their fight against segregation. Their determined efforts brought recognition from the national party, and in 1956 both Hood and Shores attended the national convention as delegates. Later, the Democratic Council won some recognition from the white State Democratic Committee because of a legal ruling by Judge Hobart Grooms, father of Angi Grooms (Proctor), who sat with Arrington on the city council.

The black group experienced growth and increased political power under the leadership of David Hood. The organization had eight units in the county when Hood took over, but by the mid-eighties there were forty-seven. The dramatic developments in civil rights buoyed blacks, especially the passage of the 1965 Voting Rights Act, which ended the systematic elimination of black citizens from the ballot box. But with growth and increased activity, however, came some internal problems and some dissatisfaction among its supporters. Black political power brokers showed no less inclination to avoid controversy than did their white counterparts.

One of the council's severest critics was editor Emory O. Jackson of the *Birmingham World*. Jackson had despaired of the "old black leadership." In a number of editorials he called for change, and in 1973 he had suggested the formation of a black leadership conference that would work for improved city services in the black community. The *Birmingham World*, wrote Jackson on 3 March 1973, almost as an affront to men such as Arthur Shores and W. C. Patton, "is proud of the new community leadership coming forward." His disappointment with black leadership had much to do with what he called the "grits-eating crowd" of the Community Affairs Committee of Operation New Birmingham. "Our leaders," he warned, "closed-door and others, need to be warned that Negro voters are growing impatient with bandwagon politics."

Before his death Jackson launched a scathing attack upon the Democratic Council. He had consistently complained that the group really made no demands upon politicians—did not "hold their feet to the fire." He maintained that the council should have systematic evaluations of politicians, especially those on the Birmingham City Council. Moreover, he charged that the organization was often uncritical in its screening of candidates who ran for government office, and he criticized the group for its failure to publicize the yardstick by which it measured office seekers. Jackson speculated that the council had not formulated any meaningful goals, and to him that failure represented "[defective] political action and perhaps is responsible for the unsatisfactory situation of the Negro group which represents 42 percent of the Birmingham population." The editor, who won recognition for his fight against police commissioner Eugene "Bull" Connor in 1963, said that some formerly strong leaders had been weakened by their method of operation. Some of the editor's barbs went toward A. G. Gaston and David Hood, who sat on Gaston's Savings and Loan board of directors, and toward Arthur Shores and W. C. Patton.

Jackson subjected Shores in particular to harsh attacks. At one point during the attorney's council years, the editor called on him to support the goals of the black community or resign. Shores's hesitancy in endorsing affirmative action and his initially lukewarm support of a black cable company greatly irritated Jackson. The *World's* editor viewed Shores as a symbol of the old, staid leadership that had lost its drive. "For some unknown reason," he complained bitterly in one editorial, "organizations like the NAACP, the Alabama Christian Movement for Human Rights . . . and the Metropolitan Business Association no longer speak out on issues vital to blacks." Jackson wrote perceptively in July 1973 that Birmingham had a hidden black leadership that "is building strength where it counts while some of the have-it-made black leaders are allowing their potential to dwindle away."

Arrington had become part of that new, youthful black leadership to which Jackson alluded. Like the black editor, he was a member of the Progressive Democratic Council, and he had once been encouraged to run for office by David Hood. In time Arrington also became a critic of some council actions, especially the slate-selection process, and that issue, more than any other, caused him to sever times with the organization. Under council procedure the president appointed a screening committee that decided which candidates to recommend to the body. In making choices, members of the committee considered such factors as background, experience, education, and contributions to the community.

Arrington served for a time as a Hood-appointed member of the council screening committee. In 1977, he dissented from the endorsement of a group of candidates that included the name of a person he opposed. Hood requested that Arrington introduce the slate to the organization, but a speaking engagement in Tuscaloosa prevented him from performing this task. Upon his return to the city, Arrington discovered that the slate remained intact and that the person he supported, Jeff Germany, had been completely overlooked. This failure, according to Arrington, violated an agreement to place Germany on the ballot in place of one of the other candidates. Hood's explanation, however, was different. He maintained that "Dr. Arrington offered an amended report [to the selection committee report] to include the name of Jeff Germany . . . [and] the council overrode that." Shortly after the conflict the disappointed Arrington set up the coalition, although he also remained a member of the council. The break created obvious tensions between Hood and the founder of the new organization, although Hood denied that there were any hard feelings. "There has been no real animosity," he said seven years after the break, "despite what may appear to be the case." And Hood pointed quickly to the support his group gave Arrington in the 1979 runoff election, ignoring the council's failure to endorse Arrington over Vann in the primary.

The break between Arrington and the council involved more than the conflict over Jeff Germany and the city-council slate. What Councilman Arrington wanted was greater participation by young black people in politics. Like Emory O. Jackson before him, Arrington was concerned about a once-aggressive black leadership whose energies, time and too many hard battles had sapped. The old black leadership struggled to maintain its power and influence, and it often gave little opportunity to others in making community choices. The hoarding of power greatly disturbed Arrington and younger members of the council.

Organized by Arrington in 1977, the Birmingham–Jefferson County Citizens Coalition quickly eclipsed the Democratic Council in political power. A kind of "holding company" of organizations for black groups, it wanted "to speak with one voice on issues that affected black people in Birmingham." Nonpartisan, it included Democrats and a few Republicans, such as Justice Oscar Adams of the present Alabama Supreme Court. The coalition, like the council, had units throughout the city and a political screening committee with representation from the various communities. Arrington used citizens' participation groups as a base, and he wisely cultivated their presidents. That approach represented a masterful political stroke, since it gave the new organization access to thousands of black voters. It was fundamental to give community leadership a voice; and in a subtle criticism of the council, which also reflected Arrington's philosophy, the future mayor of Birmingham remarked after the establishment of his group that, "when you give people the opportunity to participate, they usually let their leader move without overbearing restrictions, but they do not want to be closed out on key decisions."

Hood and the Democratic Council had originally joined the coalition. Continuing friction, however, finally forced a complete break. A staunch Democrat, Hood disliked Republican participation from the outset, especially the role of Judge Adams in addressing some issues. On the other hand, Arrington continued to bristle when Hood tried to close him off from the council, to keep him from speaking of the coalition at regular meetings. Moreover, Arrington could still see the old-guard leadership at work. So with the exit of the Jefferson County Democratic Council went the political arm of the coalition, which now became its own political organization. Some cooperation has been evident between the two groups, and with only a few striking exceptions, they have supported many of the same candidates. There can be little doubt, as Arthur Shores stated in 1983, that the coalition "became more powerful than [anyone] expected." The council, said Shores, had become too complacent.

The growth of the coalition's power and influence disturbed the leadership of the Democratic Council, and it also had a political impact on white politicians who needed to win its allegiance. The 1979 mayoral election had shown Arrington's ability to mobilize for political action and to operate effectively at the grass-roots level without large sums of money. What concerned many whites was the unity the coalition achieved in the black community, despite the circumstances that led to its creation. While the organization attempted to acquaint citizens with the major issues that faced the city's black community, politicians such as John Katopodis dubbed it a "machine," concerned principally with getting people to the polls. Supporters, of course, rejected what they considered a narrow, unobjective view of Arrington's group. And they contended that such an analysis was an elitist view or that it symbolized a fear of political mobilization in a city where blacks had rapidly approached an electoral majority.

The coalition and race were the major issues in the 1981 council election. Community revitalization, crime, city services, or economic development never really occupied center stage in the contest. As the press carried reports of the coalition's backing of an all-black slate, some whites organized to prevent a "takeover" of the city. A member of one white political-action group mirrored the position of many whites when, conceding a need for black representation, he saw an all-black slate as "a racist thing." Forgotten in the emotionalism of the election was the support of an all-white-slate by a political group in 1979, when Arrington ran for mayor. It availed little to speak of Arrington's past endorsement of white candidates or the coalition's past enthusiasm for an integrated slate. The possibility of sharing more political power sent tremors through white Birmingham, for a black-dominated council conjured up social horrors, just as Arrington's election had done. Blacks had "won" in 1979, and now they stood at the political threshold of all-out victory. For some whites, racial disaster knocked, and fear struck those who had given little thought to historic white domination of the council and city government.

At the time of the election Arrington was not the coalition's chairman. He did have enormous influence within the group, although the organization did not blindly approve every one of his requests. And the group and its creator found it relatively easy to agree on issues and upon candidates for office. Political organizations have usually endorsed candidates for office who supported their general philosophy or programs and who advanced proposals to address specific issues. The coalition was no different.

The mayor saw the election of candidates antagonistic to his programs as a blow to progress, as a means of turning back the clock of reform and racial harmony. Sensitive to this possibility he wrote members of the black clergy in September 1981 that the city-council election "will directly affect and influence all of us." He asked for their cooperation and support, since the contest would have "far reaching effects [upon] our economic, social and political survival . . . in Birmingham–Jefferson County." He requested a select group of businessmen to meet with him at the A. G. Gaston Restaurant to discuss city problems and the importance of the forthcoming council battle. The mayor spelled out his major concern when he wrote them on 24 September 1981:

> We face a great challenge in our city. It is a challenge to continue the city's progress and to avoid the racial division which threatens to move the city backwards. There are extremist forces in our City which, while speaking of unity and cooperation, have been raising money and organizing workers to take control of city government. How we shall deal with this and similar threats is a matter of utmost importance.

The mayor's effort in support of coalition candidates gave rise to greater political activity within the white community, especially among conservative, propolice groups. The strongest of these organizations was led by James Parsons, the former police chief Arrington had rejected in his bid for his old job. Determined to stop the mayor's "steamroller" by electing conservatives who would "stand up to Arrington," Parsons's group spoke for the FOP and those whites who felt they had lost grip on their city. "Law and order," however, served as a convenient issue, especially with the police-chief controversy at hand and with the emphasis on crime in Birmingham. But law and order really masked the attempt to achieve greater control over the council and the city's black mayor.

The coalition's all-black slate included incumbent William Bell, Patricia Davis, Eddie Blankenship, Charles Crockrom, and Roosevelt Bell. The mayor could not easily reject his organization's choices, but he wrestled hard with the reelection campaign of Nina Miglionico. Miglionico had largely supported the mayor's programs, and she had demonstrated the soberness of action and political balance that had won her genuine affection in many quarters. Although she had adamantly refused to agree to an out-of-court settlement of a suit brought by the family of Bonita Carter, she and the mayor had worked harmoniously on most other major issues that faced the city. While not the classic stereotype of the American racial liberal, Miss Nina harbored few of the antiquated social notions that once characterized Birmingham and that still lingered to disturb life in the Magic City. A lawyer, she was a real booster of Birmingham and prided herself in guarding the city's finances and the administration of equal justice. Although she was a quiet woman of small stature, she could display a toughness that belied her gentle appearance.

Miglionico partisans expressed dismay at her exclusion from the coalition's slate. Not only had the organization endorsed all blacks, but it had now ignored one of the more moderate councillors up for reelection. The coalition had initially opted for the endorsement of only five candidates, since more would contribute to the dilution of the black vote and, consequently, aid those opposed to the mayor and to changes in government. Lewis Spratt, chairman of the coalition in 1981, had difficulty explaining Miglionico's exclusion to the press. While he noted that the mayor had declared Miss Nina one of the ten or twelve persons up for election with whom he could work, Miglionico actually did not have an interview with the coalition's screening committee. Some effort did take place to reconsider the initial slate, with the possibility of removing Patricia Davis. But Davis's supporters united, and the coalition's political-action committee left the slate intact. Councilman David Herring, not up for reelection but ideologically close to Miss Nina, thought the mayor had actually pledged to do more in his friend's behalf. Herring excused Arrington from any blame, but others contended that his lieutenants could have acted more persuasively in pressing the councilwoman's cause.

The Miglionico problem cried out for some kind of creative solution. Less than a day after the publication of the coalition's "final" endorsements, a flyer surfaced with a slate of candidates that also included Miglionico! Some of the councilwoman's supporters, however, accused the coalition of not widely circulating its second ballot. Even Miglionico claimed not to have seen the preelection sample ballot although one of the mayor's aides, Willie Davis, supposedly received one at a church service. Spratt now encountered more difficulty in explaining Miss Nina's first exclusion, then the later unusual inclusion of the white candidate. Skirting the issue, he told one reporter that his group had given support to the best candidates who would work for all the people.

Not even the best political scientist could predict the outcome of a primary contest where thirty-seven candidates competed for five seats on the Birmingham City Council. Arrington and supporters had invested considerable time and energy in the campaign, and so had their opponents. Rarely in the recent history of the city had a contest attracted such attention and generated so much emotionalism. When the voting ended, the coalition slate had scored a thunderous victory that momentarily shook up white Birmingham. All of the group's candidates were among the top ten contestants for office, with the popular William Bell topping the field. Only two whites, John Katopodis and Bill Myers, came within the top seven! Even E. C. "Doc" Overton, who had sat on the council since its creation in 1963, went down to defeat. And an endorsement by the now-weakened Democratic Council could not prevent his twelfth-place finish in a race that sent only the top ten to the runoff. Miglionico, however, survived the battle of the slates, although it is not certain how much the coalition's second sample ballot aided her, since longtime black supporters may have again voted for her without an endorsement. With the help of black votes in 1977, Miss Nina had won a council seat without a runoff.

The 1981 primary contest undoubtedly had some relationship to Arrington's performance as mayor and how some citizens perceived his role in the campaign. While that relationship is difficult to measure, the election did clearly reflect the continuation of some notable political patterns in the city, but also some deviation from past practices. In many ways, noted one analyst, the council primary (and the later runoff) offered few surprises. As a rule, "white voters chose white candidates and black voters preferred blacks." As had been the case since the late seventies, blacks turned out in a higher percentage than did whites (48 percent and 43 percent, respectively).

Black voters showed more of a tendency than whites to cross over. Miglionico received 18 percent of the black vote, Overton nearly 11 percent, and Katopodis 6 percent. Other candidates received a much smaller percentage. White crossover ballots for black candidates were much fewer. The city's liberal Southside—the "swing" vote—where Arrington had done well in 1979, was less inclined to vote for blacks in the 1981 council race. Only Helen Shores Lee among black candidates received more than 20 percent of the white vote, a testimony, some alleged, to her endorsement by a propolice group and to her conservative posture. (Interestingly, the conservative former police chief Bill Myers won nearly 71 percent of the white Southside vote.) With one exception, all candidates had more than a 6 percent crossover vote in the primary in the 1977 election. According to Tom Fletcher, Birmingham City Council administrator, "Crossover [voting] was generally less prevalent in the council election . . . than in 1977"; and he noted that, while race had previously been a factor, a larger percentage of voters did cast their ballots on the basis of race in 1981. He reasoned correctly that the highly publicized slates of endorsed candidates had a significant effect on both blacks and whites.

The strength displayed by the candidates Arrington supported in the primary did not automatically spell victory for any of them in the runoff. The mayor recognized that a solid black vote alone would not produce a majority on the council unless some whites split their ballots; and there was no guarantee that blacks would deliver a solid vote for coalition candidates. The mayor was also a realistic politician who could count. Of the 146,862 registered voters in Birmingham in 1981, only slightly over 47 percent were black. Total victory for coalition candidates would require a unified black vote and support from some white areas (for example, the Southside). Complete victory would mean a council with six blacks and three whites. For a black to expect general white support from across the city, however, amounted to wishful thinking, if history was any guide. Arrington also knew that an increase in the number of whites at the polls with little crossover voting (which had been the case in the primary) could actually reduce the number of blacks on the council, leaving only Jeff Germany on that body.

A large number of possibilities existed, and Arrington was determined that coalition candidates not lose by default. To support those contestants solidly, the mayor sent a letter to some citizens who apparently did not vote in the 13 October primary, urging them to cast their ballot in the 3 November runoff. He did not specify individual candidates, but he wrote that "we almost lost the city Council Election . . . to those who admit . . . they would move our city backward." That contest, he said, "we could have easily won with just a few more voters going to the polls." The mayor stressed his fight for racial equality, and he mentioned the attack upon his administration by conservative-backed candidates pledged to fight his administration.

A mail-out during the campaign on the police-chief controversy also brought a heated attack from some of Arrington's opponents, especially antagonist John Katopodis, whose reelection candidacy could suffer in case of heavy white crossover voting. During the fight over the selection of a police chief, it will be recalled, Arrington had explained his position in an open letter to the public. Between the primary and the runoff election, the Birmingham Community Development Office reprinted the mayor's long letter as a flyer and mailed it to some citizens, many of them in the politically strategic Southside area of the city. Katopodis saw a perfect opportunity to profit politically from this action. Determined to exploit the issue for maximum advantage, he chose a council meeting to attack the mailing of the flyer by the mayor. Although Arrington had not spent city funds in sending the correspondence, the city had paid for printing the police-chief flyer. In a dramatic political gensure, Katopodis forcefully insisted that the mayor repay $850 of mailing charges and that the state's attorney-general's office investigate the matter. The Harvard-trained councilman now seemed on a political high. He then turned to a "Report to the People," a publication produced by the mayor's office and sent to some citizens. Katopodis made an "educated" guess that the mayor had stuffed some of the reports with sample ballots, a charge that bitterly angered the man once described as "cucumber cool."

Criticism of the mayor did not soon end. One woman wrote the mayor to accuse him of racial discrimination, since she had not received material from him. "There is just one qualification I have that may exclude me from [your] list," she said; "I am white." Katopodis tried to make clear Arrington's direct association with the coalition slate by focusing on the correspondence. The mayor's endorsement of an all-black slate, said the white councilman, had proved divisive; and "somebody ought to call his hand" and say to him, "You ought to cut that stuff out." Katopodis's harsh rhetoric did not subdue the now-hardened Arrington. He would not pay the postage for the flyer, and it was none of Katopodis's business what he sent out from his own personal postal box. The 29 October 1981 *Birmingham News* joined the chorus of criticism because of the police-chief mailout, and in some of its editorials the paper observed that no precedent existed for the mayor's action. His endorsement of the five candidates in the contest, wrote the newspaper's editor, added "a strong and extremely distasteful political overtone to the whole episode."

White citizens requested the mayor to reject the coalition's slate or to declare for an integrated one. Attorney George C. Longshore wrote the mayor before the runoff that it was not too late to correct the misconception among moderate whites that he wanted an all-black city council. "You *must* urge the voters," he emphatically told Arrington, "to consider candidates without regard to race and you must disassociate yourself with racially exclusive slates" or the city would return to "the racial abyss we all worked so long to leave behind." Longshore ended his 29 October 1981 letter in a hostile key, noting that he had voted for Arrington in 1979 but "might not do so again unless you . . . stop mouthing about only having one vote in the Coalition." Then Tommy Charles wrote in the same vain when he admonished: "Go for a bi-racial slate more strongly than just saying the empty words where you [urge] voters to look beyond racial lines." Charles also concluded his letter with direct, but not necessarily hostile, language. The mayor, he said, should endeavor to decrease polarization in the city. The businessman told Arrington, in language that misrepresented black churches, "All you have done is convince this moderate that you are either not capable of doing the job you so earnestly sought and won, or you lack the courage to face the black electorate with anything more than what they are accustomed to hearing from the pulpit—'Whitey's the bad guy get rid of him.' " E. M. Friend, of the well-established law office of Sirote, Permutt, Friend, Friedman, Held, and Apolinsky, wrote that the mayor had the support of his firm, but he was "profoundly disturbed" that Arrington had not done more to prevent racial polarization.

The mayor's reply to his political critics indicated that the campaign would be long, tough, and bitter. He did not—and politically could not—dump coalition candidates without serious repercussions; and he blamed much of the polarization on the distortions and misrepresentations of John Katopodis and the city's two major newspapers. Arrington noted that he had not abandoned merit in the assessment of candidates, and he expressed the hope that voters on 3 November would rely upon qualifications for office and not solely upon race. The mayor emphasized that he had no desire to control the democratic processes that the coalition had used in endorsing candidates. He had fought hard to get one-third of the coalition to support Nina Miglionico, but that support had gone unappreciated by the councilwoman and her followers.

In the primary the coalition had scored a stunning victory, but in the runoff it almost met with political disaster. White crossover votes in the city were no more in evidence in the runoff than they had been in the primary. At the end of election day four whites and one black, William Bell, had emerged victorious. Arrington's antagonist John Katopodis, in need of a victory to better position himself for a run against the mayor, regained his seat on the council. Joining Katopodis and Bell were Miglionico and newcomers Bettye Fine Collins and Bill Myers. "No one today," said the 4 November 1981 *Birmingham News*, "is shocked by the way the election turned out."

Of the runoff candidates only Miglionico garnered any significant number of crossover votes. Undoubtedly her past strength among blacks and her endorsement by the Progressive Democratic Council helped her win a sizable vote (nearly 30 percent in some black boxes) in the black community. Support by the respected outgoing black councilwoman Bessie Estelle, who acted as a cochairperson for her, certainly did not hurt the campaign. Miglionico, still chafing at what she considered exclusion by the coalition, saw the election outcome as a white backlash against the mayor's endorsement of the five black coalition candidates.

Perhaps political scientist Edward Lewis of the University of Alabama at Birmingham best explained white voting behavior. Whites, he said, had always had control of city government, and they felt threatened at Arrington's push for a majority of blacks on the city council. Convinced that the police-chief battle hurt the coalition ticket, Lewis maintained that Arrington might have been wise to play down the coalition and to have exercised more verbal restraint. Whites, he said, had become "quite paranoid." But polarization in the city had existed all along.

The election disappointed the mayor, but he saw it as only a temporary setback to the sharing of political power in Birmingham. Few whites, he implied in one of this postelection statements, had taken time to ask why four or even five blacks should not sit on the council. Many voters had written off well-trained and civic-minded black candidates as "nonmeritorious," when white Birmingham had elected two political newcomers who had no experience in elective office. Arrington was neither contrite nor apologetic for his role. He expressed pride in the coalition's role in political and social reform in the city, and he offered those whites unwilling to change little solace—the organization would remain a continuing force in Birmingham politics! Blacks already were a majority in the population, and in time they would probably constitute more than half of the electorate. But Arrington concerned himself more with shared power than with political domination. Many whites, he noted philosophically, still stood in the past, "grasping at the wind hoping to stop political change."

From Arrington's perspective what had really taken place in the election of 1981? He placed much of the blame for polarization on the news media, which prematurely reported his backing of the coalition slate. The mayor further charged newspapers with portraying the black community as a political monolith. But Arrington did not discount other developments that had significance. The police-chief controversy had an impact on the outcome as well as the statements and efforts of people such as James Parsons, John Katopodis, and George Seibels. Why had the coalition become the focus for such strong attacks, Arrington asked? The answer was because it could become "a unifying force for blacks, . . . expressing its own ideas of how this city's total welfare might best be served."

The year 1981 was only a short step away in time from Arrington's victory two years earlier. Edward Lewis was right in noting that polarization had already appeared before the council contest. Unfortunately, the people of the country may have read too much into Arrington's mayoral victory. For Arrington and the blacks of Birmingham, the contest of 1981 did not represent total defeat, but rather another step in the tough transition of attitudes about power and race in Birmingham, and in much of America.

Postelection observers speculated about the relationship between the black mayor and the white-dominated city council. In many ways "a lot had changed, yet nothing had changed." The council had one less black, but councils before had also contained a white majority. Arrington, of course, had enjoyed a small advantage with his first council, since he had worked with many of its members when he served in that body. He had cultivated genuine respect among most of them, even with those who sometimes disagreed with him. The council had in fact achieved an amazing degree of consensus on many major issues, despite what sometimes appeared to an outside observer. Given the political grandstanding that sometimes took place, it was easy to understand why unaccustomed council watchers could leave city hall with the impression that chaos and sharp tongues were the hallmarks of that august body.

The council elected in the heated 1981 contest had a slightly different ideological hue than Arrington's first. Among those of moderate-to-liberal views were Miglionico, Germany, Herring, and Bell. The conservative Yarbrough had begun to show a less critical posture toward Arrington than in his previous years on the council, and he would become more supportive during the period before the 1983 election, when he needed the mayor's support and that of the coalition. Pete Clifford found it hard to disguise his essential conservatism. And the presence of both Collins and Myers had the effect of moving the council toward the political right of center, although

Collins was probably less of an ideologue than the former chief. Ideology, however, had less to do with issues that came before the council than did the possible effects a policy or program would have upon the person on the street and life in the city. The council did split over racial issues as John Katopodis once correctly observed in assessing Arrington's first council. "Race is the most salient issue," he said. "We divide more often on race than any other point."

The terrible division on the council did not materialize. Some councillors tried to solidify their political positions for the 1983 election, and that factor produced a lot of verbiage and political fireworks over small issues, but the disruption and the governmental logjam some critics had forecast never developed. Nor did the council and the mayor fight protractedly over city-employee relations, as some had foreseen. With minor exceptions, Arrington received support from the council on his handling of personnel matters and his establishment of the city's own health-benefit program after dropping Blue Cross–Blue Shield. In contract negotiations with city employees some council members "made noises" in support of their political backers, but few of them tried to strong-arm Arrington into conceding all that the Federation of City Employees requested in contract talks. Council members knew well the precarious state of the Birmingham budget.

The mayor also achieved council support on programs and policies designed to yield important long-range results. It backed neighborhood revitalization and recognized the need to attract industry and business to the city by acquiring land for industrial parks. From the beginning, support existed for the mayor's effort to reduce crime, although the council did not grant him all the money he requested near the end of his first term for additional police personnel. Nor were some members on the council inclined to put the Bonita Carter affair behind them by settling the suit brought by the young woman's family.

As Arrington's first term neared an end and as the 1983 mayor's race came closer into view, council politics and rhetoric became more strident. The selection of a council administrator offers an idea of the Arrington-Katopodis political battle that had gradually taken shape, which concluded only with the mayoral clash of 1983.

The appointment of a council administrator had attracted more attention than the complaints by some council members about the poor public-relations posture of Arrington's new chief of police, or Yarbrough's unsuccessful efforts to fly a Christian flag in a council chamber supported by the taxes of persons from many faiths.

The council position took on political significance with the resignation of Tom Fletcher, who accepted a job with a business partly owned by Pedro Costa, father of the city's master plan. The leading candidate for the job, who quickly emerged after Fletcher's departure, was senior staff member Vicki Rivers, a graduate of Tuskegee Institute and Southern University Law School. Rivers came to the council in 1981 as an administrative aide from the Birmingham Legal Service Corporation. She had developed a good relationship with most councillors, but some viewed the quick-witted black woman suspiciously as an Arrington partisan. Serious controversy surfaced when John Katopodis as council president tried to appoint another council staff member, Richard Finley, who, in the words of an Arrington aide, "disliked the mayor with a passion." Whether Katopodis had made that assessment of Finley's attitude toward the mayor is irrelevant, but it is significant that Arrington supporters were suspect of Katopodis's actions.

Miffed by the Katopodis move, Councilman Yarbrough attempted to strip the president of his appointment power, and that move in turn set off a clash between pro-Katopodis and pro-Arrington forces. "There are those," said Yarbrough, "that have such hatred in their heart that anything the mayor's for, they're against it." For a former foe of the mayor who had fought him on vital issues, Yarbrough's language was indeed strong. Katopodis accused the councilman of "snuggling" up to Arrington to win reelection. He was a "pawn" who wanted an endorsement from the coalition.

The clash ended with the council's selection of Rivers by a 5-4 vote, but her appointment only further fueled the fireworks that were exploding over Birmingham in the 1983 political season. But 1983 *had* arrived. Birmingham still stood. The world was not upside down. And Arrington still served as mayor in a city that was struggling to turn its back on the past.

8

The Man Up Close: Values, Reform, and Racial Imperatives

.

The civil rights movement that engulfed Birmingham in the 1960s and the 1970s gave Arrington hope that the city and the nation would overcome the crippling legacy of racial discrimination. That faith had not suddenly become part of his thinking, or that of other blacks, with the appearance of the nonviolence crusade. Its roots went deep into black history, and Arrington kept as confident of the future as black abolitionists had been of their eventual victory over slavery. That faith, too, had its origins in an ethic that said that obstacles to human progress would ultimately yield to the triumph of the human spirit. It received consistent nourishment, too, from a belief that kindled hope that the American people would turn to their Constitution and give real meaning to full citizenship under the Fourteenth and Fifteenth amendments. The evolution toward greater freedom in America had sometimes confronted the grim reality of violence and inhumanity, but Arrington never doubted that justice would win out, that the universal law of humanity stood on the side of black people and against the evil of oppression. He contended that discrimination, like slavery, would become a thing of the past that practically all decent people would eventually deplore.

The steadfast faith that anchored Arrington as he surveyed Birmingham in the 1960s also had deep roots in black religion and in his own personal beliefs. Martin Luther King, Jr., had ingeniously taken what many long considered an orthodox Christian faith, combined it with the teachings of the Indian leader Mahatma Gandhi, and produced a powerful social movement in America. Historically, black ministers in the South had preached of God's deliverance of his children, and although the clergymen had to address political and social issues cautiously, they had little trouble communicating to their members the message of the brotherhood of all humankind. Religion, then, became a powerful tool for social reform, and Arrington's background and his association with Miles helped to shape his social ideas.

The towering figure of Lucius Pitts, a minister and president of Miles, had a profound impact on Richard Arrington. After he accepted the presidency of Miles in 1961, Pitts became one of the city's most respected leaders. From the beginning of his tenure at the school, the forty-six-year-old native Georgian seemed destined to make an indelible imprint upon race relations in the city and to serve as a role model for young black students and faculty members who studied and worked at the institution. It was difficult in the sixties, however, to provide leadership to a school that needed to get accredited and to assist in community affairs. But Pitts had remarkable energy and unusual diplomatic skills. He won support from a black community that had young activists who desired immediate changes and from more cautious, conservative leaders who tended to laud the progress that had already taken place. Pitts also received valuable support from whites, and his successes at Miles and later at Paine College in Georgia attest to his skill in dealing with them. Although he walked a thin line in handling the ideological differences within the black community and the conservatism of white Birmingham, Pitts never abandoned his quest for the absolute equality of black people. Bigotry and intolerance, he constantly stressed, had no place in America, for they were anti-intellectual and harmful to the national fabric.

"Brother Lucius," as close friends and associates called Pitts, encouraged the development of Arrington's leadership potential. "He was always trying to inspire young people, by his own examples," said Arrington many years after he had left Miles. On one occasion when he cautioned the president about the risks he took in "trying to build Miles and fight white folks at the same time," Pitts remarked, "If Negroes like you are going to be anything in Birmingham and stand tall for dignity and pride, then some black man's got to bell the cat." And then teasing his young protégé, he remarked, "I guess this good looking black man from Georgia will have to do it until boys like you get ready."

When Arrington entered Birmingham politics, Lucius Pitts had already left the city for Paine College. His influence, nevertheless, continued after his departure. When Arrington initially decided to run for the city council, newspaperman Vincent Townsend of the *Birmingham News* suggested to the candidate that he ask Pitts to write a letter to the paper endorsing his political effort. The college president did just that, and Townsend printed the correspondence. "The kinds of things I am doing in Birmingham today, as mayor," Arrington said in 1986, "are the kinds of things Lucius Pitts said I could do." Pitts had understood the essence of dreaming, and he knew the meaning of struggle. Like Arrington, he had been a sharecropper's son. And like Arrington, he understood the meaning of place; he could appreciate the vision of a southern land free of provincialism and bigotry. Perhaps no one did as much to convince Arrington that Birmingham was the place for him as did Pitts.

Life at Miles after his return to the small school greatly taxed Arrington's energy. But he was a man of much energy, and despite a busy schedule as a teacher and dean, he engaged in a variety of civic activities. As he acquired greater visibility in the city and increased his credibility, organizations called upon him repeatedly to speak, to serve on boards, and to lead drives or campaigns. Teaching required great creative ingenuity, and the detail connected with administration and personnel problems represented a significant physical drain. The young scholar had left Oklahoma with visions of an active teaching and research career, but within three years it became clear that the latter would have to take a back seat to other duties. With his acceptance of the directorship of the Alabama Center for Higher Education, Arrington's scholarly ambitions suffered virtual death. He needed large blocks of time for careful investigation and reflection to become a productive scholar, and that he could not obtain. But if he had abandoned the personal ambition of scholarship, he had become endeared to the philosophy that "you have to serve and care about people and try to make an impact on the lives of others."

Arrington's busy activities placed some strains on his relationship with his wife, Barbara, especially after he accepted the ACHE job. By the time he took his new position, he and Barbara had been married for eighteen years, but severe friction had not been very evident. His active life as a graduate student had not troubled Barbara particularly. While they were in Detroit, Barbara had worked part time as an assistant dietician at a local hospital, and she consumed much of her time with the arrival of their second child, Anthony. (Their first offspring had died at birth.) The two years spent in Detroit proved delightfully challenging as the young couple witnessed life outside Birmingham for the first time, away from the home of the senior Arringtons. Although they lived alone, close relatives in the city made adjustment to the urban area much easier for them.

Even the tensions associated with graduate training and a different environment did not dampen the happiness enjoyed by the couple. "I mean those were good years," Barbara recalled enthusiastically over twenty years later. The two found time for recreation and pleasure on the weekends, when they went to church, took in a professional baseball game, or saw a movie. Since they had no automobile, they did most of their travel in the city by bus. Although they came to Detroit only for a short time, Barbara grew to appreciate life there, and she secretly wished to remain in the Motor City. However, Richard accepted a job at his alma mater, and Barbara and their son, Anthony (Tony), found themselves headed back to Alabama. "I liked being away, but I always wanted to do what Rick wanted to do—whatever it took to make him happy," she commented in retracing the family's past.

Graduate-school years in Oklahoma brought far less joy to Barbara. Norman had only one or two permanent black residents in 1965, and less than a hundred black students attended the University of Oklahoma. "I didn't like it," she said of the nearly all-white town. For a time a feeling of isolation existed, and for a southern black woman thrust into a nearly all-white community, the fear was stifling. Barbara worried not only about herself but about the family's three children, Tony, Kenneth, and Kevin. Schools in Oklahoma, of course, had been integrated for a decade, and Norman was a university town with a racial atmosphere that was moderate compared to some other cities in the state. Yet, Barbara worried about the children's treatment and their response to this new environment. No black teachers worked in the city, and only a few black role models existed in Norman; no black protest or self-help group had a local organization in the small town of thirty thousand. A lot of understandable fears surfaced that Barbara had not considered before leaving Birmingham.

Some of her anxieties faded as Barbara met both black and white friends in Norman and nearby Oklahoma City. The area called South Base Apartments, where the Arringtons lived on the sprawling University of Oklahoma campus, constituted a little community unto itself, composed essentially of married couples. There it was possible to meet other wives whose husbands also busily pursued degrees in various fields. They were bound together in the barracklike structure of South Base in the common hope and the occasional misery that characterize graduate-student life. The friendliness of the community reminded one of the casual atmosphere in the Deep South, and truly, total isolation only came by choice, a fact Barbara discovered within a short time. Although she never really grew to enjoy Norman, life became more tolerable after Barbara widened her circle of friends. These acquaintances helped her to endure life away from her Alabama, where she had a strong sense of place. Visits to Oklahoma City and Langston, Oklahoma, and shopping with a black friend took Barbara from an ever-present white environment. Some fears eroded, too, with her discovery of an educational system that placed no unusual emphasis on color.

Barbara took pride in her husband's progress, and she wanted to do whatever it took to assist him toward a degree. There was, however, a seeming loneliness in the Oklahoma environment that she could not completely shake, and with Richard hard at work with his studies she sometimes "felt stress." There had also developed within Barbara a highly demanding love that reflected an intense possessiveness that later proved troubling to both spouses and that eventually ripped the delicate emotional cords that bound them gently together. In a reflective moment Barbara described the real strengths and weaknesses of this all-consuming feeling: "I was lonely every minute I was away from Rick because I loved him and I liked to be with him all the time. But there were so many things I didn't understand at that time . . . because I wasn't mature. If I had to go through that again, it would be so much different. I would understand more. I may . . . have been selfish. I don't know."

A young family created unity and happiness and helped to ameliorate some of the external stresses that inevitably came as Richard tried to broaden his professional horizons. Both parents had grown up in highly disciplined families, and the rearing of their offspring reflected in part their own upbringing. Despite a busy schedule Richard took time out with the children, and although he usually appeared reserved and never highly expressive in public, he was often playful with them, rolling on the floor and laughing heartily at an amusing joke. He prided rules and insisted that the children keep them, but spankings did not come in liberal doses for disobedience. Even when unruly behavior disturbed him or when the children broke the house rules, he would not "go all to pieces." He talked things out, but his benevolence could be taxed. Usually, however, he left most of the discipline to Barbara, who was, in the opinion of one of the children, less strict than her father.

Even the strong attachment to their children and the belief in the necessity of a strong family unit could not obscure marital problems that came after the return to Birmingham in 1966. Ironically, Richard's growing community involvement and Barbara's religious views played a pivotal role in creating family tensions. While he was at Miles, most of his work had been confined to the campus, but the directorship at ACHE took him across the state, and to cities around the country in search of money and grants to aid consortium programs. While Barbara understood her husband's mission and the desire for achievement at ACHE, she believed that the real breakdown in their relationship came "during the time he took that job at ACHE—that's when it started." Barbara then drifted even closer toward conservative religious beliefs.

In the early years of marriage, Barbara and Richard had attended the same church, Crumbey Bethel Primitive Baptist. About the time Richard entered politics, however, she joined the Holiness Church, and at that point some of the children (Anthony, Angela, Erica, Kevin, and Kenneth) worshiped with each of the parents in separate institutions. This change in the Arringtons religious life had an impact on their relationship. It measured in many ways their distance from each other. Barbara's religious allegiance per se did not present a problem, but the effect it had on her behavior in the secular world did aggravate the troubles the family faced. "Things just really got out of hand when I got saved," she confessed, and "I got to the point where I really didn't like politics, not being [brought up] in it. That was something new for me."

Barbara could never become adjusted to political life, and that inability troubled her, since she wanted success for her husband. She felt uncomfortable around people, and she lamented the lack of privacy as she became more submerged in religion. Although politics often took him away from the family, "Rick always found some time to be with us." The real problem came, as she put it, because she was "in Holiness and he was in the World," and she "simply couldn't cope." Barbara had found security and happiness in religion. And whatever meaning one assigns the force of religion in the Arringtons' life, there is little doubt that Barbara's abstention from politics—even to the point of not voting—greatly disturbed Richard. Tragically, the practice of religion had become a divisive force in the lives of two people who had sought unity and happiness in a society that had often conspired to produce sorrow.

Incompatibility tugged aggressively at a fragile marriage. Communication suffered as Barbara and Richard tried to maintain balance and order in their own personal lives and in the family unit. For a time they succeeded, although they reached a point where "we didn't discuss [very much]." The inevitability of separation stared disappointingly at them. Divorce came in 1974. The last year of the marriage had greatly taxed the couple, but Barbara found much security and pleasure in her faith. Yet, the couple felt the deep pain that came with the unsuccessful attempt to remedy marital difficulties. Much of Barbara's sorrow, however, had come before the divorce. "It was sort of painful during the time I was there, but once we made up our minds that we wanted to divorce each other, well, it wasn't painful anymore. I had gotten over the pain. I was ready to go." Love had died a slow, agonizing death.

Marital failures often leave deep wounds and bitter hatreds that long endure. Barbara and Richard, however, avoided the antagonisms and the consuming anger that sometimes accompany the end of a relationship. "I really didn't feel evil toward him . . . not at all," Barbara said in 1983. Cordiality prevailed after the separation, and Richard returned to do maintenance around the house or to fix things for the children. Displaying a generosity made possible perhaps by the passage of time, she blamed herself for much of what eventually happened. "I think the whole problem was me—not being mature." Life with Richard had been enjoyable until the final years. "When a man comes home and he shows you that he loves you and he takes care of you," she said rhetorically, in language that told of another era in marital relationships, "what more can you ask?" Her avoidance of politics and public functions bothered her in the years after the divorce. There were times during the marriage, she said, "when a wife should have been there, when she was needed."

In July 1975, Arrington married Rachel Reynolds, a native of Montgomery, Alabama, and an accountant at ACHE. Reared after her mother's death by her grandmother Hattie Douglass, Rachel finished high school and then attended Alabama State University, where she received a masters degree in business administration. She moved to Birmingham in 1966 and worked for the Federal Bureau of Investigation and the Federal Reserve Bank before joining ACHE in the fall of 1970. She remained at the educational consortium for nearly twelve years before she embarked on a business venture of her own.

Rachel's broad social and political interests and her view of the world complemented those of her husband. Her own background as a poor child in Monroe County, Alabama, made her sensitive to the plight of the less fortunate and an advocate of social change that would provide opportunity for citizens closed out of the economic system. The quiet-spoken mother of three children (Patrick, by a former marriage, and Matthew and Jennifer), Rachel believed strongly in the idea of self-reliance, which showed in her advocacy of small business and by the establishment of her own enterprise. Quietly confident and a believer in her own individuality—qualities that sometimes made her appear aloof to those who did not know her well—Rachel, with her special abilities and her public involvement, proved to be a political asset to her husband.

Politics and a busy life have not weakened the hold religion has had on the life of Rachel and Richard. God and religion have always been more than abstractions to Richard Arrington, and he has been a strong supporter of the church as a vital institution in creating strong communities and a humane society. He refuses to belabor the notion of God or to intellectualize his belief in a supreme being. His position is not anti-intellectual, but it is a manifestation of religious faith, his experience of living in an empirical world, and the existence of unexplained phenomena in the universe. "I can't get around the fear of God," he admits, for his rearing has seared that factor into his very fiber. Whether God had anthropomorphic features or not hardly engages his continued religion interest. "You *explain* God," he once said reflectively, "in relation to the things you understand and what you know." Arrington had seen God at work as a boy growing up in Alabama, and he had witnessed his work and been a recipient of his goodness as he struggled to establish leadership in Birmingham.

Arrington has maintained a preference for an emotional worship, compared to a low-key variety that frowns on an "amen" or a spirited hymn that sends the church "a-rockin'." Not surprisingly, he has remained at Crumbey, although some people predicted that he would move to another church after his election to the mayor's office. While there were larger, more institutionalized churches, Arrington had grown up at Crumbey, and he felt a spiritual and historic obligation to remain there and to "make a difference." Although his schedule as mayor sometimes limits his level of involvement, he still takes time to engage in a variety of activities, including an occasional "foot washing," a Primitive Baptist ritual.

Religion has made serving in office easier for Arrington. The first years of his tenure brought a number of problems and criticisms, especially during the police-selection controversy and the council election of 1981. The mayor found himself on the verge of frustration during those times, but he turned to his inner faith to avoid the anxiety that could have affected his performance. "I don't know how I would have made it through my first two or three years in office," the Oklahoma-trained scientist remarked after his first term. When his son Kenneth became involved with drugs and received a suspended sentence, he again called on the religious faith that had long guided him.

Arrington has made no effort to foist his religion upon those around him. He has, however, been willing to share his faith with those who requested his participation in religious services, and as mayor he has met with citizens at prayer breakfast activities. A source of "strength and inspiration," these services are not highly organized, complicated gatherings. "We simply get together once each month at a dutch breakfast," he told a fellow mayor from Jacksonville, Florida, "and I am allowed to make some non-political remarks." The mayor believes that prayer could help in solving the city's problems. He wrote the Reverend Collias Stacy that he had experienced "firsthand what prayer can do," and therefore he had made it a practice to "consult . . . with the Lord prior to making . . . [crucial] decisions."

A rumored threat on Arrington's life disturbed the peace that flowed from religious conviction and the mayor's view of the world. On 22 March 1980, Police Chief Bill Myers suddenly placed Arrington under heavy security during a meeting at one of the city's local hotels. Myers, however, refused to comment publicly on his actions or to indicate whether the mayor had recently received any serious personal threats upon his life. When Arrington underwent questioning about the matter, he forcefully pledged not to bow to intimidation, and he said that threats would not prevent him from carrying out his responsibilities as an elected official. Intelligence reports had revealed that someone might try to kill the city's first black mayor. "If the rumor turned out factual," Arrington said, he would also use outside law officials "to try to get to the bottom of it and to identify the people who are responsible."

Arrington's hard-fisted law-enforcement fight against small shothouse operators led to speculation about the connection between the threats on the mayor's life and illegal liquor operations in the city. With Chief Myers anxious not to give away any of his intelligence information, rumors surfaced and took on more dramatic form with each retelling of the details. The mayor could not assert that shothouse operators were involved in the threats on his life, but if that was true, he said, it only pointed to the need to redouble the effort to rid the city of them. More perhaps was involved, he noted, than the sale of illegal booze. Shothouses represented "penny-ante operations" and could involve other crimes such as gambling. With an estimated two hundred illegal houses dotting Birmingham's landscape, a large potential for crime existed, but Arrington had no intention of reducing his fight against lawbreakers because of threats. When told that someone had allegedly placed a ten-thousand-dollar contract on his life and that he was a likely subject for a "hit," the mayor confidently played it off with the quip "Do you think I'm worth $10,000?"

Allegations that threats came from some shothouse owners did not alone prompt the thorough investigation that followed and the increased security for the mayor. Some harassing phone calls and crank mail had come after his election, but hardly any of them had unduly alarmed city officials. "I don't do this on just any telephone threat," Myers said in defending the actions to protect Arrington against possible harm. On the basis of the information available to him, the chief had given top priority to the chief executive's safety. If history served as any guide, law-enforcement officials stressed optimistically, nothing would take place, but they prepared for any eventuality. Past bomb scares, death threats on policemen, and the city's history of violence from another era created tensions that made security measures imperative. The 25 March 1980 *Birmingham News* applauded the protection given the black mayor, and it lamented the actions of the "insane fringe" that menaced government through harassment of officials. The city and the people of Birmingham, said the *News*, would not abide such tactics or give in to threats by those who lived beyond the edge of civility.

Though outwardly calm, Arrington felt the obvious stress that came with the knowledge that somebody "out there wanted to get you." The death of other public officials in America and the availability of handguns caused considerable concern by citizens and law officers who understood the criminal mind. Reporter Kitty Frieden may have overstated her case for dramatic effect in noting figuratively that Arrington operated in a fishbowl and that he encountered a cramped life-style. But, unquestionably, the mayor and his staff at city hall labored under greater restraints, and his aides became more circumspect in giving out general information about his activities.

The increased threats on the mayor's life brought added pressure to his family. The burden of office in a Birmingham still undergoing social and political change had already brought some understandable stress, but somehow those anxieties appeared more tolerable than the pressures created by an unknown person who could strike at any time or at any place against the mayor or individual members of his family. Rachel Arrington did not easily disguise her fear. Arrington could joke that he had no need to worry about the matter, since so many other people looked after his welfare, but his wife felt differently and displayed less calm. "I do not take it as lightly as the mayor," she said during that tense period. She worried constantly. "I'm not content at work. I don't sleep," she confessed. While the mayor peacefully reposed, Rachel stayed awake contemplating the many possibilities of harm. The guard stationed at the Arringtons' house affected family life and sometimes inadvertently interfered with privacy. What disturbed her most, however, was the insensitive inquiry of some schoolteachers who asked her children about the threats.

Possible harm to the mayor had led to the assignment of full-time guards—the husband-wife team of Billy and Gwendolyn Webb—to protect him. A more elaborate security arrangement would have greatly restricted movement at city hall. One plan called for the use of a metal detector at the building and for a limitation on the number of entrances. Under the arrangement, employees on the mayor's floor and above would have had to wear identification badges. Undoubtedly the plan would have greatly curtailed access to city hall, and its implementation would have proved time-consuming and frustrating. The mayor agreed with a local citizen that "making a fortress of city hall . . . is not the way to answer the threats." Arrington squashed the proposal and instead opted for the protection of the Webbs, who remained with him until they became embroiled in controversy.

Arrington refused to let attempts at intimidation, racial animosities, and the city's past history dampen his passion for peaceful political, social, and economic change. Much like other black leaders in the South, he saw a close connection between general reform and racial change. By the time of his election he had developed mature thoughts on the nature of American culture and the role of black Americans in achieving their own freedom. The race problem he believed had been, and remained, preeminently a moral question, for injustice damaged self-fulfillment and robbed the individual of the opportunity of achievement in a free society. The racial system in the South had unjustly exalted whites at the expense of blacks, and it had established a kind of "super affirmative action" program that went unchallenged for many years. The "black revolution" of the sixties and seventies, which addressed this old order, Arrington often said, had not completed the task of liberating black people—it had merely begun the journey toward freedom. His political challenge, then, was to build on what others had started— that vision composed part of his moral mandate. To ignore racial abuses when he had the power to effect change would have meant a betrayal and a rejection of black people's history. He would use his voice and his energy to remove from blacks the lingering oppression that demeaned them and that affected the quality of their lives.

Arrington's march toward reform came slowly. The seeds of reformism, however, may have always been embedded within him. "My concern about the plight of black folk," he once commented, "was probably shaped long before I even knew it." As a boy, he had read the newspapers and had wondered why blacks received unusual coverage when they had committed crimes or when they were subjects of ridicule but not when they performed notable acts of achievement. His own experiences and observations rejected the images painted by a racist press determined to maintain a status quo built on racial stereotypes of blacks that sometimes bordered on the subhuman. He knew in fact that strong black men and women existed in his own community who valued law and order, cared for their families, supported churches and lodges, and recognized the worth and need for community cooperation. He concluded that black poverty and political powerlessness, the handmaidens of the southern system, were inextricably tied together and that both conspired to make blacks the mudsills of society.

Direct confrontation with a harsh social structure helped to shape Arrington's view of society and the world. Segregation and discrimination had a way of stripping black men and women of their individuality and forcing black parents to provide a shield to guard against embarrassments that inevitably came with the operation of the southern system. Racial restrictions made liars of many parents, who dared not tell their children of their inability to command personal services or to use public facilities. Arrington still remembers how he lied to his children about a trip to an amusement park in Birmingham's Westside during the era of segregation. When asked why he would not take them for a visit to the facility, he could not muster the courage to say, "You can't go out there because you're black." Lying to them, but not to himself, he would dismiss his children's request with the promise, "I'll take you later." He also vividly recalls the opening of a Jack's fast-food restaurant near one of the city's housing projects. Responding to a commercial jingle to patronize the place, his children asked to go there to purchase a hamburger. Birmingham's future mayor, however, had decided not to demean himself by "going to that little back room they had back there for black folk." So he lied to them again, suggesting, "We'll go one day."

Arrington's plight, of course, was that of other blacks. To live within a segregated society implied compromise and insult in practically every aspect of life in Alabama and other Deep South states, for the laws that controlled behavior there came from all-white legislatures that believed in white supremacy. As Arrington discovered more about the southern system as an adult and as a parent, it became more callous and more offensive to him. Although that system had been designed to condition him to live in a separate society that in practice was unequal, something had gone terribly wrong. The system did not co-opt his mind, but it admittedly created some doubt in him and forced him, for a time, to question his ability to compete with whites, who had enjoyed greater opportunities. In a strange way the old southern social arrangement created a quiet rebel, for Arrington found it increasingly difficult to live comfortably with the imposed degradation that came with second-class citizenship. As he gained more education and greater status, however, his own life contradicted the contention that black personal improvement and self-reliance led to white acceptance. Despite his achievements, he was still a "Negro" to many whites and an outright "nigger" to the true bigot.

By the time he completed his doctoral work and returned to Miles in 1966, Arrington had developed ideas remarkably consistent with those of the civil-rights movement. A believer in the nonviolent philosophy of Martin Luther King, Jr., he prided the notion of orderly reform in society, although he recognized the value of creative tensions in molding an atmosphere for change. American democratic government had undergone evolution over time, and it was unwise, Arrington contended, to look at it as a static organism. He saw it, rather, as the result of a logical progression toward the ideals of justice and equality. Freedom as perceived in the Western world could not be denied to those who struggled for it. Victory for American blacks would surely come. True liberation was only a matter of time, but he did not underestimate the difficulty of the task. Arrington remained acutely aware that black people's hatred of the old southern system and their petition against it would not alone shake the foundation of segregation's strong citadel. The walls would not come tumbling down as the voices of protest cried out for "freedom now" and as nonviolent demonstrators sang "We Shall Overcome." He knew that white men had killed to maintain "their way of life" before the advent of the movement of the sixties, and he had little doubt of their will to kill again to maintain their privileged places in society.

Arrington argued that the federal government must play a direct role in the liberation of blacks from white oppression. Prejudiced white attitudes and institutional racism had become so ingrained that only sweeping national legislation could address the major problems created by three and a half centuries of American history.

The piecemeal legislation of Congress had not abolished discrimination, and many whites across America continued to argue against the passage of federal measures because laws would not "change men's hearts." But, laws, said Arrington, could change people's *behavior*, and that was a central issue. Government existed as a medium to regulate relationships between citizens, to guarantee fair and equitable treatment, and to keep men and women from pursuing injurious antisocial actions. A change of heart within individuals, Arrington critically maintained, was purely coincidental to the process of effective enforcement of just law. Those who spoke against stronger remedies to confront racism, he said, had become trapped in their own argument, since restrictive legislation already existed that had negatively shaped race relations and that made bigotry a noticeable feature of regional and national life.

The passage of the 1964 Civil Rights Bill and the Voting Rights Act the following year reaffirmed Arrington's faith that America would fulfill its democratic promise of equality and justice for black people. These measures had come only after great sacrifice and suffering, but the struggle for their enactment had created a unity among blacks that had produced further social changes and altered the political power relationships between blacks and whites. The availability of public accommodations without regard to race had not simply restored dignity to a group of people that had given the country their loyalty, but at another level it had exalted the integrity of black parents who no longer had to lie to their children about attendance at local amusement parks or the right to purchase a coke or a hamburger at a fast-food restaurant. No longer would America have to make apologies for business establishments that willingly catered to foreigners or gave them services but denied the same services to black citizens.

The Voting Rights Act of 1965 was the most revolutionary statute in black political life since the passage of the Fifteenth Amendment. Rarely did Arrington pass up the opportunity to stress its significance to young black people in speeches across the country following his election to office. Indeed, he represented the living embodiment of the changes that came through voting. Few things bothered him as much as political lethargy, especially among younger blacks. Like other leaders, he pinned much hope on the power of the ballot. When he spoke to a group of black students in Birmingham on 15 January 1980, he sketched the difficulty blacks had once encountered in acquiring the ballot:

> I . . . went off to graduate school and I always wanted to vote because all my life I had watched people in the community; and we studied a long list of questions, hoping that we would know the answers when we got down there [to the court house]. It didn't make any difference what kind of degrees [blacks] had. There were people with Ph.D. degrees, and M.D. degrees, and teachers, and they would go down to the court house to register to vote and some man [would be] sitting there with a third grade education telling you [that] you don't know enough to vote.

Blacks could assist in setting themselves free through the ballot. People had lost their lives, their jobs, and their property to achieve the vote, and to disregard the responsibility of voting was to renege on a commitment to build on the legacy that both black and white champions of freedom had left behind. Arrington scolded those who talked of freedom and complained of continuing racism and oppression but who failed to vote. "It's that kind of hypocrisy that we don't need," he told a group of black college students after he became mayor of Birmingham. "I say today," he stressed, "don't blame white folks, don't blame anybody else if you don't make it, if you don't set yourselves free." If blacks did not take advantage of the suffrage, they had to bear the burden of continued oppression. Liberation through the ballot would free blacks and a nation that still labored under a psychology of race inherited from the past. Political apathy fostered policies that could reenslave the race; and those who regarded voting with almost studied indifference, the mayor said repeatedly to blacks, were "killing the dream . . . Martin Luther King . . . held for us."

Mayor Arrington spoke out forcefully in defense of the Voting Rights Act when conservative politicians tried to weaken it. His testimony before the House Subcommittee on Civil and Constitutional Rights of the Judiciary Committee clearly revealed the faith he invested in the measure and the need for its extension. No civil-rights legislation, he told committee members in June 1981, had been so fundamental in protecting the basic constitutional rights of citizens and in correcting the continuing effects of the illegal denial of constitutional guarantees than the 1965 law. The measure had ensured an increased number of black politicians, and it had underscored the notion that very few things in a democracy superseded the right to vote. In arguing against efforts to amend the act, Arrington stressed that the legislation had brought the country "a long way down the road towards . . . full and equal protection of every individual's and every group's right to participation in our political system." The measure had adequately demonstrated its ability to remedy many of the serious problems of political disfranchisement, and the Congress should not weaken it.

The Voting Rights Act, Arrington testified, had served as a catalyst to black voting, and it had destroyed the idea that blacks had no real interest in their own political destiny. But the mayor carefully described complications that still affected black voting negatively in his own Alabama and in other states. Unabridged access to the ballot, he said, had not yet become a reality in all areas of the South, and the Congress should consider amendments to strengthen the measure. Some places in the South, for example, did not employ adequate numbers of deputy registrars to meet the needs of various communities. Other localities had extremely short hours and a limited number of days for voters to register. People who lived in remote areas or who worked for long periods of the day found it difficult to register, and consequently, political access for them was virtually nonexistent. Other problems proved equally as frustrating: gerrymandering, annexations of areas and redistricting, and the use of unfair reidentification programs.

The mayor realized that politics alone could not bring black freedom. The active support of the black middle class, he preached, was crucial to the movement for equality. A spirit of service and altruism had to guide the actions of all blacks who had escaped discrimination and poverty. The black middle class had to live by the unselfish mottoes "I want for my brother what I want for myself" and "each brother's joy is joy to me." A generous altruism would aid the cause of black economic liberation and raise the race to new heights with the confidence that future generations of blacks would never experience economic deprivation. Repeatedly, Arrington carried this gospel to various cities across America, anxious to remind successful blacks of their responsibility. Much like the black scholar and leader W. E. B. DuBois, he believed that the talented among the race had to provide the leadership that led toward real emancipation and a democracy that lived up to its promises. The black middle class had to keep the sacred trust "to help the masses of people get home to full freedom."

Arrington forcefully articulated the theme of middle-class responsibility at a Southern Christian Leadership Conference convention shortly after his 1979 mayoral triumph, and it became a part of many of his public speeches to black groups. He scolded those who had forgotten their past or who had abandoned the fight for equality. "Some of our brothers and sisters who marched into the fire hoses and the dogs in the 60s have still not enjoyed the fruits [of equality]," Arrington told SCLC members. He chided a black middle class that ignored poverty, and he called for financial support of groups such as the NAACP and SCLC, which had historically protected blacks against inequality. Those organizations had made it possible for black Americans to acquire new jobs, and Arrington harshly criticized those in the middle class who "won't give them one thin dime." Part of the problem, Birmingham's mayor told a church gathering in Cincinnati, Ohio, in the summer of 1980, was the illusion that black people had continued to move ahead, when they in fact were standing still.

Arrington used an address at the 1983 Alpha Phi Alpha national convention to elaborate more fully on the role of the middle class and black leadership. He appropriately entitled his speech "Keeping the Sacred Trust." The black leader had chosen a good platform, since Alpha Phi Alpha, a fraternity to which Arrington himself belonged, had long prided itself in strong leadership and social service, producing a large number of black reformers. Individual achievement, he told his Alpha brethren, had merit, for it signaled the beginning of group excellence. But middle-class blacks had too often demonstrated evidence of a kind of myopia, a tendency to focus only on their own successful situation, without remembering the "hell holes, cotton fields and ghettos" from which they had come. They had ended the fight too soon. History had shown that an ethnic group could not gain real freedom with some of its members quasi-free and others oppressed, for society found it difficult to distinguish between the partially liberated and those who were not. Arrington spoke eloquently and sensitively to the fraternity, which had been formed in 1906 at Cornell University: "The script in freedom's journey calls for the black middle class to pick up the torch and with *skills* and [courage] . . . to advance the cause for freedom." Here was an altruistic philosophy, but one consistent with the efforts of those blacks who had fought for liberation at other times. "We must keep the sacred trust," he told fellow Alphamen gathered in Atlanta, for "the night is dark, the hour is late, and we're still a long way from home."

Self-reliance also permeated Arrington's philosophy as much as his emphasis on the middle class. He knew the hazards of overemphasizing the idea of individualism in a society that had reduced opportunities for a black person and that had placed an exaggerated emphasis on racial identification. Liberation, nevertheless, would come, not by eradication of racism alone, but also from the desire of black people to achieve economic security and educational progress. This theme, of course, had been prevalent in black history before Arrington. It had enjoyed currency in America since pre–Civil War days, reaching its greatest articulation under the leadership of Booker T. Washington, although he couched it in an accommodationist mold. Practically every black leader, including black nationalists, had echoed the theme, but usually in connection with American capitalism. Arrington's ideas represented part of a tradition in black thought that had been a part of black life for many decades. Self-reliance, however, did not lead him toward a kind of racial chauvinism that exalted separation. While he prided political unity, to be sure, Arrington remained throughout an advocate of political cooperation and reasonable compromise. His support of white Democratic presidential candidate Walter Mondale in 1984 over the candidacy of black civil-rights leader Jesse

Democratic Candidate Walter Mondale and Mayor Richard Arrington, Jr.,
exchanging views on politics during the 1984 presidential race. (Courtesy Mayor
Richard Arrington, Jr.,)

Jackson showed the difficulty that could arise in holding simultaneously two central ideas—the necessity for black unity, on the one
hand, and the need for political cooperation with whites, on the
other.

Black self-reliance also meant strengthening the institutions of
the black community. No contradiction really existed between his
philosophy and that of integration. Frederick Douglass, Roy Wil-
kins, Martin Luther King, and other black leaders had shared his
belief. America had long existed as a pluralistic society, and the
country had profited from different national and ethnic groups. In
this tradition, Birmingham's black mayor called for aid to black institutions of higher education, churches, and community self-help
groups. With integration some blacks had shown a tendency to de-

266

sert organizations that had long supported their cause and that had been vital to the black community in the years of segregation.

Education and its relationship to the philosophy of self-reliance merited much private and public comment from Arrington. Students at a Birmingham junior college may have been shocked to hear Arrington comment critically on the educational deficiencies of some persons who sought out jobs with the city. He had grown "a little tired of young folk coming out of college . . . [who] can't fill out an application form" and who could not write a coherent essay. Racism had had a negative impact on the lives of blacks, but they could not allow it to incapacitate them, for some black people in past generations had succeeded under far more difficult conditions. Quality education could help liberate them, could give them another chance in life. The mayor's language permitted little misinterpretation from his young audience. They had to seize the educational moment. "If you think that all you need to do is to come here [to Lawson State] and stay long enough to fool enough folk and get a piece of paper, and go out of here and don't know much more than you knew when you came . . . then you're fooling yourself." They were helping to reenslave themselves. He felt certain, however, that an educated, self-reliant people with justice on their side would not fail to get home to the promised land of full equality.

Arrington's emphasis on self-reliance did not excuse white Americans from the responsibility of correcting racial injustice. He was careful not to stress unduly what individual black improvement could achieve. Arrington remained keenly aware that many white people who claimed that racial barriers would fall as blacks achieved more education and wealth were the same ones who worked to restrict black opportunity. Through the eyes of history he had also seen how a philosophy of self-help had sometimes directed black thinking away from the fight against political and social poscriptions imposed by the white community. He avoided this mistake. He prodded blacks, constantly encouraging them to exalt excellence and achievement, but he also laid before the white community the imperative of linking the *ideal* of racial equality to the democratic *practice* of equality.

The formation of the Jefferson County Citizens Coalition also had a direct connection to Arrington's idea of self-reliance. As earlier indicated, the organization developed from special problems with another political group, but it had racial unity as an ultimate goal. If blacks in Birmingham appeared to follow Arrington's leadership and that of the coalition with a zeal that many whites could not comprehend, the attachment resulted from history and a philosophy of self-reliance, not from blind political ignorance. The long period of political denial and the methods employed by white southerners to retain their power and special privilege made possible black unity in the Magic City. Roughly two decades before Arrington's election in Birmingham, political scientist James Q. Wilson had written in *Negro Politics*, "When the social, economic, and political demands of a group are linked with a protracted and bitter struggle for the franchise, the members of that group are more likely to acquire a permanent sense of political identity." Birmingham's blacks gave substance to the assertion, and to the contention that "Negroes . . . , when they vote, can cause a startling change in style, if not the substance of . . . politics."

In Arrington's view the Democratic party offered the best chance for continued social reform and for policies that encouraged self-reliance. Arrington's political allegiance, of course, greatly resembled that of other blacks in the South and across the nation. Since Franklin D. Roosevelt's New Deal of the 1930s, black Americans had remained inseparably tied to the Democratic party. They had said good-bye and good riddance to the Grand Old Party of Abraham Lincoln in the presidential election of 1936. Since the latter part of the nineteenth century, the Republican party had become increasingly characterized by a view of government that stifled strict enforcement of the Fourteenth and Fifteenth amendments and by "lily whiteism" in the South. The political transformation of blacks that took place in the thirties involved more than New Deal largess to cure the debilitating ills of a harsh depression that threatened the country. It had much to do with a conception of government. After the 1930s, black leaders argued that a national government rigidly devoted to decentralization and states' rights had never significantly benefitted black Americans. Richard Arrington continued to share that view in the 1980s.

Arrington had no close involvement with the Democratic party before he entered politics. Of course, he had been a member of the black Jefferson County Progressive Democratic Council before organizing his Citizens Coalition, but despite the respect accorded him, he had hardly been an influential power within the council. Arrington recognized that white southern Democrats, who practically dominated the region's politics until recent years, held extremely conservative racial views, and so did southern Republicans. But the national Democratic party had a social philosophy, he believed, that paid allegiance to the working class and that addressed measures to overcome the handicaps of past racial policies more sensitively than did the GOP. Although he may not have regarded himself as the traditional kind of American politician, his triumph in Birmingham clearly established him as a leader and a shaper of ideas and brought him to the attention of national Democratic politicians. He had a large following, and he could get people to the polls to vote. And that clout partly explained why Democratic president Jimmy Carter had wasted little time in telephoning him following his 1979 victory, and why the following year Arrington gave Carter his full support against the conservative Republican candidate, Ronald Reagan. But Arrington faced a much harder decision in the 1984 Democratic presidential primary. The front-runner in that campaign was Walter Mondale, vice-president under Jimmy Carter. In the primary, Mondale received a challenge from civil-rights leader Jesse Jackson, who garnered support from a large number of rank-and-file blacks.

Realistically, Jackson had little chance of victory, but his candidacy took on an emotional meaning for many blacks in America, not because of possible victory, but because of the civil-rights leader's courageous battles and the symbolism of his campaign. Jackson's candidacy demonstrated his appeal to many blacks, and it invigorated the Democratic primary contest by registering thousands of new black voters. It also challenged the attitude of the "dumb black syndrome" that existed in some white quarters, and it said even more about the continuing frustrations and anger over recent setbacks to civil rights in America. Arrington disappointed some of his followers in not supporting Jackson, who had been one of Martin Luther King's close lieutenants. But the mayor had to weigh the cost to his city of supporting a man who had little chance of winning. He did use his influence, however, to get the Alabama Democratic Conference (which also backed Mondale) to support Jackson as a vice-presidential candidate. Much like other big-city black mayors, Arrington faced the tough choice between realistic politics and racial unity, and little room existed for compromise. While his support of Mondale produced some strains among blacks, it did give him a greater role within the party. He served for a brief time as chairman of the Democratic Platform Committee during the 1984 Democratic Convention; and rumors abounded before the presidential election about a possible cabinet position in case of a Mondale victory. Reagan's landslide win ended all speculation.

Arrington's intensified emphasis on politics and self-help mirrored the reversal of fortunes for blacks in the 1980s. National public opinion on civil rights changed dramatically, yet blacks had not achieved full freedom. Unemployment reached near-crisis proportions in many parts of America, and affirmative-action programs, instituted to redress racial grievances, came under severe attack from a conservative national administration and from those who had opposed legislation to correct the wrongs of past discrimination. Statistics on poverty, income, health care, life expectancy, housing, and other indicators told the story of a people who yet had a long way to go before arriving at freedom and equality. Many black Americans who believed they had beaten the system became comfortable in their new status, but Arrington cautioned that they had misread progress.

Richard Arrington has never doubted the achievement of black equality within the system of American capitalism. His argument has not been with the prevailing economic structure but with greedy capitalists who tolerated injustice. His support of small-business enterprises, industrial parks, and a tax structure conducive to business all flow from the basic philosophy of a man who wants blacks to have an opportunity to compete and share in American capitalism. Although he has not forgotten the role labor once played as a part of the liberal Democratic coalition that helped push civil-rights legislation, he has remained keenly aware that many laborites and union groups have strongly opposed affirmative-action programs, particularly those in the construction and building trades. In sum, Arrington believes that the economic policies of the Democratic party and a responsible capitalism balanced with labor hold out the greatest hope of an American economy where eventual black equality is possible.

The mayor's success in Birmingham provides a meaningful commentary on the impact of the role of personality in politics. To some old-line politicians it is still puzzling how the man, a "nonpolitician," could amass such power and influence. Although quiet and unassuming, he had already gained some visibility through his work at Miles and his association with President Lucius Pitts before entering the political arena, but he had not craved attention. Indeed, he struck some people as shy in public gatherings. While at Miles, and later as director of ACHE, he had spoken widely and had participated in a variety of civic and service activities, including those of the Urban League, Goodwill Industries, the United Negro College Fund, the United Way, and many others. This involvement brought him into contact with large numbers of citizens and community leaders who saw him close up and were able to assess his intelligence, his social views, and his politics. But despite the laudations of those who worked closest with him, few ever attributed to him the extroverted qualities or the charisma often associated with many other successful American politicians.

The perception of Arrington as a soft-spoken intellectual did not hurt him in an age when civil-rights rhetoric had cooled significantly. In the more volatile sixties he may have encountered difficulty securing and maintaining the attention of those who believed that rhetoric had an inherent value and that, if it could not move mountains, it could at least frighten some whites into action. A man of deliberate manner, Arrington prided objectivity, and he was inclined to say nothing in a heated moment rather than unleash an emotional barrage. Dr. James T. Montgomery served with Arrington on the Community Affairs Committee in the 1970s and knew him well as his personal physician. "When we were on CAC together," Montgomery recalled, "I could say some things to the white power structure, but I tended to anger them." Arrington could articulate the same things "so much better" and get attention. As many would later learn, Arrington was low-key yet intense, a person who could stubbornly cling to certain principles. That quality gave him a toughness that belied his quiet demeanor; and it won praise from blacks in particular, who applauded his fight for affirmative action and his struggle against police brutality during his council years.

Harsh attacks and controversy did not easily ruffle Arrington. Occasionally he sat in council meetings or other gatherings seemingly oblivious to the swirling debate around him. Some people interpreted his behavior as a kind of coldness, even arrogance. One observer, noting the mayor's ease in handling his duties, commented, "He is not the kind of person I would expect to have a stroke at age fifty-five." For an executive who involved himself with many details of his administration, Arrington's calm was baffling. A key to his balance rested with organization and his philosophy of life, but to some it existed because he was a nonpolitician who had only temporarily left his natural habitat to wander in a strange and exciting world.

By the time Arrington faced reelection in 1983, Birmingham had moved a long way from the rigidly segregated society that Martin Luther King had confronted in the Magic City two decades earlier. The force of the mayor's own personality, shaped by "old-fashioned" American values of religion, personal integrity, and hard work, had helped him alter the politics of his city. Birmingham would never be the same. Would the city continue to thrive as Atlanta and New Orleans had done in the South, or would it witness continued white flight and severe industrial and business decline like Cairo, Illinois, and Gary, Indiana, in the North? The politics of race would have much to do with the outcome.

9

A New Day Cometh:
Reelection to Office

•

Richard Arrington's decision to run for reelection to the mayor's office in Birmingham went beyond the narrow considerations of local politics. In the two decades after the Voting Rights Act, blacks voted in increasing numbers, and they slowly consolidated their power by returning politicians to office that supported their cause. In 1983, altogether 236 black mayors had won election to office, most of them in small towns of the American South. Large northern cities —Chicago, Detroit, Newark, Oakland, Hartford, Gary, Los Angeles, and Washington—had black chief executives. In the South, Andrew Young, former civil-rights activists and ambassador to the United Nations, had inherited the leadership of Atlanta from its first black mayor, Maynard Jackson, who had served two terms. And Judge Ernest Morial ran cosmopolitan New Orleans with the skill and class that had become his trademark. In the upper South Roy West had earned the top spot in Richmond, the former Confederate capital. Of twelve big-city black mayors in America in 1983, four of them presided over large municipalities in the South.

If the election of black southern mayors meant the consolidation of the black vote, it also said something about a change in the political behavior, if not the attitudes, of southern whites. Cities of the region had not crumbled with black incumbency, and the chaos predicted by doomsday prophets did not come to pass. But big-city black mayors clearly had no magic wand for the many problems that

273

faced both black and white urbanites. The delivery of services, the fight against crime, and the necessity of providing effective public transportation remained as much of a challenge for them as it had in previous years. Black mayors and their black constituents discovered the limits of power and resources. The election of blacks also gave whites the valuable experience of sharing power and of seeing black people function close up as humans and as decision makers who directly shaped their lives. And that factor was as true in Birmingham as it was in Hartford, Connecticut, or Chicago, Illinois. Although past prejudices disappeared slowly, some reduced fear of black involvement in government at top levels did take place.

Birmingham, of course, had always been a very special story. A "tough city to crack" in the early days of integration, it had never been very wealthy in a region known for its poverty. But Arrington had determined not to let the city's past, or the deep economic troubles that plagued the nation throughout his first term, trap him. After more than a decade in public life, he had helped to encourage progress and change in the physical appearance of the city and in political behavior. Birmingham had become a more livable place, with parks and recreational facilities that ranked well with other municipalities in the South. Beautification of the city had become a goal not only of downtown businesses but of many neighborhood organizations that wanted improvement in their surroundings. The city's library doubled its physical size during the Arrington years and, despite limited funds, continued its emphasis upon reaching out to localities. Various types of museums and an outstanding symphony gave a visibility to the arts that refuted the picture of cultural depravity that many northerners still believed existed in the region. The University of Alabama in Birmingham had become a sprawling center for important medical research and also a special cultural mecca with its own identity. Arrington believed that the university could develop as an important contributor to an emerging high-tech economy. Yet, Birmingham still had a national image that did not readily endear it to those even vaguely acquainted with its history. In his many speeches out-of-state, especially in the first year after his election, Arrington had tried to reshape the thinking about his city. Birmingham was no longer "Bombingham," but part of the past still remained in people's minds. Not surprisingly, then, the question of the city's image and how to improve it became a consideration in the 1983 mayoral election.

Those who carefully followed Birmingham politics correctly predicted that Arrington would seek reelection. His accomplishments and his strong political base made it easier for him to arrive at a decision to run. The issues that had proved most troubling had not cost him any significant support among blacks, and he had worked hard to mend the damage that had occurred during the 1981 city elections. The belief that his job remained unfinished guided his decision; and the reality of the toughness of Birmingham politics did nothing to discourage him. He had, of course, won in 1979 by a margin of only two thousand ballots and had received only some 10 percent of the city's white votes. In 1983, blacks constituted an even larger number of the registered voters, thus increasing Arrington's essential power base. If he could increase his white votes, he could win reelection without the kind of tragic event that had provided the political catalyst that united blacks in 1979.

Rumors prevailed in the black community that white political aspirants would try to entice other blacks to run against Arrington. A local radio announcer accurately gauged the temper of the community when he denounced anyone who would betray his people as a "Judas goat." Another irate citizen called into a talk show to exclaim that a black person who would take money to compete against the mayor should be "tarred and feathered and run out of town." A noted clergyman at one of Birmingham's largest churches could not resist comment on the alleged efforts to split the black community by having other blacks in the mayor's race. Arrington, he said, would receive 99-1/2 percent of the votes in the black community. The other one-half of 1 percent needed " a good psychiatrist." Arrington approached the potential political problem more philosophically in commenting, "I've talked with some of these people who have been approached, but there's nothing bad about that." He expected people to "put stalking horses in the race to run other folks down."

Arrington's first announced foe, Sonja Franeta, created no political fear among his backers. A member of the Socialist Workers Party, Franeta had little if any chance of emerging victorious in a Birmingham that had never provided fertile ground for left-of-center politics. A machinist at a local plant, the thirty-one-year-old woman seemed as eager to promote her party as her chances of victory in the city's nonpartisan election. Franeta attacked both the Democratic and the Republican parties as tools of big business, and she called upon workers to support her strong independent labor party. Recalling earlier days in the fight against management, she echoed the well-known battle cry of the labor movement that "an injury to one is an injury to all."

Throughout her campaign Franeta recounted a number of major national and international issues. She made an appeal to black people by pointing to the continued problems of the black community, but her mild attacks upon Arrington, the "capitalist" who protected the interest of business, were not destined to win her many votes. Arrington, she said, was too tied to the Democratic party to help the working people, and he would not "lead the kind of fight needed to halt racist attacks." If the mayor would run an independent race "with a working class program," she said, "I would drop my campaign and support him." Arrington had no intention of doing so. Like the socialist candidate in the 1979 mayoral race, Franeta would receive little attention and few votes in the 1983 contest.

Discussion had centered upon two men as possible Arrington opponents, former Police Chief Bill Myers and Birmingham City Council president John Katopodis. Myers and the mayor had differing political views, and the two had clashed before the chief left office. Myers's conservative political outlook gave him strength, and his election to the city council was an indication of his popularity. His support on the Eastside, where he had worked in the 1981 council race, could provide a strong political base if he decided to run. Although he lacked long years of service in elective office, he had been involved in decision making, and he had led a department that required poise under pressure. Moreover, Myers exuded confidence, with his piercing eyes and his relatively lean physique; and he gave the impression of a person not likely to panic in the political warfare that took place at city hall. Myers, however, ended speculation about his candidacy in April when he announced, to the surprise of no one in the Arrington camp, his support of Katopodis. Myers recognized that he would badly split the white vote if he entered the mayoral contest. The former chief, nevertheless, rejected the contention that he had based his decision on whether or not Katopodis had a better chance of defeating Arrington. Polls showed in April 1983 that Arrington would beat both men decisively in a race, although Katopodis would fare better than Myers in a head-on clash.

The possible candidacy of John Katopodis did not alarm the Arrington forces. In fact, preparation for either Myers or the council president required no considerable adjustment, since many of Katopodis's beliefs bore a remarkable resemblance to those of Myers, although some people perceived him as slightly more liberal than the former chief of police. In early April Katopodis had already tipped off his candidacy in a letter to supporters that alerted them to his forthcoming run for city hall. He discounted the polls that showed Arrington ahead of him by a substantial margin, noting confidently that "all worthwhile endeavors are difficult." He would run against Birmingham's first black mayor. To aid him, Myers helped create a group called Politically Interested Citizens (PIC), a combination of two white eastern-area organizations, VOTES and PAC East.

Arrington's reelection campaign really began the day he took office. Little thought entered his mind about a quick return to academe. He never wrestled with the decision to run again, nor did his wife, Rachel, who had given him constant encouragement. Yet, despite his determination, he was cautious not to begin his reelection bid too soon, for few things could damage a campaign more than a weary populace that stayed at home on election day. Before his announced plans, however, the mayor had begun to raise funds and to talk with confidants about his reelection. In the fall of 1983, Jessie Lewis, former newspaperman and president of Lawson State Community College, had guided a fund-raising effort called "Mayor's Celebrity Banquet." That affair raised over $100,000, and plans were already afoot for other activities to keep the city's first black mayor in office.

Arrington's 1983 campaign organization differed markedly from that of 1979. A skimpy budget had forced him to keep operating expenses at a minimum when he initially ran for mayor, and except for the hundreds of grass-roots volunteers, his campaign would have foundered. But now he was the incumbent, with even greater visibility. Many people, of course, wanted to continue to identify with the social and political transformation then taking place in Birmingham, and they more willingly contributed. Funds flowed in more readily than before—and they were necessary, for Arrington estimated a campaign cost in excess of $200,000. Jessie Lewis complained privately that the long-victimized black community had to do much more in support of candidates if it wanted to apply maximum pressure on the system for change. With roughly $100,000 in the coffers before the campaign officially got underway, Arrington seemed financially ready for battle with those anxious to replace him at city hall.

The operation of his campaign headquarters showed clear signs of more financial support than in 1979. The very appearance of the building reflected greater funding and in-kind contributions that came from businesses. Arrington's downtown headquarters underwent a remodeling and reflected the professional, businesslike atmosphere that came with the management of Rachel Arrington, who now directed Arrington's central location. Rachel brought added organization and efficiency to the campaign, and with her training as an accountant, she quietly but unobtrusively helped to manage finances. While neither the 1979 contest nor the early fund-raising activities of the 1983 campaign encountered problems, the mayor wanted to ensure the absolute financial integrity of his second mayoral effort by a systematic accountability for funds.

Confident in his ability to get necessary finances, Arrington began formal preparation in early summer for the ensuing mayoral battle. The incumbent chose a twenty-five-member campaign committee that represented a broad cross section of citizens. Co-chaired by white corporate executive Terrence B. Sheehan and by Bernice Johnson, a retired black school teacher, the committee consisted of thirteen whites and twelve blacks. The group included businessmen, educators, clergymen, attorneys, senior citizens, a civic leader, and a representative from the Physicians' Wives Association. Arrington chose one of his former aides, Mike Graffeo, to head his campaign, while the manager of his 1979 contest, Tony Carter, served as field coordinator.

Strategy for the election began to take shape in June, when the mayor met with his campaign committee. He arrived at that meeting in good spirits on a hot, sunny day in Birmingham and with the kind of enthusiasm that would characterize his entire campaign. Dressed casually, he appeared relaxed among friends, joking back and forth with those responsible for making his effort a success. He spoke with no political misgivings, resolute in his belief that he would triumph over John Katopodis. "I am going to be visible," he told his partisans, indicating his intention of running a hard-working campaign.

Arrington's "pep talk" to his election committee was designed, predictably, to inspire confidence and enthusiasm, but it did much more. He stressed the need to recruit volunteers, to keep headquarters informed of problems, and to raise funds. But most of his remarks were those of a candidate who expected a tough, but victorious, battle. He had a good record, and it was not by accident, he said, that those good things "just happened." He took a disguised jab at John Katopodis when he said that he could work well with people and that his experience as mayor had a built-in value. "Good things begin with vision," he exclaimed, practically forgetting that he spoke to the committed. He rattled off accomplishments as if to reemphasize the necessity of repetition. His administration had helped to lower crime. Housing construction was a plus, and peace and tranquility reigned. Neighborhood revitalization had made great strides and he had fostered a good environment for business. Arrington also praised those who had worked tirelessly to make progress possible and he rebutted the assertion often advanced by the opposition that he had little imagination and even less innovative spirit. He had come to office during economic stringency and had steered the city toward progress and away from spending that would have made little economic sense. He paid tribute to the Vann administration that had envisioned many far-sighted projects, but Arrington stressed that he and his staff "had put stuff in place." The record spoke for itself.

Cindy McCartney, Arrington's political consultant, spoke of campaign strategy at the June meeting. She underscored the need to secure the mayor's base and to spend time in targeted areas. "Forget East Lake," she exclaimed, to a low-key chuckle from those who knew the voting behavior of that area. "We are not going to get voters there," except as "icing on the cake." McCartney rightly assumed that Katopodis would "probably raise small, scattered issues." She warned against urging the opponent's people to go to the polls and against peaking too soon. "Talk about the mayor's record," she instructed. Mike Graffeo echoed McCartney's comments, but he also reminded the committee that legislative races would drain both volunteers and money, and he urged a determined effort to get a good portion of both.

Arrington had decided upon an official announcement date during the June meeting. The mayor's schedule, finances, and local activities all entered into the decision for a 15 August kickoff. When some two hundred supporters gathered at the city's Hyatt Hotel, Arrington appeared enthusiastic, and he sounded a note of optimism. In his formal statement the mayor spoke in general terms about the campaign, but he did foreshadow some major themes in the forthcoming contest. Despite the national recession, he informed his supporters that Birmingham had made progress in many areas and that he had presided for four years over a city where racial peace prevailed. But greater work remained to bring people together; and he pledged to rally citizens toward that end by conducting a campaign that would give him a broad base of support. Anticipating his opponent's later attack, he emphasized the decline in crime in the city during his years in office, and he cautioned against a campaign based on negativism and race.

The mayor and his planners did not underestimate the political savvy or the organizing ability of John Katopodis. From his council seat, Katopodis had a first-hand acquaintance with city problems, and he had helped shape the destiny of Birmingham by his participation in the legislative give-and-take at city hall. If he struck some people as verbally aggressive and if at times he tended to antagonize those around him, he also provoked thought from those who opposed his ideas. While his arrogance and his occasional abrasiveness irritated some people, few who knew him questioned his devotion to the city. By 1983, this man—who actually considered himself shy—had endured two council elections and a mayoral contest. A seasoned campaigner, he ably confronted difficult and sometimes hostile questions, or cleverly evaded them. Not devoid of wit, Katopodis easily turned a phrase, and occasionally he had the ability to laugh at himself.

Katopodis entered the campaign with a thorough knowledge of the mayor's record and his mode of operation. He knew his black opponent's strengths and his weaknesses. Whether he could exploit the latter, of course, depended a great deal on Katopodis's own talents and the people's knowledge of the importance of the issues. As a contender, he could attack programs, even successful ones, without belaboring specifics. The average citizen may have cared about taxes or city services, but most were too encumbered with the process of living to get bogged down in the debate over the financial intricacies of such things as Block 60 or hiring at Arlington Museum. Katopodis, of course, had few doubts about the public mind. He had been a part of government for six years, and he could take credit for its success; on the other hand, he could blame the mayor for the failure of programs, poor leadership, or bad advice. In fact, Katopodis would state during the campaign, "I could legitimately take credit for every single thing that the mayor has taken credit for . . . [because] the city council has funded every one of those programs."

The council president put together a strong, well-funded organization. He chose an insurance executive, Bill Decker, to run his campaign, although much of the nuts-and-bolts operations came under the control of Steve Moon, a former member of the Birmingham police department. The candidate also secured the services of Nancy Powell, who served as his executive secretary at the Alabama School of Fine Arts. Powell left her job to help canvass the community and to organize volunteers, a job not totally foreign to her, since she had worked in other campaigns. While the "brain center" of his campaign was his headquarters on the city's Southside,

Katopodis also had offices in two other sections of Birmingham. Although he did not have a campaign office anywhere in the black community, he did recruit a black cochairman, William Hamilton, a minister and an Arrington antagonist.

The mayoral election of 1979 and the heated city-council race two years later had given adequate evidence of the influence of race in Birmingham. In 1983, two fair-campaign groups worked to prevent racial bitterness and to hear complaints brought by the candidates. The first, the Committee for a Fair Campaign, sprang from the Community Affairs Committee of Operation New Birmingham, a biracial nonpartisan organization that worked for progressive programs in the city. Headed by Luther Smith, a former Salvation Army official, the committee asked candidates to sign pledge cards that committed them to fair play. Cynics predicted that the fair-campaign efforts would go the way of national prohibition—unenforced. To some, the committee's goals were similar to "baseball, mom, and apply pie," for any candidate that rejected them would end up a loser.

Jeff Norrell, a history professor, chaired a second group—the Fair Campaign Committee, sponsored by the Young Men's Business Club. Norrell hoped that bringing the two candidates together would prevent misunderstanding and would diffuse volatile situations. Truly, the only real enforcement power that either of the campaign groups had was a public opinion that prided a healthy image different from that of the "old Birmingham." Race, however, would remain a factor in the 1983 race, but the publicity given the establishment of the two committees probably had a wholesome effect during the election contest. It is likely, too, that the integrated council slates and the experience of the 1981 race had relieved the city of some of its racial venom. Time perhaps was having its favorable impact on the Magic City.

John Katopodis needed more than time to defeat Richard Arrington. From the beginning his campaign faced an uphill battle. But the candidate had no illusion about his monumental task, and he found it both realistic and politically convenient to assume the role of underdog. In dramatic fashion he compared his race with Arrington as a kind of "David and Goliath" contest. But, he asked an audience rhetorically, "who won that one?" Katopodis would need a powerful slingshot and many political rocks to knock his opponent out of city hall. Arrington, on the other hand, had everything to gain by playing the role of statesman. He had to be visible, but he did not have to assume an aggressive posture unless his high ratings in the polls began to plummet or unless he had to defend his administration against absurd charges. Katopodis had to win away the mayor's office, and given Arrington's record, that task would be difficult.

The first weeks of the campaign produced few fireworks, much to the surprise of those who had witnessed recent mayoral campaigns and the 1981 city elections. The political air, wrote a reporter in mid-August, "is markedly quiet." For a while the two candidates operated in political slow motion, carefully allocating their time to avoid the use of valuable energy until the final two or three weeks of the battle. Peaking too soon, as Cindy McCartney had warned the Arrington camp, could prove fatal. Winning the war was more important than victory in a few skirmishes. Katopodis used almost a shotgun approach to many issues in the early stages of the campaign, as if to test whether they would float. Anxious to find issues, he had raised a question about the mayor's six-second cameo appearance in a mass-transit television commercial, but that challenge faded quickly when editors removed Arrington from the short film. He then turned to that nebulous commodity called "leadership," telling the press that he could get the city moving again.

Arrington welcomed discussion of the leadership theme. He had already been tested, and his actions stood fully exposed to the public. Exploiting the suspicions some harbored of Katopodis's erratic nature, the mayor spoke often of the *quality* of leadership. As a person who had survived in a rugged political arena, Arrington said that he was "going to be talking about what I have done in 12 years of city government." He turned to peace in the city, stating that it was no accident. It had a relationship to honest leadership that treated all parts of the city fairly, that promoted harmonious relationships between people. During his four years in the mayor's office, he had grown in leadership capacity. To Katopodis, however, the mayor had been a divisive factor during the 1981 city-council election. Hoping to gain from that episode, Katopodis pictured that event as a "head-on collision between the mayor and myself where he [Katopodis] emerged as a force for harmony." Arrington, of course, had already expressed some disappointment in not moving sooner to heal the divisions that came during that period.

Cindy McCartney had been right in asserting that Katopodis would raise a number of scattered issues during the contest. Campaign funding was one of those. The source of funds in a political contest is a legitimate consideration when money is used to influence policy decisions or to exact favors illegally from government, but such was not the concern of Arrington's opponent. In late August, Katopodis criticized the mayor's fund-raising activities, although he claimed no misuse of money within the Arrington camp. He had become disturbed with the dollars that had flowed into Arrington's coffers from outside the state. Indeed, the mayor had requested help in his campaign from friends beyond Alabama, including Mayors Andrew Young of Atlanta and Marion Barry of Washington, D.C. Businesses such as Atlanta Life Insurance Company also aided Arrington, as did his national fraternity, Alpha Phi Alpha. Ozell Sutton, president of Alpha, put the case for the organization's action when he said that "one of the problems with black mayors and what they do [is that] the big campaign money in a given city dries up for them." The Alphas had given money to Arrington and to other blacks, including Mayor Tom Bradley of Los Angeles, to advance the black community through the political process. A black mayor, said Sutton, was not merely a chief executive but a "symbol of the aspirations of an entire people." Progress had come to Birmingham because of Arrington, and funds from his group could help sustain it. "Dick Arrington," he noted, "has done an exceptional job bringing Birmingham [into] the 20th Century."

To defeat Arrington, an opponent had to win a large majority of white voters, since little likelihood existed of black defection from the mayor. For Katopodis to win 8 percent of the black vote, as he projected early in the campaign, would amount to a political triumph of astronomical proportions. Arrington believed his opponent could muster no more than 2 percent of the black electorate.

Whatever the number, Katopodis conducted essentially a campaign to win white votes, and his appeal to the black community never showed great vigor. He worked to broaden his own base among white voters, and he wasted little time on a group unwilling to separate from its traditional allegiance.

Katopodis attempted to make crime and the economy major issues. In the 1979 race he had won the support of the Fraternal Order of Police in the primary, and now he again tried to exploit the law-and-order theme. He tried to benefit from his past history by alluding to his "long history of support for the police." With an apparent reference to Arrington's attacks against the police, he reminded citizens that he had not been a critic on the city council, "continually demoralizing our police officers who were doing the best they could under difficult circumstances." Katopodis also charged that morale had been negatively affected by Arrington's criticism. The times, however, had changed. And so had police brutality and the level of crime in Birmingham. Katopodis could not easily ignore the decline in criminal activity. He tried to play down the role Arrington's administration had assumed in the reduction of crime, stressing the overall drop in crime statistics for the entire nation. He charged that the method of keeping records accounted for the decrease, but figures were too revealing and too accurate to ignore the active role Arrington had played.

Arrington had given his strong support to high-intensity lighting in neighborhoods, and he had increased law-enforcement personnel in his effort to make the city a safe place to live. The police department had also reassigned some officers to street duty. Moreover, it will be recalled, he had taken a personal role in highlighting certain kinds of crime in the early part of his administration. Arrington was aware that not only the actual existence of crime but the belief that crime abounded had an unfavorable effect on the city. His goal, then, had been not simply to reduce crime but also to produce within Birmingham a *perception* of security.

Birmingham's assault on crime had yielded results that eclipsed the national decline and thus frustrated Katopodis's attempt to make it an issue. While there had been a reduction in crime across the nation during 1980–83, there were cities, Arrington pointed out, where crime had increased during the same period. The mayor attributed much of Birmingham's success to leadership at city hall, the diligent work of his police department, and to citizens' programs such as Block Watch and Crime-stoppers. When a representative of an anticrime group wrote the city council in June 1981 that the increase of crime in her area "is reflected city wide," she was responding to past trends, not to the reality of the present. Crime had already begun to drop in the city. The writer, incidentally, also labored under the assumption that business had continued to leave the city and that new establishments failed to come to Birmingham because of a supposed increase in crime. Another citizen also wrote Arrington authoritatively about the same time stating "I know . . . crime is up."

Figures on crime told a more objective story. For the ten-year period before Arrington came to office, crime in Birmingham had been on the upswing, compared to the nation as a whole. It did not begin to decline until 1980 and at a pace that exceeded the national average. By mid-1982, it was declining at a rate of 8 percent in the Magic City, compared with 5 percent for the nation.

Beyond the issue of crime itself, there had been improvement in the professionalism of the police. As a councilman, Arrington had worked to end police brutality, and he had insisted upon professional conduct and courtesy from law officers. A sharp critic of the police department, he had endeavored to achieve a level of performance and behavior that honored the humane treatment of citizens accused of crime. A badge, he believed, did not grant the right to brutalize citizens, nor did it give license for attack from those who would abuse law officers. This view of the operation of law enforcement had led to favorable results during Arrington's first administration, and it successfully rebutted the sometimes cryptic charges of John Katopodis. Police officers under Arrington used less deadly force in making arrests, and charges for resisting officers and for assaults decreased. Police brutality complaints had also dropped by 75 percent during the mayor's term in office. Katopodis struggled to address this kind of hard evidence. He could allude to Arrington's council years, but that era had gone. Arrington was now mayor, the person responsible for a police force that had in actuality reduced crime.

Mayors of large cities have some direct control over law enforcement, but their power over the economy is less direct. In many ways they are prisoners of national forces and the inevitable workings of the private-enterprise system. Yet, they may be able, depending on the extent of their influence, to shape the course of business and industry by establishing a healthy environment for growth and economic development. They can also focus attention on employment and greater industrial activity. Whether in a small town or a sprawling metropolis, mayors are boosters, servants who must put their city on parade and tout the strength of their people and the people's resources. Often the first impression of a city is its mayor, and to some degree he or she carries personally the image of the place and its possibilities for progressive business and industrial development. Aware of the need to project Birmingham as a vibrant city that had entered modern life and not the municipal backwater pictured in some minds, Arrington traveled widely in the early months of his administration to carry a different, more accurate, updated message. While his educational background, training, and years in public service made him suited for the purpose, the city's dark racial history often made the man himself the message.

Arrington had faced unenviable economic conditions upon coming to office, and some serious problems still lingered when Katopodis again decided to run against him. In 1979, the "double whammy" of recession and high inflation had staggered the nation, and cities suffered as they struggled to meet their responsibilities and financial obligations. In Birmingham, steel reflected the national state of the industry as companies closed or cut back operations and as related enterprises laid off workers. United States Steel became only a skeleton of its old industrial self, with only tall smokestacks to remind one of its past prominence. The quiet conditions that prevailed at some plants in the area, especially at the works in Fairfield where Arrington's father had worked for many years, provided an eerie lesson about the precarious state of the area's economy. The cutback in steel, with its multimillion-dollar income and payroll, produced a tremendously adverse ripple effect in the Birmingham economy. Years would need to pass for the city to achieve the realignment and the diversity in the economy necessary for sustained growth that depended less heavily upon a single industry.

Katopodis and his followers turned to prevailing economic conditions in assailing the mayor's record. They pointed to a high rate of unemployment that had ranged from 15 to 16 percent in the two years before the 1983 election. A number of businesses in metals and manufacturing had closed their doors or reduced their activity. Some downtown retail businesses and a few large corporations had also opted to build their office complexes outside the Magic City. Arrington, the argument ran, had at least an indirect responsibility for some of these occurrences, since he "never made the local business connections necessary to create a good business environment."

Arrington did not deny the continuing problems in the economy, but he highlighted the achievements of his administration. "The bleakest aspect of the year," he said of 1982, "has clearly been unbearably high unemployment which gripped us in the midst of the transition from dependence on heavy industry to a more diversified economy." He lamented the terrible state of industrial decline that had harshly affected Birmingham and that had helped bring high rates of joblessness. "I don't know of any local area," he said, "that can control that issue [unemployment] solely when the nation as a whole is in a near depression." Arrington, however, did not succumb to a spirit of pessimism, nor was he insensitive to the debilitating effects upon individuals and their families. "I do not underestimate [the] severe human need in our midst," he stated candidly, and he did not overestimate the role the city could play in resolving economic problems that depended so much upon private industry. While the city, in conjunction with state and local agencies, had taken steps to cushion some of the harsh economic blows to citizens, much rested upon changes in the American economy. The mayor stressed that Birmingham was laying a local economic base for a quick recovery once the country took an upturn. The problem for Katopodis on the unemployment issue, in particular, was its linkage to the national economy. As one political observer noted, "People don't expect the mayor to solve it."

Whether affected by national or local conditions, the state of the economy had a direct effect on the city's budget and revenues. Possible new taxes and the management of resources were subjects for Arrington's opponent, and he raised them, but neither ever became an overriding issue in the campaign. Katopodis warned citizens of an impending deficit crisis forecast by a local Chamber of Commerce study, and he implied that Arrington wanted to sweep the matter under the rug. Only by shifting some expenses to its federal revenue-sharing account, he said, had the city succeeded in balancing its operating budget in 1983. The chamber study called for some changes in tax rates or in the level of services offered by city hall. Either approach posed political difficulty.

Katopodis's approach to the budget called for improved management, retrenchment in expenditures, and a more effective system of taxation. He would trim some city services and revise the licensing code and he would not waste money on "frivolous" lawsuits such as the one brought by Arrington against the Jefferson County Personnel Board over the selection of a police chief. Katopodis, like Arrington, recognized the need to expand the city's tax base dramatically, and he called for careful study of the occupational tax. He contended that that particular tax served as a disincentive to investment and, consequently, a drag on revenue. Therefore, he argued, the city should either "reduce or replace" it, although it accounted for 20 percent of Birmingham's operating revenue. Katopodis did not favor a sales-tax increase, since, in his judgment, it would place Birmingham at a serious disadvantage with outlying business areas.

Arrington saw a solution to the city's budgetary problem through economic growth and some adjustment in taxes and the tax base. Katopodis's allusion to effective management and retrenchment did not greatly disturb the mayor. Arrington had brought savings to city hall without layoffs, relying heavily on attrition and efficiency, which became almost an obsession with his aide Len Gedgoudas. But the city needed more than that. "We're going to have to look for [taxes]," he told a local newspaper frankly two weeks before the election, since "I don't know any other way to meet the high needs [of the city]." The mayor carefully refrained from pinpointing the specific source of any new or increased taxes, but given his comments, a higher sales tax seemed a likely possibility. Katopodis, who opposed such a tax, charged that the mayor had wasted "thousands of dollars" of taxpayers' money through such nonessential projects as renovation of the city-hall snack bar and the purchase of experimental garbage-collection equipment.

The city had lost money in its determination to make the Block 60 project a reality, and naturally that project surfaced in the election. Although John Katopodis had been a party to the development effort through his position on the city council, he placed the bulk of the blame for its collapse upon Arrington and his staff. That project had called for building a $125-million multiuse complex in the very heart of the city's downtown. Block 60, however, had failed when one of the major owners in the area refused to sell his property at a price that had been previously agreed upon. The collapse dealt a severe blow to the mayor and his staff and the legal aftermath that saw the city in court with suits brought against it made defeat of Block 60 even more painful.

During the election, Katopodis paraded himself as a champion of the project who had made a desperate try to save it. Unfortunately, he contended, the administration should have exerted greater energy to win over Block 60 property owners and to explain the development to the city's citizens. When Katopodis told a reporter that Arrington "made a mistake in selecting a developer who did not have the financial capacity to keep the promises made to the city," he simplified the Block 60 issue, for a crucial consideration had been one of the property owner's unwillingness to sell his property. Katopodis maintained that the mayor turned his back on suggestions presented to him to salvage Block 60. As the project was crumbling, Katopodis criticized, Arrington turned a deaf ear, content that the best way to handle the disaster of Block 60 "was to let it die and then try to pass the blame on to someone else."

The details of Block 60 did not possess the emotional punch to attract sustained attention from any appreciable number of citizens. Most objective voters were not likely to separate Katopodis completely from the project or blame the mayor totally for an undertaking essentially in the hands of a private developer. Block 60 and the city's master plan had received great play in the press, and interested citizens had had an opportunity to follow the details and to respond to the mayor or to their councilpersons. Arrington contended that Katopodis had damaged Block 60 by negative statements about the developer and that his political allies, Bill Myers and Bettye Fine Collins, had contributed to the failure by refusing to sign an agreement following the mayor's successful negotiation with a local bank to acquire money to purchase land.

Initially, Block 60 had looked appealing as a possible campaign issue because of the publicity, but by the summer of 1983, it had no more attraction to the voting public than youth gangs or, say, one-man garbage pickup. To many voters, it appeared that Arrington had merely done what the master plan had decreed and what the council had sanctioned.

While Katopodis waged an attack of scattered issues, as Mc-Cartney had predicted, his style and his message drove away some voters. When discussing policies sanctioned by the city and carried out faithfully by Arrington, Katopodis succeeded in antagonizing the black community. His lukewarm support of affirmative action for women, blacks, and other minorities gained him little following among blacks. But he counted on the influence of the Reverend William Hamilton to help chip away at some of the mayor's support base.

Before the commencement of the 1983 mayoral race, Natalie Davis, a professor at Birmingham-Southern College, had prophetically commented upon the forthcoming contest. She characterized the election as a "turf battle" between blacks and whites in a city almost equally divided along racial lines. Davis had articulated what black people suspected when she said that "the issues are going to be couched in terms of Arrington's performance, but I think underneath the issue will be race." Like McCartney, Davis had predicted a campaign that would lack a strong, solid issue, and that fact, she said, would focus attention more sharply on race. The Fair Campaign Committee, of course, had been born in an effort to play down such an emphasis, but it faced a difficult ordeal.

The candidates in the 1983 mayoral contest could not keep the shadow of race in the closet of time. Katopodis had signed a fair-campaign pledge, and he later declared in statesmanlike fashion that he turned down opportunities to use race to his advantage in the election. Nonetheless, race was exploited. How close its usage came to racism often depended on the eye and ear of the beholder. For example, black people still remembered Katopodis's harsh statements during the Bonita Carter shooting, although he had apologized twice before the election. Yet, he had never suggested re-opening the issue or settling out of court with the Carter family. To many blacks, his opposition said more than his words.

The manner in which Arrington's opponent raised one specific instance of image disturbed even those blacks who otherwise may have agreed with him. During the campaign *People Magazine* published an article in its 12 September 1983 edition about the mayor's security guards, the interracial couple Billy and Gwendolyn Webb. Written by Peter Carlson, with photos by Harry Benson, the article had as a theme the sweeping changes that had taken place in Birmingham since the era of the sixties. The romance, marriage, and life of the Webbs provided a convenient background for discussion of the city's social progress and racial tolerance. Carlson wrote in his September 1983 article that "the Webbs story is a contemporary Romeo and Juliet tale set against the backdrop of the Southern Civil-rights revolution." The author brought to his work a knowledge of history and an engaging literary style. He did not attempt to open old wounds, and on the whole, he effectively delivered his essential message—Birmingham had changed.

Unfortunately, Carlson's message became lost in the heated rhetoric of politics and race. The *People* article carried several historic photos and some pictures of the Webbs. One of the shots was of Mrs. Webb lying face down on a bed, fully clothed, as her husband leans across her. How sensual the pose appeared, or whether that sensuality—if any—was inappropriate for a married couple, depended upon those who saw the article. Certainly, the photo was not sexually explicit. Why photographer Benson chose that particular shot for the story, however, is anyone's guess. Undoubtedly, the picture would have had far less relevance had not Birmingham been in the middle of a political season that pitted a man who desperately needed white votes against a black incumbent.

Katopodis called the magazine piece "tasteless," although he never publicly stated the reason for this characterization. He raised the issue at a forum with Arrington only a few days after the edition of the popular journal went on sale. Arrington had provided an opening for Katopodis's comments when he pointed to a story in another journal that carried a favorable column on the city of Birmingham. In pressing his often-repeated theme of peace and harmony, the mayor told a group that "we are no longer a city at war with ourselves" and that Birmingham had an even greater potential for progress. Katopodis, anxious to offset the mayor's positive image of his administration, asked whether any of his listeners had seen the article on the Webbs. "Do you think that this is the image we ought to have of the city of Birmingham?" he queried his audience. Whether the candidate was alluding to the image of a city undergoing favorable reform or to the photo, Katopodis, perhaps inadvertently, interjected the element of race. Interracial marriage had long been a disturbing subject for many southerners, and the Arrington camp believed that Katopodis had attempted to use it for political gain.

Once again Katopodis's distance from the black community and his almost single-minded concentration on white votes blinded him to opportunities among blacks. He showed little political creativity in trying to exploit the Webb issue, which he may have partly done had he worked more skillfully at the task. Obviously, Katopodis wanted to embarrass Arrington and, of course, win votes. His objective did not deceive blacks, and even some of those at city hall who supported the mayor but disliked the Webbs rallied to the couple's side. Blacks close to Arrington had come to regard Gwendolyn Webb as an ambitious woman with political goals that she wanted the mayor to help advance. She had become gradually more involved in political matters, a development that concerned the mayor. In the judgment of some, the Webbs viewed themselves as part of the mayor's official team—which they were not. They had once been casual friends of the Arringtons, and perhaps this relationship created the eagerness for power that often comes with living close to it.

With considerable skill Katopodis sent out reminders of race without appearing to make racist comments. For example, blacks had witnessed considerable police brutality before 1979 and Arrington, of course, had led the fight against it. When the mayor observed that police brutality had dropped drastically during his years in office, Katopodis sought maximum political benefit among the strong propolice element when he exclaimed, "Bull! It [police brutality] never was that high." Although he had retracted his comments on the Bonita Carter family suit, it was difficult for many blacks to accept the notion of his supposed liberalism.

As expected, Katopodis mounted a fierce verbal assault upon the Jefferson County Citizens Coalition, Arrington's powerful political organization. The attack was actually a continuation of the councilman's past charges against the group that had nominated an all-black slate in 1981 and that had refused to endorse his black friend Helen Shores Lee. When asked why the mayor had fared so well in the majority white city council, Katopodis played down his opponent's ability to persuade. Arrington had prevailed because "he is able to call in IOU's and he is able to apply pressure that I'm not able to apply." He had a *machine* that dictated that, "unless you go along with us on issues that we think are of importance—no matter what the merits of the issue are—you're not going to be endorsed in the next go-around." The coalition, Katopodis confessed, had developed into the most effective political organization in Birmingham.

In his search for a central issue, Katopodis returned repeatedly to the 1981 city election and the coalition. A reporter who covered the mayoral race correctly observed one month into the campaign that "one weapon he [Katopodis] is using . . . is to remind the voters of the all-black slate of council candidates in 1981" that the mayor and the coalition backed. The white candidate saw the powerful hand of the black political organization wherever he turned—and it troubled him. For him the important issue in the campaign was this octopuslike political machine that stretched its tentacles throughout the city, grasping all it could by force or favor. In a sweeping allegation, the embattled candidate, far behind in the polls in early October, claimed that Arrington's coalition controlled "every single [city board] appointment." And he inferred that the machine had exploited poor blacks to gain political power.

Arrington could tolerate charges of machine politics, but he found other allegations irritating. He did not accept the extravagant contention that the Jefferson County Citizens Coalition was worse than the old Richard Daley machine in Chicago. "It's based on patronage, on ignorance," Katopodis bitterly criticized to the embarrassment of many intelligent blacks associated with the group. He also condemned the organization the mayor had founded as undemocratic, designed to keep in power only a small number of people. "You could put Michael M. Mouse, alias Mickey, on [the] ballot and he'd be elected," Katopodis quipped flippantly. Simmie Lavender, president of the coalition in 1983, deemed particularly offensive Katopodis's charge that intellectual honesty had faded from politics.

Among Katopodis's wildest claims was that the coalition drove William Cody, public-school superintendent, from Birmingham. The Citizens Coalition, he contended, dominated the school board, with two members—Ossie Ware Mitchell and T. L. Alexander—directly connected with the politics of the black political organization. Only one board member, Martha Gaskins (a confirmed Katopodis supporter), he said, represented a sane and rational voice. The candidate's charge quickly backfired when Cody declared from his new job in Maryland that "there's not one iota of truth" that the coalition had anything to do with his leaving. He had left for professional reasons.

Katopodis's attacks on the coalition and his racial remarks reflected the plight of a political figure who desperately craved victory. An analysis of his statements on race displays a harshness that destroyed, at least in black minds, any notion of his essential desire to redress past racial wrongs. With the charged atmosphere he helped to create, it should not have surprised anyone to see a more virulent form of attack on Arrington and the coalition. During the campaign city-council candidate Russ Vann wrote the following rambling, widely distributed allegorical piece, "This Is Just a Fairy Tale, Isn't It?"

Once upon a time, in the city of Birming, in the land of Ham, there ruled a King named Richard. Now the king ruled over the people who were of two types, the nights and the days. The king, a night, claimed that he served all the people equally, regardless of type. But the people knew better.

For as in any kingdom, there were dragons which threatened the countryside. But an elite group called the Dragonslayers [police] risked their lives time and again to protect the people. Some of the Dragonslayers did such a good job that they came up for promotion. Alas, King Richard blocked their promotions because they were days and not nights, so much for serving the people equally.

Four years ago, King Richard was chosen to rule with the help of some of the days. Two years later, the king decided to show his appreciation. Five members of the Council were to be chosen. King Richard backed a slate of five nights. He forgot that it is the people, not the king, who choose and he ended up with four days and a night.

King Richard immediately claimed that it was the evil Sir Coalition, not the king, who wanted five nights and no days. He forgot to mention that Sir Coalition is his right hand man. Sir Coalition operates by getting nights to vote only for other nights. However, the storytellers [media] are saying that Sir Coalition may include one or two days on his list this time; an obvious ploy to improve the king's image.

Unfortunately, some of the days are closer to sundown tha[n] others and may fall for such a trick. The storytellers will be taken in immediately. After all, they have always thought that nights voting only for nights is happily ever after stuff; but days voting only for days is worse than dragon droppings.

But this is supposed to be a fairy tale, so where are the fairies? It is strongly rumored that the King's Council contains one or two fairies disguised as council members. Whether good or bad fairies is hard to say since it is hard enough to spot them, much less tell whether they are good or bad.

On October 11th, *you* decide if there will be 4 more years of King Richard and Sir Coalition.

Unruffled by the atmosphere of the campaign, Arrington followed his political game plan to perfection. By the second week in October, only one major hurdle remained before the final showdown in the Magic City—a televised debate. In mid-August the League of Women Voters of Greater Birmingham had extended invitations to the two major mayoral candidates for a face-to-face meeting. Katopodis had little to lose from such an encounter, and although polls showed Arrington ahead of his opponent, the mayor probably would have hurt his campaign had he declined the women's offer. The league scheduled the debate for the Sunday immediately prior to the 11 October election, the first of its type in the city's history. In 1979, mayoral candidates had traded remarks broadcast over radio, but the use of television brought to the local election in Birmingham a format adopted in national presidential elections.

The league excluded mayoral candidate Sonja Franeta. The Birmingham women argued that they were following national precedent in selecting only major contestants to debate the issues. Franeta unsuccessfully requested the city council to adopt a resolution objecting to her exclusion, and Mayor Arrington issued a statement that supported the candidate's participation in the debate. In his opinion it would "better serve the interest of the voters of this city." A spokesperson for Katopodis also voiced no objection to Franeta's appearance in the debate, but the league, nevertheless, gave no ground.

Few surprises appeared during the debate for those citizens who had followed the unfolding 1983 political drama. Arrington's aggressiveness struck many observers. Although he led in the polls, he seized the offensive as if he actually trailed in the race. By contrast, Katopodis appeared unusually calm—almost out of character—to those who knew him. The volatility of the candidate, to which the media had alluded, rarely showed through, although he sometimes chose the harsh word or phrase rather than a more palatable euphemism. For example, he spoke of Arrington "cronies" who would fill vacancies at city hall if abolition of civil service ever became a reality, and the institution of a "spoils" system, and of "frivolous" lawsuits. On the whole, however, Katopodis tried to present a statesmanlike image. The debate was his last chance before the election to prove wrong his critics who accused him of having a razorlike tongue, or at least to demonstrate to them that for a limited time he could keep his temper in check.

The debate served to sharpen the differences between the two candidates to a citywide audience and to give citizens an opportunity to judge their mental quickness. To take one position on an issue and then change it at the next community forum was now impossible, for people from throughout the city had their attention riveted on their television sets. Although both candidates had addressed the deficit, for example, their replies to the question on that issue during the debate were more forceful and more direct. Arrington admitted the city needed an additional revenue source. Some kind of tax increase would be necessary, although he did not anticipate the high deficit predicted by the Chamber of Commerce study.

Like Arrington, Katopodis agreed that the long-term solution to the city's economic problems had much to do with expansion of the tax base. Previously, however, he had talked of revamping the licensing code, better management, and efficiency to help solve the deficit problem. But Katopodis now stated more emphatically, "I am against a tax increase," for it would negatively affect business. On another matter, the possible reform of civil service, an issue that had gotten little play during the campaign, except through the indirect discussion of the police-chief selection controversy, Arrington made a case for change, while Katopodis supported the existing system. Katopodis feared that revamping the system would lead to the appointment of political friends, a comment that may have encouraged some citizens to think of Arrington's supporters in the coalition.

Occasionally, Arrington seemed to catch Katopodis completely off guard. When the police-chief issue came up, the incumbent hurriedly answered that a previous mayor had appointed other department heads from outside the state but that the issue of hiring a nonresident assumed importance only when he took office. Katopodis had stated a preference for choosing local people to head the city's departments. He also spoke of the need for aiding middle-income citizens and support for residential revitalization. Arrington brought forth an array of facts, concluding that the value of new homes built in the city during his tenure totaled $100 million. The city, he said, had assisted with 72 percent of that amount, 40 percent of which went to *middle-income* citizens.

Image and race surfaced in the television debate, but they hardly received the attention of unemployment, crime, the deficit, revitalization, and education. Katopodis had attacked the national media on several occasions for turning to Birmingham's past racial history. Arrington accused his opponent of conveniently trying to forget history. It was not healthy, Arrington warned, to "stick our heads in the sand" and to say "Stop talking about Birmingham." Citizens of the city had emerged as a stronger, more aggressive people, and persons confident of the future and of progress had no desire to sweep the past under a rug or to say to those who remembered history to "go away and leave us alone." Katopodis, determined to capitalize on history himself, turned again to a favorite theme he refused to let die—the 1981 council race. But he was hardly ready for an Arrington rebuttal that came with devastating quickness and that trapped Katopodis in his own logic. On the one hand, Katopodis had attacked the media for talking about the past, but Katopodis himself had criticized Arrington for his role in the 1981 council election.

Arrington admitted frankly that he should have acted sooner to avert some of the racial divisiveness of the 1981 council election. But the mayor responded to Katopodis by focusing on the council president's contradictory position. Arrington put the rhetorical question that made his point so plainly that no viewer could miss it. "Does he want to bring the division [between the races] back again," the mayor asked, "by constantly talking about it?" The Arrington administration, he stressed, had presided over a peaceful community.

The 1983 mayoral debate may have had a long-range positive effect. In this first televised forum of its type in Birmingham, two southerners—one black, the other white—had stood "toe to toe" battling each other, matching intellectual wits over policies to govern a population equally divided along racial lines. That encounter in itself had real, historic meaning.

Arrington had gone into the debate again assured of the support of the city's two largest newspapers. Both the *Birmingham News* and the *Birmingham Post-Herald* had backed him in 1979 over his opponent, Frank Parsons. Some difficult times, however, had come since that election and the political clash of 1983, and the press had seemed reluctant to support him on some issues, especially the 1981 council election. "To be candid," the editor of the *News* wrote a week before the debate, "some doubts arose during the first part of the Arrington administration as to the mayor's ability to win the city's confidence that he intended to perform in the best interests of the city as a whole." The *Birmingham News* said that the first black mayor of Birmingham had reacted too sensitively to criticism of his policies, assuming that color caused it. At times he appeared unwilling or unable to widen the bridges to the white community, but the mayor had matured "impressively" and had grown in his office. Katopodis must have been disappointed with the paper's conclusion that Arrington had proven "not only an effective administrator but, increasingly, a public figure commanding the respect of the entire community."

The *Birmingham Post-Herald* too, saw some weaknesses in Arrington, but the quality of his leadership tipped the scales in favor of him. A "telling difference," said the *Post-Herald* "is the personality and leadership style of the two men." The journal believed that Arrington had a much better chance of building political coalitions on the city council than did his opponent. Katopodis, said the paper's editor, had a much more "volatile personality" than Arrington did. "There is," the editorial critically observed, "no mistaking his mood." Katopodis's style was more suited to service on the city council than to the mayor's office. Arrington was not a figurehead for others, and during his four years, said the *Post-Herald*, he had become an increasingly effective mayor.

Arrington's endorsement by the city's two large dailies elicited a blistering attack from Katopodis. Those who watched closely the newspapers' coverage of the campaign must have been surprised at Katopodis's contention that the media had engaged in a "conspiracy of silence." During the contest Katopodis told a political forum that the *Birmingham News* had endorsed his opponent because that paper had persuaded the city to build a parking deck adjacent to its building. Katopodis alluded to an agreement between the city and the *News* for the rental of a new city-owned parking garage. He remarked to a group of citizens, "No, I don't have the endorsement of the *Birmingham News* because I have never voted to build them a parking deck at your expense." Katopodis's language contained a challenge to the city's papers: "I'm going to work hard to bring another newspaper to Birmingham, Alabama, to give the *Birmingham News* the competition it's been needing for years and years."

On 12 October 1983, Arrington supporters gathered at the Boutwell Auditorium in downtown Birmingham in anticipation of victory. Many of those who came had spent a long, hard day working at headquarters, in the office on the Southside calling voters, or encouraging block captains or other volunteers in the campaign. On the day of the election, Cindy McCartney and others had risen early to handle last-minute details. They had profited from the experience of 1979, and election day 1983 went without undue problems. Predictions of rain worried Arrington, but projected temperatures in the sixties buoyed him. Campaign workers made an effort to get the elderly and the handicapped to the polls early to avoid long lines. The most crucial consideration, of course, was whether Arrington supporters would go to the polls in great numbers. Katopodis needed a small black turnout, whether because of rain or some other inclement weather condition, but large numbers of whites.

Arrington whipped his opponent decisively. More than 70 percent of the registered voters went to the polls to cast ballots. Arrington won slightly over 60 percent of the total vote, while Katopodis trailed far behind with 39 percent. Sonja Franeta had no real impact on the outcome of the election with her 170 votes. It was a whopping victory for the black incumbent in a contest that saw 2 percent more registered voters go to the polls than in 1979, when Arrington narrowly edged businessman Frank Parsons.

Birmingham citizens voted along racial lines in the mayoral contest, which surprised no one. Katopodis had admitted the need for black voters, but he could attract only a small number of their ballots, and with the white turnout less in some places than he expected, victory escaped him. Of the city's black voters, 77 percent went to the polls, most of them voting for Arrington. Clearly, however, Katopodis's campaign comments about Arrington and race-related issues did not prevent a sizable number of whites from crossing over to vote for the black politician. Cindy McCartney had been correct, however, in her prediction that Arrington would register few gains in the eastern part of the city. While voting on the Southside proved unusually light compared with black sections and the city's total as a whole, Arrington improved upon his 1979 performance in the white community, winning as much as 33 percent of the vote in some places, even in Katopodis's own home box! The mayor had received about 10 percent of the white vote four years earlier, but in 1983 he increased this figure to 12 percent. While that increase did not appear remarkable, given the emphasis on race, it provided a testimony to changing political behavior in Birmingham.

Crossover voting in the race for city-council seats was much more evident than in the mayor's race. Arrington had stayed free—at least publicly—of involvement in the council race. The coalition, however, had endorsed all of the winning candidates in the primary race: David Herring, Russell Yarbrough, William Bell, and Jeff Germany. In previous years, the field of office seekers had been large, but in 1983 only eighteen persons filed for open positions. No doubt the fact that five incumbents were up for reelection discouraged many newcomers from running. William Bell quipped that the reason so few people sought the $9,300-a-year post was because "they know it's a thankless job." And Herring slyly noted that he had informed possible contenders that "this isn't the year." Heavy financial demands in running a successful campaign probably adversely influenced some would-be candidates, while others did not want to struggle for attention when the spotlight would shine mostly on Arrington and Katopodis.

The coalition's endorsement of all incumbents up for reelection in 1983 except conservative Pete Clifford came as no surprise to those who follow affairs at city hall. At first glance Yarbrough's endorsement may have temporarily stunned those who knew his basically conservative record. He had often clashed with Arrington over police brutality while on the council. But as the 1983 council election approached, Yarbrough had shown a willingness to work with the mayor, often casting crucial votes on issues the mayor favored. "These fat cats running around Birmingham . . . bellyaching about the power of the Coalition," he said in defense of the organization, "are people who can't get the Coalition's support." Yarbrough had grown increasingly antagonistic toward John Katopodis, although he had helped engineer his election as president of the council, ousting the moderate Miglionico. He later labeled the decision to support Katopodis one of his biggest mistakes. Arrington, however, was not misled into believing that Yarbrough had forever done a complete political reversal. After the election, said one Arrington supporter, Yarbrough would "become as conservative as he always was."

The coalition endorsed two black nonincumbents who had previously run unsuccessfully for a council seat. Both Roosevelt Bell and Eddie Blankenship had a history of civic service, and no one questioned their loyalty to the mayor's programs. A manager in the Social Security Administration and a neighborhood president, Bell (unrelated to William Bell) played a leading role in the revitalization that came to that community. Blankenship, a minister, had recently served as interim director of the Birmingham Urban League, a position he resigned upon declaring his candidacy. He had also worked as a special assistant for three years to Mayor David Vann. The coalition had faced a difficult choice in considering Bell and Blankenship along with four incumbents. Finally the organization decided to endorse all six candidates, including Yarbrough. In a tough runoff race Blankenship defeated Bell for the fifth seat on the council, thus adding another black to that body.

Helen Shores Lee had coveted a coalition endorsement, but it escaped her, as it had in 1981. The daughter of the distinguished civil-rights attorney could not shake a history that continued to frustrate her political hopes. The coalition, and much of the black community, seemed determined not to forgive or forget her support of John Katopodis in the 1979 mayoral primary. Lee tried to distance herself, at least publicly, from Katopodis in 1983, saying that she did not want to be judged on any past associations with any political candidates. After Lee met with Arrington, she told the press, "The mayor is well aware . . . who I plan to support." If she decided to dump her friend Katopodis for Arrington, her switch from 1979 did not swing the coalition to her side. She remained what someone called "a political outcast in the black community." Only time perhaps would make Helen Shores Lee an acceptable political name among her own people.

The election theoretically strengthened the mayor's position on the council. All the incumbents had shown a willingness to work with Arrington, but anyone could guess about Russell Yarbrough's future political allegiance. Some believed he had begun to "mellow with age" and that he would be less combative, if not less conservative. Much would depend upon his future plans and his perception of the coalition. Herring, a longtime Democrat and moderate, could be counted on for support of most administration measures, although he sometimes complained of an impending budget crisis. Both Bell and Germany were politicians of independent mind and could demonstrate their obstinacy, but they had an unquestioned commitment to the mayor's programs. With the addition of Blankenship, the old coalition pieced together by Myers and Katopodis, already virtually shattered, faced complete annihilation. If the mayor had supposedly lost ground in 1981, he had now regained it.

His election secure, and with a council that was close to him philosophically, Arrington set out to shape his program for the next four years. Since the mayor had an experienced staff returning to work with him, he anticipated devoting more personal attention to some specific goals. He wanted to continue his efforts to change the city's image, to show Birmingham as a "progressive, harmonious . . . city pursuing a common set of goals." Economic development and public education would also occupy a great deal of his time. Arrington also proposed to spotlight areas of possible cooperation with other cities within the Birmingham metropolitan area, and he pledged to support state legislation that would aid the city. He also formed a committee to address the issue of women's rights. "I am increasingly aware," he wrote in December 1983, "that women in our community face special obstacles and problems which require a greater responsiveness and sensitivity on the part of both the public and private sectors." The mayor later appointed Mary Jones to work with a commission to help resolve problems related to women.

Arrington's reelection and the city-council race of 1983, which scored such an overwhelming victory for the Citizens Coalition, had revealed more than the power of one man or the strength of the political organization he created in 1977. They said much about the continuing political consciousness of blacks in Birmingham and about the white community, which had again taken halting steps toward the sharing of political power. The return of some crossover voting in the election flashed a hopeful sign for the city's political future, but the casual observer could easily make too much of that development. Suspicions nurtured by history yet prevailed.

In 1983, Arrington again showed the power of his personality and leadership in mobilizing a large number of blacks who formerly believed they had no real stake in the system. For blacks, Arrington represented more than just another political leader. He was that, certainly, but he was also a calm voice for reason who could help repair the fragile threads of democracy in Birmingham that the sharp edges of an unjust system had nearly cut apart. Arrington was, then, Birmingham's great hope, a voice commanding an ugly past to stay still, to yield to progressive forces bound to assert their will and to usher in a new day.

10

Consolidation of Power: Arrington's Second Term

·

With his landslide victory, Arrington confidently began his second term. At the beginning most of his senior staff members chose to remain with him, but he would lose three key aides by February 1988. Undoubtedly, the greatest loss to the administration was the resignation of Edward Lamonte, the mayor's executive secretary. Lamonte enjoyed an enviable reputation among a diverse constituency that included both blacks and whites. Initially, he had joined the administration for a "few years" after the mayoral election of 1979, but he remained until August 1987. Although he had been the mayor's point man on a number of projects, especially Block 60, he had managed to maintain his credibility with both the business and the financial communities.

The executive secretary's resignation led to some speculation at city hall about his replacement. A longtime mayoral aide, Virginia Riley, appeared a logical choice to some to assume Lamonte's position, but a possible Riley appointment bothered some blacks at city hall who easily associated her Deep South accent with a southern past that many had tried desperately to forget. There were also persons who believed that the mayor's aide Willie Davis had earned the job and should move up to replace Lamonte. His elevation, however, did not seem likely, and rumors existed at the time that the black aide would leave the administration. Indeed, Davis did resign to go into business in January 1988. Previously, Len Gedgoudas, a bureaucrat with a passion for detail, had also left city hall to become director of the parking garage. Following Lamonte's resignation, the mayor reorganized his staff, although he did not appoint anyone to the executive secretary's position. Five whites, (Scotty Colson, Ellen Cowles, Mikes Miles, Virginia Riley, and M. H. Walker) and six blacks (Leonard Adams, Eric Calhoun, Benjamine Greene, Jesse Huff, Mary Jones, and Lewis White) served on Arrington's staff at the beginning of 1988.

Inadequate financial resources troubled the city during Arrington's second term in office. The American economy still suffered from the twin blows of inflation and recession that hit urban areas hard during the 1970s. Although Birmingham had been able to maintain basic services and to keep city personnel employed without layoffs, reduced revenues again confronted the city with difficult choices. The mayor sought to cut the cost of government and to increase productivity through measures that included, among other things, limiting the overnight use of automobiles by city employees and the closing of some city fire stations. Nevertheless, the city paid a heavy cost for retrenchment. Not only did Arrington have to defer important public-works projects, but he had to delay, or to completely forgo, repairs to some city vehicles, in reality postponing that expenditure until a later date. City expenses forced the mayor to support a sales tax increase in 1983 and to dig into his capital expenses for operating funds.

Cutbacks in federal money came at a time when Birmingham still struggled to convert from an economy that had relied heavily upon steel. Arrington complained that cities across the country were being asked to shoulder a large percentage of the cuts in an effort to balance the national budget. Yet, federal programs such as the Community Development Block Grant, Revenue Sharing, and the Urban Development Action Grant experienced reduction, or total elimination, during the mayor's second term. Under increasing pressure from the business community and from the public at large, Congress passed the Gramm-Rudman Act in 1987, which mandated additional reductions in federal spending according to a prescribed timetable.

The need to promote economic progress in the face of these cuts and the desire to foster cultural programs in the city prompted Arrington to push for a $65-million bond referendum in 1986. To pay for it the mayor proposed additional property taxes, which would have slightly increased a citizen's tax bill. A $100,000 house, for example, would have been taxed an additional $50. With this revenue Arrington wanted to undertake several major projects that he could not begin because of the cutback in dollars from Washington. The mayor proposed to spend the majority of the funds from the referendum on schools and museum construction ($49 million), while the remainder would go to park and neighborhood development, drainage projects, parking facilities, sanitary sewers, and industrial parks.

Arrington and supporters of the bond issue defended it by pointing to a reduction of approximately $11 million to the city from federal revenue. Unless citizens passed the referendum, they said, the city would have to trim more severely projects that had once received support from federal monies. "Without the bond issue," Arrington told one neighborhood group, "we won't have much money for our capital budget," and that would mean fewer funds for the neighborhoods, which had experienced community improvements during his tenure. Councilman David Herring echoed the mayor's message when he boldly asserted, "If we are to continue growing, we've got to pay for it." The property tax, said councilwoman Linda Coleman, was a small price to pay for sustained progress in Birmingham. If the city was going into debt, exclaimed Coleman's colleague and Arrington loyalist Jeff Germany, it was also opening the door for more jobs and the possibility of attracting people to the Magic City.

Some city-council members, nevertheless, did not anxiously embrace the referendum. The price of its passage, they contended, came too high. From the very beginning Arrington encountered strong opposition from Bettye Fine Collins, Bill Myers, and Russell Yarbrough. The conservative Yarbrough, who had received support from the pro-Arrington Jefferson County Citizens Coalition, turned to an often-repeated argument heard time and again in certain ideological circles: generations yet unborn would pay for the loose spending of this era. He admitted that the city had progressed under Arrington but asserted that city officials could do more to trim the budget before asking the people to tax themselves.

The referendum gave rise to an opposing group that eventually emerged as a contending political force to Arrington. Shortly after the city council voted to refer the bond issue to the people, a number of citizens led by attorney Robert McKee and accountant J. A. Boohaker formed an organization called Tax Busters. Although Tax Busters drew many of its members from the anti-Arrington Eastside, it attracted persons from other sections of the city. While the organization included persons opposed to the bond issue, it also contained citizens opposed to a number of Arrington programs.

Waste at city hall became a key word in Tax Busters' attacks upon the city administration. The leadership of Tax Busters pointed to city consulting fees that allegedly went to Arrington's friends, large amounts of money for city-employee travel, and a $1-million loan approved by the city council to bail out the Birmingham Stallions professional football team. A loan for the building of a water theme park also drew criticism, as did the construction of access roads to the new Birmingham racetrack built in the eastern portion of the city.

Tax Busters found a ready ally in George Seibels, former mayor and persistent Arrington antagonist. Seibels complained that the referendum would create a record debt, and he worried about an increase in prices that would supposedly come with a rise in taxes on business if the measure passed. Rental property, the former mayor alleged, would also rise. In a tone that characterized old wars with Arrington, Seibels wrote the *Birmingham Post-Herald* on 5 July 1986:

> If you rent, your rent will go up because landlord tax rates are twice [those of] homeowners. Taxes on all businesses, groceries, gas, clothes, furniture, etc. will go up and so will their prices. Taxes on electricity . . . and telephone will go up and, sooner or later, so will utility bills. If you own your own home you will pay double taxes. First your own tax increase and next all the price increases. It will be the consumer, rich, moderate or poor, who will bear the burden of the increased taxes.

The support of the referendum by the *Birmingham Post-Herald* and active community groups such as the Progressive Alliance gave Arrington optimism. The alliance included a number of leading citizens in Birmingham such as Neal Berte of Birmingham-Southern College, Emily Norton of the National Organization of Women, Odessa Woolfolk of the Center of Urban Affairs at the University of Alabama in Birmingham, and Frank McPhillips, an attorney, who chaired the group. While the alliance had as one of its major objectives the improvement of the city's racial image, it also wanted to promote economic development. Since the government in Washington had cut back funds to the city, McPhillips and his organization argued, Birmingham had to assume a greater role in supporting its institutions and maintaining its facilities. Passage of the bond referendum, they said, would ensure continued economic growth.

The mayor's optimism about a favorable bond vote proved ill-founded. He had hoped that the variety of projects the referendum would fund, coupled with only a modest increase in taxes, would assure success. The biracial appeal of the Progressive Alliance, he also believed, would aid his efforts and would help counteract the negative reaction of those who viewed the referendum as a burden principally upon middle-class whites and businesses. Arrington later confided, however, that some citizens viewed the measure as essentially a black proposal, since only one white council member, David Herring, had voted for the issue.

Voters went to the polls and administered the bond referendum a resounding defeat. Arrington had anticipated a large turnout from the black community, since bond money would have benefited the school system, which was overwhelmingly black, and would have helped fund a civil-rights museum. Nevertheless, many black citizens turned a deaf ear to the administration's radio appeals, leaflets, and phone calls. In the end only slightly over 21 percent of eligible black voters went to the polls, while the number of whites who voted almost doubled that of blacks. When the political smoke cleared on what was surely one of Arrington's most stinging defeats, the city's voters had said no to increased taxation for what administration officials deemed essential progress.

The bond referendum was not a vote of confidence on the Arrington administration, as some of the mayor's opponents maintained. Rarely is a vote on a single issue in a city with Birmingham's form of government a commentary on voter approval or disapproval of a mayor. But Councilwoman Bettye Fine Collins spoke for many whites on the city's Eastside when she exclaimed that the 8 July vote was a "no confidence" vote for Richard Arrington. Her colleague and council ally, Bill Myers, probably came to the heart of the issue in stating that "the failure of the resolution had little to do with 'no confidence.'" Council president William Bell was partly correct, too, when he said that the failure of the referendum resided in "inadequate communication," but he was more accurate in suggesting that advocates of the measure did not succeed in "getting the people stirred up." Also, an important reason for the defeat of the measure was the inclusion of too many programs in the bond issue. Some persons who opposed one particular proposition may have found it easy to vote against all of them. Other citizens simply did not want more taxes.

Arrington's proposal for a water theme park also encountered objections, despite the administration's strong economic arguments for it. The mayor stressed that the park would provide additional employment in the city, especially among area youth, create more revenue, and increase recreational activity for citizens. Proponents of the park believed that its nearness to a new racetrack in the city would further enhance its drawing potential. To Arrington and his supporters the proposal seemed a sure bet to attract customers hungry for social activity in a city that had too little of it.

The water theme park was a public-private venture, and that particular arrangement again brought forth considerable opposition. After advertising for proposals to build the facility, the city settled upon a company called Big Splash. Under a plan outlined by the administration, Arrington proposed to loan the company $3 million at 8 percent interest for fifteen years. Since state law prohibited the city from loaning funds directly to a private business, the mayor proposed to channel the money to Big Splash through the Alabama State Fair Authority. In April 1985, the city had used this procedure in making a loan to the Birmingham Stallions football team of the now-defunct United States Football League.

Bettye Fine Collins and other city-council members who op-

311

posed Arrington's proposed plan said that it violated the spirit of the law that prevented direct loans to private businesses. They complained also that the administration had not adequately informed citizens about the project and that city officials did not know enough about Big Splash. David Herring, chairman of the council's Finance Committee, worried that the loan to the company would greatly reduce the surplus in the city's capital budget. Herring, who often voted with Arrington, believed the city could lose its money if Big Splash went under, since a local bank held first mortgage on the company's assets. The mayor's aide Willie Davis, who handled the project at the time, tried to ease these fears, noting that an appreciation in the park's land values would protect both the city and other creditors, should the effort fail.

The narrow 5-4 council vote for Big Splash forecast future trouble for the park. In an 18 February 1986 editorial the *Birmingham Post-Herald* strongly attacked the water-theme proposal. Although it did not quarrel with the policy of government support for certain private business ventures, the paper accused Arrington and the council of acting in "unseemly and foolish haste" in pushing through the plan. No one was really sure, it noted, how good the Birmingham market was for a park. The city might discover that it had bought a "pig in a poke." The council's action was "dubious at best." City government, the *Post-Herald* proclaimed in a 4 March edition, "is not a bank; it has no business lending money for this purpose." The newspaper's reluctance to condemn public-private projects outright may have resulted from its insistence that the city support the Birmingham Barons baseball team, which later left Birmingham for Hoover, a nearby suburban community. Arrington and Davis argued correctly that some council members, including Collins, had voted to extend loans for other projects that even exceeded the amount approved for Big Splash.

As Arrington pressed for his project, residents who lived in the area of the proposed facility organized to stop the city's $3-million loan to the proposed builder of the park. Led by a group that called itself the Jefferson County Citizens for Responsible Government, opponents of the park attempted unsuccessfully to bring Big Splash to a public vote. But the mayor did witness momentary defeat when a case against the park came before Judge Jack Carl's Jefferson County Circuit Court. The Arrington administration had had other problems with Carl, and again it felt his judicial sting when he heard arguments on Big Splash. In a preliminary injunction the judge ruled that Birmingham could not loan Big Splash the $3 million approved by the city council until he had decided on a class-action suit filed against the park by Councilwoman Bettye Collins. Carl's injunction not only threatened to delay completion of the project, but it also raised questions about building it in the proposed location and, indeed, about whether the city should build it at all. Thus, Arrington abandoned plans to construct the park on the Eastside, but the mayor still remained determined to erect a facility. At the beginning of 1988, talk prevailed about building a park at the fairgrounds on the city's Westside.

Horse racing, much like the water theme park, received support from Arrington as a means of improving the city's economic condition. An interest in developing a racetrack in Birmingham had long existed, but the reality of gambling on thoroughbreds did not come clearly into view until state representatives John Rogers and Earl Hilliard of Jefferson County pushed hard for legislative approval of a racing bill. In 1984, the Alabama legislature gave Jefferson County permission to hold a referendum on horse racing, which citizens approved a year later. Enthusiastic supporters formed a group called the Birmingham Turf Club and announced plans to build a track at a cost that eventually exceeded $80 million. Led by a wealthy businesswoman named Judith Thompson, daughter of the founder of the successful Thompson Tractor Company, the turf club successfully raised the money it needed and hired a builder with the expectation of constructing a "major league track, second to none in the United States." Advocates of racing maintained that Birmingham would soon take on an image that would shatter past notions of a backward city in an equally backward state still struggling to overcome its terrible racial past and a history of relative poverty.

Although the mayor did not share the economic projections of possible income from the track that some promoters optimistically predicted, he did see this new industry as an important contributor

313

to the city treasury. Hotels, restaurants, and other businesses would eventually develop to accommodate the track; and receipts from racing would aid not only the city but charities and other institutions. Arrington wrote for the *Birmingham Times* on 5 March 1987 that "the big intangible is the improved image that the city of Birmingham will surely inherit." The mayor expressed pride in the role city government had played in bringing about racing and in the philosophy that undergirded public-private projects.

Racing began in Birmingham on 3 March 1987 with praise for the turf club's beautiful new facility. One local citizen happily proclaimed that horse racing would become "the biggest money-maker in the history of Birmingham." It would achieve the impossible in Alabama—eclipse football! William Killingsworth, turf club consultant, happily proclaimed that Birmingham would become the "racing capital of the south." Many of the thirteen thousand people at the track's opening races probably came out of curiosity; others, yet neophytes at gambling, came to make a quick "killing"; and still others came for a wholesome outing and to enjoy the beauty of well-trained horses dashing around an $80-million Magic City track. Whatever the reason, track promoters found hope in numbers. Perhaps Thompson and Killingsworth had guessed right on racing in Birmingham. Certainly Arrington and the city council hoped that their investment in building access roads to the turf club would yield anticipated economic returns.

Within weeks of the Birmingham Turf Club's opening, discouraging economic signs appeared. Low turnout at the track and the failure of bettors to wage larger sums on the horses produced a major problem. But the reasons for the track's dismal performance go deeper. Unquestionably, projections of average attendance at the races and the amount spectators would wager on the horses (referred to in racing circles as the "handle") proved far too optimistic. In retrospect, it is difficult to comprehend why those closely involved with the turf club accepted the figures advanced by marketing consultant Killingsworth.

The enthusiasm for the track, however, may have momentarily blinded some people to the reality of numbers—and in racing, numbers mean almost everything! Buoyed by his own hopes for Birmingham's track, consultant Killingworth predicted an average nightly racetrack attendance of 8,300 spectators, and a per-capita betting of $130. He badly missed his mark. The track's performance came nowhere near Killingsworth's projections. Some supporters were first inclined to blame the poor financial showing on the usual problems associated with a new business, but it soon became clear that more than this simple explanation was involved.

Marketing and the psychology that accompanied it also had much to do with the track's declining fortunes. The very name Birmingham Turf Club "turned some people off," for it had the ring of elitism. Among Birmingham's blacks in particular, a group the track needed to cultivate, that elitism was fatal to the success of racing in Birmingham. Promoters of the turf club also failed to take into consideration that the socioeconomic background of Birmingham differed significantly from some other cities that had tracks. The working class still constituted a large portion of the city's population, and that particular fact should have guided the thinking of those who wanted to promote racing in Birmingham. The Birmingham *Post-Herald* came close to the truth when it wrote on 4 April 1987 that:

> the [Birmingham Turf] Club aimed a little too high . . . in marketing. Average working people, who should comprise most of the betting pool, are not inclined to pay $4 for a hot dog and a glass of beer. Fancy private (i.e. members only) dining rooms, fees for parking and programs, and all that propaganda about "the sport of kings" will not bring the lunch pail crowd out to the races. We realize that a certain amount of elitism may have been necessary to attract investors, but investors and high caliber businessmen won't keep the track running.

Before the end of the 1987 racing season in October, the turf club had tried a number of things to increase attendance and betting at the track. None of them really proved successful. Sunday racing and the sale of liquor, some argued, would do much to aid the ailing track, but approval for such suggestions remained infinitely remote in an area where the Sabbath remained sacred. The possible elimination of the track's contribution to charities and the sale of track

315

stock out-of-state seemed only stopgap measures rather than long-range solutions to the monumental problems that faced racing in Birmingham. At the beginning of 1988, discussions abounded over the possible conversion of the horse track into a dog-racing facility. To some the best solution—since Judith Thompson had now left Birmingham—was to find a buyer for the track who would start anew.

Arrington hoped that the annexation of land to the city would yield better results than the first season of horse racing had shown. His view of annexation was also pragmatic. He wanted to expand not just to increase the size of the city or to bring in additional people but to add those areas that offered the best opportunity for possible commercial and business development. The effort to acquire land, however, created problems for Arrington and the city.

One of the most frustrating legal developments Arrington faced in his annexation program was an Alabama Supreme Court decision that involved the so-called long lasso doctrine. This particular case grew out of the efforts of Tuskegee to annex a dog track located some fourteen miles away in another county. Stymied by surrounding areas, Tuskegee very cleverly decided to annex the roadway that led from the city to the track. In short, the city used a "long lasso" (a roadway) to "rope in" (connect) a distant piece of property to its boundary.

In enunciating the doctrine, the 1985 Alabama Supreme Court created an open door for any city that wanted to use Tuskegee's approach to annexation. A year later, however, the court reversed itself, leaving in limbo past long-lasso annexations. By 1987, Birmingham had annexed twenty-two thousand acres of additional territory, mostly by conventional means, with the likelihood that the Arrington administration would continue to incorporate more territory, no matter what the courts decided about long lasso. The city's efforts, however, raised some racial questions, and some outlying white areas organized to resist any attempt at annexation. Some whites opposed adding any predominantly black section of Jefferson County to the city. In reality, only a small number of people lived in areas annexed by the Arrington administration before 1987.

Economic progress through growth and the need for quality education were closely linked in Arrington's mind. The mayor knew, for example, that businesses wanted to locate in areas that had a vigorous educational climate with efficient and intelligent workers. The development of such an environment was particularly important for the new Birmingham, since the city, like much of Alabama, labored under a history associated with educational poverty and low academic achievement. Unfortunately, under state law the mayor had only limited control of the public schools. By and large the administration of Birmingham schools rested in the hands of a five-member board of education appointed by the city council.

Economic stringency affected the administration's goals for the city's schools. Without good teachers and adequate facilities, Arrington contended, Birmingham and the rest of the South could not overcome the educational limitations that had long plagued the region. In spite of a determined effort, however, the bond proposal that would have aided the schools experienced a crushing defeat. Had the measure passed, city schools would have received $25 million and a decided boost toward excellence. The continued reduction in federal funds that went to the cities compounded the problem, and as a consequence, Arrington had to cut back on educational-enrichment programs designed to strengthen the curriculum. The mayor, nevertheless, could point with pride to higher national examination scores of the city's children, although Birmingham still needed to achieve consistent and uniform quality in its public schools.

Controversy over the forced resignation of Birmingham's first black school superintendent, Walter Harris, created community tensions, produced instability in leadership for a considerable time, and consequently, frustrated Arrington's goals for the schools. After a national search in 1983, the Birmingham Board of Education invited Harris to head its school system, which was nearly 85 percent black. Although he held a doctorate in education and had been employed several years in Florida as the principal of a high school where he raised the performance of his students, Harris had little experience in operating a system the size of Birmingham. At the time of his appointment, however, he received enthusiastic support from the school board.

Within two years disappointment with the black leader appeared, and in June 1985 the board asked the superintendent to step down. That decision was not unanimous, and throughout the controversy there would exist a 3-2 division within the board that rarely changed on crucial votes related to the educator's tenure. Members of the board who staunchly opposed the superintendent were Louis Dale, Martha Gaskins, and Belle Stoddard. T. L. Alexander and Ossie Mitchell consistently voted to keep Harris.

The mayor wanted to avoid involvement in the Harris controversy because of his sensitivity to possible charges of political intervention into school-board affairs. But the outcry from the public and the board's unwillingness to state publicly reasons for the request for the administrator's resignation caused Arrington to question openly the decision to dump him; and eventually the mayor came to support Harris's retention. Arrington's detractors complained that he had intervened in an effort to win black votes for the forthcoming bond referendum that would give money to the schools. Others interpreted the controversy within the narrow context of race, but that view was too restricted, since blacks on the board were split over Harris. Indeed, what surprised many people was that a board with a 3-2 majority of blacks had permitted the forced resignation of the black administrator without substantial charges of gross incompetence.

Arrington became more outspoken as the board adopted an intractable position in its decision to dismiss Harris. In a two-part series for the *Birmingham Times* in December 1986, he discussed the board's decision, its insistence upon "independence" in action, and the performance of Walter Harris since coming to Birmingham. Arrington hammered hard at the refusal to state reasons for the black's dismissal. City boards, he wrote for the black newspaper, were "not so independent that they don't have to explain to the public their reasons for their actions." Even the school board had to answer to someone. "What we have is a board making a decision which affects a total community," Arrington wrote, but that refused "to tell why it is acting as it is."

The mayor praised Harris's administration of the schools, and he tried to pinpoint the source of some of the educator's problems. He lauded the superintendent for opposing the "social promotion" of students and for a strong testing program that measured the development of academic skills. Harris also had courageously closed some underused schools, encouraged businesses to cooperate in special programs, and worked to broaden the participation of parents in the city's institutions. While those accomplishments seemed notable, Arrington believed that the black administrator experienced problems because of his failure to bring his own top-level personnel to Birmingham; and his insistence on high standards also produced a problem. Harris's critics, on the other hand, characterized him as abrasive and prone to make changes without adequate investigation or appreciation for delicate diplomacy. Morale, they contended, suffered.

Arrington's defense of Harris did not succeed in changing any votes on the board. Not only did the board vote to end Harris's tenure at the end of his 15 June 1987 contract, but it gave one of his subordinates, John Cantelow, an eighteen-month contract as interim superintendent. Cantelow, an assistant superintendent and longtime veteran of the school system, had served twice before as interim head of the school system. Although the mayor respected Cantelow and had no argument with him, he criticized the way the board made the appointment. By extending Cantelow a contract, said Arrington, the board in effect sealed Harris's doom by tying the hand of any future body that might want to reverse the decision to dismiss him and by delaying a permanent selection of a superintendent for a year and a half.

Belle Stoddard's retirement from the board after ten years' service offered the mayor and Harris partisans their only remaining hope—a new member who would vote to keep the superintendent! The Birmingham City Council, not the mayor, appoints members to the school board, but it was logical to assume that, given the mayor's influence with the present council, he could win at least five votes for a pro-Harris nominee. Although persons on both sides of the issue made much of objectivity and principle in the consideration of possible board members, clearly the issue in the minds of most was an eventual vote that would determine simply whether Harris would stay or leave.

Over a dozen persons applied for the position vacated by Stoddard. A majority of the council members believed the appointment of a white nominee would maintain a healthy black-white balance on the board, but Councilman William Bell, whose Administration Committee handled the nomination details, did not exclude anyone from the process. Harris supporters experienced renewed hope when Robert G. Corley permitted his name to be placed in nomination for a seat on the school board. Corley appeared ideal. He was white, a calm, thoughtful intellectual with a Ph.D., and a liberal who had quietly fought to bring about progressive changes in Birmingham. The University of Virginia graduate had once been employed by the Birmingham Public Library, but at the time of his nomination he was serving as executive director of the Birmingham chapter of the National Council of Christian and Jews. A soft-spoken man of quiet demeanor, he had been known to defend Arrington's administration, and only a few months before the Harris controversy he had privately confessed his disappointment that some persons still viewed Richard Arrington as anti-white.

Whatever took place between Corley and Councilman William Bell when the two met to discuss the nomination to the board and a possible vote on Harris will probably remain debatable. What is really important is that a majority of persons on the council believed Corley would vote to keep the superintendent. However, the nominee stated emphatically before his appointment that "nobody has asked me to take a position." But sources close to the mayor believed that Corley had studied Harris's case and was prepared to vote for his retention. Not surprisingly, then, when Corley's name came before the council, all five of the votes of council persons who leaned toward Harris—Roosevelt Bell, William Bell, Eddie Blankenship, Linda Coleman, and Jeff Germany—went to Corley along with that of Herring, who stated that the Harris controversy per se was unimportant to him. After his selection, Corley told the press, "I'm going into this . . . with an open mind."

In a tension-charged atmosphere the board voted on 9 June 1987 on motions to overthrow its past decisions. Corley lined up with Dale and Gaskins, as had Stoddard before him. Weeks after the event the new board member said that advice he received convinced him that Cantelow had a legal contract and, equally as important, a pro-Harris vote would only prolong turmoil. Even if Harris had returned, operating the system would have been difficult with a 3-2 split. Harris's supporters bitterly denounced Corley. Charges of betrayal filled the air. "He has paid Judas," cried Abraham Woods as he pledged to continue the fight. In January 1988, months after the vote, Corley quietly explained that he had not voted on Harris's competence but that he was more concerned about procedure and the legalism of the issue. Arrington, of course, had been precisely correct when he noted that the board had tied the hands of future bodies by granting Cantelow an eighteen-month contract. But the votes were now in, and the practical Arrington could easily recognize the ruins of the fields.

The increasing power of Birmingham's black mayor eclipsed any momentary defeat in the Harris case. Neither his image nor his influence greatly suffered. Perhaps nothing testified to Arrington's growing political stature as much as his role in the formation of the Alabama New South Coalition. For nearly a quarter century before creation of New South, the Alabama Democratic Conference (ADC) had been virtually unchallenged as the most powerful political voice among the state's black voters. Led by Joe Reed of Montgomery, ADC's influence touched practically all sections of the state, but it enjoyed enormous strength in the so-called black-belt region of Alabama. But rifts had appeared in ADC ranks, and some of the dissension had to do with Reed's leadership style and his alleged tendency to "hog political power."

By the mid-1980s, the revolt against Reed had assumed noticeable proportions. The *Greene County Democrat* of John and Carol Zippert reflected the antagonism toward Reed in the black-belt area of Alabama. In a biting 23 December 1985 editorial, the paper accused the black leader of reducing decision making at ADC conventions to "floor shows and planned power plays by . . . his blindly loyal sycophants." The most severe criticism of Reed, however, was the charge that he ran a "one-man show" and that he made no real effort to attract young, new leadership with a progressive political outlook. The *Democrat* wanted a different kind of organization that would bring a "breath of fresh air to black politics in Alabama." Not surprisingly, the Zipperts assumed an important role in the creation of the group that challenged Joe Reed's powerful influence in the state.

Revolt against Reed began to take on institutional form in December 1985, when Arrington and other influential persons from across Alabama met in Selma. Those present included Senator Hank Sanders and his attorney wife, Rose, who had become articulate voices for change in the black belt. Senator Michael Figures of Mobile, a notable Reed detractor, also showed up, as did Senator Fred Horn and Representatives Lucius Black, Jenkins Bryant, James Buskey, George Grayson, Lewis Spratt and James Thomas. None of them, however, was more disillusioned by Reed's leadership than Figures, unless perhaps it was a nonofficeholder named J. L. Chestnut, a fiery civil-rights attorney from Selma who served as ADC's vice-chairman. "Thousands and thousands of Alabamians," Chestnut told an audience "are now insisting on genuine leaders and not political manipulators." The state's blacks wanted a "new dealer dealing the cards."

Reed reacted predictably to revolt within his organization. Part of the problem, he said, was "grand jealousy." The formation of the new group would split the black vote and that result would mean reduced political power. Black office holding would suffer. While Reed did not blame Arrington outright for the problems within ADC, he believed the revolt would quickly collapse without the support of the powerful Birmingham politician. Reed reserved much of his venom for Figures, whom he saw as the chief culprit.

When over one thousand persons poured into Birmingham's Boutwell Auditorium in January 1986 for the founding convention of New South, the sounds of change filled the air. A diverse group of persons came from over the state. Longtime civil-rights activists joined hands with college professors, politicians, and plain folk in an effort destined to have an impact on electoral politics in the state. Arrington played an important role in shaping the structure of the new organization, and the striking resemblance between the new group and the Jefferson County Citizens Coalition was not merely coincidental. The constitution of New South, written essentially by Hank Sanders, created a kind of umbrella organization under which local, civic, and economic groups in the state could participate and coordinate their efforts "without losing their local identity or autonomy."

Arrington emerged as a clear choice for the presidency of the new organization, although there had been earlier speculation that Figures, Sanders, or Senator Earl Hilliard might receive considerable support for the leadership of New South. Arrington moved quickly to dispel the notion that the group existed to promote only black interests and to contest Reed and ADC. But the mayor could not disguise the resentment many persons had for Reed, even though Arrington was committed to work with him for the "political good of the black community." Some New South members, however, refused to cooperate with the Montgomery politician at all.

One of Arrington's most difficult political decisions came shortly after the formation of New South and during the 1986 Alabama Democratic primary. As expected, the new organization backed mostly Democrats, and some of its choices were different from those of ADC. A crucial battle came when New South considered the endorsement of one of three major Democratic candidates for governor—Bill Baxley, Charles Graddick, and George McMillan. Arrington had a long-standing friendship with McMillan, who had been among the first whites in Birmingham to support him in his 1979 mayoral bid.

The mayor favored McMillan in the Democratic primary, but the inability of the candidate's campaign to catch fire raised questions about his electability. Indeed, opinion polls had shown that McMillan could not possibly overcome the strength of Baxley and Graddick. Blacks in New South had their share of idealism, but they were also practical politicians who knew the meaning of power in achieving goals for the black community. Getting elected was the first step toward any understandable political reality! New South endorsed Baxley and that decision stunned McMillan and his friends, who felt a sense of betrayal. McMillan partisans believed that Arrington could have carried the day for his friend had he "stood his ground" at the New South Convention and battled for him.

McMillan supporters responded angrily to New South's failure to endorse McMillan. In one of the strongest letters the mayor received, Rev. Larry R. Horne, pastor of Shawmut United Methodist Church, blistered Arrington for his disloyalty. "I used to have respect for you," he wrote on 12 May 1986, "but you have totally destroyed that through your abandonment of sacred principle for unholy expediency." New South had shown "unbridled cowardice" by relying on the polls in making its decision. An endorsement would have helped to change the polls that showed McMillan trailing his opponents. Arrington had made "a pack with the devil," and the decision to support Baxley would "come back to haunt you." Horne confessed shame at being a native of Alabama, just as he was embarrassed to admit, "I am a native son of Birmingham."

Horne's letter, as cutting as it appeared, probably did not provoke as much of a response as the correspondence of Marie Jemison, one of the mayor's political backers. In a tone different from that of Horne, she wrote to Arrington on 31 May 1986:

> I have . . . supported you for along time and this [letter] is hard for me to write but I must. You have lost much support in [Birmingham's] white community because you did not stand up for McMillan. When I saw you . . . [recently] you said you would work to get the Baxley supporters out. But instead because of expediency, you went over to Baxley . . . [a man whose reputation has been seriously questioned]. Had you said "I will remain loyal to a friend" you would have kept 50 [percent] of the delegates and the endless gratitude of white [Birmingham].

Many of the local and state candidates in 1986 backed by the youthful New South enjoyed success. Unfortunately, however, the contest for the gubernatorial nomination produced a heated contest and an eventual court fight between Baxley and Graddick that virtually ruined the Democrats' chances against Republican Guy Hunt in the general election. When Baxley prevailed in the courts, Republicans took heart. The GOP won the governor's office for the first time since Reconstruction.

Despite the frustration that resulted from the gubernatorial contest, New South had gotten off to a fast start. Not even the 1988 presidential candidacy of black civil-rights leader Jesse Jackson proved highly decisive. Both New South and ADC backed the hopeful Jackson. Arrington could optimistically predict a bright future for the organization because it was broader than partisan politics. Although the group had political objectives, it had also established other important goals. For example, it created study committees to examine such problems as teenage pregnancy and crime; and it had a strong program that trained youth for community, state, and national leadership. Attorney Rose Sanders, a remarkable woman with boundless energy, took special interest in black youth and actively coordinated summer leadership camps.

As Arrington worked to strengthen his New South organization, he did not forget the pressing realities of Birmingham politics. And one of those realities was a reelection campaign in October 1987. The most serious challenger to emerge to contest the mayor was Robert (Bob) McKee, an attorney and founder of Tax Busters, the group that led the successful campaign against Arrington's 1986 bond referendum. A Birmingham native, McKee graduated from Howard College (now Samford University) and subsequently took a law degree from the University of Alabama. Although he had never held office in Birmingham, he had once served on the city council of Tarrant City. The strength of Tax Busters' defeat of the bond issue and the encouragement of friends convinced McKee he could triumph over a man who had become one of the most powerful black politicians in the country.

An ideal situation for McKee would have been the appearance of a strong black candidate in the mayoral contest. Indeed, before Arrington officially announced his candidacy for reelection, rumors existed of white efforts to get potentially strong black persons into the race. Some speculation centered upon Councilman William Bell, but when Arrington supporters confronted him, he strongly denied any intention of contesting the mayor. The politically astute Bell knew that strong white support for a black councilman did not necessarily translate into votes in a mayoral contest. Moreover, he recognized that the Jefferson County Citizens Coalition would view his candidacy as nothing less than traitorous.

Bell did not challenge the mayor, but two other blacks did enter the race. Neither, realistically, had the slightest chance of winning.

Richard Finley, a longtime Republican and businessman, had served on the city-council staff. John Hawkins, a socialist and coal miner, had little name recognition, and even had citizens known him, conservative political voters in Birmingham would not have rallied to his political cause in great numbers. Neither black candidate could generate much enthusiasm for his campaign. Hawkins talked of issues often unrelated to daily life in the city, and Finley could not isolate any issue that damaged the mayor's strong hold on the electorate.

McKee hammered away at waste in government and at crime. Repeatedly, he turned to city loans to private concerns, to consulting fees the Arrington administration had paid out, and to travel by city politicians as prime examples of "waste." But McKee had difficulty painting the personally thrifty Arrington as a wasteful or wild-spending administrator. The mayor's defenders quickly noted that city government was a cooperative enterprise, with the city council bearing responsibility for approving most projects; and they also stressed that some council members who backed McKee's campaign had voted for loans and other projects that they now termed "wasteful." Although crime had a better chance of becoming a major issue than waste, McKee's inexperience in politics and Arrington's skill in rebutting his opponent's contentions worked to the mayor's advantage.

Arrington spelled out his approach to his campaign in July 1987, when he met with his campaign committee. He would not let the opposition dictate the contest and he would attempt to highlight his record. From the outset the mayor appeared confident, almost eager to get into the political contest. He believed he could beat McKee or anyone else who entered the race (including Councilman Bill Myers, who ultimately chose not to run). With support from the business community and a campaign chest that already exceeded $100,000 in July, Arrington was relatively confident of adequate funds to run a good race. He would be free to concentrate on the issues and would leave his wife, Rachel, to coordinate the campaign. Now comfortable with politics and her role as the mayor's wife, the attractive first lady became a valuable asset in both the black and white communities. She had grown to feel at home in Birmingham, and her love and knowledge of politics had grown to match that she had for her husband. Now less sensitive about the past, she had become a confident woman of considerable influence and power.

Arrington and his political consultant, Cindy McCartney, adopted a strategy similar to that of previous campaigns. Again, they would not write off the usually anti-Arrington Eastside, to be sure, but they would regard any votes gained there during the election as a bonus. To expend enormous amounts of time and energy in that section, they concluded, would represent bad management of time and resources, although the mayor had made a determined effort to cultivate the area during his incumbency. As before, Arrington's strategy called for winning a sizable white vote on the city's Southside, which had a moderate-to-liberal history and which had given him his slim, winning margin in 1979.

Some small signs of dissatisfaction existed within the black community that Arrington could not ignore. While no black person of significant stature had risen to challenge his political control of the city, complaints had surfaced over the seemingly slow pace of social and economic change in the black community. Some black businessmen in particular grumbled over the lack of support to enterprises in black areas; and when a national study appeared before the election that showed Birmingham lagged behind some other cities in black businesses, their voices became more strident. Unfortunately for Arrington, the study did not attempt to measure the progress black business in Birmingham had made during his years in office.

The mayor moved swiftly to advertise his record of support for minority enterprise. Rachel Arrington and her staff distributed a detailed brochure that listed a large number of businesses that had benefited between 1980 and 1987 from the $70 million in city contracts for projects. The Arrington campaign also stressed how the establishment of programs such as Minority Business Assistance and the Business Assistance Network had aided black people. Despite an affirmative-action plan for minority contractors that the courts had rejected, the administration had achieved 20 percent minority participation in city contracts. And the mayor did not let blacks forget that, as a councilman, he had introduced the first affirmative-action ordinance in the city's history. McKee found that he could not exploit whatever dissatisfaction that existed within the black community. After the campaign the white candidate said he attempted to reach out to blacks but met a harsh rejection.

In the end the mayor's record of stability, economic progress, and racial peace proved too strong for his challenger. Arrington was the incumbent, and that position has significance at a time when things are going well. The mayor cited record levels of construction that had brought valuable employment to the city and he turned to neighborhood and commercial revitalization and to annexation of valuable land to the city that would eventually broaden Birmingham's tax base. When Donald Newton of the Birmingham Chamber of Commerce praised the mayor for his excellent leadership of the city and for his "fair treatment," his statement provided political capital for the black leader.

A thorough knowledge of the city and political experience gave Arrington a decided advantage over McKee. During the latter stages of the campaign, Arrington's political savvy showed through. He addressed a wide range of issues that showed his mastery of detail and his interest in all phases of city life. He talked of the city's concern for women and the establishment of the Commission on the Status of Women under Mary Jones; and he delighted in the part his administration was playing in fighting teenage pregnancy. McKee said little, for example, of cultural development of the city, while the mayor pointed proudly to expansion of Birmingham's cultural district.

In a low-key campaign Arrington defeated his opponent with record numbers. The mayor received 51,909 votes to McKee's 28,825. Finley and Hawkins, with less than 1 percent of the vote, had no significant impact on the contest. A historic 64 percent of the voters who went to the polls supported Arrington. Although race did not surface as a major consideration during the contest, observers could see it in voting patterns, as in previous contests since 1979. Arrington had hoped to increase his strength in the white community, but he could garner only 10 percent of the white vote, much of it from the city's Southside. Significantly, he could have won the

The Birmingham City Council, 1988. (Courtesy Mayor Richard Arrington, Jr.)

1987 mayoral election without any white votes, which had not been the case in his other two races. McKee's supporters angrily denounced those whites who had stayed at home and not voted, but had there been a turnout of all eligible white voters in Birmingham, victory in all probability would still have escaped the challenger. Perhaps Councilman Bill Myers came close to the truth when he said in the 15 October 1987 *New York Times* that "there just isn't enough anti-Arrington feeling out there, and [the mayor] is a statewide figure . . . who can deliver."

Arrington's victory had again helped rewrite the political history of Birmingham. And so did the city-council election, held at the time of the mayoral race. In 1985, Arrington's Jefferson County Citizens Coalition had supported five persons for the city council: Roosevelt Bell, a past president of Bush Hills Neighborhood Association; Eddie Blankenship, a strong advocate of economic development; Linda Coleman, former teacher and former president of Smithfield Estates Neighborhood; Antris Hinton, former mayor of Brownsville; and Bill Myers, former Birmingham police chief. Only Hinton, who as mayor of Brownsville had led the successful fight for annexation of her city to Birmingham, had failed in her election bid, following a runoff with Bettye Fine Collins, bitter critic of the coalition.

Roosevelt Bell, Blankenship and Coleman had joined William Bell and Jeff Germany to constitute a 5-4 black majority on the council in 1985. That majority had shown its power by the election of William Bell as president over longtime council member David Herring. Collins's narrow victory over Hinton had left her on the council along with three other whites: Herring, Myers, and Yarbrough. The intense, quick-witted, and sometimes provocative councilwoman had taken pride for the moment that she had defeated the coalition, but she did not delight in having to run again in 1987, when the mayor's organization would surely remember her harsh statements about the black politician and his "machine."

If a feeling of impending political doom had overcome anti-Arrington forces after the 1985 city elections, it affected them even more after the 1987 city-council races. The results of those contests gave the mayor even stronger backing on the council, since all five council winners—William Bell, Jeff Germany, Mike Graffeo, David Herring, and Antris Hinton—received coalition endorsements. Hinton had had to wait only two years to avenge the defeat Collins had administered her. The election also saw the end of Russell Yarbrough's eighteen years on the city council. In 1985 he had accepted without complaint the coalition's support, but when he failed to receive it in 1987 and lost, he blasted the organization and the "one-man control" of Richard Arrington. In his years on the council Yarbrough had combined a deep, old-fashioned conservatism with verbal bombast and a deep love for his city.

Arrington felt comfortable with a council endorsed by the political organization he had founded. Realistically, such a council gave him considerable political power. But power also carried some costs and some risks for the mayor, especially since most of the black councilpersons were relatively young, ambitious, independent, and politically astute. No less than three of them probably wanted to become mayor. The sober, realistic Arrington shared no illusions about politics, race, or the will to power. He knew that honest political differences over fundamental policies would eventually arise with black members of the council, as had happened with white councilpersons.

Richard Arrington, Jr., spent little energy playing the role of political soothsayer. If he ran the city well, with efficiency and fiscal responsibility and with an eye toward developing a diversified economy and a safe community, then the political future would take care of itself. His experiences as mayor had not dampened the buoyant spirit of optimism he had brought to government. With a deeply held sense of place, he had long believed in the possibilities of Birmingham, and he could not measure how far the city had come—how much it had changed. He and the people could continue to mold a new order if they did not weary and if they were willing to tackle the imperfections of democratic government and the daily problems that conspired to frustrate the good life.

Appendix

Birmingham Mayors and
Council Members, 1963–Present

In 1963, Birmingham adopted a mayor-council system of government, according to which the mayor serves a four-year term and
may be reelected. Since the introduction of this system, four men
have held the office of mayor: Albert Boutwell†, elected in 1963;
George G. Seibels, Jr., elected in 1967 and 1971; David Vann, elected
in 1975; and Richard Arrington, Jr., elected in 1979, 1983, and 1987.
Nine members sit on the city council. The mayor-council law
stipulated that, in 1963, the four candidates who received the highest number of votes would serve a four-year term, and the other five
candidates who gained office would serve for two years. In subsequent elections five members of the council were elected every two
years. Of these five, the four who received the highest number of
votes served a four-year term; the fifth served for two years. From
1963 to 1988, thirty persons have served on the Birmingham City
Council. They are listed below, with dates of service on the council
and, as appropriate, years served as president of the council.

Arrington, Richard, Jr.; 1971–79
Bell, Roosevelt; 1985–present
Bell, William A.; 1979–present, president 1985–present
Blankenship, Eddie; 1983–present
Bryan, John E.;† 1963–71
Clifford, W. B. (Pete); 1978–83 (elected November 1978 to fill unex-
    pired term of Hawkins)
Coleman, Linda; 1985–present
Collins, Bettye Fine; 1981–87

Corcoran, Liston A.;† 1965–74 (died in office)

Douglas, R.W.;† 1965–68 (died in office)

Drennen, Alan T., Jr.; 1963–69

Estelle, Bessie Sears;† 1975–81

Germany, Jeff; 1979–present

Golden, John T.; 1963–65

Graffeo, Mike; 1987–present

Hawkins, Don A.;† 1963–78, president 1971–78 (died in office)

Herring, Samuel David; 1974–present (elected February 1974 to fill unexpired term of Corcoran), president 1983–85

Hinton, Antris J.; 1987–present

Katopodis, John; 1977–85, president 1981–83

Langford, Larry; 1977–79

Miglionico, Nina; 1963–85, president 1978–81

Myers, Bill; 1981–present

Overton, Dr. E. C.; 1963–81

Proctor, Angi Grooms; 1971–77

Seibels, George G. Jr.; 1963–67

Shores, Arthur; 1968–77 (appointed June 1968 to fill unexpired term of Douglas)

Vann, David; 1971–75

Wiggins, M. E.;† 1963–71, president 1963–71

Woods, T. W.; 1963–65; 1967–71

Yarbrough, Russell; 1969–87

† deceased

Membership of the council after the thirteen council elections appears below. For each term, the name of the council president appears in italics. Names of councilpersons appointed or elected to fill an unexpired term are shown in parentheses underneath the member they replaced on the council.

Term	Incumbents	Elected to 4-yr. term	Elected to 2-yr. term
1963–65	—	Bryan Hawkins Seibels *Wiggins*	Drennen Golden Miglionico Overton Woods
1965–67	Bryan Hawkins Seibels *Wiggins*	Corcoran Drennen Miglionico Overton	Douglas
1967–69	Corcoran Drennen Miglionico Overton	Bryan Hawkins *Wiggins* Woods	Douglas (Shores)
1969–71	Bryan Hawkins *Wiggins* Woods	Corcoran Miglionico Overton Shores	Yarbrough
1971–73	Corcoran Miglionico Overton Shores	Arrington *Hawkins* Vann Yarbrough	Proctor
1973–75	Arrington *Hawkins* Vann Yarbrough	Miglionico Overton Proctor Shores	Corcoran (Herring)
1975–77	Miglionico Overton Proctor Shores	Arrington *Hawkins* Herring Yarbrough	Estelle

1977–79	Arrington	Estelle	Langford
	Hawkins	Katopodis	
	(Clifford)	*Miglionico*	
	Herring	Overton	
	Yarbrough		
1979–81	Estelle	Clifford	Wm. Bell
	Katopodis	Germany	
	Miglionico	Herring	
	Overton	Yarbrough	
1981–83	Clifford	Collins	Wm. Bell
	Germany	*Katopodis*	
	Herring	Miglionico	
	Yarbrough	Myers	
1983–85	Collins	Wm. Bell	Blankenship
	Katopodis	Germany	
	Miglionico	*Herring*	
	Myers	Yarbrough	
1985–87	*Wm. Bell*	R. Bell	Collins
	Germany	Blankenship	
	Herring	Coleman	
	Yarbrough	Myers	
1987–89	R. Bell	*Wm. Bell*	Hinton
	Blankenship	Germany	
	Coleman	Graffeo	
	Myers	Herring	

Essay on Sources

This biography relies heavily upon primary sources, personal interviews, and newspapers. I have used the public and private papers and the campaign files of Richard Arrington, Jr. When I began my research, most of Arrington's public papers were then located in city hall, but since that time most of them, except for the more recent years, have been moved to storage facilities within the city. The Arrington Papers have no classification number, since they have not been deposited with a library. I have also used extensively the papers of former mayors David Vann and George G. Seibels, Jr., located in the Department of Archives and Manuscripts, Birmingham Public Library. The records of Operation New Birmingham, also at the library, have been helpful. These papers, of course, have been properly classified, and I have given the appropriate document numbers when an item is mentioned in the chapter sources.

For convenience I have cited the above papers in the following manner: Arrington: Public Papers; Arrington, Private Papers; Arrington: Campaign Files; Vann: Public Papers; Seibels: Public Papers; Operation New Birmingham: Papers. The Miles College Special Collection (Birmingham) gave me some limited help in tracing the history of that college. The clipping files of the Birmingham City Council and those of the Joint Center for Political Studies (in Washington, D.C.) were also helpful in tracing Arrington's political history and in understanding the contours of black politics in America. Robert Corley, a member of the Birmingham Board of Education, permitted me to use some of his personal correspondence. George Seibels also shared with me items in his personal possession. The Department of Archives and Manuscripts of the Birmingham Public Library has some city-council records, but I have depended upon the City Clerk's Office for most official documents, especially minutes of council meetings.

Without many formal interviews with Mayor Richard Arrington,

Jr., over the past eight years, this book would never have taken shape. Informal interviews, however, often proved equally as valuable in understanding the man and the city of Birmingham. From June 1982 through May 1983, I made regular trips from Tuscaloosa to Birmingham to see the mayor function at meetings of the city council and to study that body as it carried out its work. During the summer of 1983, I lived in the city and worked from a desk at city hall. Consequently, I had the opportunity to converse with staff members, council persons, and city employees. Since 1983 was an election year, I chose to follow Arrington across the city to his various engagements, which gave me a chance to observe his activities and to note carefully his responses to city issues. The 1983 summer experience has enabled me to provide a firsthand account of many developments that transpired during that period. I continued to work out of city hall on my many subsequent trips to Birmingham. Residing in the city afforded me the opportunity to talk with black and white citizens at lounges, shopping centers, restaurants, churches, and other places, who were unaware of my attempt to understand better the city and its black mayor. My anonymity, I hope, contributed to the ideal of objectivity toward which this work strives.

Many public officials and citizens graciously agreed to interviews. Except where specifically indicated, all interviews took place in the Birmingham metropolitan area. Persons who appear in the text or whose interviews are cited in the chapter sources are Barbara Arrington, Richard Arrington, Jr., Richard Arrington, Sr., James Baker, Roosevelt Bell, William Bell, Eddie Blankenship, Harley P. Brown (Norman, Oklahoma), Lemorie "Tony" Carter, Linda Coleman, Robert G. Corley, Willie Davis, Arthur G. Gaston, Len Gedgoudas, Jeff Germany, Richard Goff (Norman), Michael Graffeo, Benjamin Greene, David Herring, David Hood, Cluff Hopla (Norman), Jessie Huff, Mary Jones, John Katopodis, Edward Lamonte, Larry Langford, Simmie Lavender, Robert McKee, James T. Montgomery, William "Bill" Myers, Frank Parsons, W. C. Patton, Vicki Rivers, George Seibels, Jr., Arthur Shores, David Vann, Billy and Gwendolyn Webb, Lewis White, Roger White, Abraham Woods, and Odessa Woolfolk. Persons interviewed but who do not appear by name in the text are Edward Bell, resident of Sumter County, 10 January 1982 (Livingston, Alabama); Mary Gaines, secretary, Arrington Campaign Headquarters, 8 March 1983 and 21 March 1988 (Montgomery); and Olivia Williams, resident of Sumter County, 10 January 1982 (Livingston).

Popular articles on Arrington in magazines such as *Ebony*, *Down Home*, and *Birmingham* have been of limited use. Newspapers, however, have been of inestimable value to me. The small paper *Our Southern Home*, of Livingston, Alabama, enabled me to understand social life in that town in the 1930s and 1940s. The *Birmingham World*, established in 1931, and the *Birmingham Times*, founded in 1964, were the eyes and ears of the black community of the Birmingham area, including Fairfield, during the decades after the Arringtons moved from Livingston. The *Birmingham News* and the *Birmingham Post-Herald* followed Arrington's career after his entry into politics in 1971, and those two papers provide the best commentary on city life for the period covered by this book.

Chapter 1

For an overview of Alabama history, I have relied upon Virginia Van der Veer Hamilton, *Alabama: A Bicentennial History* (New York: Norton, 1977), and Lucille Griffith, *Alabama: A Documentary History to 1900*, rev. ed, (University: University of Alabama Press, 1972). Valuable for its chronology down to 1941 and for its description of Alabama places, especially Livingston and Sumter County about the time the Arringtons lived in the region, is Federal Writers' Project, *Alabama: A Guide to the Deep South* (New York: Hastings House, 1941). The history of Sumter is outlined in some detail in Works Projects Administration, *Inventory of the County Archives of Alabama: Sumter County*, no. 60 (Birmingham: Alabama Historical Records Survey, 1940). Useful also is Robert D. Spratt, *A History of the Town of Livingston, Alabama* (Livingston: N.p., 1928), and Hazel L. Stickney, "The Conversion from Cotton to Cattle Economy in the Alabama Black Belt, 1930–1960" (Ph.D. diss., Clark University, 1961). The senior Arrington's experience with the WPA was similar to that of other blacks. Harvard Sitkoff, *A New Deal for Blacks: The Emergence of Civil Rights as a National Issue* (New York: Oxford, 1968), provides the best general coverage of that subject.

My comments on social life in Livingston are based on a variety of sources. *Our Southern Home* painted a good picture of rural life during this period. I have turned also to interviews with the Arringtons: Ernestine and Richard Arrington, Sr., 8 July 1981, 10 June 1982, 20 July 1983; and James Arrington, 12 November 1983 (Orangeburg, South Carolina). Reflections of Richard Arrington, Jr., on Sumter are sketched in the *Birmingham News*, 31 July 1981. Two books in particular shaped my view as I worked to isolate the strands of southernism and the importance of sense of place in Arrington's life and the lives of other blacks: James Seay Brown, Jr., *Up before Daylight: Life Histories from the Alabama Writers' Project, 1938–1939* (University: University of Alabama Press, 1982); and Mary Virginia Pounds Brown, *Toting the Lead Row: Ruby Pickens Tartt, Alabama Folklorist* (University: University of Alabama Press, 1981). While these two works do not focus specifically on blacks, they do provide an understanding of social life and the attachment many Alabamians, including blacks, had to place. Finally, no one should ignore the classic study by James Agee and Walker Evans, *Let Us Now Praise Famous Men* (Boston: Houghton Mifflin, 1960).

Chapter 2

Valuable for material on Birmingham and Fairfield are Leah Rawls Atkins, *The Valley and the Hills: An Illustrated History of Birmingham and Jefferson County* (Woodland Hills, Calif.: Windsor, 1981), and Marjorie Langenecker White, *The Birmingham District: An Industrial History and Guide* (Birmingham: Birmingham Publishing Co., 1981). See also Malcolm C. McMillan, *Yesterday's Birmingham* (Miami: Seeman, 1975), and John C. Henley, Jr., *This Is Birmingham: The Story of the Founding and Growth of an American City* (Birmingham: Southern University Press, 1960). Serious students interested in writings on Birmingham prior to the 1980s should see Ruth S. Spence, *Bibliography of Birmingham, Alabama, 1872–1972* (Birmingham: Oxmoor, 1973). A brief but fine work on Fairfield is Marvin Y. Whiting, ed., *Fairfield: Past, Present, Future, 1910–1985* . . . (Fairfield, Ala.: 75th Anniversary Celebration Committee, 1988). Comments on TCI are based essentially on interviews with Ernestine and Richard Arrington, Sr., 12 July 1981 and 9 August 1982. The description of the boyhood days of the Arrington children is also from those same interviews and from James Arrington, 12 November 1983, and Richard Arrington, Jr., 27 December 1981.

The profile of E. J. Oliver is drawn from the James and Richard Arrington, Jr., interviews cited immediately above. See also the semi-autobiographical work of Edmond Jefferson Oliver, *The End of an Era: Fairfield Industrial High School, 1924–1968* (Fairfield: Privately printed, 1968). The high school principal's book is the best description of the educational environment for blacks in his city during Richard Arrington's school years. A historical context for understanding the educational environment in Fairfield and other parts of the South is best provided by Henry Allen Bullock, *A History of Negro Education in the South from 1619 to the Present* (Cambridge: Harvard University Press, 1974).

Historian Carter G. Woodson believed that black history would aid and abet societal reform, and this idea helped guide the establishment of the Association for the Study of Negro Life and History. The association's *Journal of Negro History*, first published in 1916, reflected Woodson's beliefs. Oliver and a number of other southern black educators shared the scholar's philosophy, although they did not publicly articulate it. For decades Woodson's book *The Negro in Our History* (Washington: Associated Publishers, 1922) remained the most popular school text on the subject.

There is no good, comprehensive history of Miles College. I have made use of several interviews with Richard Arrington, Jr., in creating a picture of the school during his years there. But I have also turned to a brief history, "Miles College," written in 1955 by the school's president, W. A. Bell. The account is in the Miles College Special Collection. An informative undated brochure, "Miles College," in my possession, was also valuable. Comments on the marriage of Barbara and Richard Arrington and the challenge of those early years are based on several personal interviews: Ernestine Arrington, 8 July 1983; James Arrington, 12 November 1983; and Barbara Arrington, 16 July 1984. The most detailed description of those years was offered by Richard Arrington, Jr., 29 December 1981.

Arrington's performance as a graduate student was traced in three lenthy interviews with professors at the University of Oklahoma (Norman) on 16 November 1982: Harley P. Brown, Richard Goff, and Cluff Hopla. In a 22 June 1981 interview Arrington described his reaction to the zoology department at the University of Oklahoma. The description of Norman, Oklahoma, is drawn essentially from my own research on Oklahoma and my experience as a student at the university during the 1960s. See also George Lynn Cross, *Blacks in White Colleges: Oklahoma Landmark Cases* (Norman: University of Oklahoma Press, 1975). Arrington's ACHE experiences were covered in two interviews with him, on 29 December 1981 and 6 April 1988.

Chapter 3

The literature on the civil-rights movement in the South, which created monumental social and political changes in the region, is vast. That movement, of course, is only of general concern here, but several works help to explain the developments that brought into existence a new Alabama and a new South. A superb overview is Harvard Sitkoff, *The Struggle for Black Equality, 1954–1980* (New York: Hill and Wang, 1981). Some readers may want to begin with Martin Luther King, Jr., *Stride Toward Freedom: The Story of the Montgomery Story* (New York: Harper, 1958), which spells out the principles of nonviolence upon which King based his movement. The story of King and his work has garnered much attention in recent years. Only two studies demand attention here: David L. Lewis, *King: A Biography*, 2d ed. (Urbana: University of Illinois Press, 1978); and the Pulitzer-Prize-winning study by David J. Garrow, *Bearing the Cross: Martin Luther King, Jr., and the South-*

ern Christian Leadership Conference (New York: Morrow, 1986). Robert G. Corley, "The Fork of the Road: Birmingham's Interracial Committee and the Conflict over Segregation, 1950–1956," unpublished paper delivered at the Alabama Historical Association meeting, Birmingham, Alabama, 22 April 1983, and in my possession, is a perceptive work that has much to say about race relations in the city before King. Howell Raines, ed., *My Soul Is Rested: Movement Days in the Deep South Remembered* (New York: Bantam, 1977), has several interviews that deal with Birmingham, including one with civil-rights leader Abraham Woods, who still leads the Southern Christian Leadership Conference in the city. The 1963 Birmingham demonstrations produced much journalistic attention. Readers may want to consult Martin Luther King, Jr., *Why We Can't Wait* (New York: New American Library, [1964]), for a commentary by the man who ultimately engineered victory in the city.

The fight to abolish the commission form of government has been sketched by Leah Atkins above in *The Valley and the Hills*, but I have referred often to the *Birmingham Post-Herald* and the *Birmingham News*. Of invaluable assistance also was the unpublished paper of John L. Wright, "Birmingham Chooses the Mayor-Council Form of Government," which he graciously sent me. In 1971, Wright interviewed several important persons involved in that historic development: David Vann, an attorney; Sidney Smyer, Jr., businessman and community leader; Duard LeGrand, editor of the *Birmingham Post-Herald*; and Clarke Stallworth, city editor, the *Birmingham News*. The topic is treated in more detail in Mary Phyllis Harrison, "A Change in the Government of the City of Birmingham" (M.A. thesis, Montevallo University, 1974). A copy of the thesis is also in the Birmingham Public Library. "A Report on the Administrative Organization of Mayor-Council Government, Birmingham, Alabama," Bureau of Public Administration, Tuscaloosa, Alabama, 1963, is in my possession.

Harry Holloway, *The Politics of the Southern Negro: From Exclusion to Big City Organization* (New York: Random House, 1969), is a penetrating study. See especially the chapter "Birmingham, Alabama: Urbanism and . . . Politics of Race," which discusses in detail Jefferson County, black leadership, and local attitudes in the

1960s. Arthur Shores had a distinguished career as a civil-rights attorney and public servant. He deserves a biographer. For my commentary on the lawyer I have turned essentially to newspaper articles, a personal interview with him on 10 August 1983, biographical material in my personal possession, and an interview in Raines, *My Soul Is Rested*. Shores's appointment to the council created heated debate in the city. For example, Jesse T. Todd wrote Mayor George Seibels on 21 November 1968, that "If the people of Birmingham wanted a Negro councilman, they could and would elect one." S. Patrick Ballard wrote Seibels in a similar vein on 5 December 1968. Both letters are in Seibels: Public Papers, 19.5, Department of Archives and Manuscripts, Birmingham Public Library. Most of the letters Seibels received, however, supported appointment of Shores.

Arrington has recounted his decision to run for office in 1971 in a 29 December 1981 interview. The *Birmingham World* closely followed the black politician's career during this period. The *Birmingham Post-Herald* endorsed Arrington on 6 October 1971 and on 1 November of that same year prior to the run-off. Four years later the *Post-Herald* on 3 November 1975 again gave him its support.

For many years Arrington has written a column for the *Birmingham Times*. I have had available to me the originals of these articles, some of which differ slightly from the edited versions that appeared in the newspaper. Arrington's stand on affirmative action and other issues that faced the council and the city is best traced through these writings. The *Birmingham News*, 30 December 1973, has an excellent article that examines Arrington's position and that of the opponents of affirmative action. Mayor Seibels's stand is best reflected in his "Veto Message" of 23 December 1973, a copy of which is in Vann: Public Papers, 1.4, Department of Archives and Manuscripts, Birmingham Public Library. The mayor's legal contention on affirmative action and that of his city attorney is contained in J. M. Breckenridge to Don Hawkins, President, Birmingham City Council, 20 December 1973, Vann: Public Papers, 1.4, Department of Archives and Manuscripts, Birmingham Public Library. Arrington's dissatisfaction with the mayor's pursuit of affirmative action led to continued attacks. Drafts of the black politician's columns to the *Birmingham Times* contained repeated references to Seibels's unwillingness to act within the ordinance. One of the mayor's last notable responses before he left office came in his "Statement . . . to the [Community Affairs Committee] on the Fair Hiring Program for 1974," in Seibels: Public Papers, 10.34, Department of Archives and Manuscripts, Birmingham Public Library. A rebuttal to Seibels by a group of blacks, with statistics supplied by Arrington, is found in the "Resolution [of the] Greater Emancipation Association" of 1 January 1974, Vann: Public Papers, 1.5, Department of Archives and Manuscripts, Birmingham Public Library. Seibels discussed affirmative action and other issues of his administration with me in a 31 May 1988 interview.

For the discussion of cable television, I have depended upon the periodic reports of Arrington to the *Birmingham Times*; and I have also relied upon a 20 December 1983 interview with him. For Arrington's 1975 reelection the columns of the two black Birmingham newspapers for this period have been the best source. Pledges Vann made during the 1975 contest appear in "Campaign Promises," Vann: Public Papers, 5.14, Department of Archives and Manuscripts, Birmingham Public Library.

Chapter 4

As the leading figure in the city who was against police brutality, Arrington collected a great deal of information. The issue of police abuse is traced best in his reports to the people in the *Birmingham Times* articles, especially for the period 1971–75. Overwhelming support for Arrington's work against brutality is reflected in the city's black press. A good example is the *Birmingham Times*, 5 August 1972 and 19 July 1975. A summary of the cases of alleged police brutality is included in an appeal to black citizens for support by the Committee Against Police Brutality. The committee urged citizens to write Mayor Seibels and the city council. See the summary in Seibels: Public Papers 19.13, Department of Archives and Manuscripts, Birmingham Public Library. See also Walter F. Jackson, chairman of the Black Youth Caucus of Miles College, to George Seibels, 29 February 1972, and George Seibels to Walter F. Jackson, 6 April 1972. Both letters are in Seibels: Public Papers, 16.32, Department of Archives and Manuscripts, Birmingham Public Library. A representative example of the clash between Arrington and Seibels is Richard Arrington to the Honorable George G. Seibels, 22 June 1972, and George G. Seibels to Dr. Richard Arrington, 13 July 1972. See in Seibels: Public Papers, 19.7 and 19.8, respectively. Arrington often kept detailed notes of his activities in anticipation of an eventual memoir. I have used those notes in discussing A. G. Gaston and specific brutality cases. A. G. Gaston, *Green Power: The Successful Way of A. G. Gaston* (Birmingham: Southern University Press, 1968), is the revealing autobiography of the black millionaire, which also tells much about Birmingham and the fight for social, political, and economic change. Gaston's book is an absorbing narrative of triumph and influence of a black person who achieved great wealth and who wielded notable influence in one of the South's most segregated cities.

Years will pass, perhaps, before historians can completely unravel some of the details of the Bonita Carter shooting. My interest here, of course, has been the relationship of her shooting to Arrington's fight against police brutality and the impact the young woman's death had on his political career. Arrington's role is spelled out in a 12 June 1984 interview with him. I have carefully read the newspaper coverage of the Carter shooting, but many of my fundamental conclusions derive from the report of the "Testimony before the Ad Hoc Committee . . . in the Matter . . . Surrounding the Death of Bonita Carter. . . ." The findings of the so-called blue-ribbon-committee that convened on 28 June 1979 may be located in Operation New Birmingham: Papers, Department of Archives and Manuscripts, Birmingham Public Library, 172, Box 1, folder one-9. Some of the deductions I have made come from Mayor David Vann's 17 July 1979 "Statement . . . on the Death of Bonita Carter," which followed the special committee's investigation. See in Vann: Public Papers (uncataloged section), Department of Archives and Manuscripts, Birmingham Public Library. During the research on this book, the Carter family had legal action pending against the city of

Birmingham. Therefore, many persons closely connected with the event refused an interview. Abraham Woods, however, did discuss the role of SCLC in a 10 July 1983 interview at St. Joseph Baptist Church in Birmingham. An interview with committee member Dr. J. T. Montgomery, 13 July 1984, also helped clear up some puzzling questions about the investigation. David Vann's interview of 27 February 1986, however, added little to the story of the shooting, which generated more press coverage than any other such incident in the recent history of Birmingham.

Public opinion in the black community, of course, became crucial as political sentiment developed for Arrington. Therefore, I have given special attention to both the *Birmingham Times* and the *Birmingham World* for the period June–November 1979. The prevailing anger within the black community may be sampled in an undated, printed handout called "Project B.O.N.I.T.A." distributed by the Grassroots Coalition, an organization chaired by John C. Harris. See in Arrington: Campaign Files (1979).

Chapter 5

The historic 1979 mayoral election, like the unfortunate Bonita Carter shooting, led to an outpouring of words. The city's newspapers conducted a number of interviews with the major candidates, especially Frank Parsons and Richard Arrington, once the two reached a runoff. See, for example, *Birmingham Times*, 20 September 1979, and *Birmingham News*, 10 and 11 October 1979. Of inestimable value to me were my personal interviews with the major candidates: Richard Arrington, 29 December 1981; Frank Parsons, 5 July 1983; David Vann, 27 February 1984; John Katopodis, 10 August 1983; and Larry Langford, 8 April 1988. Tony Carter gave me an inside look at the campaign in his 8 January 1981 interview. A key to Arrington's political success has been his methodical approach to problems, his organizational skills, and his appreciation for detail. For a look at how he organized his campaign in 1979, see the document "Campaign Plans," in Arrington: Campaign Files (1979). Revealing, too, are the many letters the candidate received from average citizens. Arrington was able to use his column in the *Birmingham Times* to his political advantage. See, for example, the draft of his column "Inside City Hall," 18 September 1979, in a collection of drafts of newspaper articles in Arrington's possession. Two unsigned, popular articles that focused on the widespread community support for the Arrington campaign are "On Becoming an Informed Electorate," *Fox Trapper* 1 (November 1979): 4–5; and "Dr. Richard Arrington . . . the Man Who Should Be Mayor," *Fox Trapper* 1 (October 1979): 3–4. Frank Parsons's more zealous black supporter, Richard Cunningham, explained his allegiance in "Why I support Frank Parsons for Birmingham's Mayor," *Mirror* 4 (October 1979): [8].

Arrington's historic victory brought congratulatory letters from across the country. Those letters may be found in Arrington: Campaign Files (1979). For representative examples of out-of-state responses to the Arrington triumph, see *New York Times*, 13 October and 14 November 1979; *Washington Post*, 31 October 1979. A good, popular article on the significance of the election is Alex Poinsett, "A Big Change for Birmingham," *Ebony* 35 (February 1980): 33–42.

Chapter 6

Rachel Arrington discussed the details of the planning for the inauguration in a 6 January 1983 interview with the author. I have used press reports to describe what took place in Birmingham on the historic day Arrington took office. Peter Moss and Franklin Tate wrote colorfully of the occasion in the *Birmingham Times*, 15, 16, 17 November 1979. But see also the editorial in the *Birmingham News*, 14 November 1979. Arrington talked of the preparation of his brief speech and plans for the day in a 23 February 1983 interview.

Arrington discussed staff appointments in great detail in a 15 January 1981 interview. Interviews with Edward Lamonte, 9 August 1983; Willie Davis, 3 March 1986; Len Gedgoudas, 8 August 1986; and Jessie Huff, 25 February 1986, also aided in writing this chapter. Lamonte has received attention in Merrill Moates, "Leaving the Classroom for the Real Thing," *Birmingham* 22 (July 1982): 14–16.

Arrington employed a cautious approach to new initiatives, while pledging to continue many of the projects David Vann had begun and for which he had voted while on the council. Reporter Kiddy Freiden discussed the new mayor's goals in the *Birmingham News* on 18 and 21 November 1979, and on 16 and 20 December 1979. For a commentary on Arrington's response to the challenges of his administration, see Milton C. Jordan, "A Black Man Runs Birmingham," *Black Future* 2 (September-October 1980): 28–31. The administration's self-assessment appears in a June 1982 document, "Mayor Arrington's Record of Achievement," in Arrington: Campaign Files (1983). The day-to-day problems of government and the major issues that occupied the mayor's attention are discussed in the staff interviews with Lamonte, Huff, Gedgoudas, and Davis. The mayor's appointment secretary, Caroline Knowles, spoke of her boss's schedule in a 30 July 1987 interview, and again on 8 April 1988. During the summer of 1983, when I resided in Birmingham, I had the opportunity to witness the daily operation of government at city hall and to make my own assessment of its functions, successes, and failures.

Many reasons for the death of Block 60 may remain long hidden from the historian. So many half-truths, claims, and counterclaims appeared that a definitive position on the project at this time is impossible. My concern here, of course, has been with Arrington's support of the undertaking and with possible political problems for him. Besides relying on newspapers, I have turned to Ed Lamonte, the mayor's aide who handled Block 60, to guide me through the maze of transactions that went into this project.

Chapter 7

Arrington's relationship with the police while on the council invited careful scrutiny from the press once he occupied the mayor's office. His position on crime had been spelled out during the 1979 campaign, but he reassured citizens by issuing a strong crime message. For an excellent commentary on Arrington's crime program, see the *Birmingham News*, 7 December 1979. For a copy of the shooting policy that Arrington approved, see "Firearms Discharge Policy . . . Revised, July, 1980," in Arrington: Public Papers (1980). Chief Bill Myers refused to discuss his resignation, but Mayor Arrington freely talked of the problems with the head of the police in a 10 July 1983 interview. The press occasionally overdramatized the conflict between the chief and his boss. However, the columns of the *Birmingham News* and the *Birmingham Post-Herald* are the best newspaper sources for examining the differences between the two men.

The heated police-chief controversy prompted much correspondence from the citizens to the mayor. More positive letters than negative ones reached the mayor's office, and only a few of the latter contained racist language. Arrington's position on the appointment is spelled out in many letters. A good example is the mayor's letter to James C. Lee, Jr., 15 September 1981, and his correspondence to Sandra Scales and Deborah Rivers, 2 November 1981. Both letters are located in Arrington: Public Papers (1981). The mayor's "Open Letter to the Citizens of Birmingham," which appeared in the *Birmingham Post-Herald*, 17 October 1981, may also be found in Arrington: Public Papers (1981). Former mayor George Seibels indirectly attacked Arrington when he appeared before the Jefferson County Mayors' Association in early September 1981. A digest of Seibels's comments appears in the minutes of the Jefferson County Mayors' Association for 20 August 1981. See in Arrington: Public Papers (1981). By October the *Birmingham Post-Herald* had come to view the Jefferson County Personnel Board as a problem. See the editorial "Board Is Obstacle," in the 17 October 1981 edition of that paper. For the appointment of Chief Arthur Deutsch, see the *Birmingham News*, 11 November 1981, and the *New York Times*, 10 November 1981.

Arrington is the best source on the Jefferson County Citizens Coalition. While he discussed the organization with the author on a number of occasions, the most extensive interview on the subject took place 16 June 1983. A personal copy of the constitution and by-laws of the coalition enabled me to understand its structure. The Simmie Lavender interview, 26 February 1986, was also valuable, as well as one with Benjamin Greene, 8 April 1988. Both men are previous presidents of the organization. Interviews with David Hood, 20 July 1984, and Arthur Shores, 10 August 1984, provided the best commentary on the Jefferson County Progressive Democratic Council, although I made use of the *Birmingham World* for the early period of the organization's development. James Q. Wilson, *Negro Politics: The Search for Leadership* (Glencoe, Ill.: Free Press, 1960), is a study that aids in comprehending the historical basis for the political unity of black America in more recent times.

I have followed the 1981 city-council election through correspondence and special items in Arrington: Public Papers (1981) and the local press. In an inteview on 16 June 1983, the mayor discussed his role in the contest. A highly sophisticated political analysis of the 1981 council contest is contained in a 22 October 1981 "Memorandum" of Thomas M. Fletcher to members of the Birmingham City Council, in Arrington: Public Papers (1981). On the rough-and-tumble of politics at city hall during this period, see Joyce Deaton, "Fire and Smoke at City Hall," *Birmingham* 21 (September 1981): 36–62.

Chapter 8

Arrington's respect for Lucius Pitts is clearly revealed in his 24 February 1986 interview and in an updated portion of a speech in the Miles College Special Collection. My characterization of Pitts is based on biographical material in the above collection. For editorials that lauded Pitt's devotion to education, see the *Augusta Chronicle* and the *Augusta Herald*, both 27 February 1974.

I have had to depend upon personal interviews for much of this chapter. The principal figures in the story permitted me to probe their lives and to discuss matters not normally open to the public. A number of formal and informal interviews influenced my comments, but the most useful (listed in alphabetical order) were Barbara Arrington, 16 July 1984; Ernestine Arrington and Richard Arrington, Sr., 8 July 1981; James Arrington, 12 November 1983; Rachel Arrington, 6 January 1984; Lemorie "Tony" Carter, 8 January 1981; Jessie Huff, 25 February 1986; Caroline Knowles, 30 July

1987; and Lewis White, 25 July 1983. I have not listed every interview with the subject of this biography, since almost every conversation with him touched on various aspects of this chapter. Two articles in particular focus on Rachel Arrington: Jeff Hardy, "Rachel Arrington: Birmingham's First Lady, Her Own Person," *Down Home* 3 (Fall 1982): 35–36; and Barbara Bryant, "Rachel Arrington: Lady of Beauty," *Fame* 2 (June 1983): 17–18. During the period 1963–66, I had the chance to observe Arrington when we both matriculated as graduate students at the University of Oklahoma.

Arrington's racial, religious, and social views are reflected in many of his speeches. The mayor's office made available a special folder of Arrington's speeches, which proved indispensable in the formation of my ideas.

Chapter 9

Mayor Arrington permitted me to attend the initial meeting of his reelection committee on 25 June 1983. I often made later observations from a desk at his campaign headquarters. On 10 August 1983, I interviewed John Katopodis, and Sonja Franeta on 25 August 1983. The issues Franeta emphasized are delineated in "Vote Socialist Workers" and in "Where the Socialist Workers Campaign Stands." Both are in my possession. On 4, 5, and 6 October 1983, the *Birmingham News* carried long, informative articles on the candidates, which focused upon their lives and the issues of the campaign. Very useful also was Kelly Dowe, "Birmingham's Mayor Richard Arrington," *Down Home* 3 (Spring 1983): 10. Some of my conclusions about the 1983 campaign evolved from my study of the tape of the 9 October 1983 television debate between Katopodis and Arrington. For the city-council race of 1983, I have relied almost exclusively upon newspaper coverage and a chapter, "Overcoming the Politics of Polarization in Birmingham," in *Strategies for Mobilizing Black Voters: Four Case Studies*, ed. Thomas E. Cavanagh (Washington, D.C.: Joint Center for Political Studies, 1987), especially pp. 70–94.

Chapter 10

This chapter depends partly upon three extensive interviews with Richard Arrington that I conducted on 17 and 18 July 1987 and 7 April 1988. For an understanding of recent population trends and the changing face of Birmingham's economic landscape, I have called upon Odessa Woolfolk, director, Center for Urban Studies, University of Alabama at Birmingham. My 6 January 1988 interview with Woolfolk covered not only the topics above but a range of issues related to city life and politics. The "State of the City Address, 1982–87" and the "Mayor's Report to the People, 1983–87" helped me isolate some of the central issues the executive faced during the period. Councilman Eddie Blankenship, chairman of the city council's Industry and Jobs Committee, took the leadership in convening public forums on economic development. The "Proceedings" of the 1987 forum describe the economic challenges to Birmingham and offer recommendations from knowledgeable persons concerned with city life. A printed copy of the document may be found in the Birmingham City Council office. For an article much broader than population trends and segregation after 1954 in Birmingham, see Bobby M. Wilson, "Racial Segregation Trends in Birmingham, Alabama," *Southeastern Geographer* 25 (May 1985): 30–43.

A 6 January 1988 interview with Robert Corley helped me understand the complexity of the Walter Harris controversy. Corley also made available to me personal files that shed some light on the conflict.

The creation of the New South attracted much attention, especially after tensions built between that group and Joe Reed's Alabama Democratic Council. Arrington's 18 July 1987 interview on that subject has been a major source of information. I have perused documents on the New South in Arrington: Public Papers (1985–88). I was able to comprehend the intensity of the opposition to Joe Reed within the New South after my attendance at an 18 July 1987 meeting of the organization's executive council. The *Greene County Democrat* of John and Carol Zippert was among the harshest of Reed's critics. Margaret Edds, *Free at Last: What Really Hap-*

pened When Civil Rights Came to Southern Politics (Bethesda, Md.: Adler and Adler, 1987), has an excellent commentary on Alabama's New South group as well as the 1987 Birmingham city-council race.

A poll by William Kimmelman had much to do with Arrington's optimism as he approached reelection in 1987. Indeed, the press reports of the poll's favorable findings may have influenced some opinions. A copy of Kimmelman's 13 June 1987 poll, "A Survey of Birmingham," is in my possession. Arrington's 5 January 1988 interview and that of Robert McKee, 7 April 1988, focus on the 1987 mayoral race. Beatrice Horn Royster, "Mayor Arrington: His Record and the Economic Future of Birmingham," *Black Business Network* 2 (Spring 1983): 2–4, attempts to contrast the old economy of Birmingham with the new diversified structure that Arrington promoted. I have also examined the Arrington Files in the Joint Center for Political Studies, Washington, D.C., and also the Birmingham City Council Clipping Files.

The sharing of power through the political process remained an important concern for Arrington and other black politicians across America. William E. Nelson, Jr., and Philip J. Meranto do not deal specifically with southern cities and politics in their *Electing Black Mayors: Political Action in the Black Community* (Columbus: Ohio State University Press, 1977), but their chapter "Black Mayors: The Dilemmas of Power" is applicable to Arrington and the South. An unpublished bibliography on black politics compiled by political scientist Sharon Fluker of Vanderbilt University guided me to relevant literature in the field. Of great value also was her unpublished work "Black Succession in City Politics: Racial Bloc Voting and Non-Racial Election Strategies," a copy of which is in my possession.

Index

LIBRARY
ST. LOUIS COMMUNITY COLLEGE
AT FLORISSANT VALLEY